The Struggle over Lebanon

The
STRUGGLE
OVER
LEBANON

by TABITHA PETRAN

MONTHLY REVIEW PRESS
New York

Library of Congress Cataloging-in-Publication Data
Petran, Tabitha.
    The struggle over Lebanon.
    Includes index.
    1. Lebanon—History—1975   .2. Lebanon—
Politics and government—1946-   .I. Title.
DS87.P49   1986   956.92'044   86-18284
ISBN 0-85345-651-8
ISBN 0-85345-652-6 (pbk.)

Monthly Review Press
155 West 23rd Street
New York, N.Y. 10011

Manufactured in the United States of America

10 9 8 7 6 5 4 3 2 1

For Peter Kilburn, a kind and gentle librarian and a close friend whose murder in Lebanon is in many ways symptomatic of all those other deaths, both Lebanese and Palestinian, which have occurred since the fighting began.

Contents

Preface and Acknowledgments

Work on this book began in 1976 when the first phase of the civil war was at its height. In the months and years that followed, including the dark days of the 1982 Israeli siege of Beirut, I have received help and advice from a great many Lebanese and Palestinians whom I would like to thank but for whom any kind of public acknowledgment may present certain dangers. They alone can know how deeply indebted to them I am, and how much I respect and admire them.

Throughout the writing of this book I have used the resources of the Jafet Library at the American University of Beirut. This is one source I can acknowledge and I do so most gratefully. For even in the most difficult periods the library remained open and its staff provided assistance far beyond the call of duty. The insights of such correspondents in Lebanon as David Hirst and Eric Rouleau in explaining the complexities of Lebanon and the Palestinians have been invaluable. Invaluable also has been the work of a Lebanese friend, George Geadah, to my understanding of the evolution and failure of the Lebanese Marxist left.

In the United States I wish to thank Karen Judd, my editor, for the thoughtful care of her work on my manuscript, as well as my other colleagues at Monthly Review Press for their patience over the many delays and difficulties engendered by recurrent warfare and ruptured communications.

Matar, who have lived with this book in Lebanon, then Australia, and finally in the United States. Their assistance and encouragement have been invaluable and have helped decisively in ensuring the publication of this book.

A Note on Transliteration and Sources

Every book dealing with the countries of the Middle East or the Arabs in general is faced by the problem of transliteration from Arabic. Elaborate systems have been devised by scholars to give accurate English representations of the letters in the Arabic alphabet, but without exception these systems are painful to the nonspecialist reader and a nightmare to typesetters and printers alike. Furthermore, familiar names, such as "Beirut" and "Gemayel" can appear in strangely unfamiliar forms (Bayrūt, Jumayyil, *Dj*umayil) if such systems are followed consistently.

Consequently, the transliteration of Arabic names in the following pages has been made as simple as possible. Where a familiar form of the word already exists in English, such as "Gemayel," it has been adopted. Where one does not exist, the twin criteria of simplicity and consistancy to the Arabic original have been utilized, and diacritical marks have been dropped.

A book such as this, which especially in its later chapters is in fact dealing with contemporary events, relies on a wide variety of sources, many of them oral. In some cases this can lead to difficulties of attribution and footnoting. In the present case these difficulties have been exaggerated by the destruction of many of the author's research notes in Beirut, and by her eventual departure from Lebanon, after a residence of over twenty years, with little more than hand luggage. As a result, some of the later chapters are not as heavily footnoted as the earlier ones.

Tabitha Petran, Long-time foreign affairs correspondent for *The Guardian* (New York), *Photo History,* and the newspaper *PM,* has reported from the United Nations, India, Afghanistan, France, England, the Soviet Union, and many of the countries of the Middle East. She is the author of a highly acclaimed study, *Syria,* published in 1972. Born and raised in Mexico, Petran lived in Syria and Lebanon from 1962 until 1986.

Introduction

Israel's cynically styled "peace in Galilee" invasion of Lebanon in the summer of 1982 was intended to eradicate a Palestinian political threat, and not, as it claimed, a military one. In the fifteen years following the June 1967 war, in which it seized and retained an area three times larger than the Israeli state itself, the Israeli army killed at least 10,000 Palestinians and Lebanese, most of them civilians inside Lebanon. In the same period, according to Israeli police sources, 282 Israelis were killed by the Palestine Liberation Organization (PLO).[1] As Israeli army spokesman Brigadier General Yaakov Even put it in 1981, "We are the aggressors. We are penetrating the so-called borders of the so-called sovereign state of Lebanon, and we go after them wherever they hide."[2]

Israel's Expansionist Aims

The 1982 invasion was also intended to realize Israel's long-held expansionist goals in Lebanon. Lebanon has always been for Israel, in David Ben Gurion's words, "the weakest link" (and the most desirable) in the "Arab chain" surrounding it.[3] Almost from the moment the Zionist state was established its ambitious leaders entertained projects to break this link by creating in central Lebanon a Maronite Chistian state under Israeli tutelage, while itself annexing the entire area south of the Litani River. At a meeting of senior officials of the Israeli foreign and defense ministries on May 16, 1955, called to discuss this project, the then chief of staff of the Israeli Defense Forces (IDF), Moshe Dayan, declared (as recorded in then Foreign Minister Moshe Sharett's *Personal Diary*):

11

the only thing that's necessary is to find a Lebanese officer, even a major will do. We should either win his heart or buy him with money to get him to agree to declare himself the saviour of the Maronite population. Then the Israeli army will enter Lebanon, occupy the necessary territory and create a Christian regime which will ally itself with Israel. The territory from the Litani southward will be totally annexed by Israel. Dayan recommends that this be done immediately, tomorrow . . . .[4]

This scenario was drafted long before the appearance of the Palestinian resistance. Lebanon's attraction for the Zionists lay in its relatively abundant waters (Litani River); its strategic position as the commercial gateway to the Arab hinterland, a position Israel coveted for itself; and the weaknesses and divisions inherent in its sectarian sociopolitical structure, making it relatively easy prey. Not "tomorrow" but twenty years later—when the 1975–76 civil war erupted in Lebanon, a war that Israel's escalating aggressions did much to bring about—did Israel find its major (Saad Haddad) and assign him a role that soon secured an Israeli presence inside Lebanon's southern border. This strategic advantage, coupled with its developing alliance with rightist Maronite Catholic leaders and their militias in central Lebanon, proved crucial to Israel's drive to establish its hegemony in Beirut.

For Lebanon was not and never had been an integrated and united country. Its loose political organization—along sectarian, communal lines—has long invited ambitious neighbors to employ divide-and-rule strategies to gain hegemony there. This structure also admirably suited the political and economic strategies of the colonial and imperialist powers, as well as the profiteers of the parasitic economy that developed in Lebanon under their aegis. Lebanon's economic vocation has been to serve as a relay station, an intermediary between Western metropoles and the markets of the East, in particular the Arab hinterland. Its economy—relying always on external factors—evolved as an economy of services, producing a bourgeoisie of middlemen, commission agents, bankers, brokers, and so on, all uninterested in and incapable of building a national productive economy. Incapable also, therefore, of providing the leadership to integrate society on a nonsectarian national basis. No ruling class dedicated to national concerns ever developed.

The Sectarian System

"This is our 1789." In 1975 Kamal Jumblat thus defined the objectives of the Lebanese National Movement (LNM) he headed. For the idea of equality animating the French Revolution, the principle of the sanctity of the individual and his possession of certain inalienable rights as a citizen enunciated in the Declaration of the Rights of Man and of the Citizen (and raised even earlier by the Levellers in the seventeenth century and by the American Revolution)—all these were still without application, even largely without meaning from a cultural point of view, in the Lebanon of the late twentieth century, a Lebanon often identified in the West as (along with Israel) the only real "democracy" in the area.

The French Revolution—attacking all collectivities of special privilege, including those of sectarian communal organization—swept away the stratified society of the Middle Ages that inhibited advance in Western Europe. Not least among the rights of the citizen it established was the individual's emancipation from the corporate controls exercised by sectarian communal institutions. In proclaiming, on September 27, 1791, full citizenship for Jews (as it had earlier for Protestants), the French National Assembly emancipated Jews from subjection to the Jewish communal organization. "On its march towards consolidation," wrote Professor Salo W. Baron,

> the modern state encountered no small obstacle in Jewish communal organization. The material as well as the spiritual power possessed by communal leaders represented vested interests of considerable magnitude. . . . The modern state has had to batter down this refractory group, this nation within a nation.[5]

In Lebanon a stratified society, based on sectarian communal institutions harking back to the medieval world, remains in place, effectively blocking progressive evolution. Therein lie the roots of violence and dissension marking much of its history. The violence of 1975–76 expressed at once frustration over this blockage and a furiously resisted attempt to remove it.

Sectarian communal institutions in the Orient originated in remote antiquity. The heads of these communities had by the time of the Islamic conquest of the seventh century acquired a temporal and spiritual status imposing them as the authorities with whom the conquering Arabs dealt. Islam's decentralized system of government gave these religious communities a large measure of autonomy and officially recognized their patriarchs as the religious and temporal authorities of their respective communities. In the Ottoman Empire these communities became "states within a state." Each community (known as a millet) was self-contained, with its own schools, personal status laws, courts, taxes, levies, and so on; the patriarch of each community collected the only tax owed the central government, the capitation tax. Ruling without interference from Ottoman authorities, patriarchs acquired over their co-religionists absolute social and political power. Their tyranny and avarice and the degeneration of their communal institutions had, by the nineteenth century, become notorious.

These self-governing sectarian communities offered the colonial powers an avenue through which to extend their influence in the Ottoman Empire. The relationship between the colonial powers and the heads of these communities became that of patron to client: France "protected" the Maronite Catholics; Austria, the Greek Catholics; Russia, the Greek Orthodox Christians; England, the Jews and the Druses. Missionaries inciting secessions from established communities contributed by creating additional clientele for the powers. The patron–client bond tying sectarian leaders to one or another of the European powers disrupted coexistence among the minority communities, nurtured hostility between them and the Muslim majority, and troubled their relations with the Ottoman authorities. In Mount Lebanon, where bitter strife among rival Christian communities had become by the nineteenth century at least as common as between the Christian, Muslim, and Druse communities, contemporary observers noted that Lebanese Christians in general and even Maronite Catholics were divided into "as many groups as there were private interests. . . profoundly hostile to one another," and that this enmity was "encouraged and upheld by the consuls of the powers. Each wishes to have an exclusive interest in the country."[6]

The idea of converting one or another of these Christian or Jewish communities into non-Muslim entities or "states" to serve as bases for colonial penetration made its appearance as early as the end of the eighteenth century. In 1799 Napoleon called for "the return" of Asian and African Jews to Palestine, in order that they might there promote French interests.[7] In the 1830s and early 1840s Britain saw its control of the route to India endangered by the French-backed Egyptian occupation of Syria and appropriated this same idea. London granted consular protection to the Jews in Palestine, and studied a project to install Jews scattered throughout Europe in Judea and there re-establish the Kingdom of Israel. Only after investigation proved this project impractical did Britain abandon it for the time being and begin, as an alternative, to cultivate the Druses of Mount Lebanon.[8]

Mount Lebanon's transformation into a "Christian entity" under European protection began in 1860. Following Druse massacres of Maronite Christians in Syria and Mount Lebanon, France, the recognized protector of Catholics in the empire, dispatched a "rescue mission" with the consent of the signatories of the 1856 Treaty of Paris and established Mount Lebanon as an autonomous province.[9]

World War I provided the conditions for the realization of these French and British projects. In 1919, under cover of League of Nations mandates, Britain and France set out to build sectarian, non-Muslim states to solidify their control in the former Arab Muslim domains of the Ottoman Empire. In a Palestine then more than 90 percent Arab, the British worked with European and American Zionists to lay the foundations of an exclusively Zionist Jewish state. They simultaneously created the Transjordan Emirate (after the 1948 Palestine war, the Kingdom of Jordan) as a future receptacle for the indigenous Arab population of Palestine which was scheduled, in the imperial scheme, to move out as Jews from Europe and the Americas moved in. This at a time when the tiny Jewish community in Palestine was for the most part anti-Zionist, and the majority of Jews elsewhere were hostile or indifferent to this movement.

Greater Lebanon, or *Grand Liban,* was created in 1920. The French divided Syria into sectarian statelets, amputating and annexing parts of it to Mount Lebanon to constitute *Grand Liban* as a "national home" for the only sect located wholly in the new entity, the Maronite Catholic. Among the Maronites, France nourished a belief in a Phoenician origin and a non-Arab identity. Since Lebanese emigrants were then mainly Maronite, Greater Lebanon was so named to indicate that it extended beyond its boundaries to include all these emigrants—much as Israel was later to claim to represent all Jews in the world. British and French sectarian state-building differed, however, in one important particular: the Maronites were undeniably Arabs, albeit a minority with an embattled psychology, and were indigenous to the area; the Zionist Jews were not.

British and French strategies in Palestine and Lebanon denied the indigenous peoples their inalienable rights in order to consolidate the power of sectarian authorities through whom these powers intended to assert their control. In Lebanon the inhabitants became virtual prisoners of the sectarian communal institutions to which they perforce belonged—and still do. There was (and is) no law covering nonbelievers.

The Lebanese state was constituted as a grouping of sectarian communities; today fifteen are officially recognized.[10] Each of these communities has its own power structure, its own laws governing marriage, inheritance, and other matters of personal status, its own courts and judicial procedures, its own deputies in parliament, its own political parties, frequently its own schools and distinct educational orientations often hostile to that of other communities, its own hospitals, health, and social agencies. Prohibition of civil marriage within Lebanon—and the fact that the personal status laws of the various communities forbid marriage between Christian and Muslim, and sometimes also among the different Christian sects—contributes to maintaining the clannishness, even a structural cleavage, between the sects. So to a limited extent, does their geographical separation.[11] In this system real power rests not in the hands of the state but "in the hands of sectarian institutions without the responsibility of the state but which practice its prerogatives . . . a system incompatible with democracy . . . and human rights."[12]

Lebanon's economic and political structures are two faces of its dependence on external powers. The society lacks the potential for progressive evolution, lacks even the capacity to resolve internal conflict without resort to external intervention. The landing of American marines in Lebanon in response to President Camille Chamoun's appeal for help in settling the 1958 civil war underscored this fact. General Fouad Shehab, then chief of staff of the Lebanese army, was elected to the presidency under American auspices, and steered Lebanon away from Chamoun's extreme pro-West (especially pro-British) policies to reach a carefully measured accommodation with Egyptian President Gamal Abdel Nasser's neutral position. At the same time Shehab attempted to reorient the Lebanese economy somewhat away from its vocation as a banking center, transit station, and playground for the region's oil rich and their Lebanese partners and agents. Shehab sought to permit the development of an economy capable of meeting at least some of the needs of its people. Although he did not achieve this goal, Shehab's initiatives contributed to animating social forces whose needs and demands the sectarian system could neither accomodate nor forcibly suppress. These forces, however, had yet to develop the capacity to lead society out of the impasse.

Shehab's successor, Charles Helou (1964-70), turned away from his predecessor's reformist goals. He provoked a social polarization that was sharpened by the impact on Lebanon of Israel's attack on and crushing defeat of Egypt, Jordan, and Syria in the June 1967 war. This war activated Palestinians not only in Jordan, where the resistance was then based, but also in Lebanon, where Palestinians in growing numbers joined the resistance and attempted minor raids into Israel. Israel's subsequent military thrusts into Lebanon—some on a large scale, like the December 1968 raid on the Beirut airport— further divided Lebanese into pro- and anti-Palestinian currents, the former often disadvantaged Muslim Lebanese, the latter predominantly petty bourgeoisie of the Maronite Catholic community.

This polarization accelerated during the early years of Suleiman Franjieh's presidential term (1970–76), as the rich became richer and the less-well-off poorer. The Western powers—the United States in the lead—and pro-West Arab regimes generously assisted in arming and training the rightist, mainly Maronite Catholic, militias. This growing threat, underscored by Israel's multiplying military incursions into Lebanon, provoked a gradual coalescence of leftist and progressive groupings under Kamal Jumblat's leadership. The Lebanese National Movement, which started to come together under the impetus of Shehab's reforms, gathered momentum. It joined with the Palestinian resistance to fight against Israel's aggressions and to a limited extent became involved in support of the social demands of the disadvantaged.

The early 1970s proved to be years of rising social and political ferment, marked by strikes, protest marches, and meetings in the cities or even at times in the countryside. This sociopolitical awakening reflected the worsening situation of the disadvantaged; it also owed something to the presence and example of the Palestinian resistance which, especially in the south, provided protection against the private militias of landlords and businessmen. This popular awakening, however limited, provoked among the socially and politically advantaged, especially the Maronite Catholic community, the fears that prompted the acceleration of the training and arming of the militias of the rightist Maronite parties, especially the Kataeb (Phalange).

These deepening national, social, and political antagonisms erupted into civil war early in 1975. In this nineteen-month war the Palestinian–Lebanese National Movement alliance ultimately met defeat at the hands of the mainly Maronite rightist militias supported by Israel, Jordan, Syria, Arab oil monarchs, Egypt, and the United States. When Arab rulers brought the civil war to an end in November 1976, they did so in the context of their consistent policy aimed at eradicating popular, democratic, and national currents in the Arab world. Their total passivity in the summer of 1982—no Arab government came to the aid of the Palestinian and Lebanese Arabs under assault by one of the world's most powerful armies, not one even moved to convoke a summit conference to define a common stand—issued from the same policy. Moreover, popular demonstrations in Arab countries in support of the Lebanese and Palestinian people did not achieve the dimensions of earlier years. This relative decline in popular protest did not testify to the isolation of the resistance and its allies, but rather testified to the cruel repression autocratic Arab governments have inflicted on their peoples and to the dismantling of popular national, cultural, and political organizations.

The Problem of the Palestinians

Israel launched the 1982 invasion "with the total accord of the United States," according to both Foreign Minister Yitzhak Shamir and Defense Minister Ariel Sharon.[13] This was true even though the PLO had strictly observed the cease-fire of July 24, 1981 negotiated by American envoy Philip Habib, which followed Israel's devastating bombardments of Palestinian and Lebanese civilian quarters in West Beirut and its fortnight of strikes at bridges, communication centers, and towns throughout the south. Western intelligence sources revealed that the Israeli offensive of June 1982 was aimed from the start at West Beirut and was to have been concluded within less than a week.[14]

What was the political threat that provoked this action? The Palestinian political threat to Israel appeared in two places and in two forms: in the West Bank and Gaza, where revolt was mounting against the Israeli occupation by an indigenous population overwhelmingly loyal to the PLO; and in Lebanon, where the Palestinians under PLO leadership had achieved "the first truly independent period of Palestinian national history."[15] The evolution of a Palestinian state-in-formation as the PLO, bringing together all the institutions of the Palestinian people, assumed many of the functions and something of the structure of a state. Annhilation of the PLO in Lebanon, Israel believed, would solve both problems. Just to make sure, Israel at this time purged the Palestinian leadership in the West Bank of PLO sympathizers.

The invasion underlined the crucial importance the Zionist state attaches to destroying the national identity and national history of the Palestinians. This became obvious in its savage bombardments of West Beirut, directed first of all at Palestinian quarters and the refugee camps; in its inhuman treatment of Palestinian prisoners, civilian as well as military; and in its systematic attempts to obliterate every evidence of Palestinian culture and humanity. The Israeli army practice of encouraging its soldiers not only to loot, but to defecate and leave heaps of excrement throughout Palestinian cultural and other institutions, homes, and offices, was apparently intended to under-score Prime Minister Menachem Begin's characterization of Palestinians, in the Knesset on June 8, as "beasts walking on two paws."[16] One of the institutes so treated was the Palestine Research Center, which since its founding in Beirut in 1965 had assembled a valuable and largely irreplaceable collection of Palestinian archives, manuscripts, and books. The Israeli army seized and took to Jerusalem the entire collection (along with office equipment and supplies), leaving in its place only heaps of its soldiers' excrement. The materials were subsequently returned to the PLO in the course of a prisoner exchange. But the Israeli point was clear: one Israeli officer told correspondents outside, "There are no intellectuals among Palestinians."

The Palestinians are the most highly educated people in the region, indeed, one of the most educated people in the world. And the PLO, in achieving the vision of a Palestine shared on the basis of equality among Muslims, Christians, and Jews—a vision, even, of a democratic, secular state in all Palestine—has contributed to the political education of the people in this region, posing a challenge to Zionism that could in the long run prove fateful. Hence the imperative for Zionism and the Zionist state to dehumanize as well as displace the Palestinian people.

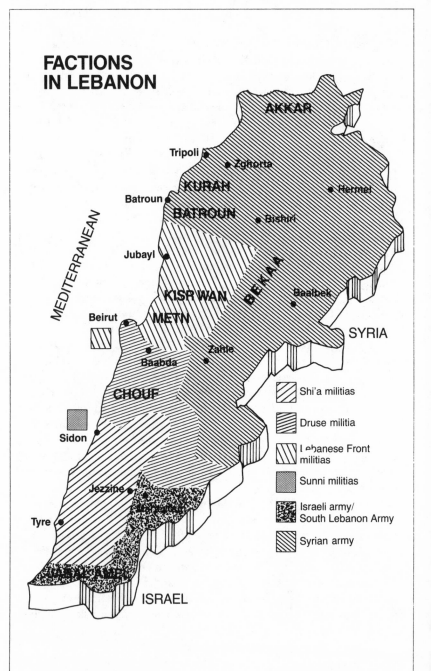

FACTIONS
IN LEBANON

AKKAR

Tripoli
● Zghorta

KURAH

Batroun
BATROUN

● Hermel

● Bishiri

Jubayl ●

KISRWAN

BEKAA

● Baalbek

Beirut
METN

MEDITERRANEAN

SYRIA

Zahle ●
Baabda ●

CHOUF

Sidon ●

Jezzine ●

Tyre ●

JABAL AMEL

ISRAEL

Shi'a militias

Druse militia

Lebanese Front
militias

Sunni militias

Israeli army/
South Lebanon Army

Syrian army

Map by Patricia Onorato
Arab Studies Quarterly, Fall 1985

$$\begin{bmatrix} \text{PART} \\ 1 \end{bmatrix}$$

SEEDS OF DESTRUCTION

[1]

From Empire to Colony:
Mount Lebanon and *Grand Liban*

The present crisis of the Lebanese state must be seen against a long
and complicated history. Conflicts between Christians and Druses in
the Levant go back to the sixteenth century. Incorporated into the
Ottoman Empire in 1516, the rugged and isolated terrain of Mount
Lebanon made it a haven for survivors of lost causes, dissidents, and
heretical sects of both Christianity and Islam, from the Byzantine,
Arab, Mameluk, and Ottoman empires.

From the end of the sixteenth to the beginning of the nineteenth
century Mount Lebanon's history was essentially one of two communities: Druse and Maronite Catholic. Shi'a Muslims, who in earlier
centuries had occupied a large part of the Mountain, had been driven
into peripheral regions by the expanding Druses and Maronites. The
Druse, a splinter sect of Islam born in the eleventh century, sought
refuge from persecution in a valley at the foot of the Anti-Lebanon
range. Druse participation in the wars against the crusaders gave rise
to a warrior aristocracy, among which the Ma'an emirs emerged as
paramount following the Ottoman conquest. In the seventeenth century, the great Druse leader Fakhr al-Din II (1586–1635) brought all
Mount Lebanon under his rule, giving it a distinct political life and a
solid economic base, its thriving economy attracting immigrants from
other areas.

In the eighteenth and nineteenth centuries, however, Druse power
was gradually sapped in clan conflicts, while that of the Maronites
rose. The Maronite sect originated in the Orontes River valley in
Syria with a seventh-century split in the Melkite church (Eastern
church of Byzantium) that may have reflected "a revolt of rural Syrian
Christians against the traditional urban ecclesiastical control."[1] The

sect's tenets spread in the century following the Muslim conquest into the northern districts of Mount Lebanon, finding a receptive audience among the rural population. During the Crusades, Maronites of the Mountain became allies of the European Christian intruders, and in the twelfth century united their church with Rome.

Three main features shaped the modern character and development of the Maronite community. First, its virtual monopoly over the silk industry, revived by Fakhr al-Din II, facilitated Maronite economic ascendancy and political cohesion, and encouraged the development of a Maronite bourgeoisie, providing a livelihood for peasants, workers, artisans, and merchants. As a result, a growing Maronite population gradually filtered southward to become numerically predominant in traditional Druse areas.

Second, due to land donations by notables and acquisitions by the monastic orders, the Maronite church by the end of the eighteenth century had become "the largest, most organized, and wealthiest organization in the whole of Mount Lebanon," strong enough to free itself from dependence on the feudal lords with whom it had been allied.[2] Close links to the Catholic powers, France and Italy, increasingly benefited the Maronite community. Following the so-called capitulation treaties, the first of which was concluded by Suleiman the Magnificent with France in 1535, Christianity became a passport to profitable association with Europeans and their enterprises. As Catholics, Maronites won French consular protection and employment as interpreters, clerks, and commercial agents in consulates and in the trading stations of French companies.

Finally, of the major sects in Mount Lebanon, the Maronite community alone was located almost exclusively in the Mountain, and so acquired a geographic as well as a religious identity. As these identities over time effectively merged into one, Mount Lebanon became for the Maronites their "historic homeland" and a national tradition and national myth evolved, assiduously cultivated by the Maronite church.[3] This national identity ran counter to the personal and kinship ties of feudalism. It also made for a Maronite self-image as a community distinct from, and superior to, its neighbors, who were often perceived as enemies—Muslims mainly, but also at times other Christians. Thus by the mid-nineteenth century the goal of a politically united Mount Lebanon under Maronite leadership had been defined.[4]

Erosion of the Feudal Order

The Egyptian occupation of Mount Lebanon and Syria (1831–40) accelerated both the advance of the Maronite community and the erosion of the feudal order. Ibrahim Pasha's political policies of enforcing equal rights for Christians and Jews, employing Maronites throughout his administration, and permitting the Maronites alone to retain their arms, greatly benefited the community. The same was true of his economic policies: the Mountain's foreign trade, reoriented from Asia to Europe, expanded enormously, making Beirut the principal port of the eastern Mediterranean and the center of more and more European merchant, trading, and banking houses.

The result was to radically alter the status of the Maronite and Druse communities: Maronites who had been the serfs of Druse sheikhs before the arrival of the Egyptians had become the chief moneylenders of these same sheikhs by the time they departed.[5]

Yet it was following a widespread popular rebellion by all sects against the Egyptian occupation that a British–Ottoman military expedition ousted the Egyptians in 1840. The popular upheaval produced, as one Middle East scholar has noted, the first written document in which the different sects refer to a common territory as their country: "We the undersigned Druses, Chrstians, Mutawilah (Shi'as) and Muslims who are known as inhabitants of Mount Lebanon".[6]

The departure of the Egyptians was followed by two decades of turmoil, marked by clashes between Druses and Maronites and by an experiment in partition. This was the dual *qa'im maqamate,* which administratively partitioned the Mountain between a Druse and a Maronite *qa'im maqam* (lieutenant-governor), each ruling over his own sect and responsible to the Ottoman governor in Beirut. Partition sharpened sectarian cleavages, and a second outbreak of Druse–Maronite fighting in 1845 led to a revision of the terms of the *qa'im maqamate.* This reinforced the power of both the feudal families and the heads of the sectarian communities.[7] So began the process by which sectarian institutions, based on religious communities, partially replaced and were partially combined with feudal institutions.

Continuing violence and upheavals over land, taxes, and feudal privileges climaxed in the 1858 peasant revolt in Kisrwan, center of the French-owned silk industry. Maronite clerics took a leading part in inciting the peasants and townspeople against the sheikhs and in defining their demands. Among these were demands for an agrarian reorganization similar to that carried out in France during the French Revolution, political rights, and an end to the rule of feudal sheikhs. Under the leadership of Tanios Chahine, a blacksmith, insurgent peasants appointed responsible leaders in all Christian villages to recruit a peasant liberation army. This army drove out the sheikhs, pillaged and burned their homes, confiscated their crops, occupied and cultivated their land, and established self-ruling communes, some of which managed to endure until 1861.

As the movement spread, Druse sheikhs as well as Maronite aristocrats and church leaders incited sectarian fears and hatreds to immunize peasants against radical contagion. Thus, class conflict was soon transformed into a sectarian war. Massacres of Christians in turn provided the pretext for European intervention: a French military expedition arrived in Beirut in mid-August 1860.

The Special Regime, 1860–1915

In a matter of months, France, Britain, Austria, Prussia, and Russia imposed a colonial condominium, known as the Special Regime, over Mount Lebanon, with the professed goal of protecting the Maronites from the Druses—and from Ottoman officials. Legitimized by the so-called treaties of capitulation, signed by the Ottoman emperor, its statutes secured for the Mountain's inhabitants special privileges (if not autonomy, as they claim): these included exemption from Ottoman military service; placing the Mountain off-limits to Ottoman armies; and internal recruitment of its own police militia under a Maronite commander.

Integration of Mount Lebanon into the world capitalist market, via Lyon and the French silk industry, accelerated the break-up of the old feudal *(muqata'ji)* system and the consolidation of the sectarian system. The result was the creation of a "confessional sectocracy," which has endured to this day.[8]

The Special Regime quickly abolished the privileges of the ruling feudal families. Tax collection became the responsibility of salaried officials under the Ottoman government; tax assessment among districts and villages was the responsibility of the Administrative Council, a body comprised of twelve members representing the six sects then present in the Mountain. Its composition consecrated Maronite domination and the leading role of the church: four of its members were nominated by the Maronite church. The Druses were represented by three members; the Greek Orthodox by two; and the Greek Catholics, Sunnis, and Shi'as by one each.

Abolition of tax-farming ended the grip of the feudal families on landed property. Peasants were relieved of paying feudal dues and rendering feudal services, clearing the way for differentiation among the peasantry and the emergence of a well-to-do peasant stratum. Reduction of land taxes to well below the levels of surrounding regions permitted the development of small and middle peasant ownership.

Yet feudal influence and loyalties survived and were assimilated into the sectarian system. Every governor of Mount Lebanon from Daoud Pasha on put members of feudal families in high administrative posts, guaranteeing their continued political influence.[9] During the period 1864–1914, according to one study, twenty-three out of thirty-seven *qa'im maqams* came from feudal families and fourteen from the bourgeoisie; of the 337 *mudirs,* 260 were of feudal and 77 of peasant origin. Some who lost their base in land found a new one in the developing capitalist economy—as financiers, commissioners, merchants, or representatives of foreign capitalist interests. This small elite came to constitute a "money feudality" alongside and often still linked to the traditional landed feudality, and was thus absorbed into the political structure.[10]

During the fifty years of colonial condominium rule, Lebanon's economic development was subordinated to European interests. Its role in silk production changed from that of an integrated industry, involving the whole transformation process from mulberry tree to woven cloth, to one of silkworm-breeding and cocoon-reeling to provide the raw material for French silk manufacturers. By the turn of the century it had become virtually a single-crop economy with a single-crop trade. One author has calculated the annual loss from the export of cocoons before reeling and of silk thread rather than woven cloth on the eve of World War I at a sum 125 percent higher than the total annual income of the Mountain's population.[11] Forty percent of the cultivable land was devoted to mulberry trees: 40 percent of its population derived income directly from silkworm breeding; silk ac-

counted for nearly three-fourths of the Mountain's total goods production and two-thirds of its exports.[12] When French demand for
Lebanese silk all but vanished around the turn of the century, the
Mountain faced a serious economic crisis, and except for a brief
period in the early 1930s, the decline proved to be permanent.

Shoemaking, weaving, tobacco curing, and cigarette making, which
had started to develop under the stimulus of the break-up of the
feudal order, were also crippled by the invasion of European goods
and money, which inhibited local capital accumulation and hence the
ability of local manufacturers to invest in technical and organizational
improvements.[13]

With the decline in silk, the stunting of industrial development, and
the unprofitability of agriculture, emigration on a large scale began in
the 1860s and gathered momentum in the last two decades of the
nineteenth century and the first two decades of the twentieth. Some
120,000 Lebanese, more than a quarter of the Mountain's then estimated population of about 400,000, had emigrated by the end of the
nineteenth century, and almost 40,000 more left between 1900 and
the end of the Special Regime in 1914. The Regime had shaped
Mount Lebanon's economic system toward one of importing capital
goods and exporting people.

On September 8, 1914, the Ottoman government unilaterally canceled the treaties of capitulation, thus terminating the Special Regime
in Mount Lebanon and restoring direct Ottoman rule. In November
Istanbul declared war on the Allied powers, and in 1915 Ottoman
armies occupied Mount Lebanon.

The French Mandate and the Creation of Grand Liban

The Turkish occupation of Mount Lebanon lasted until 1918, during which period an Allied blockade of the Syrian coast severed the
umbilical cord of the Mountain's economy. Tens of thousands died in a
famine estimated to have reduced the population by about one-fifth.
Lebanese and Syrian speculators made fortunes, however, which they
used in part to buy land from starving peasants for a pittance.

In 1920 France declared the creation of Grand Liban—adding large
tracts of extra territory to the Mountain redoubt. This was necessi-

tated in part by the fact that the Special Regime had destroyed the Mountain's ability to feed its population, which the famine made dramatically clear. It also reflected the desire of French capitalists to acquire Arab markets by creating a partially Muslim political entity as access. In addition to the port cities of Tripoli, Beirut, Sidon, and Tyre, *Grand Liban* included the largely Shi'a Muslim Bekaa Hermel plains and the Shi'a and Druse regions of Rashaya and Hasbaya in the south (including Jabal Amil, one of the most sacred Shi'a shrines), all annexed from Syria. This new state was slightly more than twice the size of Mount Lebanon; the population of the annexed areas was slightly greater than that of the Mountain.

The new entity was not born in harmony. The trauma of the famine had strengthened sectarian complexes in Maronite regions, which were the most badly affected. A belief spread among Maronites that the "Christian-hating Turks" had deliberately created the famine "to wipe out the Christians" and that relief aid—which had been assigned for distribution by French missions—offered proof of Christian brotherhood. Such sentiments, reinforced by Allied propaganda picturing the Allies as "liberators of the Christians from Muslim domination," helped to further the isolationist current in the Maronite community.

Muslims, Orthodox Christians, and Druses, however, opposed both Lebanon's detachment from Syria and Catholic domination. An Allied investigating commission in 1919 concluded:

> In Mt. Lebanon . . . the Druzes and the Greek orthodox desired union with Syria because they were afraid of Maronite domination and also feared France. But so did the Protestants and some other Christians, who sincerely believed in Syrian nationalism. . . . Finally the Moslems of Mt. Lebanon, like those of Syria proper, desired union.[14]

Moreover, the populations of the annexed regions of Syria were bitterly resentful of the union with Mount Lebanon, concluded without their consent or consultation, and contrary to the stated principles of the Allied powers.[15] Among their grievances was the fact that "hardly 17 percent of Greater Lebanon's tax revenues are paid by the Mount Lebanon district while the remaining 83 percent are collected in the annexed parts" and go to "pay an organization . . . the great majority of whose civil servants are Lebanese from the Mount Lebanon district." As late as 1937 Muslim politicians were still trying to eliminate the tax inequities between Mount Lebanon and the rest of the country.

The New Feudalism

France based its rule on the political and religious leaders of the sectarian communities. The religious leader of each sect became his community's spokesman. If a community did not have a chief cleric, it was encouraged to name one. Only after the establishment of the Lebanese state did the Sunnis, for example, acquire a mufti of their own who was then recognized by France as the spokesman of the Sunni community. At official ceremonies thereafter, the French high commissioner was accompanied on the right by the Maronite patriarch and on the left by the Sunni mufti. This "balance" was more apparent than real, as the Sunni mufti lacked the professional manpower and organization as well as the financial resources of the Maronite patriarch.[16]

Each community also had a political *za'im,* a term used in feudal times for the overlord who, in return for the personal loyalty of his followers, assumed obligations on their behalf. This relationship of fealty, in Lebanese sociologist Samir Khalaf's words, "though predominantly a feudal institution . . . is still very much alive in both form and content in contemporary political life. . . . There is hardly a phase of the political process untouched by it."[17] The term "political feudalism," as popularly used in Lebanon today, refers to the survival and importance of the personal and communal ties of fealty in political life.

The sectarian allotment of public posts and seats in parliament, as well as the allocation of electoral districts on a sectarian basis, cemented the alliance of each sect's religious and political chieftains. These provisions are crucial to the operation of the system, since the deputy's chief function—to provide services to his clientele—requires control of people on the one hand, and access to the pork barrel on the other, both assured on a sectarian basis.

The Rise of the Maronites

The chief beneficiaries of the Special Regime were the upper ranks of the Maronite Catholic and Greek Catholic communities.[18] Educational advantages of the Christian communities increased as French missions multiplied in pace with the arrival of rival Anglo-Saxon missions. Of 650 primary schools reported in Mount Lebanon at the end of the nineteenth century, only 13 were Muslim or Druse. (Muslim education did develop, but mainly outside Mount Lebanon.) Remittances from Maronite emigrants, which under the Special Regime became second only to silk as a source of income, improved housing and living standards in Maronite villages, contributed to the survival of small and medium peasant ownership in the Maronite Mountain, and in general elevated the status of this already privileged community.

The French further weighted the system in favor of the Maronite community from the start of the Mandate. The Maronite share of public posts and favors throughout the Mandate and after has remained disproportionate to their numbers. Maronite districts always received the largest share of government expenditure for roads and other development projects, and at Maronite insistence all presidents of the Republic have been Christians: in 1932, at the demand of the Maronite patriarch, the French prevented the election of a Sunni Muslim to the presidency by dissolving the Chamber of Deputies (which elects the president).

These Maronite privileges never had a basis in demographic reality. A highly dubious 1932 census (the last one taken) revealed the population to be about half Muslim and half Christian. Christians could claim a majority at that time only by including overseas emigrants and recently arrived immigrants such as the Armenians, who in the 1930s were hastily granted citizenship. But Muslim refugees, such as the no less unfortunate Kurds, and later the Palestinians, seldom received citizenship. The government refuses to this day to grant citizenship to the Sunni Muslims of Wadi Khaled—an area annexed by France in 1920, and cut off from the rest of Lebanon by a narrow strip of land, since the frontier follows a river. Yet a higher emigration rate among Christians, combined with a higher birth rate among Muslims, continues to enlarge what has for long been a Muslim majority.

The dominant strata of the other major communities, however, share some responsibility for this situation. They have directed their efforts to improving their own status within the sectarian system, rather than changing the system itself; thus they share in the rewards of office and ensure their dominance within their own communities. Sunni leaders, for example, whose position derives from their commitment to Arab nationalism, long ago lost their longing for union with

Syria.[19] Major-General Sir Edward Spears, head of the British military mission in Lebanon during 1941–44, writing of his 1942 consultations with Muslim leaders, expressed his "astonishment" that a proposal for Lebanon's reunion with Syria "was particularly unwelcome" among the Lebanese Muslims. "Why? I should have guessed. In the Lebanon they occupied a position of special importance."[20]

Sunni and Shi'a commoners in the annexed areas did not adjust so easily to their separation from Syria, and at the beginning resisted in both organized and unorganized ways. Their lot, already difficult, became worse under French rule. Over the last half-century village and tribal lands in these regions had been passing into the hands of landlords and notables, reducing peasants to sharecroppers or landless laborers. French rule based itself in the countryside on just such notables, adding a new dimension to the exploitation suffered by the landless. In the 1930s the world economic depression and the accompanying fall in agricultural prices worsened their plight, as it did that of the rural population of Mount Lebanon, for in both areas the land was worked by increasingly impoverished small peasant proprietors.

The economic crisis of the 1930s also closed the doors of most countries to Lebanese emigrants and drove many—some equipped with capital and technical skills—back home. Efforts by such emigrants to build modern industries were soon swept away by the deepening crisis, which also ruined existing artisanal and other enterprises. The fall in the number of silk-spinning mills in Mount Lebanon from eighty-five in 1929 to thirty in 1933 deprived the Mountain of "a large part of its former means of existence."[21] Widespread unemployment was aggravated by Lebanese workers returning from Palestine (owing to the 1936–39 rebellion of Palestine Arabs against the British rule and Zionist infiltration) and by the arrival in Lebanon of 33,000 Armenians, mainly from the Alexandretta region of Syria seized by Turkey in 1936, and 5,000 Syriac-speaking Nestorian Assyrians from Iraq. By the eve of World War II—despite the growth in population—Lebanon had attained a quantitative level of employment barely equal to that of 1913.[22] Unemployment touched off a new wave of emigration, this time of Druses and Shi'as as well as Christians. Maronite peasants looking for work moved in growing numbers down from the Mountain to the coast, especially to Beirut, where they often settled on the edges of the then Greek Orthodox quarter of Ashrafiyya, taking jobs as handymen, servants, and gardeners for the well-to-do of the Orthodox community.

[2]

The Early Years:
Independence and the National Pact

Lebanon's charter for independence, known as the National Pact, is unwritten. Jointly produced in 1943 behind closed doors by President Bishara al-Khuri and his prime minister, Riyad al-Sulh, an Arab nationalist of impeccable credentials, it was designed to assure perpetuation of the Lebanese entity in its existing form. Its terms included:

1. An independent, sovereign, and neutral Lebanon in which Muslims renounced any idea of union with Syria, or any other Arab state, in return for Christian renunciation of separatism and special ties with France or any other foreign power.

2. Muslim acceptance of Lebanon's "Christian character" in return for Christian acceptance of its "Arab face." Although these ambiguous terms provoked endless argument, the meaning was plain. The Christian and Muslim bourgeoisie were in agreement on the advantage of Lebanon's political distancing from the rest of the Arab world and on its vocation as an intermediary between international capitalism and Arab markets. This compromise smoothed the way for the bourgeoisie, Christian and Muslim, to develop lucrative commercial and financial relations with the oil states.

3. Sectarian allotment of seats in parliamant on the basis of a six-to-five Christian–Muslim ratio; "balanced" representation in the cabinet, with the offices of president, prime minister, and speaker of the house assigned respectively and in perpetuity to the Maronite, Sunni, and Shi'a communities. In the cabinet, this meant in practice reserving specific ministries to certain sects (e.g., foreign affairs and education to Maronites or Greek Catholics, defense to non-Christian sects, interior and agriculture usually to Sunnis), with other ministries being subject to bargaining. Since actual control of a department usually rests with its director-general—a permanent employee who operates

33

as head of the administration—the posts of directors-general, also distributed by sect, tended to become sectarian fiefdoms.

The National Pact was intended not only as a *modus vivendi* between the Maronite and Sunni communities, but also as a means to break a popular drive for secularization. A spontaneous national gathering in November 1943 to protest France's attempt to abrogate its commitment to Lebanon's independence displayed a national will overriding sectarian complexes. Although these reemerged when independence was achieved, the experience of the national awakening convinced many, especially the young of all sects, of the need to adopt a modern, secular political system on the Western model. A strong current demanding secularization developed, finding wide expression in the press and in parliament where a young Druse deputy, Kamal Jumblat, became a leader of the movement.

Even Prime Minister al-Sulh felt compelled to bow to this pressure. In ministerial declarations in 1943 and 1944 he called sectarianism "the strongest of the internal chains" preventing the country's advance, "the first evil to be erased from the system," and he solemnly pledged to seek its phased abolition.

He never did. The system exactly suited the needs and ambitions of the bourgeois, feudal, clerical, and bureaucratic ruling strata of the major communities. For it achieved a carefully calculated sharing of the spoils of office and power among the elites of the major sects, a share-out sufficient to unite the privileged of all major communities in the common cause of defending their privileges. In the words of the French political scientist Maurice Duverger, the sectarian system serves to "consolidate the domination of the privileged classes" since it "tends to unite the ruling classes and divide the downtrodden."[1] Most Lebanese knew nothing of the so-called National Pact of 1943 until 1946 or after. Nor were the leaders of other communities consulted about this crucial agreement concerning the country's political structure.[2]

In perpetuating Lebanon's existence as a collection of seventeen closed sectarian units, the National Pact distorted the limited operation of the "democratic" institutions established in the French-drafted 1926 constitution, which was adopted on the achievement of independence. The stipulation of a six-to-five Christian–Muslim ratio in parliament, as well as the arrangements governing the allotment of all civil service posts on a sectarian basis, for example, violate Lebanon's constitution, which restricts sectarianism to the executive branch and guarantees every Lebanese civil and political equality under the law. Further, the sectarian system inflates the power of the chief executive—already considerable under the constitution—to a position of "virtual omnipotence." The president holds at his mercy both the cabinet (which cannot take decisions in his absence) and the parliament (which he can dissolve or suspend at will). He has the almost exclusive right to initiate laws and can promulgate any "urgent" draft law not acted upon by parliament within forty days. Thus he can execute the budget and other projects without a parliamentary decision. He alone negotiates and ratifies treaties, about which he must inform parliament only if he decides that the interest and security of the state permit. As a result his position as a dispenser of patronage is unparalleled.[3]

Yet Lebanon's presidents have tended to be ineffective, if dictatorial, since a bureaucracy to execute policy has never existed.[4] Presidents usually govern by exploiting rivalries among the *zuama* and distributing favors. And since ministers lack a common program or party affiliation, they can do little more than carry out the president's will. The absence of authentic political parties has meant that the function of parliament differs from that of parliaments in the West. In Lebanon, parliament's role has been to preclude any change in the sectarian balance and so safeguard the interests of the ruling strata of the major communities. In fifty years of parliamentary life only 359 deputies, representing 210 families (about 8 percent of the total) have won parliamentary seats, and of these more than 300 have "inherited" their seats from a relative.[5] Parliamentary democracy, wrote the Lebanese journalist Georges Naccache in 1952, "in the present framework of our political society is the most oppressive form of government; it only mortgages national sovereignty in instituting the dictatorship of a club of notables."[6]

The Patron–Client System

The deputy's function remains that of providing services to his clientele. The political structure—state–citizen or state–political-party–citizen—does not exist in Lebanon, where the structure is *zaim*–sectarian-community–extended family. Each *zaim* has his own political machine made up of *qabadayat* (plural of *qabaday*) and their henchmen. A *qabaday* is a neighborhood or gang boss who carries out the *zaim's* responsibilities to his clientele: distributing government favors, protection, buying votes, and doing the *zaim's* dirty work in general. This relationship operates through *wastah,* a colloquial term referring to a widely prevailing system common throughout society by which a *zaim* or anyone else with influence intercedes in almost any type of affair to secure a favorable outcome for his client. The *wasit* is the go-between or middleman.[7]

The survival of the patron-client system militates against change in the political order or the development of political awareness. The electoral law requiring voters to return to their birthplace to vote maintains the system by tying voters to the traditional clan and sectarian forces in the village. *Wastah* has institutionalized corruption in the civil service, the bureaucracy, the police, and most of the administrative services, as well as among the politicians. Occasional "clean government" campaigns have always quickly expired in the vastness of the Augean stables. Corruption provided the lubricant of the Lebanese system. In the political domain, corrupt practices—ranging from vote-buying through bribery and intimidation to murder—constitute what Middle East scholar Michael Hudson has called "a kind of degenerate substitute for rationalized political organization."[8] Government authorities themselves frequently interfere in elections by arbitrary detention of opposition supporters on election day, bribery, falsification of votes, and so on.[9] Since petty officials and public employees usually owe their jobs to nepotism and *wastah,* work standards in public offices tend to be particularly lax.

The system's failure to make for efficiency in the civil service suits the requirements of the financial–commercial bourgeoisie for weak government and an uninformed and understaffed government administration.[10] For this reason, too, civil service salaries remain so modest that government employment does not, in general, attract the most qualified persons.

Governments have been, in fact, highly responsive to the needs of the bourgeoisie for a service economy. During the 1940s, under President Bishara al-Khuri, Lebanon became "a merchant republic in which the main function of government was to support big business."[11] The republic called this policy "economic liberalism." It was rather the primitive capitalism of a mercantile society without any of the palliatives the century has imposed on most other capitalist societies, a parasitic capitalism tributary to Western and international monopolies. World War II and the loss of Palestine, coupled with the Arab economic boycott of Israel, contributed to the expansion of Lebanon's service economy and Beirut's development as a commercial and financial relay station between the West and the Arab hinterland.

To the hypertrophic growth of the service sector and the growing importance of the foreign sector was added a general failure to develop the productive sectors of the economy, generating ever greater inequality of income among classes and regions. Beirut and Mount Lebanon advanced at the expense of outlying regions, whose inhabitants are for the most part mainly Shi'a Muslims. Hence the disparity between the well-to-do of Beirut and Mount Lebanon and the deprived of the hinterland—in the first place a disparity of class and geography—also appeared in a sectarian dimension. Each sectarian community had its rich and poor, but the Christian poor in general have been better off than the Muslim poor, just as the Christian bourgeoisie has in general commanded greater power and privilege than the Muslim bourgeoisie.

Yet economic liberalism coupled with the unequal political opportunities of sectarianism was attractive to the middle and lower-middle strata proliferating in the service economy, who benefited from the trickle-down effect of prosperity as long as it lasted. These middle strata—divided from each other and from those lower down the economic ladder—became the bulwark of the system's stability.

The Lebanese Army—National or Sectarian?

Any description of Lebanon's constitutional underpinnings must include the army. In 1945, when France handed control of the *Troupes Spéciales* to the Lebanese government, many spoke of a strong national army, but no consensus existed on what its character and function should be. Its character was ultimately determined, however, by the imperatives of the sectarian system and the "Christian homeland" concept on which the system was based.

The origins of the army go back to the small militia of notables— "Sons of Mount Lebanon" organized by the provincial governors during the colonial regime to "protect the Christian population," a mission which carried over into its later development. Under the

Mandate France recruited its *Troupes Spéciales* almost exclusively from its most loyal community, the Maronite Catholics. Although during the Mandate Lebanon did not have an army, a minister of war portfolio was created in 1936 in anticipation of independence. This portfolio, an unimportant one in the absence of an army, was given to a Druse notable, Majid Arslan, and in 1945 the post—retitled minister of defense—became the property of the non-Christian sects.

With the creation of an army, those functions ordinarily belonging to the minister of defense were in fact bestowed on the army commander-in-chief, a post considered to belong by natural right to the Maronite community, which also provided the majority of senior officers.[12] Thus the defense minister became little more than a figurehead.

At first the Army Command recruited volunteer soldiers among the conservative Maronite and Druse peasantry of Mount Lebanon, but since the pay was relatively modest, army service mainly attracted the economically deprived. It was the Maronite poor of the Bekaa Valley and the Akkar Plain that filled army ranks, permitting the creation of a sectarian army. Poor Muslims, mainly Shi'as from these and other poverty-stricken areas, also volunteered, but in order to forestall any chance of Muslim predominance even among privates, a Muslim volunteer was not accepted unless he brought with him a Christian volunteer. If for any reason the Christian quit during the training period, his Muslim counterpart was promptly dismissed.[13] Despite these efforts, the army eventually acquired enough Muslim soldiers and junior officers to make its use in social repression somewhat risky.

The first commander-in-chief of the army was General Fouad Shehab, a descendant of that branch of the Shehabi dynasty that had ruled Mount Lebanon from 1698 to 1841, and which had converted to Christianity. The "father of the Lebanese army,"Shehab's guiding principle was that the army command be independent of all executive control. His argument was that the army could be effective only if it were free of outside interference, isolated from the government and the rest of the country.[14] This principle probably derived from the fact that he did not want the army used to serve the ambitions of politicians, of whom he had a decidedly low opinion. Political leaders, lacking a military tradition and all knowledge of military and defense matters, were easily persuaded, the more so as they saw no threat to the Maronite power structure in an autonomous army under a Maronite commander. In 1955 President Camille Chamoun decreed the army commander virtually independent of executive authority. Twelve years later, in July 1967, President Charles Helou promulgated another law which gave the commander-in-chief total control of all defense matters.[15]

But a national army capable of defending Lebanon's frontiers against external aggression could not be built within a sectarian state. A national and integrated army depended on the abolition of the power of sectarian and clan leaderships and on the achievement of a developed political structure. Since the Lebanese ruling elite is made up of just such sectarian and clan leaderships, it has perforce shunned such a goal, and for the same reason avoided introducing military conscription. The army of a sectarian state defends that sectarianism, and as such is primarily focused on internal security, relying on foreigners for protection against external aggression.

This explains the almost total passivity of the Lebanese army in the face of Israeli penetrations into southern Lebanon from 1948 on, and the government's virtual blackout on news of bombardments of and raids into villages. After 1960, Israeli patrols undertook regular operations inside Lebanon, and gradually occupied, year by year, additional strips of Lebanese land. After 1967, when the number and extent of Israeli forays became such that a blackout was no longer feasible, these provoked almost no response from the Lebanese army. Along its sixty-mile frontier with Israel Lebanon maintained a notable lack of fortifications. Smuggling was not uncommon, Israeli goods coming in under "Made in France" labels.

The army's main task was to preserve internal order and to put down civil disturbances, deciding on its own when and how to intervene. In addition, it ruled not only over the Palestinian refugee camps but also over large areas of the country declared to be "military zones," which were generally set up on the pretext of containing "banditry" or tribal conflicts. This permitted the army to act as police for the bigger landlords and inhibit the activity of radical political groups. Only army units were allowed to move freely in and out of these zones, with all other movements subject to army permission.

Throughout the 1960s and until 1971—when the zones were abolished—they covered half the country, contributing greatly to the obstruction of political and administrative unification of the people. The zones were mainly, although not exclusively, located in impoverished areas where the population happened to be predominantly Shi'a Muslim. There, under cover of military rule, the army maintained "social peace" and was empowered to enter houses, confiscate belongings, and make arrests without warrant.[16]

The lawless turbulence of these earlier years of independence did not greatly assist the Lebanese people in developing a strong sense of national identity, and the nascent political formations which appeared at this time further encouraged, rather than diminished, the sectarianism and the factionalism of this "feudal" tradition.

[3]

The Beginning of Nationalism(s) and the Emergence of Political Parties

The troubled decade of the 1930s produced political parties of a new type, parties influenced in style and ideology by the rising fascist parties in Europe. The Syrian National Party (SNP), better known as the PPS *(Parti Populaire Syrien)*, began as a secret organization in 1932. Its founder and leader, Antun Saadeh, a Greek Orthodox from Dhour Shweir (a town in the northern Metn where the Greek Orthodox population had been established for centuries) advocated a doctrine of Syrian nationalism dedicated to the reunification of "natural Syria," complete secularization, and the eradication of feudalism. This mission, especially its emphasis on secularism, articulated the orientation of a community—the Greek Orthodox—based in the context of geographic Syria and hence destined to permanent coexistence with a Muslim majority.[1] Its anti-feudalist program accorded with the needs and hopes of rural middle and lower-middle strata that came to make up the bulk of Saadeh's following. Like other political leaders emerging in colonial countries in the 1930s Saadeh was receptive to fascist ideas, insisting on leadership by an elite and firmly believing in the "superiority of the Syrian nation," defined to include geographic Syria and sometimes also Iraq and Cyprus.

Saadeh was absent from Lebanon for nine years during the critical period of World War II, independence, and the loss of Palestine. During his absence the party had acquired a more "Lebanese" orientation and a new legitimacy. On his return, Saadeh promptly reoriented it, renaming it the Syrian Social Nationalist Party (SSNP), and launched a series of trenchant attacks on Arab nationalism, the bankruptcy of which he considered demonstrated by the creation of Israel. While this policy won him some support among Palestinian refugees, it alienated Lebanese Muslims and provoked government anxiety, especially after the rise to power in Damascus of SSNP-supported Colonel Husni Zaim in March 1949. A clash in Beirut between Maronite militiamen and SSNP workers in June of that year provided a pretext for the government to arrest some 2,500 alleged party members.

Saadeh fled to safety in Damascus, where President Zaim promised to arm the SSNP and back it against the Lebanese government. The party leader proclaimed a rebellion on July 4 and invited the Lebanese people to join his "popular revolution." But the popular support he expected did not materialize; Zaim did not fulfill his promises, and the rebellion was swiftly crushed. Saadeh was handed over to the Lebanese government and executed within twenty-four hours, as were also six of his supporters.[2]

Subsequently reorganized in Damascus, the SSNP had its revenge on July 16, 1951, when it assassinated Lebanese Prime Minister Riyad al-Sulh in Amman. In Lebanon the party had sufficiently recovered by 1952 to take part in the movement that ousted President al-Khuri and elected Camille Chamoun. While officially banned, the SSNP resumed its activities more or less openly, its vehement anticommunism and anti-Arab nationalism undoubtedly tempering official fears and hostility.

The PPS and its doctrine of Syrian nationalism provoked the hostility of Maronite Catholic Lebanese nationalists, who in November 1936 formed the Phalanges Libanaises—a name which was gradually replaced by its Arabic equivalent, Kataeb, after 1943. The organization's founder, Pierre Gemayel, participated in the 1936 Berlin Olympics as captain of a soccer team. Impressed by the Hitler Youth and other paramilitary youth organizations in Europe, Gemayel returned to Lebanon to found the Phalanges Libanaises as a youth sporting club. It combined features of the Hitler Youth, Franco's Falange, and a traditional *zaim* grouping around the Gemayel family. Its mottoes were "God, Fatherland, Family" and "Lebanon First." Gemayel, a pharmacist, was elected its leader in April 1937. Like the PPS, the organization was authoritarian, its leader all powerful; the emphasis was on obedience, unquestioning discipline, and military training. Its members paraded in uniform and gave the fascist salute.[3]

The Kataeb's mission was to promote Lebanese nationalism. While it professed to be nonsectarian, its membership remained overwhelmingly Catholic and its officials all Catholics. Its political positions coincided exactly with those advanced by the Maronite community. Unlike other Maronite political' organizations whose strongholds lay in Mount Lebanon and its villages, the Kataeb was originally urban-based, representing the middle and lower-middle strata of Beirut and a few larger towns. In time it rallied similar strata in the mountain villages. Poor in relation to the Christian elites, these Christian classes have always been economically and politically privileged in relation to their Muslim counterparts. The Kataeb's driving force has come from its promise to maintain this relatively privileged status, which was translated in the Kataeb lexicon into an inherent right integral to Christian security.

Formation of the Kataeb promoted the almost simultaneous appearance of a Sunni Muslim counterpart, al-Najada (Helpers), organized by a journalist, Muhieddine Nsouli, as a paramilitary youth group. Its aim was to revive and promote Arab and Islamic culture, but it never attained a level of organization and response in the Sunni community comparable to that of the Kataeb in the Maronite community.

After independence, the establishment of a Jewish state on Lebanon's southern border was an inspiration to those Maronites who had long nursed the hope of making Lebanon a national home for the Christians. Their tendency to equate Lebanese with Maronite sovereignty, and to see Arabs—always identified as Muslims—as a threat, was greatly heightened by the arrival of more than a hundred thousand Palestinian refugees uprooted by the conflict with Israel and denied permission to return home.

Maronite nationalists saw in Zionism a kindred movement, and in the 1930s openly welcomed the prospect of a Jewish state on the southern frontier. This, they claimed, would break the hostile ring of Muslim Arabs which an independent Arab Syria and Palestine might otherwise form.[4] As early as June 1937 Maronite Patriarch Antoine Arida, and later Lebanese President Emile Edde, met with the Zionist leader Chaim Weizmann. According to one study of the Weizmann archives: "The Patriarch expressed his desire to see friendly relations established with the Jews. The President, on hearing from Weizmann that the Royal Commission had proposed a Jewish state . . . asked Weizmann to promise that the first treaty of friendship to be made by the Jewish state should be made with Lebanon."[5]

At the end of World War II, this current worked for a national home for Christians in Lebanon. Patriarch Arida himself endorsed a 1946 pamphlet, "Lebanon is the home for the Christians of the East," which spoke of "the grave danger" facing Lebanon because of "the ambiguity that arises from such false concepts as Arab, Arabism and the Arab outlook." The Maronite archbishop of Beirut, Ignatius Mubarak, in an August 5, 1947 memorandum to the UN Conciliation Commission, demanded that "Lebanon as well as Palestine should remain a permanent home for the minorities" in the Arab world, and that a Jewish state should be established in Palestine and a Christian state in Lebanon.[6]

Such sentiments have continued to animate that part of the rightist leadership which has dominated the Maronite community since 1943. Much as the Zionists envisaged Zionist Palestine as part of a wall of defense in Europe and Asia, an "outpost of civilization against barbarism," so rightist Maronite leaders unabashedly evoke a Christian-dominated Lebanon as "the bastion of civilization" against the "backward hordes of Islam."

Yet unlike the Zionists, most of whom are alien settlers in the Middle East, the Maronites have been a genuine part of Arab society for a thousand years and more, making a contribution to, and deriving much from, this society.[7] Maronite isolationism expresses an extreme form of sectarianism, designed to maintain the power and privilege of the ruling strata of the major communities and the dominant position of the Maronite community among them.

The extreme isolationist current subsided in the early 1950s, chiefly as a result of the advance of the Maronite merchant bourgeoisie, whose expanding influence both within the Maronite community and outside it made this community reluctant to change the status quo. However, the sentiments that animate Maronite nationalism—disdain for Muslim and Druse co-nationals, condescension toward non-Catholic Christian co-nationals, and intense anti-Arabism—continued. The Kataeb Party is one of the Maronites' most extreme political manifestations, with its dedication to the formation of a "Lebanese nation" comprising residents and emigrants. By Lebanese the Kataeb means Maronite.[8] It has therefore consistently directed part of its efforts to what it called "the dispersed half of the Lebanese nation." It organized the first congress of Lebanese emigrants in 1945, and has invariably rejected a population census that does not include emigrants. The Kataeb has consistently demanded that emigrants have the right to vote, whether or not they hold Lebanese citizenship and pay taxes in Lebanon.

These policies attracted considerable support in the government, controlled as it was by Maronites and Greek Catholics concerned about their minority status. Lebanon's naturalization laws and practices permit emigrants and their children, including those born abroad, citizenship on arrival. For non-Christians the obstacles are often insuperable.[9]

While formally a political party, the Kataeb has from the beginning existed as an armed militia. Its dislike of foreigners, particularly Arabs, prompted attacks on Beirut port workers (predominantly Palestinians and Syrians) in July 1949, incidents which led to the discovery of Kataeb arms caches. This early threat to state security was further underlined by a letter seized from PPS files from the PPS director-general in Acre to Antun Saadeh on August 31, 1949. This informed Saadeh that, according to the secret police office in charge of the Galilee Brigade, the Kataeb together with Archbishop Mubarak were negotiating with Israel to overthrow the government in Lebanon, build a Christian homeland, and persecute other sects.[10] This was a month after the cabinet had unanimously decided to disband all armed party militias, but the measure was weakened by allowing political parties "to take the place of these organizations if they so wanted."[11] The Kataeb continued unofficially under the name Lebanese Social Democratic Party until 1957, when it resumed the name Kataeb.

Maronite exclusionism has long been of interest to Zionist leaders, who saw in a Christian Lebanon a parallel to their own Jewish state. In 1937 David Ben Gurion was one of the few who recognized the strategic advantages of the proposed boundaries of the Jewish state. Among these was the fact that "the northern frontier touches Lebanon," providing "a marvelous political support for the Jewish state." "Lebanon," he went on, "is the natural ally of the Jews of the land of Israel," adding that it was "not impossible to exceed the northern frontier, as the place where the Lebanon borders the frontiers of the Jewish state, which would give us the possibility to expand with the accord and benediction of our neighbors who would have need of us."[12]

The Arab Nationalist Movement (ANM)

In contrast to Maronite exclusionism and "Greater Syrian" nationalism, a number of postwar Lebanese movements began to coalesce around competing visions of pan-Arab nationalism. The

1947 partition of Palestine and the establishment of the Zionist state in 1948 resulted in the dismemberment of Palestine. Many young Lebanese felt compelled to seek an answer to what they considered the material and moral failure of the Arab countries to prevent the loss of Palestine.

In this search, the work of Constantine Zurayk, particularly *Ma'na al-Nakba* (Meaning of the Disaster), had a seminal influence among students in Lebanon, including members of the student club *Al-Urwah al-Wuthqah* (The Firm Tie) at the American University of Beirut. The club's newspaper became the voice of what was to be the Arab Nationalist Youth, later called the Arab Nationalist Movement (ANM). George Habash and Wadi Haddad, both Palestinians, Hani Hindi, a Syrian, and Ahmad al-Khatib, a Kuwaiti, were among its original members. They were convinced of the imperative of mobilizing the Arab world to recover Palestine, for which they considered Arab unity a prerequisite. Working in the refugee camps and among secondary and university students in the coastal cities, the ANM was predominantly comprised of Lebanese Muslims, although it won a growing number of Christians to the ideas of Arab nationalism. Drawn to the pan-Arabist ideas of Egyptian President Gamal Abdel Nasser, the movement allied itself with the Nasserites in 1954.[13]

The Communist Party of Lebanon (CPL) and the Peace Partisans

The ANM profited from the progressive ambience fostered in large part by the Partisans of Peace movement, launched by the Soviet Union in 1949. Owing to the Russian Orthodox church's prominent role in the movement, the Partisans of Peace won an especially warm response from the Greek Orthodox community. Within the movement friendly relations developed between some orthodox bishops and priests and the left, on the basis of a shared concern for social problems. Church notables became outspoken advocates of political reform and played a significant part in awakening a social consciousness, especially among the young.

The success of this movement enabled the Communist Party of Lebanon (CPL) to recover some of the influence it had lost in 1947, when it followed the Soviet line in supporting the partition of Palestine. This gave the Lebanese government a pretext to outlaw the party, close its offices, and arrest its leaders. With the growth of the Partisans of Peace, however—although the party remained illegal—its organization and discipline allowed it to play an important role in mobilizing popular opposition to Western military pacts.

Progressive Socialist Party (PSP)

Not all who dedicated themselves to the ideal of a modern nation in Lebanon espoused the ideologies of nationalism then current. For the Progressive Socialist Party (PSP), founded in 1949 by Kamal Jumblat, nationalism had "become in the Orient a sort of Byzantine sophism intended to lead the masses into error."[14] In its place, Jumblat proposed progressivism and socialism. The PSP defined progressivism as reconciling (within "a new popular democracy") the measures which in totalitarian regimes "assure the well-being of the masses" with those in Western law that guarantee the citizen "basic individual rights."[15]

Jumblat, who had entered parliament in 1943 at the age of twenty-six, distributed much of his landed domain to the tenants who worked it. He became an early advocate of production to satisfy human needs rather than production for profit, and the PSP reflected his ideas. A mystic versed in Indian and other Eastern philosophies, a student of Rousseau and Marx and many other Western thinkers, a humanist with a genuine concern for the downtrodden, Jumblat was no common politician. His intelligence, the range of his interests, his contacts with international movements and personalities, all brought a new dimension to the narrow parochialism of Lebanese political life.

Usually described as a leftist, Jumblat came closer to being an intelligent conservative. Throughout most of his political career he was to work more or less consistently toward the goal of transforming Lebanon from an aggregate of sects into a modern nation, acknowledging its place in, and close links with, the Arab and Afro-Asian worlds. Although an Arabist, he saw not Arab unity but the achievement of Lebanon's internal unity as the first imperative. Jumblat was highly conscious of the fact that much of the educated middle class, practically all nontraditional groups, and all the newly politicized younger generation were excluded from the political system. He sought, therefore, to reform the system to permit their participation.

To this end he was again and again to bring together progressive groups, parties, and personalities to "create the opposition that is lacking in parliament," and so set in motion a genuine political reform movement which began to challenge the Lebanese system.

The PSP remained organizationally weak, but it spread from Jumblat's native Chouf to Marjeyoun and Hasbaya in the south, and to the Bekaa Valley, the Metn, and Beirut. Although its base in the beginning was predominantly Druse, the PSP sought, and to a significant extent eventually won, an audience among citizens of almost all sects, whatever their ideas on the issue of Lebanon's identity. The party struck a responsive chord, especially among educated young people in the years after the 1948 Palestine war, when the PSP maintained an intransigent opposition to Western military projects in the area. Jumblat also developed a trenchant critique of the country's dependent service economy.

New Strains—and Regional Polarization

In 1952 a reformist coalition, the Socialist National Front (SNF), ousted President al-Khuri and brought Camille Chamoun to the presidency. The reform demands of the coalition members were wide, ranging from the PSP interest in land redistribution to women's suffrage. Chamoun's interest in reform was limited to his desire to cut the power of the political *zuama* and so enhance his own. He therefore had a new election law enacted in 1952 (and another in 1957) to break the power of the feudal notables, thereby alienating both the reform-minded and the traditional politicians.

Chamoun's real interest was in foreign policy, in part due to new pressures in the region. American policy—directed at supplanting France and Britain as the dominant power, and at keeping Soviet influence out—was rapidly splitting Arab countries, including Lebanon, into pro- and anti-Western camps. This made the kind of balance in Arab policy that al-Khuri had maintained impossible. Lebanon's course was influenced by events elsewhere in the Arab world. Two months before Chamoun's inauguration, the Free Officers took power in Egypt. Despite holding America initially in its favor, by 1954 Egypt met American cold war policy with a move toward Moscow. That same year in neighboring Syria, the end of Colonel

Adib Shishakli's dictatorship allowed new and popular forces to participate in political life, mobilizing popular opinion against American and Israeli policies. Israel's punishing raids into both Syria and Egypt in early 1955 made both these countries seek from the Eastern bloc the arms denied them by the United States.

These events had an electrifying impact on Lebanon. Chamoun, who as ambassador in London had ably spoken on behalf of the Arab and Palestine cause, now appeared to be aligning his country with the American camp. His refusal to link Lebanon to the Egypt–Saudi–Syria Defense Pact of March 1955, his friendship with Turkey, and his rejection of a Syrian demand for extradition of the SSNP murderers of the popular Syrian chief of staff, Colonel Adnan Malki, all placed Chamoun squarely in the Western camp in the eyes of many Lebanese.

The polarization of Arab regional politics intensified sectarian sensitivities inside Lebanon. Gamal Abdel Nasser's growing challenge to the West stirred Sunni Muslims to demand a united Lebanese stand against American imperialism and deepened their already existing discontent over their inconsequential share in political power. Nasser's intrepidness before the Western powers inspired the poor and uneducated of the Muslim communities, as well as the young, educated middle strata of many sects, to rally to the banner of Arab nationalism and Nasser, its leader. This in turn excited the fears of the Christian nationalists.

The American decision to withhold promised aid for the Aswan High Dam on the Nile, Nasser's nationalization of the Suez Canal Company, and the Anglo–French–Israeli invasion of Egypt combined to split Lebanon down the middle, mainly though not entirely on sectarian lines. Catholic Christians remained committed for the most part to the West; the Muslims and Orthodox Christians aligned for the most part with Egypt and the Arab world.

Chamoun did his best to maneuver out of the resulting crisis. He expressed support for Egypt's nationalization of the Suez Canal in July 1956, assuring France and Britain that Egypt's main interest was in developing the canal. And, immediately after the Israeli, British, and French invasion of Egypt was launched in October 1956, he called a conference of Arab heads of state to decide on common action, attempting to defray criticism of his failure to break relations with Britain and France.[16] While he managed thus to ride out the crisis, however, he did not succeed in closing the breach that the events of 1956 had opened up in Lebanon.

[4]

The Shehab Experiment:
The Failure of Reform

The Revolt of the Pashas

The first major breakdown in the Lebanese political system occurred in 1958. Chamoun's attempts to expand his power while reducing the influence of certain traditional leaders alienated many politicians, while his intrigues against Syria—then a lively center of democratic and diverse political currents—provoked popular resentment. The less-than-enthusiastic support Chamoun and his foreign minister, Charles Malik, gave Egypt during the Suez crisis, together with their acceptance of the Eisenhower Doctrine (whereby the United States asserted its right to intervene to preserve stability in the Middle East), contravened both the National Pact and Lebanon's "neutral" foreign policy. Chamoun perhaps revealed his real sentiments when he told Washington columnist Drew Pearson, "Your greatest mistake was not to let the Israeli army continue in Suez for another fourteen days."[1]

The creation of the United Arab Republic (UAR) by the union of Egypt and Syria in February 1958 produced a heady climate of ascendant Arab nationalism among many Lebanese who were deeply offended by Chamoun's now open anti-Nasserism. At a time when the Maronite patriarch himself conceded a 60 percent Muslim majority in Lebanon, Chamoun's policies intensified the feeling among Muslims, especially of the lower urban middle class, of being second-class citizens in their own country.[2] Rising resentment in the neglected rural hinterlands against Mount Lebanon and Beirut was also a major factor in fueling revolt.

On May 8, 1958, Nasib al-Matni, the liberal Maronite publisher and owner of the *Telegraph,* was assassinated, touching off the insurgency known as the Revolt of the Pashas. The assassination was openly blamed on Chamoun and his government, since al-Matni was a severe critic of the Chamoun regime and had been threatened with murder if he did not cease his opposition to the government. The Revolt of the Pashas—so-called because traditional political leaders assumed its command—brought together groups that had never before joined in common action: Sunnis, Druses, Shi'as, and Christians (including prominent Maronite leaders) as well as the political *zuama* of the border regions. Peasants, villagers, workers, lower-middle-class people, progressive students and intellectuals (an avant-garde denied participation in the political system) provided the revolt's foot soldiers.

Chamoun, however, was unable to call on the army to put down the revolt, since General Fouad Shehab, perceiving the dangers of involving the army in a factional struggle, tried to keep it out of the conflict in an effort to maintain a kind of balance. He attacked the insurgents only when they were too successful, and even on occasion used the army against forces fighting with Chamoun.

Chamoun thus fell back on the gendarmerie. This, however, was poorly equipped, and many among its ranks deserted to join the insurgents, obliging him to solicit the help of the Christian militias: the Kataeb and, paradoxically, the Syrian Social Nationalist Party (SSNP), the devoted champion of Greater Syria (just what Chamoun and the Kataeb professed to be fighting against). The SSNP, supplied and armed by the Iraqi government of Nuri al-Said, proved to be Chamoun's main support in what rapidly developed into civil war.

Participation by the Christian militias gave the conflict a sectarian coloring, enhanced by Chamoun himself, who realized he faced strong opposition and sought to incite Maronite fears that Christian Lebanon's independence was at stake. Among the Maronite leaders opposing him were Patriarch Bulos Meouchi, former President Bishara al-Khuri, the Franjieh clan of Zgharta, and Jean Aziz of Jezzine in the south. The patriarch's stand so angered the Kataeb and the Chamounists that they organized a demonstration against him on September 28 at the patriarchal seat in Bkerke—a demonstration unprecedented against such a religious leader.

The most important battles of the 1958 civil war took place in the Chouf, where Kamal Jumblat organized an administration (armed forces, police, supply, etc.) centered around his home in Mukhtara. From here Jumblat launched two important offensives, one in mid-May against the presidential palace at Beiteddine and one at the end of June to take Beirut. After bitter fighting, General Shehab intervened with the army to halt both. Apart from these battles, fighting was for the most part sporadic, localized, and inconclusive, in large part due to Shehab's astute refusal to risk the army by using it in an anti-guerrilla war (for which it was not trained) against the widely scattered insurgent areas.

In July 1958, American Marines landed in Lebanon, propelled not only by the Lebanese troubles but also by the desire to send a warning to the new powers in Iraq, victors in the revolution of July 14. Egypt said nothing. When a cease-fire was arranged, Shehab, credited with having kept the army neutral, proved acceptable to both sides as the only possible presidential candidate. He was duly elected on July 31, 1958. Thus once again, as in 1860, Lebanon's problems were "settled" by foreign intervention.

Shehab's Early Years

The lack of Egyptian protest at the Marine landing reflected a developing U.S.–Egyptian understanding that began with the formation of the UAR and with Nasser's almost immediate repression of the left in both Egypt and Syria. This gave Shehab room to pursue a more-or-less pro-Nasserist policy during his presidency, a policy which served to mollify traditional Muslim leaders for their failure to win most of their internal political demands.

Traditional Muslim leaders had not revolted against the sectarian system as such. Nor did they take up arms to become part of the newly formed UAR: more than once they specifically rejected any such idea, specifying that the difference between the two countries' economies made union undesirable.[3] Their hope was to cut the presidency down to size in order to obtain a balance between executive, legislative, and judicial power and to secure a more equitable Muslim participation in government and public posts.

With one exception, however, they did not achieve these modest goals. Presidential power was further inflated, and demands put forward by Kamal Jumblat, the strongest of the insurgent leaders, for a nonsectarian administration and a ceiling on electoral expenditures, went unheeded. Only the promised fifty-fifty Christian–Muslim representation in higher public posts was won, as a result of which many more Sunnis found places in the administration.

The 1958 crisis was notable, however, for the participation of the common people, irrespective of sectarian affiliation. As one author has noted:

> It was they who fought behind the barricades and in the mountains, suffered and died. Without their sacrifice, the traditional leaders would have been powerless. This has given the people a new appreciation of their importance and a sense of power virtually absent before and released them somewhat from the bondage of traditional loyalties.[4]

The Maronite rightists drew another lesson from the conflict. The civil war had barely ended with Shehab's election—and his appointment of a cabinet excluding Chamoun supporters—when the Kataeb staged its self-styled "glorious counter-revolution" (September 24–October 15) to upset what it saw as a Muslim victory imposed by the United States.[5] Through an orgy of sectarian killings and kidnappings it brought Beirut to a near standstill, threatening to destroy key installations and services if it were not given a place in government.

The Kataeb succeeded in bringing down Prime Minister Rashid Karami's government and securing a four-man government (two Maronites and two Sunnis), including Kataeb chieftain Pierre Gemayel; this was the first time the Kataeb had achieved a top position in the power structure. Thus the sectarian structure remained intact, even strengthened, as a result of the Kataeb's counter-revolution. Indeed, this was their intent, to institutionalize the structure in which they now held more power. In so doing they effectively closed the door to real change or reform.

The Kataeb's participation was in line with its usual policy of standing with whatever regime was in power, and its belief at the time in the need for a measure of social reform as a prophylactic against change in the sectarian system itself. Alone among sectarian parties the Kataeb had a grassroots base, to which Shehab's reformist ideas appealed, as well as a second-rank leadership in which not political feudalists but an educated and more-or-less modern elite then predominated. Its presence in the government thus provided Shehab's regime with the "Maronite cover" necessary to confront opposition from the majority of traditional Maronite leaders, of whom Raymond Edde, son of Emile Edde and leader of a parliamentary grouping known as the National Bloc, was the most active.[6]

The Kataeb, however, was alarmed by the civil war's challenge to Maronite supremacy and by the emergence of the "common man" freed from traditional bondage. Impelled by these fears and, above all, by General Shehab's failure to use the army in defense of Maronite "legitimacy," the Kataeb pursued what it conceived to be its mission: assuming an independent role "in defense of the state." This meant organizing on military lines and occupying itself with military and strategic concerns. In this period the Kataeb extended and consolidated its instruments of intelligence, propaganda, infiltration, and sabotage.[7] It planted party offices among Christian migrants from north Lebanon who had settled near Tripoli, and it sought to develop the small ports north of Beirut—Junieh, Jubayl (Byblos), and Batroun. All these preparations were directed against the potential "enemy within": the Muslim population and that by-no-means-insignificant part of the Christian population that did not welcome domination by the Maronite rightists.

The Kataeb owed some of its success in this period to the exclusion of its traditional rival, the SSNP, from Shehab's government of "national reconciliation." The two parties operated in much the same area, competing fiercely for the allegiance of the Christian middle and lower-middle classes. In December 1961 the SSNP participated in a coup attempt against Shehab, planned by a handful of junior Lebanese army officers who hoped to replace the military chief of state with a civilian government (presumably of SSNP leaders and their friends). The SSNP role put its leaders in prison for the rest of the decade. There, in time, they charted a new course for their party. Although the SSNP was subjected to harsh repression, Shehab refused to uphold the death penalty imposed on SSNP leaders and followed this same policy toward common criminals: in his twelve-year rule no executions were carried out, an innovation of some importance in a country which traditionally holds dear the law of retaliation.

The attempted coup had a profound impact on the SSNP's allies of 1958, suddenly aware of the paradox of their alliance with the most zealous devotees of Greater Syria. Suppression of the SSNP became the pretext for the elimination of dissent, real or imagined, both inside and outside the army. Several thousand civilians, including Palestinian refugees and Syrians, were arrested (although only 323 civilians were named in the indictment), and controls were tightened over foreigners as well as over the left. On the recommendation of a disciplinary committee set up by Shehab's brother Adel (the army commander-in-chief who had brought the charges), many officers were arbitrarily discharged from the army or forced to resign. The repression that followed the failed coup marked the beginning of the army's rise to dominance in political life.

Shehab's Attempts to Modernize

As long-time head of an army that ruled over many of the country's deprived areas, President Shehab could understand the grievances animating the insurgents as well as the imperative to develop the neglected regions. His ambition was to foster the growth of a modern bourgeoisie, Muslim and Christian. With their aid he sought to achieve a modern, centralized state capable of integrating outlying regions and playing a key role in socioeconomic development, much as Egypt, Syria, and the newly established regime of Abdel Karim Kassim in Iraq had already set out to do. On one occasion he defined the goal of his development program as that of melting all Lebanese in the crucible of a single society based not on coexistence or association of different categories of the population but on each citizen's conviction of being an integral part of a single people and totally loyal to a single country.

First, however, he had to consolidate his power. He chose Rashid Karami, political boss of Tripoli, who enjoyed close relations with the Nasser regime in Cairo, as prime minister. Except for a short period in 1960–61, during which Saeb Salam became prime minister, Karami held the post throughout Shehab's term, becoming and remaining the champion of Shehabism against the unrelenting opposition of the Catholic right. Whereas during 1958–60 Shehab faced a parliament packed with Chamoun supporters, in April 1960 he and Karami secured the adoption of a new electoral law that favored their supporters. In May, a year before the expiration of his mandate, the president dissolved parliament and called elections. The result was an overwhelmingly Shehabist parliament. When the returns were in the president resigned, declaring he had achieved his goal of reestablishing concord. This move provoked an outpouring of demands that he remain in office and he bowed to "the popular will."

Shehab was the first Lebanese president to initiate a socioeconomic program and to attempt to make all sides conform to its imperatives. It was he who commissioned a study of Lebanon's development needs by the Institut de Recherche et de Formation en vue du Dévéloppement (IRFED), the first study to document the extremes of wealth and poverty in the country and to suggest remedies. Following IRFED's recommendations, Shehab created a planning institution which endeavored to orient socioeconomic planning on a regional level. Among the infrastructure projects it initiated was the Litani River Development Plan for the benefit of the south and the Bekaa Valley. The Green Plan, a semi-autonomous government organization, was set up to encourage irrigation and expansion of the cultivated area, and an Office of Social Development was established to operate in rural areas and assist private welfare organizations. Marking an important advance, a comprehensive social security law was adopted; it went into effect under Shehab's successor, Charles Helou. Promulgation of a Money and Credit Law in 1963 prepared the way for creation of a central bank in 1964, permitting a measure of government control over the banking system.

These initiatives produced mixed results. The hydroelectric projects of the Litani River Plan—necessary for Beirut's water supply—were completed within a decade. But irrigation projects intended to provide much-needed water to poor farmers in south Lebanon and the Bekaa Valley were blocked by the opposition of Israel, the power of traditional notables and landlords, and the ruling class preference for developing the service rather than the productive sector of the economy.

Landlords and their agents determined the distribution of water to peasant lands in the south, and this authority was the key to their power over the countryside and to their election to parliament. Refusing to surrender this power, they successfully forestalled the water projects. Green Plan operations, concerned largely with land reclamation, lacked any established priorities for making possible the cultivation of reclaimed land. For its part, the five-year development plan on which regional planning depended was scrapped when Shehab left office. The demise of these projects was partly due to the fact that Shehab relied solely on Western development models, ignoring the political realities of his own country. Since he shunned radicalism of any kind, and made no attempt to reform the sectarian political system itself, in practice his efforts were directed toward making the National Pact work. He thus unwittingly gave new impetus to sectarianism. His social and economic development policy was based on strengthening private as well as public services; it therefore subsidized private schools, hospitals, clubs, and health and medical institutions. Since all such private institutions are sectarian, the structure was thereby reinforced.

Shehab's socioeconomic programs were intended to develop the deprived, largely Muslim, regions and to integrate them into the state education system, trade unions, and government service. These undertakings, too, had mixed results. In a country where more children attend private school than public, Shehab expanded the public school system, building more public schools and bringing such schools to rural communities for the first time. At the same time, new social classes, chiefly lower-middle strata, entered into the secondary schools.[8] However, the Ministry of Education, dominated by the Maronite right, opposed the adoption of a national education policy. Without such a policy regional imbalances continued: in 1970, 69 percent of all secondary schools were located in Beirut and Mount Lebanon, accounting for 44 percent of the population; curricula, designed for the children of the elites, went unchanged.[9] In addition the private schools—even those so-called free schools run by religious orders, which the government subsidized—were not subject to regulation. They continued to expand faster than public schools and to nourish a sectarian orientation.

In the political realm, Shehab sought to assure Muslims of their representation through the application of the fifty-fifty formula for the distribution of public posts between Christians and Muslims (Legislative Decree 112). As all important public posts became subject to sectarian distribution, the regulatory bodies (established in 1959 to supervise the civil service) became almost wholly preoccupied with this. The lion's share of the additional posts brought under sectarian distribution went to the Sunnis—at the expense of the rapidly growing Shi'a community, thereby creating new grievances. The reform, moreover, did not affect traditional Maronite control of the army command or of key positions in the ministries of foreign affairs, education, finance, and the interior, and so confirmed the inviolability of this control.

Application of the fifty-fifty formula gave new emphasis to sectarianism at a time when an influx of foreign capital and capitalists was also contributing to sectarian tensions. Those most affected by land reforms and nationalizations in other Arab countries were the wealthy

Christian and Jewish minorities, who brought to Lebanon not only capital but also well-developed anti-Arab, anti-Muslim, and anti-socialist prejudices. At the same time Arab oil money was moving into Lebanon, investing in land, buildings, banks, and business firms and enhancing Arab influence. Shehab encouraged the formation of and officially recognized a General Confederation of Labor, and he backed the principle of wage increases to offset price rises. He also made legislative provision for collective bargaining, a great advance for workers. Oil workers formed their own union in 1964, the first homogeneous industrial union.

The Rise of the Deuxième Bureau

Shehab's reforms were accompanied by a sinister development—the rise of the Deuxième Bureau in national security. Throughout his presidency Shehab lacked a social and political base to carry out his programs, obliging him to rely on his own political machine. On the one hand, this included many foreign experts and Lebanese technocrats under the supervision of his chief of cabinet, Elias Sarkis; on the other it included the army's Deuxième Bureau, strengthened by the SSNP coup attempt and the growing militancy of the Palestinians in the refugee camps, which it was assigned to control. In his effort to build a strong state, Shehab increased the army to 15,000 men, gave key security posts to army officers, and gave the Deuxième Bureau the prerogatives of general security.

In pursuit of state authority, Shehab authorized the Bureau—in which he included Muslim officers—to settle tribal and clan feuds in the Bekaa and Akkar regions and to tame the armed gangs and small private militias of political *zuama* that had proliferated during the 1958 civil strife. However, the Bureau involved itself in politics to undermine traditional leaders, often promoting younger rivals of the same sect. It also maintained surveillance of, and intimidated, critics and opponents. Finally Shehab created the so-called Joint Apparatus *(Al Jihaz Al Mushtarak)* bringing together the Internal Security Forces, the General Security Forces, and the army under the guidance of the Deuxième Bureau. Military intelligence was thus given the predominant role in internal security.

Without a social and political base, Shehab's reforms—all made within the confines of the sectarian system—fell victim to the pressures of the political and business oligarchy, which had regained its power after 1958. He was the first to admit his failure. Declining nomination for a second term in 1970, Shehab acknowledged his defeat in a bitter attack on the traditional forces and political institutions. The Lebanese press declaimed, "His NO to the Presidency is NO to the prevailing Lebanese system." Shehab bluntly admitted he could not change the system: "Somebody else might be able to do it but I can't." Three weeks before his death in 1973, he told the French political scientist Maurice Duverger, "Don't deceive yourself: this country apparently so balanced and peaceful lives over a powder keg. All of it will explode soon if its politicians continue to ignore its real problems."[10]

The Domination of Foreign Capital

The Shehab experience revealed Lebanon's lack of a bourgeoisie with the will and capacity to take the lead in building a modern state. The economy's subjection to foreign capital increased during the Shehab period. Capital movement into Lebanon grew from 15 million Lebanese pounds in 1951 to 105 million in 1956 and 370 million in 1966, while remittances from emigrants rose from 58.5 million in 1951 to 112 million in 1966. The rising inflow of foreign capital, together with the steady development of services such as travel and transportation, covered the widening gap in the balance of payments—the result of a chronic and ever-expanding trade deficit.

Capital inflow also stimulated an enormous growth in the country's monetary and banking structure. The number of banks (Lebanese and foreign) grew from seven in 1945 to twenty-two in 1955, forty in 1960, and ninety-three in 1964. Yet Beirut did not become a true financial center where short-term capital is transformed into long-term capital. It functioned rather as a distribution center. Inflowing capital (placed for the most part on short-term deposit in the banks) when not used to finance commercial operations, was redistributed to European industry and American financial centers.[11] This policy denied industry and agriculture the medium and long-term credits essential for development, while the banking system's excessive liquidity was partially siphoned into building. This stimulated an unprecedented building boom, pushing up rents and land prices and soon contributing to serious inflation.

Capital penetrating into an imperfectly competitive economic structure reinforced a trend toward centralization, and banks and monopolies extended their power throughout the country. Manipulating laws, administrative regulations, and the import licensing system, a few monopolies achieved control of the import trade and so also often dominated local production.

The Rural World

Capitalist penetration changed the rural sector. Capitalist investment in agriculture was directed mainly into development of a few specialized crops for export (chiefly to Arab markets): apples grown on small and medium holdings on the slopes of Mount Lebanon; citrus fruits on the coastal plain; poultry and sugar beets in the Bekaa; tobacco mainly in the south. Capitalist enterprises bought up land from absentee landlords, transforming sharecroppers and small peasants into wage laborers or driving them off the land altogether.

Large-scale imports of agricultural produce reduced the domestic production of essential foodstuffs, especially cereals, animal, meat, and milk products. Food prices increased substantially. Agricultural-transformation industries, dominated by a few large firms, developed on the basis of imported, not Lebanese, materials: soy beans and cotton seeds for making vegetable oils, rather than Lebanese olives; imported milk powders to produce milk products; imported concentrates to make vegetable and fruit juices.

Yet Lebanese agriculture remained based for the most part on small-scale, low-return farm production. In 1970, 82 percent of the agricultural land was still owned by those who cultivated it, and of these more than half owned less than one acre.[12] The remaining 18 percent of the agricultural land was rented or farmed by sharecroppers. Although some fifty or so owners had estates of 100 to 1,000 hectares, the average-sized farm holding was 2.4 hectares.[13] Small and medium farmers increasingly found themselves at the mercy of foreign and local monopolies that controlled agricultural inputs and—since state institutions supplied only 10 percent of total agricultural credit—dependent on private commercial banks and userers for short-term credit and on importers and distributors for fertilizers, seeds, pesticides, and agricultural machinery. But these distributors were often themselves usurers who charged average interest rates of about 50 percent.[14] The rising cost of agricultural inputs and the heavy burden of interest payments, which by 1970 amounted to a third or more of the credit granted, ruined many farmers.[15]

A few big operators controlled cold-storage facilities, transport, and distribution outlets, dominating the marketing of agricultural products. With no organization enabling them to stand together, each farmer faced the trading monopoly alone. The result was low prices paid to the farmer and high prices paid by the consumer. Moreover, in the absence of regulation, illegal practices flourished.

The state, lacking an agricultural policy, did not regulate or even establish norms for the marketing of farm produce. In fact, as agriculture had ceased to be one of the country's chief resources, agricultural development was not a major concern. Persistent neglect of agricultural land steadily reduced the area under cultivation. Out of a total cultivable area of 400,000 hectares (40 percent of the total land area) only 200,000 were cultivated in 1965, and barely 50,000 irrigated. This obtained even though the area of cultivable land per agricultural worker was only 0.13 of a hectare, compared to the 0.5 estimated as needed to provide sufficient food per capita. The 110,000 to 115,000 workers in agriculture in 1965 supported 30 percent of the population but received only 10 percent of gross domestic production. According to an estimate based on Food and Agriculture Organization (FAO) criteria, 20,000 of these workers were "surplus," and more than 50,000 families received insufficient returns from agriculture.[16]

The Green Plan for land reclamation and rural development launched under Shehab was almost the first evidence of state concern for agricultural problems. In the five years 1965–70, this project reclaimed a little over 11,000 hectares and brought benefits to 2,184 villages. Yet in the same period, 44,822 hectares of neglected agricultural land went out of cultivation.[17]

Dependent Industrialization

The rural-to-urban migration of the 1960s—during which 18 percent of the population of the south moved into the cities and towns—created new urban slums and widened poverty belts around Beirut and other cities.[18] Although in 1964 nearly 70 percent of the country's industries and industrial workforce were found in its suburbs, Beirut had few jobs to offer the rural migrants. Aside from petroleum-refining and cement, Lebanon had a light consumer-goods industry, one producing for a domestic market that had developed with the emergence of a relatively substantial middle class during the postwar boom in the service economy. But given the growing preference for imported goods, the limits of this market were soon reached.

Owing to the narrowness of the domestic market, industrial firms in general operated at less than two-thirds capacity. But with the sharp rise in Arab oil wealth beginning in the early 1960s Arab markets attracted Lebanese industrial exports, which grew at an annual rate of 15–18 percent in the period 1960–67. As a result of the June 1967 war, which closed the Suez Canal, congested Middle East ports, and doubled freight rates, the competitive position of Lebanese industrialists improved greatly. An export subsidy law of August 1967 gave a substantial boost to industrial exports, and in 1968 67.5 percent of Lebanon's industrial output was sold to Arab countries.[19]

This was not, however, real industrialization, since Lebanon's export industries did little more than assemble or process imported components. The contribution these industries made to national income and employment was limited to the value added in Lebanon. Moreover, by 1977 the share of Lebanese components in industrial output was steadily shrinking.[20]

In 1964 a government report conceded that the modern industrial sector was "developing too slowly to be able to absorb the growth of population."[21] It was also too slow to absorb displaced peasants and sharecroppers migrating out of rural areas. Between 1955 and 1964, employment in industries with five or more workers increased by an average of 750 workers a year, compared to the 13,000 new jobs a year estimated to be necessary to minimize unemployment.[22] According to the industrial censuses, between 1964 and 1970, despite the spectacular development in industrial exports, the number of new jobs in industry averaged just under 1,000 a year.

The development of export industries brought an ever-growing dependence on foreign corporations for machinery, raw materials, and semi-finished goods, and on foreign banks for credits. Licensing agreements and technical and marketing assistance contracts linked Lebanese firms to foreign corporations. Foreign corporations often became part-owners of the local firm. Production of export goods became concentrated in a few firms in each field. Lebanese industrial exports became an avenue through which Western finance capital, benefiting from Lebanon's cheap labor, the Arab cover it provides, and its proximity to Arab countries, could capture Arab markets.

The Crash of the Intra Bank: An Economic Turning Point

The October 1966 crash of the Intra Bank—the country's largest, boasting total assets greater than the government budget—marked a decisive turn for the Lebanese economy. Intra was the creation of the financial genius of Yusuf Beidas, a Christian Palestinian who after 1948 settled in Beirut and opened a small exchange office. From this lowly beginning Beidas developed his bank into one of the largest financial institutions in the Middle East, with important holdings in the Americas and Europe and the control of a substantial part of the Lebanese economy. Intra's rise and expansion, based on the inflow of Arab financial surpluses from the Gulf and increasingly on remittances from Lebanese emigrants in the Americas and Africa, thus posed a challenge to Western financial capital operating from Beirut.

Intra's collapse was the result of both local and international developments. On the local level, Lebanese banks in the early 1960s faced growing competition from foreign financial institutions in Beirut for funds from Arab oil states. To meet this competition they raised interest rates to depositors. This increased their overheads, reduced their profits, and involved them in medium- and long-term investments which realize higher returns but are more difficult to liquidate at short notice. Pressures on the Lebanese banks increased in 1964 when the United States and Europe, in an attempt to damp down the worldwide inflation generated by the Vietnam war, imposed a tight monetary squeeze and higher interest rates. Arab and other depositors in Lebanese banks (which paid interest rates of no more than 4 percent) transferred their funds to American and European banks which offered interests rates of up to 9 percent. All Lebanese banks, not only Intra, thus faced a liquidity problem.

But Lebanon's predominantly Catholic financial bourgeoisie, long jealous of the rising influence of Beidas, took advantage of the liquidity situation to execute a carefully planned run on Intra. The Central Bank rejected Beidas' appeal for cash aid to meet the resulting crisis, although it allotted such aid to all the remaining banks in the country. Its refusal to aid Intra was all the more striking since Intra's composition of assets and liabilities was better than that of other banks.[23] Nonetheless the Central Bank deliberately forced Intra over the brink. The *New York Times* put the matter bluntly: "The credit squeeze against Intra was spearheaded by the Central Bank."[24]

Within three years of Intra's fall, the number of Lebanese banks—owing to failures, fusions, and absorption by foreign banks—was reduced from fifty-five to thirty-eight. Within six years Western banks controlled nearly 60 percent of banking activity in Lebanon, Arab banks controlled 20 percent, and Lebanese banks another 20 percent (a proportion that was soon to sink further).[25] Lebanese savings and profits—financial resources needed to develop a national economy—were now for the most part invested in foreign banks and so used to a large extent outside of Lebanon. Within Lebanon the credit policies pursued by foreign banks favored economic sectors in which foreign capital was involved—principally trade, but also certain industrial companies linked to foreign firms—thus increasing foreign domination in these sectors.

In a letter to the Lebanese people, written shortly before his death and published in *Al Nahar* on April 4, 1969, Beidas explained that the hostility of the Lebanese financial bourgeoisie toward Intra arose from Intra's decision to give "a true Lebanese character to all those numerous projects which are Lebanese in name only but are in fact only fingers for foreign interests." Intra sought, Beidas claimed, to permit Lebanon to achieve economic independence. In doing this, he added, he knew he challenged not only powerful foreign interests but also a small, influential group of Lebanese who had depended since the days of the Mandate on serving projects in Lebanon controlled by foreign groups.

Intra's fall, however, had a further significance. It marked the start of a drying-up of the capital inflow into Lebanon from the Arab oil states. Such funds increasingly bypassed Lebanese banks to be directly invested in European and American financial institutions and other enterprises, which offered Arab capital a safeguard against its erosion by worldwide inflation. As a result, the mainstay of the Lebanese economy began to crumble. Lebanon's traditional vocation as the intermediary between Western capitalism and the Arab hinterland became in some respects increasingly superfluous; the hinterland itself became capitalized. Intra's collapse, in the words of Israeli writer Dan Diner, "marked the beginning of the collapse of the Lebanese state."[26]

[5]

The Forgotten South:
Israel and the Palestinians

To the Paris Peace Conference in 1919 the World Zionist Organization presented these "minimal territorial demands" for the projected "Jewish state": the coastal plains of south Lebanon up to Sidon's outskirts; the waters of the wholly Lebanese Litani River; the entire Jordan watershed, including the northern and eastern slopes of Mount Hermon (Lebanese and Syrian territory); the whole of the Yarmuk watershed and the Hauran plain in Syria; all of Transjordan, the Negev, and the Sinai peninsula.[1]

Since Lebanon and Syria came within the French sphere of influence, France opposed these demands for large parts of Lebanese and Syrian territory, but an Anglo-French compromise met them in part. In order to give the future Zionist state total control of one of the sources of the Jordan River, a strip of land cutting deep into what was to become southern Lebanon was allotted to Palestine, as was another strip running along the eastern banks of the Upper Jordan and the eastern shores of Lake Huleh and the Sea of Galilee.

Until the World War I peace settlement, no international frontier separated Palestine from southern Lebanon. Under the Ottoman Empire southern Lebanon was a part of northern Galilee, and like all of northern Galilee was closely linked economically to southern Syria. People living in the barren hills and mountains of the region owned and farmed much of the northern Huleh plain. Its most important towns developed as commercial centers for Palestinian–Lebanese and Syrian–Lebanese trade, facilitated by the Beirut–Haifa–Cairo railroad. These centuries-old social and economic bonds made of southern Lebanon, southern Syria, and northern Palestine a relatively prosperous economic unit; Haifa, then the most important port of the east Mediterranean coast, was the economic capital. During the period of the mandates the economic unity of the region persisted, while social relations between Arabs of southern Lebanon and those of northern Palestine continued to be intimate. Families often had branches in both countries.

The establishment of Israel in 1948 brutally cut these vital links, blocking trade routes with Arab Africa and destroying the economic entity comprised of southern Lebanon, southern Syria, and northern Palestine. The Israeli army immediately occupied twenty-two Lebanese villages and permanently annexed eight of them, shifting the Israeli frontier in some sections up to 200 meters further into Lebanon.[2] Lebanese farmers denied access to their lands in Palestine have through the years watched Israelis farming this land, which legally the Lebanese farmers still own and to which many still retain their title deeds.

Israeli Expansionism

The UN partition resolution allotted the Jewish state 5,500 square miles of Palestine. By the end of 1955 Israel occupied 7,900 square miles, and after the 1967 war roughly 30,000. This increase was the result of a systematic policy of expansion characterized by repeated terrorist operations and military attacks against Israel's Arab neighbors. Israel always called these aggressions "reprisal operations" imperative to its security. Ignoring the testimony of UN observers as well as that of Arabs, Western officials and the Western press overwhelmingly portrayed the new state as "hapless Israel, the victim of Arab aggression."

Moshe Sharett's personal diary reveals the reality.[3] Sharett records then Chief of Staff Moshe Dayan speaking of these so-called reprisals as "our vital lymph. They . . . help us to maintain a high tension among our population and in the army. . . . [I]n order to have young men go to the Negev we have to cry out that it is in danger" (entry of May 26, 1955). Sharett, then prime minister and foreign minister, writes of his worries about "the long chain of false incidents and hostilities we have invented . . . the many clashes we have provoked which cost us much blood . . . the violations of the law by our men" (June 2, 1955); and about the glorification of terrorism and revenge as the new "moral and sacred values of Israeli society" (March 13, 1955).

He makes clear the threefold purpose of these actions: to push the weak Arab states into confrontations in which their defeat was assured, and so destabilize these states and demoralize their peoples; to disperse the Palestinian people from the vicinity of Israel's borders; and to seize additional land and so reach the boundaries of Greater Israel, Zionism's unchanging goal.

Sharett also discusses in some detail the plan of Ben Gurion, Dayan, and Pinhas Lavon to destabilize and partition Lebanon.[4] In 1954 he rejected as "nonsense" Ben Gurion's insistence that the time had come for Israel to push the Lebanese Maronites to proclaim a Christian state (February 27, 1954), but he did not exclude the possibility of achieving these goals at a future date. His view was that the plan could not work at the time because Maronites would not risk war; the Christians did not constitute a majority and were not a unified bloc.

Yet Ben Gurion's scheme apparently did evoke some interest in Lebanon. According to Sharett, President Chamoun indicated he would be ready to agree given three conditions: Israel must (1) guarantee Lebanon's borders; (2) come to Lebanon's aid if it were attacked by Syria; and (3) buy Lebanon's agricultural surplus (December 2, 1955).

The plan to partition Lebanon may also have had American support. Cooperation between Israeli Special Services and the CIA was so close during the first half of the 1950s that it is difficult to believe the CIA was not informed of Israel's Lebanese projects.

Testimony before the U.S. Senate Committee on Refugees by then CIA Director William Colby (July 1976) revealed that the United States "supplied arms in the fifties to the Christians in Lebanon in the framework of the use of religious and ethnic minorities to fight against communism."[5]

Israel put the Lebanon plan aside in October 1955, Sharett reports, when the U.S. government, shocked at Nasser's decision to buy arms from Czechoslovakia after the United States withheld the promised money for his Aswan Dam Project, reportedly gave Israel a green light to attack Egypt.[6]

The South

Although the Beirut government was probably unaware of these details, Israeli designs on south Lebanon were not secret. They had a significant influence on the Maronite-dominated government's policy toward the south, namely, one of a studied neglect.

The closing of the Lebanon–Palestine frontier, together with the disruption of Syrian trade routes, meant the south was virtually isolated economically, except for the neglected coastal road. The political alliance between the government and the handful of powerful, landed families dominating the south and wanting no outside interference reinforced the region's isolation.

Thus from 1948 on the south began a cumulative process of deterioration. Trading towns stagnated, artisanal production diminished, the development of nascent agricultural industries ceased. Two projects inspired hopes for reanimating the region's economy: the construction of Aramco Tapline (Trans-Arabian Pipeline) to bring Saudi oil to the Mediterranean, and, later, an oil refinery at Zaharani to refine oil for Lebanese use. But both enterprises proved to be wholly cut off from the local economy. Aramco Tapline was originally exempt from all taxes—income, import, export, fuel, municipal—and even in 1963 paid only 3.5 million Lebanese pounds to the government and a token fee to Sidon.[7] The refinery at first refused to employ local labor, and it put the Zaharani harbor, one of the coast's best fishing areas, off-limits to fishermen. Extensive corruption involved in the construction of both projects, however, brought impressive profits to a small group of American businessmen and Lebanese politicians.

In agriculture the situation was rather different. Irrigation of the coastal plain south of Sidon induced entrepreneurs in Sidon and Tyre to buy coastal land from the estates of notable families. There they operated modern citrus and banana orchards, usually managed by nonlocal merchants or returned emigrants and employing a Palestinian workforce.[8] While this caused a boom in land values in Sidon and the plain, those who did not own land did not share in these benefits.

Outside the coastal plain and the area around Jezzine, the southernmost part of the Mount Lebanon range, the rural population inland was left with only the eroded, white, and stony land of Jabal Amel. Water for both irrigation and drinking was scarce and of poor quality. Peasants tried to wring a subsistence out of tobacco planted in the thin soil of small valleys, or from cereals sown in rock crevices, or from fig trees on the arid mountain slopes. Tobacco was particularly well adapted to these conditions, and after 1948 it became the principal source of income for the rural population. The area allotted to tobacco increased two and a half times between 1951 and 1963, and the number of tobacco planters increased more than four times. Yet expansion of tobacco cultivation did not halt the growing impoverishment of the south.

The Régie Domain

Since 1955 the Régie des Tabacs et Tombacs, originally a French concessionary company, has held a monopoly over all phases of the tobacco business in Lebanon: the cultivation and export of raw tobacco; the manufacture and marketing of local cigarettes; and the import and marketing of foreign tobacco products. The monopoly has been exercised on behalf of the government in return for a percentage of net profits: 95 percent to the government and 5 percent to Régie.[9] Régie's operations have always been oriented toward importing and marketing foreign cigarettes, since this yielded the highest profit rates. The sale price of foreign cigarettes in Lebanon could run 700–1000 percent more than the purchase price. Highly detrimental to the national tobacco industry, the policy was promoted by politicians and influential businessmen since it enabled them to acquire representation rights for well-known brands of cigarettes. Such agencies became even more lucrative as consumption of foreign cigarettes rapidly increased (more than eight times from 1951 to 1963). The share of imported cigarettes in local consumption rose from 5 percent in 1951 to more than 60 percent in 1970, not counting what was smuggled from Tangiers, Gibraltar, and Hong Kong, which reached about 40 percent of the annual sales volume of legally imported cigarettes.[10]

Régie's policy held down the quantity of home-grown tobacco needed for local cigarette manufacture. Yet until 1966 the area planted to tobacco steadily increased, first under the pressures from political *zuama* and notables, and later a local oil bourgeoisie. Tobacco could be cultivated only under Régie licensing. Régie distributed these licenses free each year to political bosses, local notables, and so on, who in turn rented or sold them to farmers. This operation netted the intermediaries not only monetary but political profits, while the tobacco farmers had to pay high fees. A large black market in these licenses developed, which intensified the exploitation of the farmers.

Since tobacco cultivation was expanding under pressure from the local notables who were getting rich, the proportion of raw tobacco available for export had to be increased. This was costly to the state, which subsidized Régie by supporting the price the company paid to farmers at two or three times the world level. Tobacco sold on the world market was sold at a loss, and the loss per kilo rose steadily.[11]

The state subsidy was intended to keep the farmer on the land and so prevent migration to the cities. Yet the great majority of farmers (74 percent in 1960) received licenses to cultivate an area of only two dunams (about 1.24 acres) or less—insufficient for providing a living. Tobacco cultivation, spread over a 200-day-period per year, is an occupation requiring the work of a family of five or six plus a number of seasonal workers. Once expenses have been deducted, a large family could receive an income of less than $100 a year.[12] Moreover, Régie and the government consistently rejected local demands to locate a tobacco packing plant in the south, the source of at least two-thirds of Lebanon's raw tobacco.

Had state policy been to promote local tobacco processing and develop a national cigarette industry, the expansion of the planting area could have provided employment and income to thousands of peasants. Instead, the peasants' inability to make a living out of tobacco was a major cause for the pauperization of the rural population and the rising migration out of the south.

In the early 1960s, when President Fouad Shehab's development program got under way, 250 southern villages with 150,000 inhabitants had no water; 445 of the region's 452 towns and villages had no electricity; half the children between the ages of six and ten had no schools, and schools providing more than primary grades were almost nonexistent; much of the population was illiterate; health, social, and sanitary services were almost wholly wanting; eighty-five villages had only footpaths, many more only dusty tracks; and almost a third of the cultivable land had been abandoned.[13] Shehab's program brought roads, electricity, phones, more primary schools, and a few secondary schools to southern villages, but these improvements did little if anything to stimulate local production. Modernization facilitated the marketing of products made in Beirut or imported from abroad, and Beirut's capitalists and merchants began to extend their domination over the region.

In 1968, four years after Shehab left office, the south—comprising 20 percent of the country's land area and 12 percent of its population—contained only 2.4 percent of Lebanon's workforce and less than 5 percent of its industrial establishments.[14]

The improvement of communication and educational facilities, however, brought the people of the isolated south into partial contact with the rest of the country. Aside from the predominantly Sunni city of Sidon, the Maronite town of Jezzine, a few Maronite and Orthodox villages near the Israeli frontier, and the Druse town of Hasbaya, the south is Shi'a Muslim. Throughout most of this century it has been the landed and political domain of four powerful Shi'a families—al-Asaad, al-Khalil, Osseiran, and al-Zein—each owning around 1,500 hectares of land. While new forces have arisen to erode the influence of these families, the families' power remained substantial. All four families usually were, and still are, represented in the higher reaches of government. The al-Asaad family, "seigneurs of Taybe," has long supplied the south's supreme political boss. The present family leader, Seigneur Kamil al-Asaad, like his uncle and father before him, has many times been a deputy and in 1972 was named speaker of the house, the highest government post open to a Shi'a.[15]

The Shi'a community as such, however, remains under-represented politically and economically deprived. Although the National Pact set the Shi'a share in parliamentary, ministerial, and other posts at 20 percent, this provision was respected only in parliament. Political discrimination has been compounded by the rapid growth of the Shi'a population since the end of World War II, the result of a high (4.4 percent) birthrate and a decline in infant mortality. Shi'a emigration to foreign countries increased in this period, but, unlike other Lebanese emigrants, Shi'a emigrants usually return home after making their fortunes abroad. Shi'a community leaders have long claimed that theirs is the largest community, a claim supported by military statistics. A 1974–75 report indicated that Shi'as make up about a third of the population, followed by the Sunnis and the Maronites.[16]

Shi'a religious, feudal, and tribal leaders in the south were the first to benefit from the partial end of isolation. This ruling class succeeded in manipulating development funds in its own interest and acquired a great deal more patronage to distribute among its clients. Expenditures of development funds and the return home of rich emigrants helped create a new professional and business bourgeoisie.[17] A younger generation of the small but now-expanding upper class—including even some of its daughters—graduated from universities and entered the liberal professions.[18]

The new elite emerged not in opposition to the traditional Shi'a ruling class but in the main as an extension of it. Its social and political attitudes, however, were more modern and somewhat more enlightened.

Progressive Politics

The south proved to be a propitious terrain for the development of progressive and non-establishment political parties. The presence of the Communist Party of Lebanon (CPL) in the south dates back to the 1940s; that of the Arab Nationalist Movement (ANM) and the Baath to the late 1950s. The ANM was solidly established in Sidon and Tyre, while the CPL was active in Nabatiye, Marjeyoun, Bint Jbeil, the port cities, and a number of Orthodox villages. The presence of the Palestinian refugees, most of whom were located in Shi'a areas (the south, the Bekaa, and the shantytowns near Beirut), helped awaken a political consciousness among the impoverished Shi'a population and turn it in a progressive direction.

Trade unions appeared in the south as early as the late 1940s; unions of fishermen in 1952; electricity workers, butchers, and bakers in the late 1950s; tapline and oil refinery workers in the 1960s. In 1957 the people of Sidon became the first to elect to parliament a man of modest social background—Marouf Saad, a former policeman and athletics teacher, militant who fought in the 1948 Palestine war, member of the Partisans of Peace movement, and a Nasserite, as well as the leader of the 1958 rebellion in the south. As the political boss of Sidon, his influence thereafter contributed to undermining the power of the great families of the south.

In the late 1950s a new personality appeared in the south. This was Musa Sadr, mufti of Tyre. Sadr realized that the radicalism emerging among the Shi'a masses could be checked only by a very modern approach that could give life to the Shi'a rite. A charismatic figure, Imam Sadr cultivated the new Shi'a elite and started organizing his community, especially its young people. He founded youth, sport, and cultural clubs, known as the Husainiyyat, which he extended into almost every village. However modest their premises, these clubs became important institutions in poor villages which had nothing else, and under the Imam's aegis they became at times centers of national and social agitation and work.

The proximity of Israel, its cross-border infiltrations and later incursions; the large number of Palestinian refugees in the south; the solidarity that in this early period often developed between the Palestinians and the Shi'a villagers out of common suffering; all these contributed to the Imam's rapid involvement in the Palestinian issue.

The Palestinian Issue

In 1948 more than 100,000 Palestinians took refuge in south Lebanon, finding shelter with relatives and friends or in schools, mosques, churches, or in caves and ruins. Those with business, professional, or administrative backgrounds—many of whom were Christians—or with technical and scientific skills and/or capital, moved on to the cities, notably Beirut. They soon played a major role in developing the Lebanese economy, especially its service sector.[19]

Most refugees were of rural origin, however, many of them peasants without possessions, skills, or education. Absorbing so large a destitute population posed a difficult problem for so small a country. The government provided food and shelter until the United Nations Relief and Works Agency (UNRWA) took over, but held the refugees to be in Lebanon on sufferance. The Catholic establishment saw in the refugees—90 percent of whom were Sunni Muslims—a threat to the fragile sectarian balance of power, and urged their prompt repatriation or resettlement in Syria.[20]

As time passed, however, both Muslim and Christian Lebanese began to exploit the Palestinians as the cheapest possible source of labor. The government issued special identity cards marked *lajje* ("refugee") to refugees registered with UNRWA, but it did not issue any specific rules or regulations governing residence, work permits, travel, or citizenship. In all these matters the fate of the refugee was determined by discretionary powers, the exercise of which followed a clear pattern. Christian Palestinians usually acquired citizenship without much difficulty. Personal connections and/or money permitted some Muslim refugees to obtain citizenship. Altogether about 40,000 Palestinians became Lebanese citizens in the thirty years 1948–78, according to Chafik al-Hout, then director of the PLO office in Beirut. As citizens, they could go into business on their own, maintaining themselves as entrepreneurs, small shopkeepers, commission agents, and so on. Those without citizenship were required to obtain work permits, issued only if the refugee was an expert or specialist, married to a Lebanese or of Lebanese origin, or was employed by a foreign company.

Most Palestinians could not get work permits and were reduced to working, if at all, illegally and at substandard wages in low-grade jobs. All Palestinians were barred from trade-union membership and from the protection provided by the social security system inaugurated in the mid-1960s. They received no compensation for accidents at work, no sick leave with pay, no guarantees that their wages would reach the legal minimum. Nevertheless their contributions to the social security fund were regularly deducted from their wages and salaries.

UNRWA rations, meager though they were (never more than twenty cents a day), enabled some to subsist on what otherwise would have been starvation wages. The influx of this mass of cheap labor contributed to a persistent surplus in labor supply, holding down wages for both Lebanese and Palestinian workers. The Lebanese bourgeoisie used the artificial antagonism thus created between Lebanese and Palestinian workers to intensify its exploitation of both. A prominent engineering consultant, Henry Edde, nephew of former president Emile Edde, later pointed out:

> We did not welcome the Palestinians with open arms or take them to our hearts. We did not make available to them the most basic necessities of life—neither water, nor electricity, nor drainage facilities, nor roads, nor social services. It is we who deliberately put them near urban areas and not on the frontiers, in response to the wishes of businessmen for cheap labor. . . . It was the Lebanese bourgeoisie, to which I belong, that advised this so that the Palestinians could be exploited in Beirut and in agriculture on the coast.[21]

A case in point is that of Tel al-Zaatar, a refugee camp located in the heart of "Christian Beirut" on the edge of a wealthy Maronite district. The camp was established in 1950 on land rented by UNRWA from the order of Maronite monks. Attracted by the availability of cheap labor, Lebanese capitalists located industries nearby. The district developed to account for almost a third of the country's industrial production. UNRWA, under pressure from the Christian bourgeoisie, acted to secure a plentiful supply of cheap labor by transferring refugees from other parts of Lebanon to Tel al-Zaatar in 1951 and again in 1955.

Seventeen camps were located on the fringes of Tyre, Sidon, Beirut, Tripoli, and the Bekaa. About a fifth of the camp population had no gainful employment of any kind, though this was a rate of unemployment not significantly greater than that experienced by Lebanese.[22] Those who did work found irregular employment in agriculture or low-grade services jobs. Few had permanent employment; many spent most of their time job hunting. The industrial workers were usually employed in small and scattered firms. The low wages received by one or two members of large families could barely provide a minimum subsistence. The camps also included self-employed proprietors such as butchers, bakers, dressmakers, and tradespeople.

Physical conditions in the camps were miserable in the beginning and in some ways became worse. In twenty years the camp population doubled while the population of the area remained the same. Inhabitants were packed into shacks, tin hovels, or dilapidated apartments, mostly without running water and bathrooms, many still without private or semi-private toilets, heating, or electricity. Inadequately fed children suffered from anemia; their only playgrounds were the alleyways of the camps.

To get a job—as well as escape the tedium and deprivation of camp life—refugees zealously pursued an education.[23] But the government did not admit Palestinians—or Kurds—to public schools at any level. Since most private schools are run by foreign missions, Christian religious orders, or entrepreneurs, and in any case charge fees beyond the means of the destitute, this meant denying the refugees access to any education other than that provided by UNRWA or by the Maqasid (Sunni) schools. Overcrowding, a high ratio of pupils to teachers, low teaching standards, excessive bureaucracy, and an aversion to teaching Palestinian national or political subjects or even mentioning Palestine—these have been the hallmarks of UNRWA schools.[24]

Until 1959 Palestinians were the responsibility of the Minister of the Interior, the Public Security Department, or the Deuxième Bureau, and they were governed by the sometimes contradictory interests of these departments. To bring some order into the situation, President Shehab established an Office of Palestinian Refugees in the Ministry of the Interior, thus making it clear that the Palestinian presence was considered a matter of internal security only. The functions of the new directorate included handling social and personal status formalities, regulating the movement of Palestinians, issuing travel documents, and appointing the local councils in the camps. This ruled out any form of autonomous organization in the camps.[25]

During Shehab's term the Deuxième Bureau, assisted by the Internal Security Forces (ISF), assumed control of the camps. Movement of Palestinians outside the camps was strictly controlled and kept to a minimum; a permit was required to enter or leave. Visits between camps required special permits, registration on arrival and departure, usually also statements of the purpose of the visit and the names of those visited.

Movement within the camps was also restricted. Residents could not leave their dwellings after 9 p.m. In some camps a 10 p.m. lights-out was enforced. Fines and penalties imposed on almost any pretext were a constant means of harassment. All political activity was pro-hibited, including fund-raising. The Deuxième Bureau often monitored UNRWA classrooms, interfered in personal and family affairs, incited bad feeling among camp residents or between them and local Lebanese, or took persons off "for interrogation," from which some returned beaten and tortured and others did not return at all. Until 1969, when they were taken over by the Palestine Libera-tion Organization (PLO), the refugee camps were "not far removed from concentration camps."[26]

The Deuxième Bureau's oppression and humiliation of camp resi-dents became such that a group of Palestinians sought and secured a meeting with President Shehab. Admitting that some Deuxième Bu-reau officers were animated by hatred of the Palestinians, Shehab attributed the Bureau's oppressive policy to the "weakness" of the Lebanese political system and the precarious balance among the sects. If the Palestinians were considered to be a sect, he is reported to have said, owing to its members' political consciousness and dedica-tion to a common cause, it would be the strongest of all. Lebanon "must therefore be excused if it sometimes deals with the refugees in a coercive way."[27]

The situation in the camps, however, did not improve. The oppres-sion suffered by the camp population increased the Palestinians deter-mination to preserve their national identity. From the beginning the refugees managed to re-create in the camps their villages of origin in Palestine, thereby preserving traditional family and peasant values. These bonds gave the camps "a robust cultural self-confidence," writes anthropologist Rosemary Sayegh, adding that in certain con-texts "insistence on preserving peasant traditions can assume a revo-lutionary character."[28]

Political Recovery

Initially paralyzed by the trauma of their uprooting, the refugees were electrified in turn by Nasser's nationalization of the Suez Canal, the 1957 U.S.-dictated Israeli withdrawal from Sinai, and the 1958 Egyptian–Syrian union. Many placed their hopes for the recovery of Palestine on Nasser's Arab nationalism. The 1961 break-up of the United Arab Republic (UAR) at one blow destroyed these expectations, bringing home to the Palestinians their own responsibility for regaining their homeland. Al-Fatah leader Abu Iyad (Salah Khalaf) later revealed that his organization's "metamorphosis into a mass movement" began with the break-up of the UAR in 1961. The disappointment over the union's failure was as great as the hopes its formation had originally inspired. Camp refugees now turned to their own secret organizations. A mounting distrust of Arab governments grew rapidly in the camps in Lebanon and in other Arab countries.

The First Arab Summit and the Formation of the PLO

Palestinian unrest persuaded Nasser and other Arab leaders of the need to bring this developing current under control. In the fall of 1963 Nasser began to explore ways to bring about a Palestine National Congress and affirm a Palestinian entity. This imperative was coupled with another: Israel's project to divert the headwaters of the Jordan River was nearing completion, and none of the Arab states— least of all Egypt—was in a position to fight. For Nasser the imperative was to call a halt to Arab quarrels, make Arab states share in the decision not to go to war, and in a common Arab action reduce the Jordan River water available to Israel.

These imperatives produced the first Arab Summit Conference, in Cairo, in January 1964, which Lebanon attended. Lebanon agreed to help counter the diversion of the Jordan River by diverting two of its tributaries and building a dam to divert water to the Litani River valley. Lebanese fears that these projects would invite Israeli attack brought offers from both Egypt and Syria to station protective troops in the country. Lebanon hastily rejected these offers.

Another Summit decision required Lebanon to double its military forces and equip them with modern arms, for which the Arab League agreed to pay 75 percent of the cost. Lebanon's acceptance was conditional on a guarantee that no Arab armed forces would enter the country without the authorization of the Lebanese government.

The Cairo Summit was the first time—sixteen years after the Palestinians' expulsion from Palestine—that Arab governments formally recognized the Palestinians' right to organize and fight to liberate their land. The participating governments authorized formation of the Palestine Liberation Organization (PLO) and its Palestine Liberation Army (PLA), both which these governments, particularly Egypt, attempted to control, with only limited success. For Palestinians the PLO had real significance; after sixteen years as "the refugees," they again became Palestinian in name, and for the first time acquired representation, however inadequate, and could make their views prevail.

The Lebanese government insisted, and the other participating Arab governments agreed, that the PLA should have neither bases nor training camps in Lebanon and that any Palestinian who joined the PLA would not be allowed to return to Lebanon for any reason whatsoever. Yet for all these restrictions, the Cairo Summit and the Alexandria Summit that followed it effectively brought an unwilling Lebanon into the ranks of the confrontation states in attendance.

On January 1, 1965, only seven months after the PLO's creation, al-Fatah (the Palestine National Liberation Movement) made its first raid into Israel, serving notice of its intention to wage an armed struggle to liberate Palestine. For Palestinians in Lebanese camps this date became the day "the revolution issued," although earlier raids into Israel by other Palestinian commando organizations had already started the resistance roster of martyrs. Al-Fatah's ideology—to have no ideology other than armed struggle—had a powerful attraction for a people with so searing and prolonged an experience of political betrayal. It restored to the refugees their identity and their history. "When the refugees spoke of their pre-1965 life as 'paralysis,' 'death,' and 'burial,'" Rosemary Sayegh wrote, "these terms were symbols of political nonexistence."[29] Above all, al-Fatah appeared to offer Palestinians a chance to take their future into their own hands, and so acquire a political existence.

[6]

Winds of Change:
The Emergence of a Sociopolitical
Opposition

The new activism that emerged among Palestinians came at the very time that a new spirit of dissent and protest manifested itself among the less-favored strata of Lebanese society, as well as among middle strata barred from participation in the political system. From 1964 to June 1967 these two currents developed significantly and to a certain extent began to coalesce.

Fouad Shehab's presidency had inaugurated a marked change in the climate of opinion in Lebanon. The findings of the Institut de Recherche et de Formation en vue du Développement (IRFED) mission, presented in a seven-volume report published in both Arabic and French in May 1961, laid the basis for this shift.[1] The report found "enormous disparities in living standards" between Beirut and Mount Lebanon and the other regions, underlining the contrast between "the ostentatious wealth" of the richest 4 percent of the population and the primitive conditions in the villages of the periphery. It pointed to the "disintegration" already under way in "economic and human entities" and warned of a "revolution of the underprivileged classes . . . coming to a boil."[2] Widely publicized in Lebanon, the IRFED report heightened awareness of the imperative need for change and reform, at least among young people, students, and the intelligentsia. Legitimating popular social demands, it provided those excluded from the social and political system with an effective weapon.

President Nasser's "socialist measures" enacted in the wake of the break-up of the United Arab Republic (UAR) in September 1961 (nationalization, land reform, allocation of half the seats in parliament to workers) and his many verbal attacks on "feudalists and the rich" also helped keep such issues on the boil. Interior Minister Kamal

Jumblat, returning from a visit to Cairo in summer 1962, proposed an increase in the number of seats in parliament from 99 to 150 so that "workers and peasants who form 55 percent of the Lebanese people may be represented," and he suggested that a worker be named minister of labor.

Although the establishment did not take these propositions seriously, Jumblat, undaunted, launched his third effort to organize an opposition front, this time on a new basis. His earlier attempts—the Socialist National Front of 1951–52 and the 1957–58 reformist front—brought together chiefly traditional politicians and notables. In 1962–63 he set out to organize among social groups excluded from participation in political institutions. The base of the new front was to be an active, politically motivated labor movement. In his capacity as interior minister, Jumblat issued a license to the Labor Liberation Front, created by former union leaders associated with the National Federation of Labor Unions (NFLU).[3]

Jumblat's Progressive Socialist Party (PSP), the Communist Party of Lebanon (CPL), and the Arab Nationalist Movement (ANM) cooperated with each other as well as with the Labor Liberation Front on specific issues, but the group did not yet share a common program. It was only after Khrushchev's visit to Cairo and the Moscow–Cairo reconciliation that the basis of a minimum common program could be discussed. A wide-ranging debate in the progressive press throughout 1965 hammered out the terms of cooperation and laid the basis for a formal front. Even before this, however, the nascent front imparted a somewhat new character to a widening movement for social demands. Other groupings of a more diverse nature became involved; demands became more comprehensive and the movement began to acquire a political orientation.

Election of President Charles Helou (1964–70)

At the same time, leading Muslim politicians set out to secure a second term for the president. When Shehab resisted, parliament elected Charles Helou, Shehab's chosen successor, over the Kataeb's candidate, Pierre Gemayel, by a vote of ninety-two to five.

Helou, however, was a weak president. A founding member of the Kataeb, he had shifted in 1945 to the Constitutional Party, which left him without a political base. His weakness gave the Deuxième Bureau free rein to run the state.

Helou's presidency covered an ever more troubled period. The growing foreign and local monopolies penetrating throughout the country widened social disparities, which in turn revealed the limits of Shehab's socioeconomic development program. The continuing Arab–Israeli conflict over the Jordan River waters, King Husain's 1965 crackdown on the PLO and the left in Jordan, and the arrival in power in Damascus of a radical Baath regime in 1966 all contributed to accelerated political and sectarian polarization. The heightened militancy of the struggle for social demands came up against the Maronite right's ever more aggressive stand against "intruders" and "foreigners" accused of undermining the Lebanese system.

Social Protest

Substantial price increases at the end of 1964 touched off numerous demands and strikes for higher wages, among them a countrywide strike by elementary school teachers, who were restricted from joining a union. Although no union came to their aid, they managed to hold out for three weeks. This remarkable feat was due in part to the help they received from progressive parties in Jumblat's grouping. The cabinet, backed by parliament, managed to break the strike by announcing that new teachers would be hired to take the place of the strikers.

Wage demands became so widespread at this time, however, that in January 1965 the government raised the minimum wage and granted a general 8 percent wage increase over the 1960 level. Attached to these reforms were various conditions that considerably reduced their attractiveness, however, especially in view of the fact that members of parliament had just voted themselves a 21.75 percent salary increase.

In addition to strikes, a wave of dismissals resulting from employers' attempts to evade the new social security law provoked considerable labor unrest. Massive layoffs were also frequent in the textile industry, as a rising inflow of unrestricted textile imports compelled companies to curtail production. Workers and owners stood together in demanding import restrictions, but the government took no action until after the 1967 war.

A student strike in 1965 illuminated the Maronite right's hard-line determination to maintain its predominance at any cost. A law degree has always been the passport to positions of power in Lebanon, and access to it has therefore been carefully limited to preserve a Catholic predominance in the profession. Only the Université St. Joseph boasted a law school until the late 1950s, when the Lebanese and Arab Universities opened law faculties, for the first time offering low-income Muslim students an opportunity to get law degrees. When the first graduating class from the Arab University received its diplomas, the Beirut Order of Advocates refused them membership, hence also the right to practice, and provoked the graduates to strike. Adverse publicity induced the order's president to declare that he would recognize the diplomas under certain conditions, and President Helou issued a decree accepting the diploma as Lebanese—at which point the Advocates added additional qualifications: possession of a Ph.D. and the perfect command of a foreign language. At the same time they raised the order's membership dues by more than 33 percent.[4]

Helou's regime was further troubled by a great increase in urban migration, much of it to squatter communities on the outskirts of Beirut. Since the Maronite church and its orders own much of the land in and around Beirut, the squatters inevitably erected their tin shacks on church property. Most of the squatters were Shi'a Muslims from Baalbek and the south, as well as poor Kurds and Palestinians. The interior minister yielded to Kataeb demands to remove the shacks but also authorized some rebuilding, pleasing neither the squatters nor the Kataeb. A high wall built around one of the communities, located on a road leading to fashionable resorts in Mount Lebanon, spared well-to-do recreation-seekers the sight of its squalor.

The Agricultural Crisis

By the mid-1960s the tightening grip of monopolistic merchants, importers, and exporters on small farmers and their produce began to create serious crises in more than one of the country's major crops. Excessive overplanting and primitive methods had much to do with the farmers' plight. But government neglect, delays in distributing promised loans, and above all rapidly rising costs resulting from monopoly control of cold-storage facilties, transport, and marketing were also crucial.

The apple farmers were a typical case. Almost 60 percent of people who worked the land grew apples, mostly on small farms, and prices had declined drastically. Rural Lebanon, however, retained its importance in political life, owing in part to the requirement that voting take place in the village of origin. Politicans could not ignore the apple crisis. In September 1965 Jumblat's PSP invited apple growers to a rally in Btakhnai, where he proposed a program for apples and other crops in similar difficulties. The party called on the government to reduce electricity rates to farmers, to break the foreign monopolies on distribution, and to reduce prices. It also called for the formation of a union of agriculturalists. The rally also demanded that the government buy and guarantee a part of the crop.[5]

One of a series organized by the PSP in the apple-growing areas, the Btakhnai rally provoked an astonishing shock effect in political circles and the local press, and even attracted the attention of the foreign press.[6] Big business quickly rallied to the defense of a "free economy," promising to prevent "socializing consequences." Pierre Gemayel insisted that the rally had been inspired from abroad "to destroy the economic system in Lebanon," and a counter-rally organized by Chamounists won the participation of most Catholic rightist deputies and big capitalists. Taken up in parliament, the issue produced an unprecedented left–right division. But when the debate ended, the apple growers were left on their own to cope with the export and import monopolies.

An Emerging Student Movement

The rapid development of public secondary education during Shehab's term, and the consequent entry of children from under-privileged families into schools that had not been adapted to their needs, soon created serious educational problems. Shrinking job opportunities in the wake of the 1966 Intra Bank crash made even more apparent the unbalanced, elitist character of the educational system. Discontent among secondary students was reflected in their growing demands for the Arabization of instruction, as well as for the reduction of exam fees and the standardization of programs.

Unprecedented strikes by secondary school students over these issues erupted during the first half of 1967. The movement began in Tyre in the extreme south, protesting mass failures in matriculation exams. A big student rally in Tripoli then opposed a rise in exam fees. Students in public and private secondary schools in Tyre and Sidon called for a general strike, which was observed in most of Lebanon, to demand a revision of the curriculum and the standardization of text-books.

The government's answer to student demands was to call on the Internal Security Forces (ISF) to halt the strikes. Clashes between the ISF and students in several cities brought Lebanese and Arab University students into the streets to protest police and army brutality. Spring vacation and a promise by the educational minister to appoint a commission to study the issues gradually ended the strike. But the commission was made up as usual of the high priests of sectarian education; the reforms it drafted increased imbalances in school programs, and the failure rate in exams became even higher. Finding itself in a blind alley, the student movement was compelled to reconsider the roots of its problems more deeply.

Seeing in student unrest "activities of the left parties," the authorities arrested and deported some sixty "alien elements" held responsible. Kataeb student branches, which had strongly opposed the strike, put responsibility on "Palestinian refugees."[7] But the fact that Catholic students were beaten—and one killed—by the ISF persuaded the Kataeb to join in protesting police brutality. Muslim and Christian students who together had participated in the strike made the dead student the symbol around which they rallied. At a time of sharpening sectarian hostility, the students achieved an important degree of national solidarity.

In this period students at the Lebanese University also began to develop a social conscience about the importance of their institution, the country's only national university. The Lebanese University had been founded in 1953 to endow with its own national university a country hitherto served by two foreign and elite universities—the American University of Beirut and the French Université St. Joseph.

In its early years the Lebanese University attracted only children of poor parents, but by the mid-1960s rising demand and efforts to raise its academic level began to have some effect. As its standards rose, the university welcomed an influx of middle- and lower-middle-class students, and within a few years its student body reflected the economic, social, and sectarian range of Lebanese society. The university, however, still lacked any directing idea; like the government it seemed to have no higher education policy.

As economic difficulties worsened in 1966, making jobs in the already saturated service economy ever harder to find, students began to demand courses more relevant to their employment needs. The "Lebanese miracle," based on the service economy, appeared to many to be specious. This perception led to the conclusion that the problem was not that of adapting university programs to the prevailing service economy but of orienting the economy to the production sectors (industry and agriculture) and for this a national university would be indispensable. This perception contributed to the radicalization of the emerging student movement.[8]

In October 1965, three weeks after the famous apple meeting, the authorities prohibited all public meetings. Soon after, the ISF used arms to disperse some 300 Palestinians gathered for a speech in front of the PLO's Beirut office. While the government hastened to start work on a new law on political parties, the ISF confiscated "subversive literature" in the offices of the Syrian Social Nationalist Party (SSNP), the ANM, the Baathists, and the Muslim Brotherhood, and imprisoned some Brotherhood leaders. Somewhat later many Palestinians were arrested for "illegal residence." One Palestinian I knew of, facing expulsion and unable to find a country to go to, committed suicide.

Inter-Arab Conflict

Left-wing and Palestinian activity was not the only danger threatening. In May 1966 Kamil Mrowa, editor and publisher of *Al Hayat* and diehard Shi'a opponent of Egyptian President Nasser, was assassinated in Lebanon. The killing, for which Saudi Arabia held Cairo responsible, brought to Lebanon the conflict between Saudi King Faisal and Nasser over the king's efforts to "contain" progressive Arab states—most recently by courting pro-Western Islamic states. Lebanon, especially the press, became one of the chief battlegrounds in an inter-Arab cold war.

In this battle the Saudis enjoyed the support of the Maronite right, itself virulently anti-Nasser, as well as that of a part of the Muslim right; Nasser commanded the allegiance of most of the popular forces and much of the Muslim community. Each side accused Lebanon of deviation in favor of the other, and both protested against the "bias" of the Lebanese press. Both subsidized one or more newspapers, and neither was ungenerous in the payment of bribes.

Throughout this period the Saudis threatened to withdraw deposits in Lebanese banks, cancel the Saudi–Lebanese trade agreement, and freeze relations if Lebanon did not cease its alleged partiality toward Cairo. Although these threats bolstered Saudi supporters, they never materialized. The pro-Nasser camp made much of the allegedly huge sums of Saudi money coming into Lebanon to buy allegiance and influence the coming parliamentary elections, while Nasser's alleged plots became the chief theme of the Catholic right.

In early 1967 a series of bomb explosions began in Beirut. They hit the United States, Jordanian, and Saudi embassies and cultural attaché offices; cafes frequented by Americans; newspaper offices, both pro- and anti-Nasser; and the homes of Syrian and Iraqi political exiles. The blasts caused slight damage and no loss of life. They were attributed to "foreign Arabs" and provided a convenient pretext for deportation of many "aliens," mainly Syrians and Kurds, at a time of rising unemployment.

The basic issue for Lebanon in the Saudi–Egyptian conflict was Lebanon's post-1958 foreign policy acknowledging Lebanon to be part of the Arab world and maintaining a moderate pro-Nasser stance. This was coupled with an effort to stay out of inter-Arab conflicts, and toward this end the government issued a law dubbed "the law of kings and presidents," which forbade the publication of any attack on Arab or foreign heads of state. As Kamal Jumblat described it:

> We are Saudis with the Saudis; Kuwaitis with the Kuwaitis; Syrians with the Syrians; Egyptians with the UAR, and we also go along with the Americans in certain basic questions such as the purchase of big aircraft, but at the same time we refuse to say a word about the crimes committed every day in Vietnam.[9]

Internal disputes also found expression in the conflict. In December 1966 Saeb Salam and the other Sunni Muslim politicians demanded the constitution be amended to provide for equitable Muslim participation in power, and succeeded in calling a constitutional conference. Pierre Gemayel threatened implacable Kataeb opposition to any attempt "to undermine the pillars of stability" by discussing constitutional change. Sunni deputies, however, did not all back Salam's proposal—the most notable opponent being Prime Minister Rashid Karami—and they ultimately shelved it, demanding electoral reform instead. As the 1968 parliamentary elections neared, reform for many took second place to winning the Maronite right's support against Karami, who had excluded Sunni deputies from high positions in his political entourage.

The right's campaign against Nasser and his Lebanese followers continued unabated, however. In an open letter to the president on March 8, 1967, Pierre Gemayel asserted that Lebanon "has been harnessed to Egypt's chariot," and hinted that his party would extend its hand "to all honorable Lebanese hands" in order to undertake "a vast national salvation campaign."[10] The Kataeb stepped up a campaign against Lebanon's participation in the Arab boycott of Israel on the grounds that Cairo was using the boycott office in Beirut to interfere in Lebanon's internal affairs.[11]

The Chamounists and Raymond Edde's National Bloc supported the Kataeb. On March 28, the leaders of the three parties that were soon to constitute the Tripartite Bloc met with President Helou to inform him that "Lebanon did not enjoy full sovereignty." They demanded a return to "nonalignment" and the adoption of the National Pact as an unwritten constitution.[12] The president's rejection of these demands gave impetus to the rightist offensive against the government's alleged subservience to Cairo and communism. Evidence of this was the fact that the Afro-Asian Writers' Conference had recently held a meeting in Lebanon under the auspices of Prime Minister Karami and that Khalid Muhieddine, head of the Egyptian Partisans of Peace Movement, had paid "regular" visits to Beirut. Declaimed Gemayel on May 10, "State encouragement of communist organizations can no longer be tolerated."[13] So successfully did the Maronite right beat the drum about the "red menace" that parliament was persuaded to postpone until June 1969 elections for city councils and village *mukhtars,* scheduled for May 1967, "owing to leftist activities."

Rightist distrust about "illegal parties" and "leftist organizations" reflected the right's growing concern about the widening movement for social change. With increasing frequency, newspapers, political figures, and ordinary citizens asked, "Are we on the eve of another 1958?"

[7]

The Debacle:
June 1967 and Its Aftermath

The operations of the Palestinian resistance achieved a new level in the winter of 1966–67. For Israel, committed to denying the very existence of the Palestinian people, this affirmation of a vigorous Palestinian existence was intolerable, the more so as Damascus encouraged it defiantly, while Nasser looked to the United Nations for a solution. Thus to nip the resistance in the bud, "do something" about the Damascus regime, parry Egyptian initiatives, and annex more Arab land, Israel attacked Syria, Egypt, and Jordan on June 5, 1967.

Israel claimed to be fighting the six-day war for survival, as Prime Minister Levi Eshkol proclaimed in the Knesset: "the existence of the Israeli state hung on a thread . . . but the hopes of Arab leaders to exterminate Israel came to naught."[1] But U. S. intelligence experts rejected Israel's claim of an imminent Egyptian attack, and both the CIA and the Pentagon had considered that "Israel would easily win if hostilities were to begin, no matter who struck first."[2] Moreover, Nasser's actions throughout the crisis were clearly intended to avert an Israeli attack on Syria.

But if Nasser did not want war, Israel did. Five years later Israeli General M. Peled announced in Tel Aviv, "The thesis according to which the danger of genocide hung over us in June 1967, and Israel was fighting for her very physical survival, was nothing but a bluff which was born and developed after the war."[3] Replying to the resulting uproar, he said there was no reason to hide the fact that since 1949 no one dared, or in more exact terms, no one was in any position to threaten the very existence of Israel. No one in his right mind, he said, could believe that the forces Israel mobilized at this time "were necessary to defend us against the Egyptian threat"; rather, they were to crush once and for all the Egyptian military. He added that "by falsifying the causes of war and confusing its true motivations, the Israeli government was seeking to render acceptable to the people the principle of partial or total annexation."[4] Former Chief of Staff General Haim Bar-Lev agreed, and even General Ezer Weizmann, at that time an ardent partisan of Greater Israel, admitted "there was never a danger of extermination."[5]

Most telling of all, perhaps, was Prime Minister Menachem Begin, who in a speech to the Israeli National Defense College during Israel's 1982 invasion of Lebanon stated that of Israel's five wars, including the "Peace for Galilee" operation, only two were really defensive, the war of independence and the Yom Kippur war; the other three, the Suez campaign, the six-day war, and Peace for Galilee were all offensive. Begin's words on the six-day war are especially memorable: "Let us be truthful with ourselves. Nasser did not attack us. We decided to attack him." At the time Begin was a member of the cabinet and so spoke with some authority. He went on to defend wars of aggression by arguing that the army suffered far fewer casualties than in defensive wars.[6]

Although fully aware of who the agressor was, the United States supported Israel. On the eve of the war President Lyndon Johnson declared the United States to be firmly committed to the support of the political independence and territorial integrity of all nations of that area. But a few days later, UN delegate Arthur Goldberg opposed UN efforts to draft a resolution demanding Israel's withdrawal to the 1949 armistice lines. He went on to demand settlement of "all outstanding questions" on "a new basis"—namely, liquidation of the Palestinian question.

Lebanon and the 1967 War

Although Lebanon had no direct role in the 1967 war, the Israeli aggression alarmed many people, especially in the south. Following the angry popular reaction to Israeli cross-border raids in 1965 and 1966, pledges to introduce military conscription, fortify border villages, and arm the inhabitants were made to parliament. The raids were insignificant compared to what was to come, but serious enough for villagers whose homes were blown up or whose sons were kidnapped and taken to Israel for "questioning." In the crisis atmosphere of May 1967, an aroused public opinion insisted that the government take its stand with other Arab states in the face of the mounting Israeli threat. Yet the government sidestepped the demand for military conscription and refused to arm the villagers.

Finally, in mid-May, Prime Minister Karami announced that Lebanon had taken the military steps to fulfill its commitments as a member of the Arab League Defense Council. Reserves were called up, recruiting centers were opened, demonstrations and meetings were banned, and internal security was reinforced.

On June 5, when the war began, Radio Beirut called on Palestinian refugees to volunteer, and parliament granted the government emergency powers for a two-month period. Commander-in-Chief Emile Bustani decreed a state of emergency, forbidding gatherings of any kind and imposing press censorship. Beirut students who called on the government to fight for Palestine and in defense of Lebanon were dispersed by the Internal Security Forces and thanked for their "national sentiment."

Throughout the war, Lebanese listened helplessly to the reports of disaster. Nasser's resignation in Egypt provoked dismay in many parts of Lebanon. In Muslim West Beirut shops and offices closed and a general strike began. The government quickly banned all demonstrations.

Soon after the war Israel attempted to make the Israeli–Lebanon border subject to renegotiation under UN Security Council resolution 242, which assured Israel of "secure borders." Lebanon rejected this, adding that since Lebanon had not been a party to the war, the cease-fire agreement did not apply. The government agreed to the presence of UN observers on the border, on condition that they be stationed on both sides and that the arrangement come under the 1949 armistice agreement rather than Resolution 242.

A Decisive Turn

The June 1967 war effected a decisive change in the Middle East. Arab unity at the Khartoum conference in August–September could not conceal the reinforcement of American influence in the area and the overwhelming predominance of an expanded Israel enjoying virtually carte blanche U.S. backing.

For Israel, the war's outcome proved crucial, since it compelled Arab states to abandon their total rejection of its presence and accept its existence within its pre-June 1967 frontiers. "Restoration of Palestine" for Arab governments had shrunk to mean restoration of the West Bank and Gaza Strip.

The very magnitude of the debacle suffered by Arab governments made their immediate surrender to American–Israeli terms impossible. Just as after the 1948 Palestine war, the Arab governments were both militarily and politically too weak to make either further war or a decent peace. This was as true of "socialist" Egypt and Syria as of "conservative" Jordan. Great mass demonstrations in Egypt demanding Nasser withdraw his resignation—echoed in Lebanon and other Arab countries—expressed the popular will to continue the battle. While this canceled much of the immediate political impact of Israel's victory, Nasser failed to use popular energies on behalf of basic reform and a popularly based national effort.

The failure of Arab governments to achieve any Israeli withdrawal whatsoever by diplomatic means radicalized the popular classes in all eastern Arab countries. The result was that, on the one hand, only the Palestinian resistance was left to carry on the national liberation war, and on the other, the conflict became to an important degree an internal class conflict in each Arab country. This was especially true in Lebanon.

The Palestinian Resistance in Lebanon

On March 10, 1968, Israel attacked the West Bank town of Karameh. Palestinian commandos, with some support from the Jordanian army, beat off the attack, lifting Arab morale and transforming the resistance in the eyes of the people into the catalyst of hoped-for Arab revolution. The battle also made al-Fatah the acknowledged leader and voice of the resistance. Thousands joined its ranks at this time.

Intensified guerrilla activity in the West Bank and Gaza had a significant impact on Israel's military and economic capacity and brought the Palestine question to the center of the international arena.[7] Yet the resistance was not wholly prepared to play the revolutionary role assigned to it by the Arab masses. Al-Fatah, its main body, was organized as a broad nationalist movement. Its leaders, for the most part from the refugee camps, had become contractors and commission agents in Kuwait or employees of the Saudi and Kuwaiti governments. Many al-Fatah leaders came from religious backgrounds; some at one time or another had been associated with the Muslim Brotherhood. The Palestinian bourgeoisie of Kuwait and the Gulf provided the main financial support, while the fighters came mainly from the refugee camps—drawn by eagerness to serve the cause and the steady, if modest, wages.

Al-Fatah accepted recruits without applying political standards and promptly integrated them into military units. Al-Fatah leader Abu Iyad (Salah Khalaf) explained: "From the beginning Fatah has been concerned to bring together all persons from the extreme right to the extreme left."[8] The policy was one of noninterference in members' beliefs as long as their commitment to the struggle was assured. This allowed a variety of political orientations and discourse—in itself a kind of political education—while permitting the leadership a high degree of diplomatic and to an extent political flexibility.

Prior to 1967 al-Fatah had stood against Nasserism, the major political movement in the Arab world, because Nasser opposed commando activity against Israel independent of his own control. Al-Fatah maintained good relations with Saudi Arabia and Kuwait and forged relations that were later to serve it well with Algeria and Syria. It cooperated with Arab governments, whatever their political complexion, on the basis of two principles: (1) Palestinian responsibility for Palestine's liberation (which Arab states should support but not direct); and as a corollary, (2) noninterference by the Palestine resistance movement in the internal affairs of Arab states.

Arab regimes quickly embraced al-Fatah, whose professed lack of ideology they found reassuring. Oil states, in particular Saudi Arabia, saw in aid to al-Fatah a means of preserving social peace at home. Palestinians made up much of the Saudi workforce and had been largely responsible for the great strikes that paralyzed Aramco's operations in 1953 and 1954. A by-product of al-Fatah's organization of Palestinians in the Gulf could be a "well-behaved" labor force.

The growing popular appeal of the resistance movement after the 1967 war prompted each Arab regime to create its own "Palestine resistance" organization. Such organizations had little, if anything, to do with the Palestine cause. They were intended to advance the aims of their patrons in inter-Arab conflicts and to contain and limit the local influence of the authentic resistance. These organizations did incalculable harm to the evolution of a disciplined and responsible Palestinian liberation movement, not only by their undisciplined behavior but also by provoking conflicts between the resistance and the local population, as well as within the resistance movement itself. This state of affairs underlined again the magnitude of the problems faced by a liberation movement which was without a land of its own from which to fight and which issued from a people widely dispersed in many countries.

Al-Fatah met this situation by trying to win the support of all Arab regimes and so maintain its independence from each—when necessary maneuvering among them. Its single purpose—liberation—was defined in the perspective of a narrow nationalism. This strategy allowed al-Fatah time to establish itself, but its relations with Arab governments risked inhibiting its relations with the Palestinian and Arab masses, as some of its leaders later came to realize.[9] This trap became clear when U.S. "peace" initiatives, beginning with the so-called Rogers Plan in June 1970 (proposed by then U.S. secretary of state William Rogers) offered Arab governments "solutions" which excluded the resistance.

Radical Currents

A radical perspective existed and developed within the resistance, among the middle cadres of al-Fatah itself and in smaller organizations. This was comprised mostly of offshoots of the Arab Nationalist Movement (ANM), whose Palestine branch had set up a military wing in the early 1960s and started commando operations in northern Galilee (in spite of Nasser's opposition). But the break-up of the United Arab Republic in 1961, the armed and ultimately successful struggle waged by the ANM's South Arabian branch (independent of Nasser's control) against the British in Aden in 1964–67, and the growing exposure to radical ideas from participation in international conferences in the "socialist world," all contributed to the beginnings of a reexamination of the premises of Arab nationalism even before the 1967 war.

Yet the ANM, having been so closely identified with Nasser, went down with him in the 1967 war. Its organization in the West Bank and

Jordan—all of whose active leaders were in jail at the time—was virtually destroyed when Israelis took over Jordanian police and intelligence files. In the Gaza Strip, however, the ANM survived the war intact. Here Palestinian commando activity went back to 1948. The camps were more crowded and the people poorer than in the West Bank, and Israel's rule was from the beginning more repressive than elsewhere. The ANM's Palestine branch, solidly based among the masses in Gaza, succeeded in arming the people—mainly with weapons left behind in Sinai in 1967.

At the end of 1967 the ANM Palestine branch established the Popular Front for the Liberation of Palestine (PFLP), under the leadership of George Habash, to wage an armed struggle to liberate Palestine. Through continuing discussion and study in the next year, the PFLP decided to transform itself into a Marxist-Leninist organization. Thereafter it experienced a number of splits, the most notable being the departure in 1969 of many of its intellectual cadres, led by Nayef Hawatmeh, to form a new organization, the Popular Democratic Front for the Liberation of Palestine (PDF). The PFLP and the PDF thereafter tried to establish themselves among the masses, but apart from the PFLP's success in Gaza, their following remained far smaller than that of al-Fatah. Even so, they had a significant influence on al-Fatah, because their ideological perspective contributed to an understanding of the Palestine and Arab national problems.

The Palestine resistance had the misfortune to be born big: it did not develop organically out of earlier combined military and political work. Although the 1967 war blew up the myth of Arab military might, it did not prompt the movement to a critical analysis of the causes of the debacle. While al-Fatah did make a real effort to create an insurrectionary situation in the West Bank after the war, the effort failed because the organization lacked roots in the area. This failure meant that henceforth the battle was to be waged not from inside Palestine but from surrounding Arab states.

After their humiliating defeat in 1967, these states projected the Palestinian resistance movement to center stage as an alternative to their own inaction. This was the only way they could hide their own military weakness and mitigate popular frustration over their political bankruptcy. An important consequence of this strategy was to give the resistance movement the right to operate in other Arab states as if it were on liberated territory. The resistance movement took this right at face value. Its exclusively nationalist perspective did not prepare it for policy changes by Arab governments when they were offered alternatives excluding the resistance. Thus in September 1970, when King Husain clamped down on the resistance in Jordan, it did not have the internal structure to withstand the assault.

This political weakness arose in part from conditions particular to the Palestinian situation. Nowhere did Palestinians live in a complete Palestine society. Widely dispersed geographically, they had become increasingly diverse. Moreover, political and ideological currents experienced by Palestinians tended to be translated into the needs of classes in their host society, not into their own needs. Exile and dispersion had cut them off from their own history, a history rich in instructive experience for the new phase of their struggle. Host governments had condemned Palestinians to political and cultural passivity, while feeding them promises of a not-too-distant liberation of Palestine by regular Arab armies.

The fact that the Palestinian resistance movement was robbed of its own country and had no land of its own as a base from which to operate blinded it in part to the need to understand the peculiar features of the Lebanese situation and to the need to take these features into account in its own development. The resulting inability of both its right and left wing to make a direct linkage between the national and social basis of struggle cost it dearly after 1970, when Lebanon became its last stronghold.

Historic ties, and a common social oppression, bound the people of south Lebanon to the Palestinians. Most Lebanese in the south warmly welcomed and supported (and sometimes fought with) the resistance fighters. Many factors contributed to the eventual erosion of this support; not least among them was the resistance's inability to give a social dimension to its crusade.

Aftermath of the 1967 War

The 1967 war deepened the basic cleavage in Lebanese society. To the Maronite right, the Arab debacle offered the opportunity to renounce both Arab nationalism and the Arab national movement and to strengthen its ties to the West. In the words of Kataeb leader Pierre Gemayel, the time had come "to internationalize Lebanon's neutrality" and make it "another Switzerland," that is, no longer part of the Arab world. By contrast, for the Progressive Front, as Kamal Jumblat's grouping was then called, it was imperative to revise outdated institutions to eliminate sectarian privileges and to allow Lebanon to assume its national responsibilities in the Arab world. In an effort to contain this division, the government imposed a strict military censorship over all publications and prolonged the state of emergency until the end of the year.[10]

Only a month after the June war, however, on July 11, the three Maronite leaders—Camille Chamoun, Pierre Gemayel, and Raymond Edde—issued a long (and heavily censored) manifesto, announcing that Lebanon stood at the crossroads: "Either it joins the extremist socialist systems, which are a first step to communism, or continues its free economic system which is part of its parliamentary democratic system."[11] The manifesto demanded that Lebanon reject the anti-American measures adopted by other Arab states, strengthen its ties with Washington, and combat socialism. A new tone, highly condescending to the Arabs and Arabism, appeared in the speeches of these leaders.

The rightist offensive was directed toward the spring 1968 parliamentary elections, the first since Shehab left office. The Triple Alliance, formed by the three leaders to fight the elections, hoped to eliminate the deputies who had dominated parliament for the past decade and bring back the Chamounists. Their platform—anti-socialist, pro-United States, and implicitly anti-Arab—won them the support of the United States and other Western powers. Their campaign pulled out all sectarian stops. Slogans in Kisrawan, giving the impression that President Nasser was running against the Virgin Mary, proved highly effective. Jumblat prophesied that the campaign "would turn Lebanon into another Cyprus where Muslims and Christians would fight each other like Greek and Turkish Cypriots."[12]

Progressives campaigned on the demands put forward at the famous "apple meeting" as well as on student and worker concerns: educational reform, free medical treatment and medicine, free compulsory primary education, and wider participation in the Palestinian liberation effort.

Aside from the sectarian campaign of the Triple Alliance, the most obvious aspect of the election was the apathy of the electorate; only some 20 to 40 percent voted.[13] Chamounists were returned to parliament in force after almost ten years of near oblivion, and the Triple

Alliance gained a narrow edge over its chief opponent, the Democratic Parliamentary Front of Rashid Karami.

This balance of forces paralyzed parliament, which could not even reach agreement on the formation of a new government. A four-man emergency cabinet of two Maronites and two Sunnis, including Shehabist Abdullah Yafi as prime minister, was ultimately formed.

Sociopolitical Polarization

The movement for social change, halted only temporarily during the 1967 war, had resumed with new strength and quickly became linked with the Palestine liberation movement. During the election campaign, secondary students in Beirut and Lebanese University students went on strike for educational reforms. A month after the Lebanese University strike began, the Internal Security Forces brutally ended it. Police with tear gas entered the campus and university buildings late in the evening, beating students with rifle butts, jamming them into police trucks, and taking them off for detention. Police violence politicized many more students.

Wide and growing popular support for the Palestine resistance movement compelled the government to change its attitude toward Palestinians. On April 27, 1968, some 150,000 people attended the funeral ceremony of seventeen-year-old Khalil al-Jamal, the first Lebanese member of al-Fatah to be killed in action (in Jordan). Pierre Gemayel felt it necessary to send six top party aides to represent the Kataeb at this ceremony; Camille Chamoun and Raymond Edde also sent delegates. The weekly *Al Sayyad* commented on May 2, 1968: "the attendance of government representatives at the funeral, the like of which had never been seen before in the history of Lebanon . . . is proof of a tremendous change in the government's attitude toward commando activity."

Recruiting offices for commando organizations opened in Beirut, attracting many Christians as well as Muslims. Prime Minister Abdullah Yafi told a big demonstration protesting against an Israeli army parade in Jerusalem that the government "will meet your demands and give arms to volunteers who join the Lebanese army to liberate Palestine."[14]

Israel's response to these developments—a series of four mortar attacks on one or another southern village in May, June, and October—provoked new demands for military conscription, fortification of border villages, and aid to the commandos. Press reports of American pressures for a prohibition of all commando activity, the arrest of Palestinians, and restrictions on their activities prompted the formation of popular committees to support the various commando groups, raise funds, and recruit volunteers.

In late October, al-Fatah and the Syrian Baath Palestinian organization Saiqa deployed small units—not many more than one hundred men—on the slopes of Mount Hermon inside Lebanon, reportedly with the approval of former president Shehab. But nine days later a Lebanese army unit attacked a group of these fighters returning from Israel, killing one Palestinian. A Lebanese military spokesman subsequently expressed regret over the incident.

The closing months of 1968 saw a proliferation of popular activities on behalf of the resistance and the people of the south. Shi'a leader Imam Musa Sadr, perceiving the sympathy of the Shi'a population for the Palestinians, now emerged as a champion of the Palestine cause, while Kamal Jumblat became head of the Lebanese Organization for Support of Commando Action.

Balfour Day, November 2, 1968, saw big pro-Palestinian demonstrations in Beirut and other cities. A few days later punitive measures taken by Jordan's King Husain against the resistance in that country provoked student protest demonstrations in Beirut, Tripoli, and Sidon. At the Université St. Joseph, whose student body was overwhelmingly Catholic, student militia under the leadership of Bashir Gemayel, the son of Pierre, attacked and beat up students joining the pro-Palestinian demonstrations. All the leaders and most of the demonstrators on both sides were Christians, Maronite, Greek Catholic, and Orthodox.[15] In Tripoli, stormy strikes and demonstrations in which a student was killed led to a week-long curfew and an even longer student strike. Counter-demonstrations by the Kataeb and other rightist students in Beirut provoked further disturbances, a government ban on all demonstrations, and a cabinet debate on calling in the army.

Military conscription was out of the question, however, owing to the Maronite veto. It would mean an influx of Muslim officers threatening the Maronite monopoly of the officer corps, and a potential armed resistance to the weak government.

Yet the private militias of the two main Maronite right parties, the Kataeb and Chamoun's Ahrar, were already undergoing training and receiving arms. In October the formation of a new rightist Maronite militia, the Zghorta Liberation Army, was announced. (Zghorta is the seat of the feudal domain of the Franjieh clan.) Purchase and distribution of arms—British-made rifles and machine guns—began in some Christian villages just after the 1968 elections. By summer, Soviet Kalashnikovs captured by Israel from Syria during the 1967 war were being sold to Lebanese at prices four times higher than they commanded in Israel.[16]

The Beirut Airport Raid

On December 28, 1968, Israel raided Beirut Airport, allegedly in retaliation for a PFLP attack on an Israeli plane in Athens. If Israeli policy was to nourish the seeds of division in Lebanon, the reaction proved the soil was fertile. The response of the Lebanese authorities to the raid revealed almost unbelievable incompetence—or tacit complicity. Immediately after the PFLP attack Israel gave clear notice of its intention to strike at Lebanon. The next morning Lebanese Transport Minister Raymond Edde warned that the airport would be the target. Early on December 28, Commander-in-Chief Emile Bustani ordered all officers and commanders to remain on alert, especially at the airport.[17] At 9:10 p.m. that same evening an Air Navigation official telephoned the Airport Security Base only to have his call shifted to the Defense Ministry, where no one answered the phone.[18] Five minutes after the Israeli attack began, Bustani phoned army leader Iskander Ghanem, who explained that his men could not reach the airport because the roads were blocked. Israeli paratroopers landed and blew up thirteen planes on the runway, fired on terminal windows, strafed the road, and within half an hour departed—without interference of any kind.

An investigation revealed that Ghanem had disobeyed orders, allowing many of his soldiers to go on leave. On hearing this, President Helou called for the file and kept it until Ghanem reached retirement age in July 1969, thus blocking any punitive measures from being taken against him.[19]

The army's humiliating inaction angered the population. In all cities, strikes and demonstrations called on the government to assume its responsibilities, introduce military conscription, allow the resistance to operate freely, and coordinate its policies with other Arab states. The government promptly banned all demonstrations, and then Prime Minister Abdullah Yafi resigned.

The formation of a new government encountered the familiar obstacle of the conflict over Chamounist participation. In late January 1969 Rashid Karami put together a government without Chamoun, and therefore also without Gemayel and Edde. Karami's statement incorporated the principal popular demands, including support for the resistance movement and commitment to a compulsory military conscription bill.

The right called for the intensification of the crisis so as "to bring down the irresponsible and dangerous government" which was "leaning ever more to the left," and also for a general strike to hand the government a vote of no confidence. But only Christian East Beirut observed the strike. In parliament Karami won a confidence vote, but not before a Chamounist deputy caused an uproar by denouncing the Palestinians as "bands of armed foreigners who were sent by the Baath and the communists to commit sabotage and sow dissension among Lebanese and turn Lebanon into an easy prey for the enemy." He warned the government that if it did not "forcibly remove" the Palestinians, civil war was inevitable. This was the first public statement of what was to become the Maronite right's favorite threat of blackmail—until civil war materialized six years later.[20]

Public opinion for the most part understood the serious implications of the Israeli attack, which exploded the myth that Lebanon could stay out of the Arab–Israeli conflict and rely on its friends in the West. A serious attempt to work out a national policy to meet the crisis seemed imperative to many, but the Lebanese political system lacked the institutions that could formulate a national policy.

Thus the crisis was handled on a de facto basis by the army command and the president, who decided that Palestinians rather than Israelis were "the enemy." Without consulting the newly formed Karami government, the army and the Internal Security Forces (ISF) rounded up Palestinians and their supporters and started a military campaign in the south to cut the Palestinian supply-line from Syria. Tension mounted sharply when the army in the Arqoub tried to surround the Palestinian forces, and arrests of Palestinians and Lebanese "leftists" multiplied. In mid-April, chasing commandos returning from an operation in Israel, the army besieged the town of Bint Jbeil when the townspeople refused to hand over the wanted men. After a three-day army bombardment of the town, the commandos, to spare the inhabitants further suffering, gave themselves up and were imprisoned in Tyre.

News of this affair sparked protest demonstrations throughout the country. On April 19 students in Tripoli and the south went on strike demanding the commandos' release. Demonstrations inside and outside the refugee camps and in most towns and cities demanded an end to army–ISF attacks and a government policy of support for the resistance. On April 22, Jumblat's grouping of national and progressive parties joined with the resistance movement in calling for a protest march the next day, but Minister of the Interior Adel Osseiran refused to authorize it.

On April 23, defying the order, some 10,000 to 15,000 marchers, reinforced by busloads of students and others from all parts of the country, gathered in a Muslim quarter of Beirut to march on the city center. As these unarmed people started their march, the ISF (later proving to be army men in ISF uniforms, since local police could not be trusted to carry out "shoot and kill" orders) met them with tear-gas grenades and hoses of hot water.[21] When the marchers, after falling back to regroup, again advanced, the forces of law and order fired at them point blank, killing and wounding many. Thus began an unequal battle that lasted for two hours. Time and again the unarmed marchers fell back, reformed their ranks, and resumed their attempt to advance in the face of ISF fire. Official figures put the number killed at twenty, the wounded at more than one hundred, the arrested at more than two hundred. Others reported much higher casualty figures. Local strikes continued for several days until the army, unable to withstand the wave of anger and revulsion that engulfed the country, released the imprisoned commandos. Interior Minister Osseiran could not explain why unarmed people should be killed for supporting the Palestine cause or even for disobeying a government order. Nor could he produce a single wounded member of the forces of law and order to back up his claim that a shot at a policeman had triggered the attack. The contrast between this savagery against their children (many of the marchers were students) and the army's failure to lift a finger against the Israeli paratroopers at the airport was not lost on the population. Alarmed by the popular revulsion, the government imposed a state of emergency, military censorship, and a ten-day curfew.

The heavy-handed suppression of the April 23, 1969 demonstrations marked a crucial turn in Lebanon. The Palestinians no longer stood alone, and they knew it. Most importantly, the government authorities and the ruling elite also knew it. The way was open for the Palestinians to liberate their camps from Deuxième Bureau tyranny and to win an official treaty legitimating their right to operate against Israel from inside Lebanon.

The next day Karami resigned, saying no government could take sides on the issue of Palestinian action without splitting the country. His resignation stripped the executive authority of its "Muslim cover" and left the country without a government for the next seven months. The long government crisis suggested that the balance of sectarian power was beginning to shift against the Catholic right, as traditional Muslim politicians were compelled to heed popular pressures. The army, unrepentant, took advantage of the seven-month crisis to hit at the Palestinians wherever and whenever it could.[22]

Army clashes with al-Fatah and Saiqa in the south in late April and early May led the executive to try to persuade Syrian President Adnan Atassi to curtail Saiqa activity in Lebanon. When this failed, Lebanese President Charles Helou asked Egyptian President Nasser to mediate. Nasser sent his personal representative, Hassan Sabri al-Kholy, to meet Palestine Liberation Organization (PLO) leader Yasir Arafat, top Lebanese army officers, and President Helou to work out an end to hostilities. The agreement that was reached provided for the release of those arrested during the April demonstrations, the withdrawal of security forces from the Palestinian camps, and new coordination between the Palestinians and the Lebanese government.

But arrests of Palestinians and their Lebanese supporters continued. Security forces still besieged the refugee camps. And on May 31, after meeting with American Ambassador Dwight Porter, President Helou announced his rejection of a Palestinian armed presence in Lebanon. Helou's insistence in subsequent consultations with Karami and others that the Palestinian commandos must be withdrawn from Lebanon "by force if necessary," doomed any attempts by Lebanese factions to agree among themselves.[23] With the approach of summer's heat all factions in parliament tacitly agreed to "freeze the crisis" for the time being so as "not to spoil the tourist season."

The summer season, however, proved less than brilliant, owing to conflicts with Syria (over the presence of Syrian exiles in Beirut), Iraq (over Beirut press reports on Baghdad's alleged persecution of its

Shi'a population), and Saudi Arabia (over the construction of a Saudi oil refinery in Lebanon).

But all attention shifted back to the Palestine problem in August, when Israeli air attacks on front-line villages in the south shook the summer's relative calm. The reaction of the villagers did nothing to allay openly expressed rightest fears over the impact of the resistance movement on the less-favored classes. The poor demanded not that the commandos leave, but that the government provide them with shelters, trenches, and arms to defend themselves.[24] This gave a new impetus to the Maronite right's charge that commando action was "a cover for open conspiracy to change Lebanon."[25]

The Israeli raids encouraged the Lebanese army to renew its attacks on the refugee camps which it still encircled. When eleven Lebanese army soldiers broke into the Nahr al-Bared camp north of Tripoli and were taken hostage by camp inhabitants, army units forced their way into the camp. The refugees, however, fought back until the army agreed to withdraw two miles from the camp in return for release of the hostages. Pressures from other Arab states, as well as the power of popular feeling throughout the country, compelled this retreat.

The army cordon remained, but Deuxième Bureau and ISF offices were ousted from the camp. Thereafter all the Palestinian refugee camps liberated themselves one by one from Deuxième Bureau and ISF control, although in each case the army maintained its cordon around the camp.

The Cairo Accord

Resumption of Lebanese army battles against the Palestinians in the southeast during the last week of October 1969 brought strong protests from Syria, Iraq, Libya, Algeria, and South Yemen, as well as an offer of mediation from Egyptian President Nasser. President Helou accepted, and the result was the Cairo Accord signed by General Bustani on November 2. On his return to Beirut, Bustani insisted that the accord be placed before the cabinet for ratification; he was promptly fired by Helou. Parliament and the cabinet approved the accord without knowing its contents.[26]

The Cairo Accord legitimized the Palestinian armed presence in

Lebanon and the resistance movement's use of part of the south as a springboard for attacks into Israel, in effect giving the resistance extraterritorial rights in that area. The fact that the accord was not made public indicated that the state was either embarrassed or afraid to guarantee its validity. Its provisions recognized very important Palestinian rights in Lebanon, including Palestinian control of the refugee camps; the right of Palestinian residents in Lebanon to participate in the Palestinian revolution through armed struggle; and the right of the resistance movement to operate from fixed bases in southern Lebanon (on the understanding that the government exercised its full rights and responsibilities in these regions). It also required the Lebanese authorities to facilitate the movement of Palestinian commandos to and from Lebanon's borders. In addition, the resistance movement was to appoint representatives to meet with the Lebanese army command on a regular basis, to establish coordination, and control the members of both organizations. Both parties were to cease all propaganda campaigns and establish joint committees.

For the Palestinians a decisive question was whether the camps would serve as "detention camps or revolutionary bases." The resistance movement established a Supreme Committee for Palestinian affairs to be responsible for PLO dealings with the government. Attempts by then Interior Minister Jumblat to negotiate a return of Lebanese internal security forces to the camps ended with an agreement, dated February 25, 1970, that allowed Palestinian organizations to handle all questions concerning the security of the resistance movement, while Lebanese security forces would be stationed outside the camps to handle civil and criminal offenses involving camp inhabitants.

The absence of central authority on both sides aggravated the difficulties of enforcing the Cairo Accord. The fact that a press leak in April 1970 divulged its contents did not improve matters, since the state still insisted on treating it as secret and thus still refused to guarantee it. Less than three weeks after its signature, following a clash between the army and commandos in Nabatiye camp, the army bombarded the camp and killed or wounded more than fifty people. No disciplinary action was taken against those responsible.

At the same time, a "deliberate attempt to discredit the resistance" got underway with the falsification of reports about commando activities.[27] On March 17, the Deuxième Bureau summoned three

Palestinian officers to an army checkpoint near Bint Jbeil and shot them dead. A week later the Bureau killed another three Palestinian officers near Beirut. And on the next day Kataeb militiamen ambushed the funeral cortege of one of these murdered officers on its way to Damascus and again on its return, killing ten Palestinians and wounding eighteen. During the next two days the Kataeb and Palestinians fought near the Tel al-Zaatar refugee camp, provoking fear that the clashes would spread to central Beirut and ignite a civil war.

Other militias, notably those led by Chamoun and Franjieh, also became active. And Israel joined the drive to undermine the Cairo Accord, its gradual escalation of incursions into Lebanon reaching a climax on May 12, when some 5,000 troops, supported by planes, tanks, and field artillery, invaded the Marjeyoun district. This provoked an unintended reaction. The resistance movement was joined by regular army units on their own initiative, and with some Syrian air support, fought side by side, turning what Israel had planned as a swift operation into a hard-fought battle. Lebanese–Palestinian–Syrian solidarity in battle demonstrated that the army—despite rightist domination of its command—was not a monolithic institution, and that within it ran a current in tune with popular support for the Palestinian cause and Lebanese Arab patriotism.

A nationwide strike on May 26, called by Imam Sadr "to make the south a part of Lebanon," paralyzed the country, proving to be the most total such event in Lebanese memory. Demonstrators throughout the country chanted: "We want arms!"

The contradiction between Lebanese sovereignty and the Palestinian right to wage armed struggle against Israel from Lebanese soil could not be reconciled short of a common approach to the problem of Israel and a common political-military strategy to deal with it. While it was clear by the summer of 1970 that the effective Lebanese authorities and the Catholic right did not subscribe to the common approach and common policy, to which lip-service was paid in the Cairo Accord, the majority of the Lebanese people at that time assuredly did. The resistance movement was becoming the rallying point for all those disaffected with the Lebanese system.

[8]

1970:
The Tide Turns

Black September

The 1967 Cairo Accord legitimating Palestinian use of south Lebanon
as a springboard for operations in Israel seemed to indicate a shift in
the sectarian balance of power inside Lebanon as well as continuing a
somewhat favorable trend among Arab governments toward the Palestinians. Developments in 1970, however, beginning with an American initiative to settle the Arab–Israel conflict, revealed the transient
character of Arab government support. Acceptance of the American
proposals by Egyptian President Nasser and Jordan's King Husain led
to an August cease-fire in the fierce "war of attrition" over the Suez
Canal. Arab states tempted by the American initiative now increasingly perceived the resistance movement as a liability.

Husain was the first to strike. In September 1970 he attacked the
resistance in Jordan, continuing a war already marked by battles in
1969 and in February, May, June, and July of 1970. The Popular
Front for the Liberation of Palestine (PFLP) had long warned that the
king was committed to ending "dual power" in Jordan by crushing the
resistance. To forestall this it had called for strengthening relations
with progressive Jordanians and placing the Palestine question before
the world. Yet the resistance had no political strategy governing its
relations with the monarchy. Through want of discipline in its ranks it
allowed repeated provocations against the king and his government,
but had no plan to take power. It did not even anticipate the king's
determination to end the Palestinian challenge to Jordanian authority
once and for all.

Al-Fatah leader Abu Iyad later admitted that the resistance was
well aware of the king's intrigues "to provoke our ruin, yet we helped

him powerfully to achieve his objective in multiplying our errors of judgment, our mistakes—and—why not admit it frankly?—our provocations."[1] Abu Iyad also revealed that the Central Council of the resistance, meeting in July 1970, decided not to take power in Jordan but rejected the logical alternative, an attempt to normalize relations with the king. Resistance leaders for the most part believed the king would not dare to attack.

Nonetheless, in military terms, the resistance did not suffer defeat. The battle of Amman began on September 16. When it ended on September 27, the resistance movement controlled roughly three-fourths of this predominantly Palestinian city; some 5,000 Jordanian soldiers, virtually all of Palestinian origin, had joined its ranks. Moreover, the Jordanian army's Brigadier General, Mahmoud Daoud, resigned on September 26, in order to remain faithful "to my beloved Palestine." Yet heavy Jordanian bombardment of the refugee camps caused very high civilian casualties. Politically, the resistance movement lost the battle through its naive misjudgment of Arab regimes.

Moreover, the ouster of the Salah Jadid government in Damascus early in November removed the one Arab government that had come to the resistance's aid. During the September battle Jadid had sent Palestine Liberation Army (PLA) units (in Syrian tanks) into north Jordan to bolster resistance positions in the area. This Syrian intervention was a limited affair: General Hafez al-Assad, then defense minister, had unilaterally denied the resistance air cover. But American reaction was spectacular. The United States sent its aircraft carrier *Saratoga* to the east coast of the Mediterranean and, as Kissinger later boasted, "we sent an armored division down the autobahn [presumably in West Germany]. We flew aircraft from the Sixth Fleet to Lod Airport in order to pick up staging plans. We put the 82nd Airborne on alert." As a consequence, "the Syrian tanks turned back."[2] American bellicosity also persuaded Baghdad to pull out the 12,000 Iraqi troops stationed in Jordan. These troops made not even a gesture of aid to the resistance movement, although Baghdad had promised they would be placed at its disposal in case of need.

General Assad seized power in a bloodless coup in Damascus on November 13. Thereafter, he gradually aligned Syria with the Arab governments following the American lead to a "political settlement," one based on Arab acceptance of the Zionist seizure of most of Palestine. Understanding perfectly the meaning of the change in Damascus, King Husain scrapped the agreement on which the civil war in Jordan had been ended and set out to methodically liquidate the resistance movement. Resistance leaders—still counting on the support of Arab governments and the good offices of the Arab Committee sent to protect them—agreed to disarm their militias in the cities. Thereafter, the resistance was pushed out of one place after another, and by July 1971 its presence in Jordan was completely liquidated.

This defeat coincided with changes in the status of the Palestinian resistance movement in Syria, where the Assad regime subjected it to more strict controls, and in Egypt, where Anwar Sadat was already embarking on a policy of compromise with Israel.

Thus Lebanon had by 1970–71 become the Palestinians' last stronghold.

The End of Shehabism

In the summer of 1970 Shehabism's twelve-year rule ended with the election of Zghorta-based deputy Suleiman Franjieh to the presidency by a one-vote margin over the Shehabist candidate, Elias Sarkis. This was hailed as the beginning of a new era heralding prosperity and peace.

Franjieh's election marked the return to power of political feudalism. Originally the "strong man" of his brother Hamid, a respected and enlightened politician, Suleiman Franjieh owed his political career to the stroke that compelled his brother to withdraw from political life. Zghorta, the Franjieh fiefdom, marks the northern limit of the "Maronite fortress," the core region of Lebanon which stretches unbroken to Jezzine at the southern end of the Mount Lebanon range. It thus lies on the edge of a peripheral northern area populated mainly by Muslims. This region, the Akkar, which suffered economic decline after its separation from Syria in 1920, remains poor and backward. Zghorta is one of its more indigent localities. In terms of identity, the Maronites of the north tend to be more tribalist than sectarian, with tribal loyalties usually taking priority over sectarian allegiances.

Economic and social interests link Zghorta and other towns of the area to Sunni Tripoli and to the Syrian cities of Homs and Hama more than to the Maronite Mountain. This helps explain the fact that during the 1958 rebellion the Franjieh clan fought beside the insurgents against Chamoun, and that Zghorta and Jezzine (whose economic interests also lie on the Syrian side) were the only two Maronite localities to support Patriarch Meouchi in his 1958 stand against Chamoun.

Zghorta was never a base for Maronite nationalism and never ranked among the Maronite elite. The sociopolitical pecking order in the Maronite community is rigid, and Maronites of the core regions of Metn and Kisrwan look down on Maronites of other regions as a lesser breed—the further from the core region, the lower down on the sociopolitical ladder. That Franjieh's election was widely acclaimed reflected the general relief at the defeat of the army's Deuxième Bureau, which had run rampant in recent years. Political feudalism expressed satisfaction over the triumph of one of its own, rather than any great confidence in the capacities of the new president.

The first years of Franjieh's rule saw the definitive abandonment of Shehab's effort to build a national industry to supply the home market and become the base of a national productive economy. This was the culmination of a trend whose beginnings we have already noted, in the growing involvement of Lebanese industrialists in production for export markets in conjunction with foreign corporations. This development meant leaving the home market to foreign imports, a major factor in driving up both prices and the cost of living at an accelerating rate in the first half of the 1970s.

Political renunciation of the effort to build a productive economy marked a crucial turning point, since a productive national economy was essential to the development of an integrated national state, to the evolution of new classes capable of leading society in this direction, and to the evolution of a secular ideology. Parasitic capitalism and political feudalism were natural partners, sectarianism serving the interests of both. But under the pressure of new social forces the partnership was beginning to show cracks.

One of the new regime's first acts was to launch a law-and-order campaign in an effort to assert state authority. Lebanon witnessed its first executions in more than a decade, with the sectarian balance scrupulously observed: one Christian and one Muslim were selected for hanging. In a drive against "outlaws," the Internal Security Forces, backed by the army, swept into the Bekaa-Hermel area and on into Tripoli. These sweeps, involving house-to-house searches without warrants, won the applause of Christian right leaders. In Tripoli, an important base of the progressive parties as well as the political fief of Sunni leader Rashid Karami, progressive political activists, and even some of Karami's followers were jailed.

Franjieh's first year in office was acclaimed as "the fattest year" economically since 1967, owing to the establishment of "law and order." The law-and-order campaign, however, suggested a different conclusion—that the traditional partnership of parasitic capitalism and political feudalism could maintain its ascendancy only by repressive measures.

"Revolution at the Top to Prevent a Revolution from Below"

Yet the new regime revealed a certain awareness of the need for a new style of government. President Franjieh designated his long-time personal friend Saeb Salam, one of the so-called Sunni political giants, to form a government. Their choice of a twelve-man extra-parliamentary cabinet of relatively young technocrats was an innovation in Lebanese political life, at once a gesture toward the partisans of modernization and reform then becoming more numerous, and an effort by representatives of political feudalism to refurbish its image and reverse its decline. Salam's call for "a revolution at the top to avert a revolution from below" became his government's watchword. Some of his ministers certainly tried to carry out needed reforms, but the Lebanese system soon defeated the would-be reformers. It was clearly not the aim of the Franjieh–Salam team to reform the system. The prime minister said flatly, "We do not accept in any way that the system be touched. We reject subversion."[3]

Finance Minister Elias Saba set out to encourage national industry and find more money for social and economic investment, and did so by raising customs duties on a wide range of imports, mainly luxury goods. This was the famous Decree 1943, which provoked a not-to-be-forgotten storm of protest from all but one of the country's business associations. (The exception was the Association of Industrialists.) Amid a vast propaganda effort orchestrated by the magnates of the service sector, merchants sharply increased prices on imported and other goods and went on strike. Within ten days they had succeeded in compelling the government to withdraw Decree 1943 and in forcing Saba to resign. Cancellation of the decree did not persuade merchants to cancel the price rises, however, which set off the inflationary spiral of the 1970s.

Health Minister Emile Bitar, attempting to reduce inflated medicine prices, found himself engaged in a bitter battle with medicine importers who refused to import, and with pharmacists who refused to sell, medicines at the lower prices; they threatened to strike unless the price reductions were rescinded. Importers and pharmacists won this trial of strength because persons close to the president opposed the price reductions. The government therefore refused to back Bitar, and he too was compelled to resign.

Public Works Minister Henry Edde, nephew of preindependence Lebanese President Emile Edde, resigned when his ministry's appropriations were arbitrarily and substantially cut without consulting him. Education Minister Ghassan Tueni quit after 100 days because the president refused to support his plan to reform the educational system. His successor, Najib Abu Haidar, also resigned, because of his powerlessness to satisfy student and teacher demands. The next education minister, none other than former Public Works Minister Henry Edde, became the first minister ever to be fired—because he attempted to carry out the reforms Tueni had started.

The technocrats' failure to achieve even the most modest reforms bore witness to the bankruptcy of the long-standing ruling partnership between the service economy's commercial and financial bourgeoisie and the great political families of the provinces, who have traditionally dominated both parliament and executive offices, and who still do. The former's rejection of any interference in unbridled free enterprise ran parallel with the latter's rejection of any real reform in state institutions.

The Army "Out of Politics"

Traditional politicians and their bourgeois partners, resenting Shehab's use of the army's Deuxième Bureau to undermine their power in his attempt to build a modern, centralized state, began a drive to "get the army out of politics." Wide popular opposition to the army's real abuses of power, especially the Deuxième Bureau's contempt for civil liberties, hid the true significance of this drive, which was also directed against other modern, central institutions created by Shehab. The drive was in fact intended to strengthen the sectarian system. Voicing popular sentiment, Kamal Jumblat sought the complete abolition of the Deuxième Bureau. This failed because the regime's aim was not to get rid of the Deuxième Bureau but rather to eliminate Shehabist influence in both the army and the government.[4]

Jumblat was more successful in his campaign to put an end to the army's interference in civil disturbances and civil life. A law was adopted by parliament in June 1971 which defined the army's role in internal security. Civilian authorities were given responsibility in this field, and only when the interior minister found the Internal Security Forces inadequate could he call upon the army for assistance.[5] The army was forbidden to make arrests, violate civil rights, or use force except in self-defense; while on military field action, the army was required to remain in contact with civilian authorities. A further law of November 1972 authorized the army to take action in civil disturbances by cabinet decree only, and at the same time increased the prerogatives of the defense minister.[6] This law also reduced somewhat the number and area of military zones, along with the authority of army officers in these zones.[7]

In practice, however, the new laws changed little. When it proved expedient, they were ignored. When General Jean Nujaim—a respected officer who had succeeded Emile Bustani as commander-in-chief—was killed in a helicopter crash in July 1971, President Franjieh brought Iskander Ghanem out of retirement to replace him.[8] Ghanem owed his appointment to the backing of Camille Chamoun. Nevertheless it was an astonishing appointment. Both Franjieh and Saeb Salam, then allies in parliament, had demanded Ghanem's dismissal from the army following his official condemnation for negligence and his failure to carry out orders during the Israeli raid on Beirut Airport.[9] Troubling questions were raised about the appointment, especially because widely believed reports insisted that Nujaim had been murdered. No proof of these reports was ever offered, but criticism of Franjieh's choice of a retired officer to command the army—especially an officer who had recently served as a paid consultant to the American military attaché in Beirut—did not die. Nor was the 1968 airport fiasco to be the last of Ghanem's curious actions in carrying out his duties.[10]

Ghanem's assumption of the army command was followed by what Rashid Karami later called "a series of appointments, transfers, and promotions which allowed Christian elements to take over all sensitive key positions in the Army," thereby converting it into an instrument of Maronite sectarian nationalism.[11] Together, Franjieh and Ghanem reinstated the "strength through weakness" policy dear to the Maronite right. The basic theme they advanced was that Lebanon's defense was impossible, the entry of Arab troops into the country would be inevitably fatal, and the Palestine resistance movement must therefore cease its activities in Lebanon.

This development coincided with a decision to formalize and expand cooperation between the army and the militias of the Maronite right. The army would henceforth provide these militias (chiefly the Kataeb) with military training, weapons, and other aid. This permitted the militias to perform a task the army alone (given that the national division on the Palestine question was repeated to a certain extent in the army's own ranks) could not perform: that of harrassing and containing the resistance movement.

The Maronite Right and Its Militias

Sharpening differences among the parties of the Maronite right came to a head with the definitive break-up of the Triple Alliance of Pierre Gemayel, Camille Chamoun, and Raymond Edde, once the strongest Christian political grouping in Lebanon. This occurred over a by-election in December 1970 for the parliamentary seat left vacant by the death of Pierre Gemayel's brother, Maurice. Refusing to back Pierre's son Amin Gemayel, the Kataeb candidate and ultimate victor, Edde campaigned for Fouad Lahoud. Lahoud was a National Liberal Party (NLP) member whom NLP leader Chamoun, eager to maintain his alliance with the Kataeb, refused to support. Differences between Edde and the Kataeb had their origins in the Kataeb participation in the Shehab regime, as a result of which the Triple Alliance had once before become inoperative. To Edde, always opposed to a political role for the army, the activities of the Deuxième Bureau had become "as dangerous as Zionism and communism," and the Maronite cover the Kataeb had provided Shehab was "a sellout." Moreover Edde, who had stubbornly opposed the Cairo Accord, was outraged by the Kataeb's vote for it.

In the wake of the Cairo Accord both the Kataeb and the NLP

stepped up the training and use of their militias. The proliferation of these militias plunged Lebanon into a multiple crisis: a *political* crisis engendered by increasingly unworkable political institutions, widening sectarian inequalities, and contradictions sharpened by Lebanon's inclusion among the confrontation states; an *economic* crisis reflected in shrinking national production, the widening domination of foreign capital, and spiraling inflation; a *social* crisis felt in the displacement of much of the rural population, in peasant revolts, and in workers' and students' strikes; and a *national* crisis engendered by the state's failure to resist Israel's repeated violations of Lebanese sovereignty. The militias appeared because the ruling partnership of the service bourgeoisie and the political feudalists was totally incapable of responding to popular demands and needs.

Not insignificant among the reasons for the Maronite right's arming their cohorts and putting them in uniform was the desire to guarantee their youthful clientele against infection by ideas of social change. Not least among the reasons for the right's strident campaign against the Palestinian resistance movement was the need to divert attention from its own adamant rejection of any change in the system at home. The rightist battle-cry, "Palestinian violation of Lebanese sovereignty," served to hide the identity of the real violators of Lebanese national sovereignty: the militias. When the Catholic right spoke of Lebanese sovereignty, it was talking about sectarian rather than national sovereignty. The sectarian system itself, with its inevitable lack of political structure and its feeble and inefficient state institutions, permitted the Palestinians much freedom of action, and it ensured that the Catholic right would try to abort the nascent alliance developing between the Palestinians and disaffected Lebanese.

This strategy served to reawaken among some Christians the historically embedded "minority-fear complex" and to persuade them of the need to accept the tutelage of the militias. The Catholic right's answer to the multiple crisis was the reinforcement of sectarianism. Implicit in this answer was a long-term goal: if rightist hegemony could not be preserved over the whole country, then partition was second best.

The Lebanese people were not easily convinced. In the south the commando presence put a stop to the Israeli practice of sending soldiers across the border to intimidate and mistreat villagers and to shoot the livestock of any who defied Israeli orders. Commando purchases provided villages with a new source of income. Many impoverished villagers came to believe their enemy and the commandos' enemy to be one and the same.

But Israel's retaliatory air strikes and artillery bombardments of Lebanese villages still created tensions between the villagers and the commandos. In Nabatiye in January 1970, after heavy Israeli attacks, townspeople demanded the commandos' departure. Other villages asked the commandos to withdraw from the village itself but to remain in the vicinity, since the commandos did afford some protection against Israeli raids. Still others worked with, supported, and sometimes fought alongside the commandos.

As Israeli reprisals became more severe, a certain myopia on the part of the resistance movement created resentment and bad feelings among the rural Lebanese. The multiplicity of commando organizations, the fact that some organizations were creatures of Arab regimes bent on inhibiting the development of a revolutionary resistance, the too-frequent lack of discipline and sense of responsibility in command ranks, all these gave the rightists a chance to achieve some eventual success in the increasingly inevitable conflict.

$$\left[\begin{array}{c} \text{PART} \\ \text{2} \end{array}\right]$$

THE CIVIL WAR, 1975–76

[9]

The Gathering Storm:
Political, Economic, and Social Crisis

The Muslim Challenge: Sunni "Participation"

The latent political conflict between the Sunni and Maronite communities over the terms of their respective shares in power, which had subsided during Fouad Shehab's regime, began to resurface during Charles Helou's presidency. A further growth of the Sunni capitalist class contributed to a renewal of Sunni demands for a more equal share in power. The 1967 Arab defeat and the aggressive anti-Arabism of the Maronite right in its wake exacerbated Sunni sensitivities. The presence of the Palestinian resistance movement put added pressure on traditional Sunni leaders to stand up for Muslim rights, since the resistance movement's magnetic attraction for the Sunni poor threatened to radicalize and draw away their chief clientele. Sunni *zuama,* the landed aristocracy, were already beginning to lose command of the Muslim streets to the Palestinians and their Lebanese supporters.

Sunni leaders adopted the slogan *al-Musharakah* ("participation") to express their demands, and they pointed for justification to the fact that Muslims clearly constituted a majority of the population. But they did not present themselves as active leaders, appearing rather more like a minority petitioning for equal rights. Sunni demands did not envisage change in the sectarian system, but Sunni leaders needed to achieve a more equitable share in power in order to maintain their hold over their community.

Rightist Maronite leaders, firm in their conviction of Lebanon as the Maronite fatherland, not only rejected Sunni demands but also tried to erode Sunni prerogatives. These efforts—evidenced especially in Suleiman Franjieh's manoeuvers to enhance his authority at the expense of the Sunni prime minister—set off a simmering political crisis.[1] Many Sunni leaders suspected that Prime Minister Saeb Salam was less than zealous in advancing Muslim rights, citing his opposition to Shehabism, his cool relations with Cairo, and his close ties with Saudi King Faisal.[2]

The "participation" campaign started with a demand to make Friday, the Muslim holy day, an official day of rest.[3] Strict enforcement of a ruling requiring all shops and souks to close on Sunday fed Muslim resentment, since it gave Christian competitors an advantage over all Muslims who did not work on Friday.

As the campaign heated up, Israel's assassination in Beirut in April 1973 of three Palestinian leaders, followed by Lebanese army attacks on Palestinian commandos, abruptly shifted the focus of Muslim demands to political rights. During the crisis President and Commander-in-Chief Helou wielded absolute power under a state of emergency, as if the Muslim community and its representatives did not exist. Prime Minister Salam resigned.

Ultimately, the Islamic associations issued a charter defining Sunni demands. These included: (1) suppression of political sectarianism, that is, ending sectarian privilege on the level of popular representation and posts in the state apparatus (this demand seemed to go beyond "participation," but was usually expressed in terms meaning just that); (2) sectarian balance in the state apparatus; (3) reform of the electoral law to eliminate political feudalism; (4) placing the army under the authority of the defense minister and creating a Command Council to assure "national balance" in the army, reinforcing its potential to permit it to defend the country; (5) dissolution of the armed militias of the parties; (6) priorities for development projects in deprived regions; (7) a general census to settle the problem of naturalization; (8) support for the Palestinian resistance movements; and (9) a favorable response to the demands of the Shi'a community.[4]

The Sunni charter thus raised many of the problems agitating the country, but its proposed solutions—although seeking to do away with sectarianism in the political domain—remained within the sectarian context.

Shi'a Muslim Demands

A more dynamic challenge to the Establishment, one aimed at economic and social as well as political reform, came from the Shi'a community under the leadership of Imam Musa Sadr. Although the Shi'as had received official recognition in 1926 as a community separate from the Sunnis, they did not acquire an officially recognized spokesperson until 1967, when Imam Sadr established the higher Shi'a Council.

Although a backward step from a secular perspective, the organization of the council gave the Shi'a community an official voice and placed it on a more equitable footing with the other large communities. Since laypeople have a role in the council, it also brought to the forefront the new Shi'a elite.

In February 1974 the council formally presented the demands of the Shi'a community: the community must receive the number of posts in government to which it was entitled under the National Pact; citizenship must be promplty granted to the tens of thousands of Lebanese, chiefly Shi'as in the deprived regions, who had long been denied it; and state negligence in defending the south against Israeli aggression must cease. The council also demanded the execution of specific development projects, most long since approved but never carried out, including the provision of schools, hospitals, and other medical facilities in the south, the Bekaa, and Akkar regions, and the amelioration of the conditions of both tobacco-growers and the poor of the Beirut slums.

These demands issued from a broad sociopolitical religious movement, *Harakat al-Mahrumin* (Movement of the Disinherited), set in motion by Imam Musa Sadr. This movement, founded in February 1973, had its roots in the changes wrought in the Shi'a community by the extension of capitalism and the service economy into the backward rural regions, by the rise of a Shi'a bourgeoisie seeking its rightful place in the Lebanese system, and above all, by the further pauperization of the already impoverished majority of the Shi'a community.

The Movement of the Disinherited spoke on behalf not of the Shi'a community alone but of all the deprived and all the impoverished and backward regions. Initially some 20 percent of its membership was Christian. Although this percentage later decreased, the movement always rallied some Christians and worked with others of whatever sect who pursued the same ends. Sadr verbally supported the Palestinian cause, the legalization of the Communist Party of Lebanon, and other political causes. His emphasis on the social dimension of his mission and his positive stand on the Palestinian resistance movement led progressives to see in him a leader who had "opted for the modern conception of man who must forge his own destiny."[5] Sadr's movement forced upon public opinion at least some awareness of the injustices inflicted on the majority by the obsolescence of the Lebanese system, the operation of unbridled capitalism, and the state's failure to defend its citizens against Israel's ever-more-punishing attacks.

The refusal of the Maronite right to entertain any of the Muslim demands, Sunni or Shi'a, not only intensified the frustrations of these communities, it also slowly pushed some of their conservative and even rightist political leaders toward an unwilling rapprochement with the national and progressive forces.

The National Movement

Especially troubling to the Maronite right was the development of a modern opposition movement oriented toward the needs of oppressed social groups. In the early 1970s Interior Minister Kamal Jumblat took two decisions that significantly changed Lebanon's political life. One was to allow clubs and societies to exist and operate without prior government permission. The second was to legalize all banned political parties.

The first, coming at a time when middle strata were expanding and old values suffering erosion, led to the appearance of many societies and clubs in villages as well as towns.[6] Club meetings and activities offered contacts outside those of family and clan and often became an avenue through which ideas and culture from the cities reached the villages, so contributing to the beginnings of a national orientation and culture.

On August 15, 1970, in the closing days of President Helou's term, Jumblat issued a ministerial order legalizing all banned political parties. These included the Communist Party of Lebanon (CPL) and communist splinter groups; the Baath parties, Syrian and Iraqi; the Arab Nationalist Movement (ANM) and its offshoots; the various Nasserist organizations; and the Syrian Social Nationalist Party (SSNP). Jumblat explained the move as "in the interest of strengthening democratic life in the country. We have put before the new president a *fait accompli.*"[7]

Infuriated by Jumblat's initiative, the Maronite right mobilized its forces to get the order rescinded. As part of this passionate effort, the Kataeb stepped up its incessant anticommunist crusade. Kataeb themes held that the "enemy" responsible for the socioeconomic crisis was "international communism," and the cause of the national crisis was the "alien," specifically the "alien Palestinian commandos." Thus as the national, progressive, and left parties moved toward a certain coherence, the Kataeb developed in a more openly fascist direction.

Jumblat's order reflected the new political climate created by the 1967 war and its consequences. The weakening of central authority in the post-Shebab period, coupled with the collapse of myths in the 1967 debacle, permitted a relatively open and stimulating political climate to develop. A shifting sectarian balance of power effected by the appearance of the Palestine resistance movement encouraged many new groups and individuals to take part in political life. Representatives of more-or-less radical Arab opposition movements suffocating under dictatorships prevailing elsewhere in the Arab world took refuge in Beirut, where they too contributed to the liveliness of political discourse.

A "new left"—which had first appeared in Lebanon in the mid–1960s largely as a result of the Sino-Soviet split—reemerged after the 1967 war to define itself gradually under the influence of liberation wars in Vietnam, Latin America, and Africa, and especially that of the 1968 "revolution" in Paris, where many Lebanese and Arabs studied. Other radical groups came out of the break-up of the Arab Nationalist movement and splits in the Baath and Communist parties. These included the Organization of Lebanese Socialists, an ANM offshoot led by Muhsin Ibrahim, and a grouping around a clandestine journal, *Lubnan Al Ishtiraki (Socialist Lebanon)*, a Marxist faction that split from the Lebanese Baath. Unlike other would-be Marxist groups that tended to schematically apply to Lebanon theses and strategies issued from other and very different societies, *Socialist Lebanon* made a serious effort to analyze Lebanon's socioeconomic-political structures scientifically. This effort was carried on, at least for a time, by the Organization of Communist Action (OCA), formed in 1971 as a result of the merger of *Socialist Lebanon* and the Organization of Lebanese Socialists. The OCA was linked from the beginning to the Popular Democratic Front for the Liberation of Palestine (PDF)—later renamed simply the Democratic Front for the Liberation of Palestine (DFLP)—the intellectual splinter group of the Popular Front for the Liberation of Palestine (PFLP).

Although originally opposed to each other, the OCA and CPL gradually began to work together on a growing number of issues, especially as the CPL moved somewhat away from Soviet tutelage. In all radical groups, Shi'as—intellectuals, workers, displaced migrants from the Bekaa Valley and the south, and students—were prominent.

The loose groupings of self-styled national and progressive parties and personalities formed by Jumblat in the mid-1960s, however, had not survived the differences, especially over the Soviet role in the Middle East, that were created by the 1967 Arab defeat. In the summer of 1970, therefore, when they suddenly found themselves legal, the progressive parties were working largely in isolation from each other. In 1969 and 1970 Jumblat had been trying to bring them together again, and on local issues his Progressive Socialist Party (PSP) and the CPL had been able to cooperate. Political developments in other Arab states soon contributed to a gradual *rapprochment* among Lebanese progressives. The entry of communist parties into national fronts with the ruling Baath parties in Syria and Iraq facilitated collaboration between the CPL and the Lebanese branches of these parties. A split in the Nasserist movement into right and left currents after President Nasser's death led to cooperation between left Nasserists and progressives in Lebanon. And so Jumblat succeeded in drawing these various parties into a coalition that would tolerate different views on the Arab situation, concentrate on social problems, and work for change in stages.

Impetus for coalition among these groups came from the Maronite right's campaign against their legalization. The government put forward a draft law on political parties so restrictive that it made the 1909 Ottoman law, under which Lebanon still operated, appear almost a model of progress. Among other things, it banned all political groups with links to non-Lebanese political organizations, prohibited student political activity, and barred civil servants, police, and workers on government contracts from membership in political parties.

The fight against this bill, which was ultimately not adopted, cemented cooperation among opposition groups working for the democratization of Lebanon. But they did not become an articulate political movement with a common program and leadership until the summer of 1975, after the start of the civil war, and they did not officially adopt the name Lebanese National Movement (LNM) until early 1976.[8]

Though usually called leftist, the movement was not so in the

European sense of the term. Properly speaking it was a broad national front, embracing ultimately a dozen or more organizations of differing orientations including the progressive as well as the more traditional. In Lebanon, an imperative for such a movement must be to replace traditional particularist ties (family, kinship, tribal, religious, etc.) that are incompatible with democracy by a national and social class identification that permits development of a secular, democratic political system. Although LNM parties had yet to liberate themselves completely from such traditional bonds, the movement itself, in bringing together Muslims and Christians of practically all sects around political principles, constituted a significant advance.

April 1972 Parliamentary Elections

Although the national movement had yet to coalesce at the time of the 1972 parliamentary elections, the vote revealed a small advance in a national direction, with national or nontraditional candidates winning in a few districts and offering competition to traditionalists in a few others. In both Tripoli and Tyre, the second and fifth cities, nontraditional candidates won the largest number of votes: in Tripoli, Iraqi Baath leader Abdel Meguid Rafi'i; and in Tyre, Ali al-Khalil, an independent. An independent progressive, Albert Mansour, won the Greek Catholic seat in the Bekaa with a vote count ranking among the highest in the country. Communist candidates also made good showings. In the Chouf, Jumblat and his slate of six were elected in contrast to the victory of only two from Chamoun's slate. In a Beirut constituency, Najah Wakim, twenty-six-year-old candidate of the Nasserist Union of Working Forces, won the Greek Orthodox seat, to the consternation of the community's leadership, which charged he was elected by Muslim votes. All of these gains came in the face of an intense rightist campaign against the "red menace."

Yet the significance of the nontraditional and national vote should not be exaggerated. When such candidates won, they often did so by running on the slate of a traditional political *zaim*. Ali al-Khalil, a former Baath leader in the south, was helped by the fact that he belonged to one of the south's most prominent families. Some national or progressive candidates failed. Marouf Saad, a Nasserist, lost the seat he had held for fourteen years in Sidon. His defeat was due in part at least to his endorsement of President Nasser's acceptance of the Rogers Plan in 1970, a stand that brought him into conflict with the resistance movement. Many conservatives and rightists won; in Tyre, the southern political feudalist Kazem al-Khalil, vice president of Chamoun's party, managed to get elected for the first time in fourteen years. Villages along the border with Israel returned the entire slate of another political *zaim*, Kamil al-Assad. The moderate Maronite deputy Jean Aziz was defeated in Jezzine by the Kataeb candidate, Edmond Rizk.

Press proclamations that the new parliament would reflect the growing conflict between right and left were confirmed as the battle over the rightist-backed political parties bill intensified. Prime Minister Salam's denunciation of Jumblat's "subversive activity," broadcast repeatedly by the government radio and featured in the press, revealed the nonsectarian character of the conflict. Parliamentary squabbles took place against a background of occasional bomb explosions, a rash of letter bombs to Palestinian personalities, strikes and clashes and massive Israeli incursions into the south—an unfolding scenario soon to become all too familiar.

Although efforts to sectarianize the conflict were not lacking, these found a relatively faint echo. Sectarianism had not yet smudged over class lines. With its strong base among Christian workers and white-collar employees, the Kataeb itself indirectly recognized this in programs promising "jobs for the unemployed," "equal opportunities for all," even "elimination of sectarian discrimination." At the same time it continued to deny the reality of class conflict and to promote its doctrine emphasizing the alleged identity of interests of the rich and the poor, the bosses and the workers, with all society being the beneficiary of the efforts and profits of the capitalists. As the developing socioeconomic crisis made this line of thought less persuasive, the Kataeb in practice relied increasingly on its expanding militia to transfer socioeconomic problems to the military plane.

Economic Crisis: The Fading Miracle

Lebanon's "economic miracle" began to lose its momentum in the last half of the 1960s, when the real growth rate in net national production fell from an annual average of 10.5 percent in 1960–65 to 2.5 percent in 1965–70, owing primarily to an unprecedented rise in prices.[9] Lebanon imported inflation along with the goods and services it bought from industrial countries and on which it spent 55 percent of its national income.[10] Nearly all its requirements in consumer goods were supplied from abroad. A 54 percent decline in food production per capita between 1950–52 and 1973–77 created an ever-increasing need for food imports, which contributed to the inflation.[11] And local merchants and monopolists did their bit to stoke the inflation by raising their prices.

Inflation combined with stagnant production to deepen fissures between social classes. The service sector accounted for 73 percent of net national production in 1970 (up from about 62 percent in 1950), while agriculture's share dwindled from 20 to 9 percent in the same period. Industry remained stagnant, at the same level (18 percent) as in 1950.

Wage levels in agriculture and industry were extremely low. In 1970, 30 percent of the population was dependent on agriculture (and another 30 percent derived some income from it). The 30 percent who were wholly supported by agriculture numbered 600,000. They received an annual average per capita income of 500 Lebanese pounds a year, allowing little more than subsistence on the threshold of starvation. The comparable figure for the 26 percent of the population supported by industry and building—580,000 persons—was 1,100 Lebanese pounds.[12]

While over half the population (56 percent) shared a little over a quarter of net production, the 45 percent of the population—1,050,000 persons—supported by the tertiary, service sector shared 73 percent, enjoying an annual average per capita income of 8,000 Lebanese pounds. Within this sector the 245,000 persons supported by commerce—barely a tenth of the population—shared almost a third of net production, with an average annual per capita income of 20,000 Lebanese pounds.

This was the situation in 1970. By 1974 net national production registered zero growth. Early in 1973—on top of the inflation under way since the mid-1960s—a "terrific inflation" set in, and by 1975 had more than doubled general price levels.[13] The inflation far outran the few small cost-of-living wage increases workers won from the government. Most critically affected were those working on the land, who suffered falling returns, rising costs, and a growing weight of indebtedness. Dependent on private banks and usurers for 90–95 percent of their credits, they paid interest rates averaging around 15 percent to the banks and 50 percent to usurers, while costs of agricultural inputs, marketing, transport, cold storage, etc., under the tightening grip of the foreign and local monopolies, soared. Peasants and sharecroppers abandoned their homes and land in unprecedented numbers to seek work in the towns and cities. Most ended up in the misery belts encircling Beirut and other cities.

By 1975, 40 percent of the country's total rural population had been forced out of their homes and off the land, including 65 percent of the rural population of the south and 50 percent of that of the Bekaa.[14] The majority of the rural refugees were Shi'a Muslims, who crowded into shantytown ghettos beside the earlier arrivals, the Kurds and the Palestinians, subsisting like them on irregular and often menial jobs for pitifully low wages.

The government itself contributed to accelerating the inflation. At a time of inexorably rising prices it did not have a monetary policy; it resorted to budget deficits and foreign borrowing to finance development projects. Meanwhile, excessive liquidity was inducing bankers to seek "secure" investment abroad (World Bank bonds, loans to the State Bank of India, the Renault Car Company, etc.) Locally, they stepped up investments in real etate, promoting extensive speculation in the purchase of land and buildings. Forty percent of all bank credits at this time were being channeled into the real estate sector.

Although a series of conferences in 1974 concluded that Lebanon's banking structure was not sufficiently evolved to cope with a bigger share of oil money, and that communications and other facilities were inadequate even for the present level of banking operations, the banking community was not deterred from trying to make Beirut a bigger money market. Nor did the rush of foreign bankers and financiers lose momentum. Financial and commercial operations were, of course, highly profitable to big merchants, real estate speculators, and landlords, and contributed to the further expansion of the service sector, though they were of little if any value to the Lebanese economy. Many consisted merely of transferring money or goods which did not even pass through Lebanon.

Pleas that the government exercise some "guidance" over investment—above all, that monetary laws be enacted to permit Central

Bank control over banks and the flow of money—went unheeded: such measures ran counter to the "free enterprise" system so profitable to the ruling elites. The same rationale inhibited any genuine government effort to control prices.

Bank vaults overflowed with deposits in search of investment opportunities, but the government could scarcely maintain—let alone extend—the public school system: it still did not provide free compulsory primary education. It could not fill the urgent need for basic health facilities or even furnish its cities with sufficient electricity and drinking water. (Water rationing in Beirut became routine in summer.) Lebanon has 600 million square meters of theoretically usable subterranean water, of which only 160 million were then exploited.[15] The road network became even more inadequate as the number of imported cars doubled every two years (from 10,391 in 1970 to 40,000 in 1974).[16] The government lacked the funds to build badly needed agricultural roads to permit the exploitation of marginal land and to construct even more urgently needed irrigation projects.

Shortage of state funds to provide essential services derived in large part from corruption in the tax system. Modestly paid workers, and employees whose income was collected at the source, paid more income tax than their wealthy employers, who as a matter of course manipulated balance sheets to avoid all tax payments.[17] A 1960 report found the tax evasion rate in the liberal professions "close to 90 percent" and "nearly 75 percent" in private enterprise and national companies; among workers and employees it was barely 3 percent.[18] Altogether, only a third of direct taxes due were collected. Fourteen years later, the London *Economist* reported that only 20 percent of direct taxes owed were actually collected.[19]

Tax laws favored the rich and well-to-do. There was, for example, no capital-gains tax on real estate deals, source of some of the highest profits. Corruption was endemic among tax collectors and functionaries, their bribes often higher than their salaries. Even businesses seeking to pay the full amount owed sometimes found difficulty in doing so, since some tax collectors demanded bribes for accepting payment.

A former minister of planning has stated that uncollected taxes each year totaled more than the state budget. The government therefore had to rely on indirect taxes, especially customs dues, which weighed heavily on the less well-off. The inadequacy of tax revenues kept expenditures on public education, health, and social facilities to a minimum. Reliance on customs dues meant little, if any, protection from foreign competition for local industry.

Corruption greased the wheels of the system but, as the political structure came into growing contradiction with the needs of the people, the inability to achieve a more effective and honest administration came to pose a threat to the system itself. Venality in government was not new, but in the early 1970s—when so many were reduced to misery, without employment, without homes—the government's connivance in the corruption and its favoritism became more intolerable. In these years the rich got richer, the poor became poorer and ever more desperate, and the government grew ever more impotent.

Social Crisis: "Revolution from Below"

The five years 1970–75 witnessed an unprecedented outbreak of rural revolts, and more strikes than in the near-quarter-century since the departure of the French. To this social agitation the state had only one answer: army and police violence would quell the "revolution from below," against which its abortive "revolution from the top" had proved so ineffective. Expressing the desperate resolve of the most exploited and neglected, these worker, peasant, student and farmer popular actions were often rank-and-file efforts. The progressive parties, Kamal Jumblat, and on occasion a handful of other deputies, backed the popular demands. Party members and students sometimes went into the countryside to lend a hand to peasants and sharecroppers standing up for their rights. Students, especially those at the Lebanese University, often tried to mobilize support at the national level for popular demands and so contributed to awakening a social and national conscience.

The "revolution from below" seldom achieved its demands, but the social ferment it unleashed shook the pillars of the sectarian system. A look at a few of these popular actions, including a significant development in the labor movement, will suffice to reveal the modest nature of popular demands and the total incapacity of the sectarian system to accommodate these demands.

Labor Militancy

In 1970 the labor movement achieved at least formal unity when all nine trade union federations came together in the General Council of Labor (GCL). More significantly, in 1971 and 1972 a rising militancy among shop stewards and the rank and file was expressed in the formation of workers' committees. This action began in the country's most compact industrial center, Mkalles, site of some 450 factories (many very small) employing roughly 30,000 workers. This rank-and-file movement then set out to make workers aware of their basic rights. In many cases these rights were legally recognized, but the government and union leaders had kept workers in ignorance of them. In meetings, tracts, and soon a paper, *Nidal al-Ummal (The Workers' Struggle)* the committees explained these rights and emphasized the need to reform the union movement.

Reform required the organization of big trade-union units on the basis of labor sectors, the adoption of democratic procedures in the unions, and the replacement of traditional leaders allied to employers and the government by authentic workers' representatives. A major aim was to stimulate an organizing drive among both industrial and agricultural workers—then constituting only around 10 percent of trade union membership—so as to expand the base of the movement and make such workers a leading force within it.

The workers' committees became the spearhead of a drive to amend Article 50 of the Labor Code (permitting arbitrary dismissals). They also stood in the front lines of the social agitation of the period, providing the stimulus and much of the work for such gains as workers were able to make. Their appearance suggested that workers were beginning to forge new relations, replacing sectarian divisiveness and paternalist influence. By 1974 the workers' committees had become a force that could not be ignored.

This organized pressure from below compelled the GCL to launch campaigns to bring down the cost of living, raise wages, and amend Article 50. In giving employers the right to make arbitrary dismissals, Article 50 canceled practically every right and protection owed workers under other sections of the 1946 Labor Code.

GCL efforts to secure amendment of Article 50 provoked such powerful opposition from employers that the GCL shelved the issue for the time being, concentrating instead on prices and wages. On

August 23, 1973, a highly successful strike, called by the GCL with the state's blessing, demanded action against wholesale monopolists, the regulation and control of the market to bring down prices, and the payment of subsidies to workers. The GCL, however, did not carry out its threat to hold a monthly general strike until its demands were met. In return for a promised increase in family subsidies, it canceled its call for a general strike a month later. Workers' committees, joined by some trade-union leaders, protested against the cancellation on the grounds that only basic reforms aimed at the monopolies, coupled with new economic and financial policies, could halt or even slow the rapid enrichment of the few at the expense of the many.

These views were almost identical with those set forth in a report to parliament in January 1974 by the chairman of its Foreign Affairs Commission, Amin al-Hafez, a respected economist. This report had placed responsibility for the soaring cost of living on "the government's failure to adopt a long-term financial and monetary policy" at a time when inflation and the influx of capital from abroad had reached "record levels." The report also sharply criticized the "superficial character" of the government's anti-inflation moves.[20]

In February 1974 the GCL again canceled a general strike when the government offered a 10 percent wage increase. For the first time ever it was unable to enforce its *diktat* on its members. Defying the GCL order, the Federation of South Lebanon Unions observed the strike. So did the workers in Mkalles, mobilized by their workers' committees. In Tripoli, union members sacked the office of the North Lebanon Trade Union Federation when it called off the strike in obedience to the GCL order. Popular demonstrations against the GCL decision occurred in Tyre, Sidon, Tripoli, and Beirut and its suburbs. This solidarity and militancy, reflecting workers' anger against their leaders, started to give a new dimension to the labor movement. Workers' committees did not give up the battle, and early in 1974 the GCL was persuaded to resume the drive to amend Article 50.

GCL negotiations with the Ministry of Labor and Social Affairs at that time produced a compromise agreement on a draft amendment of the law. Employers reacted hysterically, rejecting any restrictions on their arbitrary right to fire employees, since such restrictions would spell "the doom of Lebanon's free economy." Boutros Khouri, the president of the industrialists' association and a close friend and business associate of the Franjieh family, insisted that any amendment of Article 50 "would mean that the status of employers would not be different from that of workers."[21] Placed on the defensive by this outcry, trade-union leaders hastened to avow their devotion to the free enterprise system. Workers' committees still tried to mobilize pressures on parliament to adopt the draft amendment, but the Take-iddine Solh government did not put the issue before the House.

Curiously neglected by the labor movement was a demand for the application of the minimum wage to workers under twenty years of age, who constituted a substantial part of the industrial workforce (in large industrial enterprises in East Beirut, more than a third in 1974).[22] The 1946 Labor Code had nothing to say about the practice of paying such workers less than the minimum wage, sometimes only half the minimum, and firing them as soon as they reached the age of twenty. Coupled with Article 50 this practice meant total insecurity for young workers and pulled down the wages of all workers. It was sufficiently profitable for employers, however, for the government to write it into law in 1967. Approved by parliament and promulgated by the president on May 16, 1967, Law 36/37 excluded workers under twenty from minimum wage provisions. Ever since, every subsequent decree concerning cost-of-living increments has referred to this law, and so barred workers under twenty from receiving increments related to the minimum wage.

Peasant Revolt in the North

In mid-November 1970 Beirut Radio reported an "armed insurrection" in the Akkar Plain, some 150 kilometers north of Beirut, near the Syrian border. Traditionally a corridor for contraband trade between Syria and Lebanon, and a military zone, the Akkar remained the feudal domain of beys and aghas, descendants of officials of the Ottoman Empire. The plain's soil is fertile; the region is desolate and arid. Its fifty or more villages—many without electricity, water, and schools—are impoverished, their inhabitants often living with their animals in mud or reed huts. Big landlords reside in Beirut or Tripoli; only the smaller ones stay on their lands in the Akkar. The landlords, mainly Sunnis, traditionally divided their land into small plots to be worked by sharecropping peasants. Although entitled to half the crop, the peasants generally received only about a tenth. Additionally they often had to pay feudal dues and render feudal services to the landlord, providing eggs, chickens, milk, and other gifts, while their wives and children worked as his unpaid servants.

Capitalist penetration of this feudal system of production in the late 1960s worsened the plight of the peasants, as feudalism started to give way to large-scale mechanized production. Peasants first felt the impact of this transformation in 1969 when landowners, starting to abandon the sharecropping system, compelled them to pay cash rent and assume all expenses of production. Lacking the resources to operate in this fashion, within a year or two many peasants were obliged to return the land and become agricultural laborers. Landlords could then rent their land—of good quality and cheaper than in south Lebanon and the Bekaa—to wealthy merchants and bankers from Tripoli, Beirut, and even the West Bank. Such landowners usually reserved a small portion of their land to rent to "loyal" peasants, assuring themselves of continuing feudal services and privileges. With this exception, Akkar landlords in the early 1970s were chiefly concerned to drive peasants off the land in order to rent it for the capitalist development of specialized export crops, thus forcing peasants established in the region for centuries to emigrate or become poorly paid agricultural workers. The favorite method for compelling the peasants' departure was to evict them from their homes.

Resistance to this landlord operation first erupted in October 1969, at a moment when the Lebanese army was fighting the Palestinians in the south and when charges of Syrian intervention were rife. Peasants often resisted landlords' militias and, when landlords called on the police for help, fought them too. Beirut translated the peasants' action into "Syrian army incursion," though the only aid the peasants received came from the Lebanese branch of the Syrian Baath and from other Lebanese progressive groups.

Following the October 1969 incidents Kamal Jumblat, then interior minister, prepared a program of government aid for the Akkar peasants. This included the payment of indemnities to sharecroppers and agricultural workers; provision of housing, water, and electrical facilities; fertilizers and other agricultural inputs; and adoption of road projects. The government, however, shelved the program, and in early November 1970, soon after Franjieh became president, the Akkar landlords resumed their offensive. This time their militias and security forces came in armored cars and tanks to evict the peasants. The peasants' resistance became the "armed insurrection" reported by Beirut Radio.

The clashes eventually ended in a compromise: the state would henceforth guarantee the peasants' rent contract. Yet this compromise, like others that were to follow, was broken by the landlords. They soon resumed their efforts to get rid of the peasants, and in early 1971 new police incursions and mass arrests of peasants and workers occurred. Jumblat condemned the attacks, but no government action was taken to help the peasants.

The peasant struggle intensified as land speculation increased in the following years. Moreover, in 1972 and after, the peasants found a powerful ally in the Baarini clan, itself at war over irrigation rights and landownership with the clan of Suleiman Ali, the Akkar's leading political feudalist and a long-time deputy. The peasant struggle against the landlords, interlocked with the Baarini–Suleiman Ali clan conflict, reached such dimensions by 1974 that the government, at the demand of Akkar deputies, sent the army and the Internal Security Forces—thousands of troops, 500 commandos, tanks, armored cars, and four helicopters—into the desolate Akkar Plain to hunt down "outlaws."

For the uprooted peasants of the Akkar—as of the Bekaa-Hermel area—deprivation also had a sectarian color. Thousands of inhabitants of these two regions, where their ancestors had lived for centuries, had been denied Lebanese citizenship for no other reason than that they were Muslims. Periodic Lebanese police and army operations against them had scarcely made them feel welcome in a state which had otherwise completely neglected them. The extended family clans of these regions, accustomed over centuries to move back and forth between what is now Lebanon and Syria, inevitably retreated into Syria when under attack; there they became aware that their Syrian counterparts were far better off than they, a perception that increased their disaffection.

Agricultural Workers and Farmers in the East

In the Bekaa-Hermel region, where some five families owned more than half the land, the transition from an agrarian to a market economy dominated by big merchants was more advanced than in the Akkar Plain. The rural exodus in the Bekaa had started early in the 1950s. The chief problem of agriculturalists in this area was a tremendous rise in the prices of agricultural inputs (fertilizers, seeds, fodder, machines, etc.) beginning in 1972, and a swift upward movement in land rents. Such laws as existed governing peasant–landlord relations dated back to the Mandate or even Ottoman times, and left agricultural workers, peasants, and farmers without protection in the new circumstances.[23]

In 1973 and 1974 peasants and farmers began meeting in village mosques to try to organize and make their demands heard, and in time succeeded in forming a vigilance committee. Villages then started meeting other villages, and then groups of villages with each other. In this way preparations were made for an agricultural congress of the Bekaa, which was held on April 6, 1975. The congress adopted a set of demands and established a twenty-five member committee to create a Union of Peasants and Farmers of the Bekaa.

Agricultural workers also tried to organize, and in 1974 a Congress of Agricultural Workers of the Bekaa met. This congress took the lead in forming a National Committee of Agricultural Workers of Lebanon, which demanded application of the labor law to agricultural workers, recognition of the right of such workers to classification as full-time workers, and recognition of the National Committee as an agricultural workers' union. A second Congress of the Agricultural Workers of the Bekaa was held in May 1975, but the civil war had then already started and the vicissitudes it brought preempted the development of both projected unions.

Peasant Revolt in the South

In December 1972 a delegation of tobacco growers from the south brought to parliament a petition signed by 16,000 peasants exposing the injustice they suffered at the hands of the Régie tobacco monopoly. Régie failed to carry out its commitment to buy all their crop, for which under the prevailing monopoly they had no other market. The price paid for their tobacco remained low, although it was subsidized by the state, because it was determined without any peasant bargaining powers. Big growers, however, received higher prices. Classification of tobacco was arbitrary; often as much as a third of the crop was left unsold and hence a total loss. The peasants petitioned parliament for higher prices, the purchase of the entire crop, the right to organize a trade union which would *not* be chosen by politicians, and their inclusion in the social security and health insurance systems on the same basis as workers in the Régie cigarette factory. They also sought a reduction in foreign imports of tobacco and cigarettes, so that production could be expanded and a tobacco factory be located in the south.

Parliament's failure to support these demands provoked new protests. Ten thousand farmers gathered in Nabatiye in January 1973 to reaffirm their demands. Merchants closed their shops in solidarity and students demonstrated in support. Because the south was a military zone, the army moved in to crush this demonstration, killing two peasants, wounding fifteen, and imprisoning scores. Demonstrators withdrew only to reappear periodically throughout the day to protest and to call—for the first time—for "an end to the time of beys and *zuama*." When soldiers dragged peasants off to jail, angry crowds chanted demands for the dismissal of "the government of fascist butchers" and an end to the state of emergency in the south.

The death of the two innocent peasants rallied nationwide support for the tobacco farmers from university and secondary school students, intellectuals, progressive forces, and Imam Sadr's followers (but not the support of the General Council of Labor or the workers in the Régie factories around Beirut, who were organized in a house union). A popular march from Nabatiye to Beirut, eluding army and Internal Security Forces barricades along the way, brought some 20,000 people to a meeting at the Arab University, where Kamal Jumblat spoke on behalf of the tobacco growers.

Yet this impressive popular mobilization in solidarity with the peasants of the south proved ephemeral and at the time accomplished little. The peasants won only a slightly higher price for the crop than they had originally been offered (still lower than the price of the year before). They were still subjected to all the injustices about which they had petitioned parliament. The disproportion between the revolt—which had encouraged the peasants and much of the south—and its meager results increased peasant despair. Yet in April 1973 some peasants organized a congress of tobacco growers of the Sidon region in an effort to lay the basis for a union of tobacco growers. By the winter of 1974–75 peasants were again besieging parliament and the Ministry of Finance with petitions bearing thousands of signatures.

The Ghandour Strike

A strike at two of the Ghandour chocolate and biscuit factories in the suburbs of Beirut early in November 1972 revealed much about working conditions in Lebanese factories. Workers demanded the reduction of daily working hours from ten to eight; the payment of wages during sickness and absence due to work accidents; an end to arbitrary dismissals and dismissals for participating in strikes; a wage increase of 5 percent to offset a 15 percent rise in the cost of living; an end to body searches at factory gates; the right to join the General Union of Chocolate Workers instead of having to form a house union; and the inscription of all workers on social security rolls.

The company's answer was to call in the Internal Security Forces (ISF) to break the strike. At the Shiah plant the ISF fired on striking workers, killing a man and a woman, wounding five others, and arresting many more.

The killing of the two workers (the woman had been active in the Workers' Committee formed in the factory) provoked popular anger and wide protests. Students, some trade unions, and the progressive parties held a day-long demonstration in Beirut, followed on November 13 by a 25,000-strong march to protest against police brutality. The progressive parties, joined by the Trade Union of Syrian Workers, organized a boycott of Ghandour products, collected funds for the strikers, and helped them in other ways. Kataeb leader Pierre Gemayel, on the other hand, hastened to proclaim his support for the Ghandour brothers, as did the minister of labor and social affairs, who handled the strike for the government.

The General Council of Labor (GCL) entered the picture only to reach agreement on a return to work, achieved on the promise of a committee to study the demands, the standard fashion of burying such matters. Ghandour workers reluctantly returned to work only to be faced with the dismissal of so-called instigators at one plant and a lock-out at another. Even an administrative employee who had shown sympathy with the strikers was dismissed. Demands for reemployment of some seventy-five dismissed workers continued throughout

December and January; the GCL half-heartedly supported the return of fifteen. The company stood firm; the workers were not reemployed. The investigating committee was not heard from again.

The Educational Crisis

Nothing demonstrated more clearly the bankruptcy of the Lebanese sectarian political system than its attitude to education. Insofar as a state educational policy existed at all, it was that of the Maronite Catholic right to perpetuate Catholic advantage and Muslim disadvantage. By the first half of the 1970s this policy could produce only turmoil in the schools and universities.

A decision to cancel the system of equivalence—under which the government accepted secondary school certificates granted by Syria and Egypt—touched off wide student protests. Lebanon's baccalaureate exam tests students in French or English, the languages of instruction in most private schools. Students unable to afford private school education and without sufficient command of French or English were until this time allowed to present a Syrian or Egyptian diploma. Cancellation of equivalences in effect barred access to higher education for the unprivileged. In the eyes of many it was cultural imperialism, as well as a denial of Arabism and nationalism. Yet Lebanon's service economy needed not graduates and technicians but low-waged, unskilled workers.

The cancellation of equivalences brought the educational crisis to a climax. Secondary school students, for whom it crystallized all the evils of the educational system, promptly moved into action. They put together a comprehensive program calling for the Arabization of instruction, which they insisted was indispensable to defining a national culture and a national education policy: the elimination of grading in a foreign language; the retention of equivalences until reforms of the school system made it unnecessary; and the reform and diversification of programs to permit students to prepare for jobs or trades. The student movement spread from Beirut and its suburbs to provincial towns and rural regions, where students blocked roads and occupied public buildings to make their demands known. The rapid turnover in education ministers during Franjieh's presidency bore witness to the strength and coherence of the students' programs.

Free Private Schools

The scandal of the free private schools—which are subsidized by the state but over which it exercises almost no supervision or control—also came to the fore in the agitation over educational policy. Since the Constitution makes education the responsibility of private schools as well as the government, the state made no real effort to supervise these schools. To the free private schools, numbering almost 12,000, it paid a subsidy for each pupil. These schools often fictitiously inflated the number of pupils to get higher subsidies. Teachers in such schools were often required to turn over to the proprietors as much as half the salary they received from the ministry of education. On signing a contract teachers also had to sign an undated resignation. At the expiration of their contract they had to sign still another paper certifying that they had received the minimum wage for twelve months, although they might have received less than the minimum and that for only eight or nine months. They were often fired at the end of the year so that proprietors would not have to pay social insurance.

Early in 1974 teachers in four private schools in Bourj Hammoud— a poor, densely populated, predominantly Armenian suburb of Beirut—revolted against the kickback system, refusing to turn over their pay to the proprietors. The movement spread rapidly. Committees were formed in many private schools to fight for the end of the system. Other teachers and students rallied to their support, joining in the demand for state control of all private schools. This demand came up against the powerful opposition of the Catholic schools, which had already started organizing to fight possible state control over the private schools. Their opposition ensured that little significant change in the situation of these teachers was achieved.

Lebanese University

In January of 1970 students at the Lebanese University occupied the School of Education and the College of Law and Politics in protest against the arrest of a number of fellow students. They remained on strike for more than a month until university officials promised to act on their demands. When, by 1971, these promises had yet to be fulfilled, they resumed the strike. In the early months of 1971 strikes and demonstrations by secondary and university students seemed to be almost a daily occurrence. Deputies entering parliament heard themselves hailed by students as "the ninety-nine thieves."

Early in March thousands of students staged the largest student strike ever held in Beirut: some 10,000 participated in a student march. Three days later Lebanese University students started a strike which was to last for forty-nine days. The essential demand of all these strikes was for a *national* education system using the national language, Arabic, as opposed to the existing multiplicity of private and sectarian educational systems and philosophies using foreign languages. Not least was their insistence on a democratic educational system in which education would be available and open to all.[24]

For both secondary and university students a major concern was the development of a truly national university, open to the poor and the less well-off and offering practical scientific subjects (medicine, engineering, agricultural science, etc.). The Lebanese University did not offer such courses. The upper-class, Christian monopoly of the professions and technical education remained the exclusive preserve of the expensive foreign universities: Université St. Joseph and the American University of Beirut. A Lebanese cabinet minister in 1973 expressed his satisfaction over this state of affairs, saying that he "preferred to see the government subsidize foreign universities rather than give the national university apparatus the means of providing a substitute."[25]

Student union elections at the Lebanese University in 1972, 1973, and 1975 returned an overwhelmingly progressive leadership, and in these years the union won important gains, including national scholarships for students and student–teacher participation in the creation of new faculties of applied sciences. These reforms were not achieved without prolonged strikes, sit-ins, clashes with police, and much hard work, since the government's answer to student demands was usually severe repression. Moreover, students often fared badly in the media, which tended to ignore their constructive programs and actions and always to assign to them the responsibility for violence. Yet the Lebanese University student union in these years became the backbone of the entire student movement; it took a real part in the social conflicts erupting throughout the country and developed into a force the government could not wholly ignore.

[10]

National Crisis:
Toward Civil War

"We will make all life impossible in South Lebanon."
Moshe Dayan (*Le Monde*,
April 14–15, 1974)

The legitimacy of the Lebanese state, progressively eroded by its
inability either to resolve social problems or to suppress social protest,
was ultimately destroyed by its failure to act against Israel's escalating
aggressions. It could not (more damagingly, would not) provide its
citizens with fundamental protection or defend its sovereignty over
Lebanese territory.

In the seven years from May 1968 to April 1975 Israel committed
more than 6,200 acts of aggression against Lebanon: nearly 4,000
aerial and artillery bombardments of villages, towns, and refugee
camps; more than 350 military incursions, large and small, employing
hundreds—on occasion thousands—of troops equipped with tanks,
helicopters, and planes; as well as continual violations of airspace and
territorial waters. The year 1972 alone saw a four-day Israeli occupation of the Arqoub in January, a devastating two-day land and air
invasion in September, heavy air raids the same month against Palestinian refugee camps throughout Lebanon and Syria which left hundreds dead, as well as frequent bombardments of Lebanese villages.
Forty percent of the actions took place in the seventeen months
between the October 1973 war, when the resistance officially halted
incursions from Lebanon into Israel, and the outbreak of the
Lebanese civil war.[1]

Yet this period saw no perceptible effort by the Lebanese armed
forces to defend the country or its people. Prime Minister and Defense Minister Saeb Salam later told parliament that despite his order
to the army to resist Israel's September 1972 invasion with all its

powers, it had not done so. A Defense Ministry investigation committee criticized the army's "disorderly retreat" and the Army Command's "procrastination."[2] Along with the army's failure to fight was
the state's failure to organize, equip, arm, and control the army so that
it could do so. Former Colonel Fouad Lahoud, chairman of parliament's Defense Committee since 1972, told parliament how the defense budget allocated to the military was squandered because
Lebanon "had no defense policy" and no recognized chain of responsibility or command. While the president, prime minister, and defense
minister deferred to the commander-in-chief in matters concerning
the military, the commander-in-chief proved to be accountable to no
one.[3]

Since there was no defense policy, military procurement meant
buying weapons without any plans, or even ideas, of the use to which
they would be put. This situation constituted an open invitation to
corruption. Lahoud revealed that orders for Crotale missiles from
France, which had proved effective and suitable for Lebanon's needs,
were canceled by the president not, as the government claimed,
because they were ineffective, but "because of Israeli threats":
Lebanon's possession of the missiles would have inhibited Israel's
incursions into Lebanese airspace. Yet they were canceled just before
the October war. Noting that the Crotale missiles were replaced by
"20mm artillery which had been designed before World War II for
defense against planes whose speed was half that of sound," Lahoud
added: "What I say about artillery applies to all weapons," concluding
that "the State did not want to strengthen the Army."[4]

Israeli threats were only one factor in this affair; the other was the
regime's decision to back out of its commitments to the Arab League
and the Palestinian cause. So, as Lahoud noted, "strange things happened."[5] Lebanon's commitment to equip its army with modern sophisticated weapons had already been partially fulfilled when Franjieh took office: Mirage planes had already been delivered; land radar
was installed at Barouk; the contract for Crotale missiles had been
signed. The Franjieh regime canceled the Crotale contract and set out
to sell the Mirage planes. To justify cancellation of the Crotale contract, which entailed high indemnities, the government inspired a
press campaign intended to convince the public that the missile was
ineffective.

Still another blow to the Arab League plan soon followed. The Joint
Arab Defense Council had awarded the PLO $20 million to build air

raid shelters and fortify the refugee camps in Lebanon. The government refused to allow either, on the ground that the aid would constitute a violation of Lebanon's sovereignty. The government itself had always denied the camps protection from Israeli attacks.

The government's abdication of responsibility to defend its frontiers and protect its people discredited both the state and the army, ensuring the eventual collapse of both. The fact that the Palestinians did fight the Israeli invaders helped make the resistance movement the magnet around which Lebanon's patriots and poor began to gather. In the south, Lebanese progressive parties, chiefly the Communist Party of Lebanon (CPL) and the Organization of Communist Action (OCA), worked with the village inhabitants to organize People's Guards for self-defense. The growing convergence of the Palestinian resistance movement and the Lebanese national and progressive movement found dramatic expression in July 1972, when Israel assassinated the Palestinian writer and Popular Front for the Liberation of Palestine (PFLP) spokesman Ghassan Kanafani and his niece in Beirut: the killings were answered by the biggest political demonstration since the death of Nasser.

Less than a year later another Israeli assassination—this time of three Palestinian leaders in the heart of Beirut on the night of April 10, 1973, apparently with the blessing of the United States—shocked the country.[6] For three hours that night Israeli commandos, who had landed by rubber dinghys from the sea, directed traffic at Ramlet al-Beida on the southern edge of Beirut, circulated freely in central Beirut, passing within yards of Internal Security Forces (ISF) and army barracks and, having completed their murderous mission—which included killing nine Lebanese who got in their way—were allowed to depart without a move by the army or the ISF. Kamal Jumblat stated bluntly the next day: "There was collusion in theory and practice between the Lebanese authorities, the Israeli government, and the planners of the operation, which we admit was very, very clever and well-organized. The ISF did not move because the Interior Minister (Saeb Salam) did not instruct them to do so. We are a state with no honour."[7]

Prime Minister Salam later told parliament that he had been awakened when the raid took place: "I wonder why. It was the job of the military authorities." He then informed the commander-in-chief, Iskander Ghanem. Later that night he asked Ghanem: "What have you done about the raid on Sidon?" The commander-in-chief replied: "What raid?" When the president rejected Salam's demand that Ghanem be dismissed, Salam himself resigned.

In Lebanon's greatest demonstration ever, more than 250,000 people—roughly a tenth of the population—marched in the funeral procession of the martyred Palestinian leaders. The size and seriousness of the demonstration served notice to the regime of the consequences of any attempt to destroy the resistance movement, but the regime did not heed this warning. All the slain leaders were well known throughout the Arab world, yet official news bulletins by Lebanese radio about the April 10 events said scarcely a word about them.

If the Lebanese were stunned and humiliated by the government's inaction during the Israeli raid, a shocked Palestinian resistance movement saw its fears of a Lebanese Black September confirmed.

The Army Battles the Resistance, May 1973

On the heels of the Israeli raid came an army attempt to crush the resistance movement, confirming popular suspicions of high-level collusion with Israel. The army's attack was touched off when the resistance movement countered the army's arrest of a number of commandos found carrying explosives in late April. The resistance kidnapped two army sergeants, setting the stage for an exchange of hostages. While the prime minister designate, Amine al-Hafez, was attempting to effect the release of hostages, fighting broke out on the night of May 1. A "third force," later identified as the Kataeb, was held responsible for starting the fighting.[8] Army units seized on this pretext to surround, and to use tanks and armored cars to shell, two Palestinian refugee camps in West Beirut, Bourj al-Barajney and Shatila. On whose orders this attack was made has never been disclosed, but few doubted that the army and the Kataeb were acting in collusion.

The attack caused Syrian President Hafez al-Assad to dispatch Palestinan Liberation Army (PLA) troops to Lebanon while his foreign minister, Abdul Halim Khaddam, hastened to Beirut to mediate. A cease-fire was secured on May 7, but that evening new clashes erupted. Again a "third force" was held responsible. Security forces later rounded up some of the alleged culprits, who were reported to have "already confessed to being in the employ of Israeli intelligence."[9]

Two battles were fought in May, one of two days' duration, the second two-and-a-half days long. The 12,000-strong Lebanese army outnumbered the commandos more than two-to-one, but lacked combat experience and could not marshall all its forces for fear of splitting. Basing its strategy and tactics on its understanding of this fact, the resistance movement more than held its own against the Lebanese army.

The May battles found the resistance movement in a fairly solid position, owing to efforts underway for the past year to achieve unity among its different organizations. These battles also marked the first time that Lebanese progressive parties—chiefly the CPL, the OCA, and the Mourabitoun (a Nasserite group supported and trained by al-Fatah)—participated militarily in defense of the camps. The PFLP warned at this time that the resistance must prepare itself for a major battle in Lebanon, one to be waged by the rightist party militias and other paramilitary organizations.

Kataeb Overtures to the Palestinians and Syria

The outcome of the May battles confirmed the Kataeb's fears of the growing weight of the resistance movement on the political scene. This came at a time when social unrest made the emerging alliance between the Palestinians and the underprivileged Lebanese appear all the more threatening. In an effort to disrupt this developing association, the Kataeb initiated a dialogue with resistance leaders in late May of 1973. This dialogue, and others that followed, achieved nothing. A joint Kataeb–Palestinian declaration was prepared for presentation at the Kataeb's annual congress in September, but the Kataeb in the end refused to make it public.

Similar initiatives with Damascus and later with Cairo and Riyad had a more favorable outcome. As the intermediary between Western capitalism and the markets of the Arab hinterland, the predominantly Catholic banking and mercantile bourgeoisie had long been economically and financially involved with other Arab states, while still pursuing a policy of political isolation from Arabism and Arab concerns as such. Gradual modifications of this political stance had begun as early as the mid-1960s with the emergence of Saudi Arabia as the leader of the anti-Nasser camp, with which Lebanon's service bourgeoisie sympathized.

The trend in Arab capitals toward a "political settlement" of the Arab–Israeli conflict was underscored by Sadat's cancellation of his friendship treaty with Moscow in 1971 and his expulsion of Soviet advisers in 1972. Coupled with Lebanese social unrest and the rise of youthful, radical, and democratic national forces, this persuaded the Kataeb to seek direct and friendly relations with some Arab governments. Though they might disagree on means and methods, Lebanese and Arab leaders bent on "political settlement" faced a common problem: taming the Palestinian resistance movement and nipping the development of popular movements in the bud.

In September of 1973 Kataeb leaders began a series of meetings with the Saiqa commander, Zuhair Muhsin, who during the May events had been the target of the most virulent Kataeb recriminations. Soon leaders of the Lebanese branch of the Syrian Baath joined the talks. Syrian President Hafez Assad's subsequent invitation to Pierre Gemayel to visit Damascus struck some Lebanese newspapers as "historic," since the Kataeb had been the most firmly anti-Syrian of all Lebanese political organizations.

The Kataeb, however, did not evince a similar interest in cooperating with fellow Lebanese Muslims. In a hard-line speech delivered on the morrow of his return from Damascus, Pierre Gemayel asserted that "a scorched earth Lebanon" was preferable to a Lebanon shorn of its special (i.e., Christian) identity.[10] This was a virtual declaration of war against all Lebanese who hoped to achieve a more democratic regime. Early in 1974 Gemayel paid week-long visits to Egypt and Saudi Arabia, from which he returned enthusiastic. Later he also visited Jordan.

The Kataeb–Damascus rapprochement coincided with a political storm gathering over the arming and training of the militias. Newspaper photos showed Camille Chamoun's Tiger militia training with live munitions ranging from pistols to anti-tank rockets while Gemayel announced that the Kataeb was operating nine military training camps "under the supervision of the authorities."[11] "How," asked Jumblat, "can the authorities train members of a sectarian organization like the Kataeb? What authorities? Civilian or military?"[12] To the demands to disband the militias, Gemayel replied:

"Neither the present government or any other could shut down a single training camp."[13]

National Bloc leader Raymond Edde commented that paramilitary organizations were "creating conditions for a new outbreak like 1958." He predicted that hostilities "will be not between Lebanese and Palestinians, as some might expect, but between the political parties themselves."[14]

Syria's Role in Lebanon, May–September 1973

The crisis of May 1973 in Lebanon involved Syrian interests, as Israel's occupation of the Golan Heights placed the Israeli army in a position to strike through southeast Lebanon around and behind Syrian lines defending Damascus. The troubles in Lebanon, moreover, could not be permitted to disrupt Syrian–Egyptian plans to attack Israeli forces in the occupied Sinai and occupied Golan Heights. Sadat and Assad had already established a unified Military Command in January 1973, and by early May the overall war plan had been settled. The coming war imposed two imperatives on Syrian President Assad with respect to Lebanon: to secure Lebanese stability and—since he still needed the Palestinian card—to preserve the resistance movement while establishing control over it. Toward the social agitation sweeping through Lebanon, Assad's authoritarian regime was hardly more sympathetic than was the Lebanese ruling class. Assad did not want Lebanon torn by social strife on the eve of the war, nor did he want the social virus to penetrate into Syria. His rapprochement with the Kataeb on the eve of the October war conformed to these general aims in Lebanon.

Comments in the government-controlled Syrian press at this time—recalling that Lebanon was a colonial creation carved out of Syria—underscored the fact that Syria had never abandoned its dream of regaining influence in Lebanon, or at least the provinces lost in 1920. For this reason Damascus had consistently refused to establish diplomatic relations with Beirut. Syrian rulers almost automatically assumed what they conceived to be a natural right: to have a say in Lebanese affairs. Assad was simply more open about this than most.

The Lebanese crisis afforded the Assad regime an opportunity to settle a number of outstanding political and economic disputes with the Lebanese government. Foremost was the anticipated creation of a stable Lebanese national government. This was followed by demands for more favorable terms for Syria in handling transit trade; the expulsion of Syrian political exiles in Lebanon; an end to the "anti-Syrian campaign" in the Lebanese press; and the improvement of the status of Syrian workers in Lebanon.

The demand for a "national government" meant a government including representatives of Syria's friends among traditional Sunni politicians and the national forces. The formation of Takeiddine Solh's government on July 8 satisfied this demand. (The national movement's representative was Bahij Takeiddine, a member of Jumblat's parliamentary bloc but not of the PSP, who became interior minister.[15] On the status of the nearly 300,000 Syrian workers in Lebanon, Syria won substantial improvements (at least on paper): equal treatment with Lebanese in matters of minimum wages, sick leave, overtime, and so on. In practice, however, Syrian workers—who provided the bulk of the labor force in the construction industry—continued to be paid less than Lebanese workers and did not receive the social benefits promised. Damascus did not protest.

Syria's other two objectives, probably more important, were achieved without publicity. When the border was reopened in August and PLA troops had withdrawn, Syrian political exiles quietly left Lebanon, not to return. *Al-Rayah,* the organ of the ousted Salah Jadid faction of the Syrian Baath, was closed down. Criticism of Syria in the Lebanese press was muted.

The direction of Syrian policy on the Palestinian resistance movement became clear after a September meeting in Cairo, where Sadat, Assad, and Jordan's King Husain consumated a reconciliation between Assad and Husain which had been in preparation for some time. Al-Fatah's criticism of the reconciliation brought prompt retaliation from Assad, who ordered al-Fatah's radio station in Deraa closed, its information officers arrested, and its literature confiscated. Saiqa and PLA units stationed in Syria henceforth acted independently of the PLO, taking orders from the Syrian government.

The October 1973 War

On the afternoon of October 6, 1973, Egypt and Syria attacked Israeli forces occupying the Egyptian Sinai peninsula and the Syrian

Golan Heights. In the war's first week, Egyptian and Syrian forces, both armed by the USSR, scored impressive gains, so much so that the United States had to fly to Israel's rescue. Then Secretary of State Henry Kissinger later asserted that the United States "saved Israel from collapse at the end of the first week by our arms supply." Speaking about U.S. foreign policy to a group of American Jewish leaders, Kissinger explained: "What we wanted in October 1973 was the most massive defeat possible so that it would be clear to the Arabs that they would get nowhere with dependence on the Soviets." "What was our strategy in 1973?" he asked, and answered: "First, we sought to break up the Arab united front. Also we wanted to argue that the Europeans and Japan did not get involved in the diplomacy arena. Finally, we sought a situation which would enable Israel to deal separately with each of its neighbors."[16]

This American strategy explains much that followed. Kissinger's "step-by-step" approach after the war avoided, in his own words, "the disadvantages of bringing all the Arabs together," and permitted the United States to respond to Israel's demands for more time. To go into "a protracted stall with the Arabs," Kissinger said, "I took many trips to the area . . . with no progress, of course." Kissinger asserted that he had left the Palestine question alone in order to work on the frontier questions, hoping eventually to isolate the Palestinians. He explained that, in his view, Arab governments would abandon the Palestinians if they could recover their conquered lands.

The outcome of the October war was a bitter disappointment to the Syrian, Egyptian, and Palestinian people. The Palestinians, both the PLA and the resistance, fought on the Suez and Golan fronts, defending Mount Hermon and harrassing the Israeli army's rear lines in northern Israel. Israel's success in crossing the Suez Canal and encircling the Egyptian Third Army on the east bank and in Suez induced Sadat to agree to a cease-fire on October 22. Syria was compelled to do the same two days later. The American attempt to break up the Arab front and isolate the Palestinians was underway.

Toward Civil War

The October war accelerated the decline in Lebanon's economy. Egypt's (and soon after Syria's) economic opening to the West and rapid developments in the economic potential of other Arab states allowed them to bypass Lebanon as a go-between in dealing with Western capitalism. Egyptian and Syrian capital, which had earlier flowed into Beirut, now started returning home.

Lebanon's dependence on other Arab economies, meanwhile, increased substantially. In 1974, 75 percent of Lebanon's industrial and 86 percent of its fruit exports were to Arab countries, primarily Saudi Arabia.[17] The same Arab countries accounted for the bulk of Lebanon's tourist income, and provided jobs for the growing number of Lebanese unable to find work in the saturated service economy. By 1974 almost 100,000 Lebanese workers were employed abroad, chiefly in Arab oil countries, with their annual remittances home reaching about 100 million Lebanese pounds.[18] Internally, the ongoing inflation dissipated the support the service sector of the ruling bourgeoisie had always enjoyed among the urban middle strata—civil servants, white-collar employees, small shopkeepers and merchants— for whom the spill-over from upper-class prosperity had provided both a living and the stuff of dreams of upward mobility.

The darkening prospects for Lebanon's service economy induced a significant part of the service bourgeoisie—along with the industrial and technocratic bourgeoisie developing export markets for Arab countries—to join in a project to "modernize" the system without changing its essential character. The country's dilapidated infrastructure frustrated the economic initiative of this class and cost it heavily. Congestion at Beirut port had since 1972 cost importers 250 million Lebanese pounds a year in freight charges alone. Railroads, the road network, and the airport were all inadequate to cope with increased freight and other traffic. These businessmen insisted that the state "assume its responsibilities" to provide the infrastructure and services they needed to profit in the new circumstances.

Alongside this "reformist" trend among the economic and political elite, another trend was reflected in the intensifying military mobilization of the Kataeb and other rightist Maronite militias. In 1973 these militias recruited non-party members for the first time, opening new training camps and mounting military parades in mountain towns and villages. The Maronite bourgeoisie and political elite contributed generously, suggesting that this particular group looked more and more to the militias—especially that of the Kataeb, alone among rightist parties in having a mass base—as the most effective guardians of its privileges. The rise in status of an indoctrinated and armed petty bourgeoisie in the Maronite community somewhat undermined the position of the old established Maronite families.

Sectarian Communities in Crisis

The militias' growing boldness and provocations affected nearly all Christian communities. As early as 1969 Catholic and Orthodox students, aroused by the campaign the rightists were waging against the Palestinians, convoked a conference to affirm publicly their support for the resistance movement. In January of 1974 a Caucus of Committed Christians sought to offer Christians an alternative to what it saw as the ever more militaristic and fascistic line in the Maronite community. This initiative came from the clergy, theologians, and intellectuals involved in social action, and from social workers who opposed the social and ideological role of the Christian institutions in which they worked. One of the Caucus' main concerns was to combat the "fear complex" the right was nurturing among the Christian masses by deliberately confusing the maintenance of Christian economic and political privilege with the continued existence of the Christian communities. The Caucus also affirmed to the Muslim masses Christian support for the Palestinian cause and Christian rejection of church-state collusion. Its objective was to become a movement of opinion rather than a structure for political intervention. The Caucus achieved an important audience among the churches, and especially among Christian youth.[19]

Gregoire Haddad, the Greek Catholic archbishop of Beirut, spoke on behalf of the downtrodden, splitting the Greek Catholic community. He attacked the "minority living in insolent luxury while most Lebanese families do not earn enough for food and housing," and insisted on the need for change. This, he said, must go beyond cosmetic change and the "so-called Lebanese formula."[20]

In August of 1974 the Vatican, reflecting the stand of the Greek Catholic hierarchy, suspended and later dismissed Haddad from his post. Petitions, newspaper advertisements, and committees protested and demanded his reinstatement. When these proved to be of no avail, many, and especially the young, flocked to participate in the social action that the former archbishop continued around his journal, *Afaq (Perspectives)*.

If the Orthodox bourgeoisie, reputed to be the wealthiest in Lebanon, often stood with the Maronite right, the dominant trend at other levels was more democratic and secular, and often progressive. Orthodox youth figured prominently in progressive students movements in support of the resistance movement and among the Caucus of Committed Christians. Above all, Orthodox church leaders assumed a notable role in combatting the propagation of fear and sectarian strife coming from the strongholds of the Maronite right. Archbishops Georges Khodr of Beirut, Jean Kurban of Tripoli, and Paul Khouri of Sidon, all noted for their progressive thought and action, worked to halt the exploitation of religion in the secular domain and to promote coexistence among communities on the basis of equal rights and duties. Archbishop Khodr spoke for many in asserting that coexistence could be achieved only by the acceptance of "the concept of a national state based solely on the wish of all citizens to live together."

As the crisis deepened, Imam Sadr became the Shi'a community's most popular leader. The small group of traditional Shi'a establishment leaders was compelled to give way for the time being, while the number of Shi'as moving into the progressive and left parties increased steadily. With the exception of Kamel al-Asaad's bloc of six, Shi'a deputies promised to work for Shi'a demands, threatening to withdraw their support from the government if these demands were not met. The government's failure to act brought the Sadr movement to its zenith. Early in 1974 Sadr's rallies drew crowds of 50,000, even 100,000 people, including many armed men. Peasants from the south and the Bekaa, now subsisting precariously in the city slums, artisan producers and workers of the villages, the small bourgeoisie of the market towns—these were the Imam's most ardent supporters. In the heady ambience of his huge gatherings the Imam's speeches became ever more revolutionary: "We have no choice," he declared, "but revolution and arms."[21]

The Imam attracted support from nearly 200 personalities of all sects and factions. His efforts on behalf of tobacco growers and the oppressed in his own community, his support for the resistance movement, his careful attempt to speak in behalf of *all* the oppressed—not only the Shi'as—often brought him into tacit cooperation with progressive forces. If he did not win the progressives and leftists of his community, whose audience was then expanding, his mobilization of the largest and one of the most deprived communities in Lebanon behind demands for change undermined the basis of the 1943 National Pact.

On the Sunni side, the ground appeared to be moving under the feet of the traditional leaders. Their clientele turned in other directions, to Nasserite political organizations and to the resistance. In spite of their efforts to define their demands and take a firm stand, traditional Sunni leaders seemed to be progressively eclipsed. Kamal Jumblat's rising stature as a national political leader and spokesperson for a modern, national orientation contributed to the decline of the Sunni *zuama*.

Isolation of the Service Bourgeoisie

The sociopolitical climate deteriorated rapidly after May 1973. A rash of murders, kidnappings, thefts, shoot-outs, and clan and tribal skirmishes erupted in many areas—deformed manifestations of the impact of the socioeconomic crisis. Gangs of outlaws and criminals proliferated. "Outlaw republics" appeared in certain city quarters, and bandits reigned in isolated villages. Before these eruptions of violence the state stood seemingly uncaring and helpless.

An impatient radical reaction came from an extreme left that went underground to practice what it preached: armed action. In 1973–75 the most effective of these groups, the Arab Communist Organization (ACO), carried out a series of well-prepared and in general skillfully executed attacks on American institutions and interests in Syria and Lebanon, hitting at what it identified as the main enemy.[22] Small revolutionary groups formed in some southern towns and in the poorer quarters of the coastal cities, groups which, although not organizationally related, thought and acted on similar lines. Advocating popular political and military struggle, these revolutionaries refused to cooperate with traditional politicians, Christian or Muslim. But the influence of these small groups did not reach beyond their immediate localities.

Contributing to the formation of a new concerned public opinion was the appearance in 1974 of a well-edited, lively, modern newspaper, *Al-Safir*, which concerned itself with the needs and problems of the poor and deprived, exposing government venality and corruption, and honestly reporting the statements and activities of progressive and left parties and leaders.

In this social and political ambience progressive parties acquired many new partisans and sympathizers and a more receptive audience. This was especially true of the CPL, the OCA, and the PSP, all three of which were active in Shi'a areas, especially in the south, where they now found the bulk of their members and sympathizers. The communists' organization of home guards to stand against Israeli attacks in southern villages and the leading role played by communists in the growing number of workers' committees contributed to the widening influence of these parties.

Even so, the discontented masses remained for the most part outside the influence of any political parties. Their protests, usually spontaneous and localized, acquired national dimensions only when national issues were at stake. If the Palestinian revolution still inspired the masses of the poor, the revolution's leaders made little effort to orient popular support or to demonstrate in practice the unity of Palestinian and Lebanese goals. The progressive and left parties, especially the CPL, were seen as giving priority to electoral politics over popular needs. Electoral politics involved supporting traditional notables who had little, if anything, to offer the deprived classes.

The efforts of the emerging national movement, whatever its shortcomings, were primarily directed toward a political drive to end the threat posed by the rightist militias and their ever-more-blatant collusion with the army. Curiously, although repeatedly pointing to this threat, the national movement did not prepare itself militarily. It concentrated on advancing popular socioeconomic demands, while insisting on the need to eliminate sectarianism from the political system.

"Government of All Lebanon"

Takeiddine Solh's government—a precisely balanced team representing all traditional forces and all parliamentary blocs—took a first step toward implementing some promised reforms in 1974, when it reshuffled more than a hundred civil service posts to assure Muslims greater "participation."[23] For the first time ever Muslims were named to posts hitherto reserved for Christians, and vice versa. The reshuffle did somewhat reduce a few long-established Maronite fiefdoms in the government machine, but Solh's claim to have achieved "a breakthrough in overcoming the sectarian character of administrative posts" was excessive. The effect, moreover, was weakened by widespread criticism of the nepotism involved in the appointments. The Kataeb did not openly oppose this moderate reform, but Camille Chamoun withdrew his minister from the government in protest.

Reform proposals poured in from all sides. More than a hundred concrete proposals for electoral law reforms were submitted, most dealing with basic issues: to lower the voting age to eighteen; to limit the amount of money spent on electoral campaigns; eliminate sectarianism in popular representations; and redraw electoral districts to do away with the influence of political feudalism.

In May 1973 popular pressures persuaded President Franjieh to call a special cabinet meeting to discuss the needed reforms and the problem of the militias. This session, known as the Beiteddine Conclave, took two important decisions: to introduce military conscription, a measure hitherto always opposed by the Kataeb and its allies; and to amend the electoral law. The cabinet formally adopted a conscription bill a few days later, but parliament did not take up this issue until the end of 1975, when the civil war and the army's imminent disintegration made the matter academic. Electoral law reforms did not materialize.

The Conclave discussed political sectarianism only to conclude that no action was necessary since "the Constitution protects the rights of all citizens." The issue of "restricting the possession and carrying of arms by civilians," that is, the militias, the main reason for convoking the Conclave, was also evaded. This surprised no one. While President Franjieh presided over the Conclave, his own militia, the Marada Brigade, was training in Zghorta under the command of his son, Tony.

These meager results could not still the rising clamor for change, in particular change in the National Pact, against which more and more voices were raised. Moreover, Lebanon's supine attitude in the face of Israeli aggressions provoked troubling questions about the character of the state itself. A large-scale Israeli incursion five to ten kilometers inside Lebanon along a seventy-five-kilometer stretch of the border on April 12, 1974, presented a now familiar scenario: Israeli invasion, followed by orders to the army from the prime minister (Takeiddine Solh this time) and the cabinet to fight back. Blandly ignoring the order, the army sits on its hands. To what authority, if any, was the army responsible? Whose orders, if anyone's, did it obey? Obviously not those of the prime minister and his government, as they all could testify.

A raucous meeting of parliament on April 16 again and again raised the issue of the government's failure—or impotence—to make the army do what it was ordered to do.[24] Many deputies protested that despite the growing Israeli threat, no steps had been taken to strengthen the army, let alone reform it. The army's continuing complacent indifference in the face of Israel's almost daily humiliating violations of Lebanon's sovereignty and borders, coupled with the unchallenged arrogance of the rightist militias, provoked doubts and suspicions about the role of both and their relation to each other.

The issue came to a head in late summer when two ministers—Kazem al-Khalil (Justice), the vice president of Chamoun's Ahrar Party, and Nasri Malouf (Defense), attended a banquet in honor of that party's militia. This celebration came only a month after a clash between the Kataeb militia and the Palestinians in Dekwane, both using heavy weapons, which left ten killed and thirty-five wounded. It coincided with news reports that the militia were being trained in heavy weapons in Jordan, and with the arrival in the port of Junieh of two large shiploads of arms for the militias. In an interview with a Madrid newspaper soon after the banquet, Khalil asserted that "the Palestinians must leave Lebanon."

Jumblat now bluntly warned that the Kataeb and Ahrar were "setting the stage for large-scale violence and national strife in Lebanon" and for "a massacre of the Palestinians in cooperation with Jordan and the CIA." When the government again failed to make any move to control the militias, and the interior minister's efforts to halt the unloading of the arms shipments were blocked by higher authorities, Jumblat pulled his two ministers—Bahij Takeiddine (Interior) and Tewfik Assaf (Petroleum)—out of the government. Their departure, soon followed by that of other ministers, provoked the collapse of Takeiddine Solh's government. The government's fall again underscored the fact that the National Pact had become unworkable. Solh's government could not amend the labor law, moderate or reduce social conflicts, stem the worsening security situation, prevent the militias from becoming stronger and more provocative, or halt their clashes with the Palestinians and with other Lebanese. Lebanon's problems escaped the traditional formulas of the system. A rigid economic-political structure, incapable of evolution, could neither absorb the changes required by the new social forces that had developed within it nor suppress these forces. Solh's failure cut the ground from under the moderates seeking to reform the system without changing its essential character.

Rashid Solh's Government

Conflicts over the militias and power-sharing held up the formation of a new government. In an apparent effort to halt the Muslim right's growing convergence with Jumblat's national movement in the demand for reform, President Franjieh asked Saeb Salam to form a new government. After a three-week dispute with Franjieh over who would choose the ministers, Salam abandoned the effort.

The president then named Rashid Solh, a cousin of Takeiddine Solh who had never held a ministerial post, as prime minister. This choice angered the Muslim right; leaders Saeb Salam and Rashid Karami promptly formed a bloc to oppose the new government with independent deputy Raymond Edde. In the main, Solh's eighteen-member cabinet was a traditionalist one, a heterogeneous grouping of right and left, parliamentary and extra-parliamentary, veterans and novices, Muslims and Christians. Yet it differed from its predecessors in avoiding confrontation with the national and popular forces. Solh's cabinet was the first in Franjieh's term to include a member of Jumblat's PSP. This was Abbas Khalaf, a PSP vice-president, who became economy minister. Khaled Jumblat, a PSP ally, became minister of finance. In the rapidly accelerating crisis of subsequent months, Kamal Jumblat and the national movement constituted a major influence on Solh's government. This government attempted to make a few real, though certainly not radical, reforms. The mere attempt was sufficient to bring on the civil war.

Economy Minister Khalaf took at least partially effective steps to deal with spiraling living costs and shortages of essential commodities. In the case of sugar, for example—as a preliminary measure until ration cards could be issued—Khalaf fixed an 80 piastre price per kilo for the ordinary consumer and a 320 piastre price for industrialists. When sugar disappeared from the market, Khalaf raided sugar factories and sweetshops where it was being hoarded, redistributed the confiscated sugar to shopkeepers, and arrested the hoarders. He also declared war against monopolists of other consumer goods. To finance government price subsidies for essential consumer products, Finance Minister Khaled Jumblat won cabinet approval for increased customs duties on cars, refrigerators, and alcoholic drinks.

The prime minister acted decisively to solve the problem of the long-stalled amendment of Article 50 of the Labor Code. He simply promulgated it by decree as he was by law entitled to do.[25] The law virtually abolished arbitrary dismissal. This was a major victory for workers, especially for the workers' committees, and they were now determined to see that the law was enforced.

Solh also won parliament's approval for a long-demanded extension of social security protection to new categories of workers, and he applied to the public sector an increase in the minimum wage (to 310 Lebanese pounds a month) and a wage rise (11 percent) won earlier by the General Council of Labor (GCL) for the private sector. Finance Minister Jumblat—exercising the government's prerogative to oversee the policies of the Régie tobacco monopoly—increased the price paid to farmers for their tobacco and agreed to other growers' demands. Striking workers in Régie tobacco factories also won wage increases and a promise to reorganize work conditions in their factories within three months.

Although the government showed a greater awareness of popular needs than had its predecessors, it lacked the power and cohesion either to allay mass social unrest or to halt it. Strikes and demonstrations in all parts of the country marked the few months before the outbreak of civil war. Even prisoners went on strike, protesting inequality of treatment and the slowness of judicial procedures.

The security front also commanded attention. In parts of the country, security of life and property no longer existed; the collection of protection money and killings had become commonplace.

Kafr Shuba

On October 1, 1974, Israel officially announced its intention "to organize regular and systematic" patrols and roadblocks on Lebanese territory: "From now on we will send our troops regularly into Lebanon. For us it is a new method of preventing infiltration across our border." As if this humiliation were not enough for the Lebanese, Israeli communiques on operations inside Lebanon during the weeks that followed often ended: "Our troops encountered no resistance from the Lebanese army."[76]

The impunity with which Israeli forces disported themselves on Lebanese territory, coupled with the state's failure to provide even a modicum of protection or medical aid for the wounded, became insupportable to the local population. After heavy Israeli bombing of the village of Blida early in October, one of the victims died for lack of medical supplies at the government hospital in Tibrine. A morning meeting a week later, to commemorate the victims of this attack, chanted slogans hostile to the regime. It soon became a 5,000-strong march to Bint Jbeil, the district center, gathering adherents on the way. The angry crowd erected barricades around Bint Jbeil, cut its telephone lines, sacked the government house (Serail) when they found it empty, tore down the Lebanese flag, stamped on the picture of the president, attacked a police post and threw stones at army units.

On December 12, Israel bombarded the Sabra and Shatila refugee camps in Beirut, and the next day the refugee camp in Nabatiye, already partially destroyed in earlier bombings. Southern villages came under almost daily aerial and artillery bomardment, and were raided by Israeli commandos who blew up the homes of suspected Palestinian sympathizers. A UN-arranged "olive truce" (to permit harvesting the olive crop), from December 25 to January 31, proved ephemeral: Israeli bombardment resumed on December 28, followed by a series of heavy raids on villages in the central sector and a large-scale operation in the Arqoub. The raids, intended to turn Lebanese villages against the Palestinians, had unintended results. Palestinian commandos fought off an Israeli force of more than 300 troops, supported by troops in motorized units and tanks, in the village of Kafr Shuba.

During this week-long battle the Lebanese army was entirely absent, though it maintained barricades on roads leading to the south to prevent reinforcements and munitions from reaching the embattled Palestinians. The army did not fire a shot at the Israelis, but it did manage, two days after the battle ended, to kill three Palestinian commandos returning from a reconnaissance mission in Israel. During the Kafr Shuba battle some 800 of its displaced inhabitants marched to Marjeyoun, the district capital, to protest against the army's failure to help defend their village and the state's failure to provide them with food and blankets. When the demonstrators refused to withdraw, security forces opened fire, wounding many. Enraged demonstrators then smashed windows and doors, blocked roads with rocks, and set tires on fire, while the security men attacked them with rubber truncheons.

The villagers of Kafr Shuba demanded government protection, compensation for homes and crops destroyed, the right to return home, and the rebuilding of their village. Fearing what they saw as an Israeli attempt to turn south Lebanon into another Palestine, many were determined to return home: they insisted that they would not be stampeded into leaving as the Palestinians had been in 1948. Villagers were at first forcibly prevented from going back. Later they were told they could take food to relatives who had stayed behind. Many then returned with their belongings, expecting to stay, only to be told a few hours later to pack up and leave for good. Young men lay down on the road to try to prevent this evacuation.

The "seven-day little war of Kafr Shuba," that left Palestinian commandos still in command of the shattered village, electrified people of the south and throughout the country. The Palestinians, not the army, had stood, fought, and—for the time being, at least—had won; progressive parties and popular organizations, not the government, hastened to provide food, shelter, and blankets for the homeless. Kafr Shuba became a symbol of a common struggle of Lebanese and Palestinians together against the foreign enemy and its Lebanese collaborators—these last being identified by many as the holders of high office in army and government. "South Lebanon will be the tomb of feudalism and aggressors," read a typical placard carried in the many popular demonstrations that followed.

On January 20, at a meeting attended by thousands, Imam Sadr called for the creation of a "Lebanese resistance" to fight alongside the Palestinian resistance movement, to prevent the loss of Lebanon as Palestine had been lost. Within a few months his Movement of the Disinherited had organized such a resistance force: Amal (Hope). On January 28, south Lebanon observed a general strike to demand that the south be defended. In Beirut some 15,000 gathered for a National Day for Protection of the South. Reaction was not limited to the popular forces. Rashid Karami bitterly criticized the state's "strength through weakness" policy, declaring his support for the "double revolt of the people of the south" and predicting that for "lack of resistance we will be sacrificed on the altar of ignorance, cowardice and capitulation." In an editorial in *Al-Nahar,* publisher and editor Ghassan Tueni spoke for a broad current in asserting: "The time has come for Lebanon to enter the war against Israel." Another response came from the Maronite extremists. On January 24, 1975—six days after the end of the Kafr Shuba battle and on the eve of a meeting of the Arab League Defense Council—Kataeb leader Pierre Gemayel emerged from a conference with President Franjieh to make public a memorandum he had delivered to the president. This denounced the Cairo Accord, bitterly attacked the presence of the Palestinian resistance movement, declared the south to be "completely out of government control," and warned the Palestinians that if they "did not unify their ranks and put an end to anarchy," the state "would exercise its right to recover its authority." Gemayel added that on this point the president "is in agreement with us."

Southern villages were encouraged to send telegrams to the president demanding Palestinian withdrawal from the south. Franjieh sent his foreign minister to Damascus to try to persuade Syria to compel the commandos to halt their activities in Lebanon. But strong, even violent, popular reaction to Gemayel's memorandum frustrated these initiatives.

The memorandum drew the battle lines clearly. Behind the pro- and anti-Palestinian division was a basic schism: between a privileged ruling class, linked to the dominant Maronite Catholic sect, and forces that had arisen in the disadvantaged sectarian communities, whose basic needs the sectarian political system had proved incapable of answering. The system appeared to be approaching collapse, but no single force or class was capable of mastering the situation to its own advantage. Political feudalism was already disintegrating. The service bourgeoisie, which in thirty years had proved incapable of building a single national institution—not even a national army—was rapidly losing the support it had once had among the middle classes.[27] The stunted national bourgeoisie remained politically negligible. The middle strata—which with the downfall of colonially imposed regimes in other Arab countries had been able to take up the challenge—lacked a national structure and even any national organizations of their own. Yet the national and progressive movement had not achieved sufficient coherence and maturity to assume leadership.

The absence of any dominant force or class capable of settling the crisis in its own interests produced a growing disarray at the top. The decision of the politicians of the Maronite right to yield not an inch to the popular demand for reforms virtually guaranteed that growing incoherence would degenerate into civil strife.

[11]

Flashpoint:
The Outbreak of Hostilities

The Beginning

"We are small fish about to be eaten by a shark." So said fishermen all along the Lebanese coast in the winter of 1974–75, expressing their fear of the widening monopoly over the fishing industry by the Protein Company, of which Camille Chamoun was board chairman and general manager. The government's licensing of this company contradicted the policy laid down in the 1972 Six-Year Plan to develop fishing cooperatives in order to assure employment and a decent living to fishermen and to modernize operations. In February 1975 fishermen's unions in Sidon, Tyre, and Tripoli decided to strike: they demanded cancellation of Protein's licenses and better working conditions. While the strike in Tripoli on February 25 passed almost unnoticed outside the city, the Sidon strike the next day and the army's attempt to crush it convulsed the country for two weeks. It also proved to be the forerunner of the civil war.

All Sidon rallied to the fishermen's cause. Sidon deputy Dr. Nazih Bizri, and his political rival, ex-deputy Marouf Saad, led a demonstration in which every democratic and progressive trend participated. Passions ran high, the expression of deeply felt resentment over neglect of the city and of the entire southern region of which it is the capital. Like many deprived villages of the south, Sidon was denied development projects, investment, and industry. Throughout the south—a military zone where the Army Command reigned supreme—the people had grown allergic to an army that during Israel's frequent incursions had failed to fire a shot in their defense, and which preferred instead to harrass the Palestinians. Around 40 percent of

163

Sidon's population and almost half its fishermen were of Palestinian origin. Many of the city's inhabitants, both Lebanese and Palestinian, joined or supported the Palestinian resistance movement.

Clashes between the army and the people during the Sidon demonstration brought all the old suspicions about this army to the forefront. The government had authorized its entrance into Sidon only because the governor of the south, Henry Lahoud, had reported that the Sidon–Tyre road was blocked and "the situation out of control."[1] To the contrary, Nazih Bizri later told parliament, "The entry of the army into Sidon was itself what caused the blocking of the road."[2] Right after the first clash, in which one soldier was killed and twelve civilians wounded—including ex-deputy Saad—a Sidon delegation came to Beirut to demand that the governor be removed for misrepresenting the situation. Apparently convinced, the cabinet quickly ordered the governor to go "on enforced administrative leave" while the prime minister sent his economy minister, Abbas Khalaf, a leader of Kamal Jumblat's Progressive Socialist Party (PSP), to negotiate with the fishermen.

In all major towns strikers and demonstrators took to the streets to voice their solidarity with the fishermen and people of Sidon; in that city itself a committee was formed to keep order and negotiate with the government. Headed by Deputy Bizri, the committee grouped important personalities and representatives of virtually all parties and trends—from the Communists to the Chamber of Commerce.[3] Operating democratically, it managed during the two weeks it governed the city to preserve unity and to maintain its independence from traditional politicians. Under its auspices a popular resistance was organized and armed to defend the city.

On March 1, just as Khalaf's negotiations were nearing a successful conclusion, the army again intervened, engaging the popular resistance in a battle that left five dead soldiers, ten dead civilians, and thirty wounded. The pretext for the army's intervention was that the city had ignored a deadline for removing the roadblocks from the Sidon–Tyre highway. Prime Minister Solh had tried to cancel his authorization for the army's entry into the city the moment Khalaf informed him of the imminent success of his negotiations. But efforts to reach the commander-in-chief, Iskander Ghanem, proved fruitless. Malek Salam, a cabinet minister, demanded an investigation of Ghanem's unavailability during the crisis, and then his dismissal.

When the demand was rejected, Salam himself resigned. On March 2 the government and the committee reached an accord: Sidon agreed to remove the roadblocks once the army had withdrawn.

The Sidon events revived acrimonious debate in parliament over the need to reorganize the army and Muslim demands for an equal share in power. A draft law on reorganization of the army, although "absolutely rejected" by Maronite right leaders, was referred to the appropriate parliamentary committees for discussion. And on April 10 the prime minister sent parliament a naturalization bill that would grant citizenship to the tens of thousands of Muslims of Wadi Khaled and other regions hitherto denied it because of their religion.

The government transferred the two officers in command of the south and announced its decision to establish fishing cooperatives for the fishermen. Somewhat later, it put restrictions on areas where Protein could operate and the types of boats it could use. Yet the wave of anger sweeping through the country over the Sidon events assumed the aspect of a mass uprising against the army, especially in the south. Rightist Maronite political parties quickly organized counter-demonstrations, proclaiming March 5 Army Day. Observed only in Christian areas, Army Day for much of the population identified the army more than ever as the exclusive instrument of the Maronite sect.

The next day, Marouf Saad died of his wounds. Shops closed, barricades went up on streets and roads, and the tension became palpable. Saad's funeral in Sidon was proclaimed a day of national mourning, and became a demonstration of Lebanese–Palestinian solidarity. Saad, a veteran of the 1948 Palestine war, was buried wrapped in the Palestinian flag; Lebanese and Palestinian flags flew side by side throughout the city.

When the bullet taken from Saad's body was sent to European ballistics experts, they found it came from a rifle used by the Lebanese army. The prime minister than sent the bullet to the Army Command so that the perpetrator of the crime could be identified, but the army took no action.[4] To many Lebanese this proved that the army's Deuxième Bureau was responsible for Saad's murder.

Many of the internal ingredients that combined to ignite the civil war appeared in the Sidon events: social injustice associated with regional and sectarian disparities; state impotence and the army's deployment as an instrument of the Maronite power structure; and the emergence of a popular front for change. While both the resistance movement and the Maronite militias were visibly absent, they both would soon be drawn into the conflict.

The First Three Rounds

Pierre Gemayel's 1973 threat to "burn Lebanon rather than see its identity changed" proved not an idle one. While Kataeb gunman continued to harrass both Lebanese and Palestinians, Gemayel orchestrated the political and psychological mobilization that preceded the conflagration. In interview after interview and memorandum after memorandum he demanded the cancellation of the Cairo Accord, a plebiscite on the commando presence in Lebanon, and the eviction of the Tel al-Zaatar refugees from the Christian sector. Early in the afternoon on April 13, 1975, a busload of Palestinian and Lebanese families returning from a popular gathering in Sabra camp to their homes in Tel al-Zaatar ran into a carefully prepared ambush in Ain-Remaneh. Gunmen opened fire and more than thirty persons—including women, children, and the aged—were killed and many more wounded. The massacre—for which at the time the Kataeb was almost universally held responsible—touched off four days of fighting in Beirut (April 13–17) and a wave of violence in Tripoli and Sidon.[5] Rightist attacks were concentrated on the Palestinian camps in Beirut (Bourj al-Barajney and Tel al-Zaatar) and the Shi'a suburb of Shiyah. Fighting soon spread into the industrial sector of Dekwane, and the Christian suburbs of Ain-Remaneh and Furn al-Shebbak. In parts of the downtown and the hotel district—then dominated by the Kataeb—the conflict took the form of sniping by day and dynamiting Muslim enterprises by night.

Palestinians concentrated on defending the camps, but they and their Lebanese allies also dynamited rightist Maronite enterprises in many parts of the city. Progressive and national parties, for the most part lacking militias and militarily unprepared, participated in the fighting largely on a neighborhood basis. Mahmoud Riad, Arab League secretary-general, finally secured a truce on April 16 which ended the first round. Fighting by then had cost the lives of 250 to 350 people.

Two political currents now confronted each other. For the Maronite parties departure of the Rashid Solh government had become imperative. Coming up before parliament were a number of draft laws and measures that the Kataeb claimed would "change the identity of Lebanon," that is, modify the sectarian political structure and its free enterprise system. The Kataeb insisted that such reforms not be discussed. At the same time, Kamal Jumblat's progressives and nationalists demanded the Kataeb's isolation and the removal of Kataeb ministers from the government. "Isolation of the Kataeb" became the slogan of the Muslim streets.

The Maronite parties pulled their ministers out of the government, compelling Solh to resign. In his farewell speech Solh blamed the Kataeb exclusively for the bus massacre and the April fighting—"only the latest in a series of aggressions against the Palestinians in recent years"—and emphasized his conviction of the need for basic reform: "The evil lies at the base of the very principles of government, in institutions and in laws rather than in men."[6] He then read out the demands of the national groups, and departed. In Rashid Solh's government the new political forces had reached their apex; his departure signified that the Maronite right had deliberately closed the door to peaceful reform.

The second round began the next day, as shooting erupted in the southeastern suburbs, where the Kataeb was still blockading Tel al-Zaatar. Suleiman Franjieh abruptly formed a military government, in which Iskander Ghanem held the defense portfolio, and proclaimed his determination to stop the advance of national and progressive forces. With only the right hailing the new government, the opposition—spearheaded by Muslims—took on national dimensions. Fighting intensified; a general strike began. Traditional Muslim leaders now for the first time sent their followers into the battle and into the streets to build barricades. Calling for the military government to resign, Sunni, Shi'a, and Druse leaders decided to support the national parties' boycott of the Kataeb. That evening, Syrian foreign minister Abdul Halim Khaddam and Syrian air force commander Major-General Naji Jamil arrived in Beirut on the first of many mediation efforts. Two days later the military government stepped down, but the fighting continued.

The issue of the Kataeb's exclusion from government dominated the difficult problem of forming a new cabinet. On May 28 the president conferred this task on his long-time political enemy, Rashid Karami, a choice imposed by Karami's acceptability to both Syria and Egypt. After four weeks, Kamal Jumblat agreed to a government excluding both the Kataeb and his own Progressive Socialist Party (PSP).

Rightist and traditional, Karami's six-man cabinet included three Christians and three Muslims, with each of the six major sects represented.[7] Karami's choice of Camille Chamoun for the Interior Ministry—a key portfolio usually assumed by the prime minister in times of crisis—robbed the ban on the Kataeb of any practical meaning. As minister of interior, Chamoun refused even to consult with Karami and used his position at every opportunity to sabotage the government's policy and to advance the rightist cause. Thus not the Kataeb but only national and progressive forces were excluded. The Beirut weekly *Al-Hawadess* noted that Jumblat and Imam Sadr, "the embodiments of new currents," "the hope of all those who place their bets on the future," had no part in forming the new government.[8]

During the prolonged bargaining over the government, the third round of fighting began. If the first round was fought between the Maronite militias and the Palestinians supported by their Lebanese allies, and the second was between those militias and the Muslim Lebanese, the third was a class war, pitting the dispossessed (Lebanese, Kurds, Palestinians, etc.) of the miserable ghettos encircling Beirut against the rich, whose homes, enterprises, and possessions were looted or destroyed.

Rightist savagery toward unarmed civilians was matched on the national side as unpoliticized groups—led by a neighborhood *zaim* or his *qabadayat,* often linked to the world of crime—joined the fighting. Some of the diverse groups making up the national coalition proved unable or unwilling to control the gangs of freebooters and religious fanatics who first became active in West Beirut during the second round, committing atrocities that rivaled those of the right.[9] The heterogeneous character of the national movement, above all the fact that it was not united by a revolutionary strategy, made imposition of discipline over its many groupings difficult and often impossible.

During the first three months of intermittent civil war the national movement parties, which had yet to become politically oriented toward armed struggle to achieve their goals, adopted a defensive stance, reacting to rightist attacks rather than taking the initiative. The withdrawal of al-Fatah fighters from the battle after the first round left only Rejection Front Palestinians, chiefly the Popular Front for the Liberation of Palestine (PFLP), to fight beside the national movement. This alliance quickly proved capable of standing on its own. Its effectiveness permitted Damascus, which was inevitably concerned in the civil war from the beginning, to assume the role of umpire.

Arab and International Involvement

On September 1, 1975, Egyptian President Anwar Sadat concluded the second Sinai accord with Israel. This, in the words of an Israeli official, "put another nail in the coffin" of UN Security Council Resolution 242 (to move Israel back to the pre-1967 demarcation lines) and left Israel free to pursue its already well-advanced entrenchment in the occupied territories.[10] The accord determined Egypt's stake in the Lebanese civil war, since Sadat's solution depended on stemming the resistance movement and frustrating Syrian president Hafez Assad's attempt to build an eastern front embracing Jordan and the Palestinians. Sadat thus supported the Kataeb (continuing to do so until Syria itself became the Kataeb's ally), and he stepped up diplomatic efforts to counter the Syrian initiative in Lebanon. Fervently Islamic Arab oil states—Saudi Arabia, Kuwait, the Emirates—also subsidized the Maronite militias throughout 1975. Al-Fatah's Abu Iyad, visiting Kuwait and the Emirates in December 1975, found Gulf rulers unanimous in holding the conflict in Lebanon to be one between the right, which they supported, and the international left. They denounced the resistance alliance along with the latter.[11]

The Sinai Accord left Syria to face Israel alone, a threat underscored by some thirty-eight Israeli air raids, incursions, and bombardments of villages and refugee camps throughout Lebanon in 1975, aggressions which the United States made no effort to restrain. In this situation, the imperative for the Assad regime was to prevent Lebanon from falling into the zone of influence of any other power, Arab or non-Arab. Assad sought, on the one hand, to avert the creation of what would be in effect a Maronite Israel, a partitionist goal posed openly by Maronite leaders, and on the other, to prevent the rise of a democratic, possibly radical, Lebanese regime as demanded by the national movement. Such a development could provide the pretext for Israeli intervention and undermine Assad's own authoritarian regime.

These imperatives determined the "no victor, no vanquished" policy by which he attempted to maintain his regime's ascendancy in Lebanon through the preservation of a balance between the contending parties.

American policy came under attack from both sides. Maronite rightists accused Washington of trying to compel Christians to emigrate in order to make room to settle the Palestinians in Lebanon. The Palestinian resistance–Lebanese National Movement (LNM) alliance saw the United States involved in a conspiracy with Israel to emasculate their joint forces. Washington had never been a diehard supporter of Maronite extremists, however, and it did not now back rightist demands. [12] In the wake of the Sinai II accords, Washington worked to secure an accommodation among more moderate rightist forces, Christian and Muslim. On the Muslim right, it courted Prime Minister Karami and the Shehabist current, and on the Maronite right, President Franjieh and other Christians opposed to partition. In time this policy contributed to bringing Franjieh and Karami together on a peace plan.

Complementary to this effort, Washington tried to get Syria, the best positioned of the Arab states for influencing Lebanon, to follow in Sadat's footsteps. On October 16, 1975—a day after both Washington and Paris had separately declared their rejection of partition—the United States ambassador to Damascus, Richard Murphy, handed President Assad a message from President Gerald Ford inviting him to promote "a balanced solution" in Lebanon, assuring him of American support for such a solution, and promising to persuade Israel to accept Syrian involvement in Lebanon within reasonable limits. [13] The solution envisaged by the United States was not so remote from Assad's goals as to prevent Washington and Damascus from traveling at least part of the road together.

Sadat and Kissinger were determined to exclude Moscow from any part in an Arab–Israeli settlement, and to a large extent they succeeded. Soviet influence on the course of the civil war was minor. Moscow confined its efforts to trying to reinforce its ties with both the resistance movement and Syria, giving public support to the Palestinian–LNM alliance and military aid to the resistance movement. Yet throughout 1975 Soviet leaders repeatedly urged the Palestinians to stay out of what they perceived to be a Lebanese "family affair." [14] Later, when Syria and the Palestinian resistance movement became opponents, Soviet policy in Lebanon was virtually immobilized.

Political Goals

A lull in the fighting in the summer of 1975 witnessed the nearly total departure of Syrian workers, an exodus touched off by rightist torture and killing of Syrian workers at Beirut port. As a result, the volume of work at the port fell to 30 percent of normal, and activity in other economic sectors declined. Government efforts to lure Syrian workers back by offering them the minimum wage, legal working hours, paid holidays, sick leave, family allowances, and retirement pensions (all promised in the August 1973 Lebanese–Syrian Accord, but not yet delivered) failed. Syrian workers did not return, and with the resumption of the war in late August Lebanese workers began to leave for their villages as well.

The principal protagonists used the summer lull to set forth their political aims. The Kataeb's political program, presented in a memorandum to the president and the Maronite patriarch on August 23, 1975, contained nothing new.[15] The party presented itself as having always "worked for the secularization of the state and the abolition of sectarianism." The only concrete measure it proposed in this direction, however, was "secularization of the personal status laws." This proposal was the Kataeb's invariable response to popular demands for abolition of the sectarian privilege and dominance enjoyed by the Maronite community. It was intended to embarrass the Muslim communities, for whom personal status laws are governed by Islam, and among whom the conservatives are strongly opposed to secularization.

Other Kataeb proposals remained rooted in the conviction that Christian privileges must continue to ensure Christian security. The Kataeb insisted, for example, on perpetuating discrimination in favor of Christians in naturalization and in reiterating its standard demand that Lebanese emigrants be granted citizenship "wherever they may be."

Muslims however, were not calling for establishment of an Islamic state but, in the words of a Muslim religious leader, "for a state based on equality and nothing more." If Lebanese Muslims renounced the rule of an Islamic state in Lebanon "despite the danger that forms for their creed," he asked, cannot Christians renounce "a state of Christian privileges in Lebanon" to promote "national rule based on justice and equality?"[16]

On August 18, the Lebanese National Movement (LNM) issued a

political program, intended as a first step toward a democratic and totally secular society. Abolition of sectarianism in parliament, the executive, the judiciary, and military branches of the government and in sociopolitical practice was set as the task of the "present stage."[17]

To this end it proposed: (1) to introduce proportional representation, make Lebanon one electoral district, and so eliminate the many small electoral units that ensure clan rule, and enfranchise the large part of the population now disfranchised; (2) to dismantle the semifeudal sectarian state machine by redefining the powers and prerogatives of the legislature and executive; (3) to eliminate discrimination in naturalization; (4) to reorganize the army on a nonsectarian basis, bring it under executive and civilian control, and confine its duties to defense of Lebanon's frontiers and independence; and (5) to elect a Constituent Assembly to conduct a national dialogue on these and other proposed reforms and draft the constitutional and statutory legislation to implement them.

The LNM postponed the elaboration of a socioeconomic platform. This soft-pedaling of social and economic issues at a time when they were uppermost for much of the LNM's actual and potential constituency prevented its setting goals for which the masses were prepared to fight. Jumblat later implicitly acknowledged this to have been a mistake, urging that the LNM undertake economic and social reforms in areas under its control.[18]

Most of the LNM's financing came from Iraq, which accepted the LNM's ruling that other Arab regimes had the duty to support the Lebanese Arab national cause and to do so without interfering in their internal affairs.[19] Libya later provided financial aid on the same basis. The LNM was thus soon to be financially independent of Syria, which on occasion attempted to use aid as a form of pressure.

The disappearance of government services and authority left the LNM and the Palestinian resistance movement responsible for meeting the needs of the people in the areas under their control, known thereafter as national areas. In its efforts to mobilize the population and to stimulate popular action in these areas, the LNM almost inevitably had to take second place to al-Fatah, already long active in this field and possessing far greater resources. LNM parties established popular committees: one near the Arab University in West Beirut, where most Palestinian offices were located and where most Lebanese residents supported the resistance and the national movement; and one in Zarif, a center of Communist Party strength, which served as an assembly point for troops moving to and from the front in downtown Beirut.

As schools closed down, one or another LNM party found volunteer teachers to reopen them. Popular committees maintained dispensaries, trained civilians in first aid, civil defense, and the use of weapons and, as the shortage of food and other essentials developed, undertook their distribution. Committees flourished during the first six months or so of the war, but then began to lose their vitality. Each party tended to work alone, with the result that no practical unifying action was achieved. The committees were philanthropic rather than political and did not manage, or for the most part attempt, to develop a new type of relation with and among the people. The parties neglected the political education of their own members and recruits, who were too often trained to be loyal to the party as a name and an institution rather than to a political ideology.

In July 1976 the LNM decided to set up a civil administration in which the popular committees would be united and incorporated. Committee members were to have been elected democratically, but in practice the LNM usually appointed just over half the members of each. As Jumblat admitted, the civil administration was not very successful. Al-Fatah, because of its greater resources, continued to assume responsibility for providing essential supplies to national areas and so to a large extent controlled the direction and planning of the LNM committees. LNM efforts to add independents to these committees, the most active and respected people in each region, proved unsuccessful.

With the inauguration of the LNM's civil administration, many demanded that the LNM put its political program into effect. But al-Fatah's opposition thwarted any such initiative. Al-Fatah held that any attempt to carry out reforms would compromise relations with conservative Arab regimes, Lebanese Sunni *zuama,* and *qabadayat* (political bosses). It also prohibited any move that would disrupt its relations with the state. Moreover, it encouraged and subsidized a proliferation of small militias through which it could both exercise pressures on Sunni and other traditional *zuama* and also ensure itself an indirect presence within the LNM. Among others, it promoted the rise of young Nasserite leaders, providing them with arms and money. This goes some way to explain the eventual presence of some six

Nasserite groups within the LNM and ten or more gravitating around it, many dependent on al-Fatah or Libya and lacking a popular base. It also explains, in part, the difficulties the LNM encountered in formulating and applying an independent line. In general, such militias did little more than collect protection money, engage in rackets, and fight each other. The harm this practice inflicted on the national and the Palestinian cause was incalculable.

All these circumstances gave a defensive orientation to the LNM from the beginning.[20] This attitude led it to neglect grassroots concerns and democratic change and made it in large part incapable of directing the tremendous outpouring of spontaneous popular support in the war's early months into effective and sustained popular participation. Thousands hurried to join the national and Palestinian forces, but military mobilization resulted less in political mobilization than in eventual depoliticization. This proved especially so since, as the war progressed, the parties took in new recruits who had nothing to do with politics. Many joined up out of economic need for the regular wage; some for the opportunities to make money, win positions of power, exploit others, spy, or whatever. (After the Syrian army entered Lebanon, many of the latter type switched to Syrian-sponsored organizations, where the opportunities for gain appeared greater.)

A practical and loose coalition of organizations with minimum demands in common, the LNM did not achieve a common vision of Lebanon's future. Yet the readiness of many of its partisans to fight and die for the rights of the Palestinians and disadvantaged Lebanese ultimately weakened the Maronite right's hegemony in Lebanon, destroying the possibility of its restoration without large-scale foreign intervention.

[12]

Escalating War, Faltering Peace

The Fourth Round: The Bekaa and the North

Barely a week after publication of the Lebanese National Movement (LNM) program, the fourth round of fighting began in Zahle, the capital of the Bekaa. Greek Catholic and wealthy, Zahle is surrounded by a largely Shi'a Muslim and indigent countryside. An accumulation of many incidents—expressions of rural conflicts between small farmers and agricultural workers on the one hand and well-to-do merchants and landowners on the other—combined to touch off the explosion.

In the weeks preceding the clashes, Muslims from surrounding areas who tried to pass through the city were often attacked. Their complaints to the local authorities met no response. Culprits, if arrested by the police, were promptly set free on orders of a higher authority. Kidnappings became frequent. Progressive Christians living in the city often found themselves prevented from leaving their homes. When a Maronite militia training camp was opened nearby, the fear these militamen inspired among local Greek Catholic leaders caused them to arm their own henchmen and form the Zahle General Union (a coalition of their militias and the only non-Maronite militia on the right), thereby fanning the conflict.

The deliberate murder of a Palestinian officer and a young Syrian provoked the clashes that began on August 28. Business establishments, especially those of vegetable and chicken merchants, were blown up. Many were killed or kidnapped on the basis of the religion listed on their identity cards. Whole families were slaughtered together. These essentially social and class conflicts quickly assumed a sectarian character, as Christians and Muslims in mixed villages fought each other.

Just as relative calm returned to Zahle, an automobile accident in Tripoli set off fighting between Tripoli and Zgharta. Family and friends of these victims—all from Zgharta—hauled twelve passengers from a passing bus on the Tripoli–Zgharta road and killed them, running a car back and forth over their bodies. Zgharta-owned enterprises in Tripoli were then dynamited, as were Tripoli-owned properties in Zgharta. Kidnappings (sixty on the first day) were carried out by both sides. The Karami government—having secured the hated Iskander Ghanem's replacement as commander-in-chief by the more acceptable Major-General Nuri al-Said, and having won cabinet approval of a draft law to reform the army—could now deploy the army in a protective cordon around Zgharta designed to halt the fighting. But the initiative did not work out as hoped: on September 15, just south of Tripoli, the army killed thirteen members of the October 24 Movement.[1]

The Lebanese National Movement (LNM) responded by occupying government buildings, police stations, and barracks throughout the city. Within two days, together with the Palestinians, they controlled the city and jointly assumed responsibility for maintaining law and order. On October 9 the army attempted to enter Tripoli. After losing seven tanks and several armored cars, and facing the threat of mutiny by its Muslim soldiers, the army gave up the attempt. This fiasco in Tripoli led Commander-in-Chief Said to order an investigation; the investigation concluded that the army had been improperly deployed in Tripoli, had seriously deteriorated, and could not be trusted with internal police duties.[2] Notwithstanding these findings the army was soon deployed in Zahle, the Akkar, and on certain main roads and at strategic points in Beirut.

President Suleiman Franjieh, Prime Minister Rashid Karami, and Interior Minister Camille Chamoun each had his own conception of how to use the army, producing a confusion that reinforced the army command's habitual practice of going its own way. The result, as Colonel Henry Lahoud pointed out, was that "the army was used in a camouflaged, secret way. It was deployed piecemeal and "used to support one group against the other." Arms were given to the Internal Security Forces (ISF) and some army soldiers were transferred to the ISF. The question of whether or not to use the army, Lahoud emphasized, was determined "solely by political considerations and its collapse was due to political, not military considerations.[3]

The First Battle of Beirut

The first battle of Beirut began on the night of September 17, when the Kataeb launched an offensive against the Bourj (Martyrs Square), the center of the downtown commercial district. The battle lasted until December, a two-and-a-half-month period punctuated by a number of cease-fires, briefly and only partially observed, and less than two weeks of calm.

The first target of the Kataeb offensive was Souk Sursock, a cheap and popular fabrics market owned for the most part by Muslim merchants; then Souk Nurieh, a cheap meat and vegetables market; then Souk Azarieh, a popular bookshop and office district. National movement forces responded with an attack on Souk Tawile, a market of high-quality clothes and other goods. Exchanges of rockets, mortars, and incendiary bombs damaged and destroyed many buildings, and started huge and uncontrollable fires in which many perished. Both sides dynamited buildings and looted throughout the commercial center. Kidnappings (307 on October 1 alone) and killings at roadblocks became the order of the day.

The devastation of the souks and the commercial district affected not only the Muslim bourgeoisie but also the Christian (particularly the Maronite) bourgeoisie. Even Kataeb enthusiasts asked why the Kataeb deliberately set out to destroy the city's business center and the properties of the Christian bourgeoisie.

Several answers were advanced: to face business people, Muslim and Christian alike, with the choice of backing the right or losing their businesses and probably their lives; to give Arab states which had interests in the business district (and were all, exept Iraq, then backing the right) a pretext to intervene; to provoke army intervention; to encourage partition by destroying the commercial center and so compelling Muslims to go West and Christians East. All these reasons perhaps—plus the tremendous booty to be had from looting—played a part in the Kataeb's offensive. The destruction and looting of the district provoked a certain disenchantment with, and fear of, the rightist parties among Christian business people, many of whom moved West to establish themselves beside Muslims.

On September 20 Syrian Foreign Minister Abdul Halim Khaddam arrived in Beirut on still another mediation mission. Negotiations with Lebanese leaders, Palestinian Liberation Organization (PLO) leader Yasir Arafat, and Saiqa leader Zuhair Muhsin led to the formation of a national dialogue committee and a cease-fire. But the cease-fire lasted only two days, through the Muslim feast of Id al-Fitr. Such month-end truces had become a regular and necessary feature of the war, permitting fighters to cash their pay checks, get a rest, attend to private affairs, reorganize. When fighting resumed early in October, Karami and Arafat journeyed to Damascus to agree on a new cease-fire. The cease-fire prompted peace marches in various parts of Beirut, but soon proved as ephemeral as its predecessors.

In the wake of the Sinai Accord, violent verbal attacks between Presidents Sadat of Egypt and Assad of Syria increased, causing anxiety in Saudi Arabia and Kuwait. Moreover, Maronite political leaders increasingly demanded Arab League intervention to settle the question of the Palestinian armed presence in the country. Thus an emergency Arab foreign ministers' meeting was called for October to discuss the Lebanese crisis. However, the national movement, the PLO, Syria, and Libya viewed the conference as an attempt to Arabize the Lebanese conflict and boycotted the meeting, underscoring the dissension among Arab states.

The Cairo meeting triggered a wave of kidnappings, sniper fire throughout Beirut, the resumption of battles in the downtown district, and their extension to new areas in West Beirut. When the Kataeb tried to attack Lebanese National Movement (LNM) forces from the rear in order to relieve pressure on its forces in the Holiday Inn, the well-to-do Kantari and Clemenceau street districts, along with the poor Jewish and Kurdish quarter of Wadi Abu Jamil behind the hotel district, were drawn into the fighting. Many persons were trapped in the synagogue. A vociferous Israeli propaganda operation called for the rescue of "Jews and Christians" allegedly facing starvation and massacre at the hands of the Muslims and Palestinians. In fact, the PLO and al-Fatah kept the people in the synagogue and others in Wadi Abu Jamil supplied with water, food, and other necessities. Yasir Arafat received a letter of thanks and appreciation from the deputy head of the Jewish community, Salim al-Moghrabi. Dr. Elie Halleck, the community's leader, angrily rejected Israel's claims that "4,000 Jews in Lebanon" needed rescue. Lebanese Jews, he noted, numbered only about 1,700, and they "coexisted peacefully with the Kurds in Wadi Abu Jamil."[4]

The fighting in late October set the stage for the "battle of the hotels," or the second battle of Beirut.

Peace Efforts: Operation Serail

Amid this mounting violence Prime Minister Karami tried without success to induce parliament to meet. In desperation, on October 28, he established himself in the old Ottoman Serail (government house) located on a small hill close to and overlooking the downtown area, and invited his cabinet and all political leaders to join him, declaring he would remain there until peace was restored. Only two of his ministers, Ghassan Tueni (Greek Orthodox) and Adel Osseiran (Shi'a), responded. Arafat and a Palestinian delegation visited the prime minister to offer Palestinian cooperation in settling the crisis; Syrian Foreign Minister Khaddam telephoned encouragement. Karami then managed to put together a Higher Coordination Committee, in which the army, the PLO, and the militias were represented, to prevent excesses and enforce the truce.

During the week he spent in the Serail, Karami appeared on television nightly to report to the people. An uninspiring speaker with a flat monotone voice, he did at least give his audience the impression that he was making an honest effort. This, perhaps his only accomplishment, was not insignificant in a situation where most political leaders and many state officials talked of peace while actively directing their cohorts in battle.

The National Dialogue Committee

Meanwhile, the National Dialogue Committee (NDC) had been meeting more or less regularly throughout the battle of Beirut. The hope was that it would become a forum where differences could be negotiated rather than fought out on the streets. But selection of its members on a sectarian basis drew sharp criticism. Significantly absent was any representative of the working class.

According to Elias Saba, a Greek Orthodox businessman, economist, and former minister, who served on the committee, the challenge facing the NDC was "to provide the country with institutions that are sensitive to the need for change and capable of introducing it."[5] The NDC failed to meet this challenge. Deliberate sabotage by the Kataeb representatives—Pierre Gemayel and Edmond Rizk, who indulged in long, irrelevant, even ridiculous filibusters, and Camille Chamoun's boycott of later sessions—had much to do with this failure.[6]

In the absence of Kataeb and Chamounist representatives, who boycotted the meeting, the subcommittee on political reform came to agreement on a number of proposals, an agreement that revealed the isolation of the Maronite right organizations. The subcommittee proposed to cancel Article 95 of the constitution (sectarian distribution of civil service posts), suppress sectarianism in parliamentary representation, lower the voting age to eighteen, and set up an economic and social council—all called for in the LNM's program.[7]

The presidential palace and Chamoun's entourage promptly took to speaking of the NDC as "the supreme revolutionary command," accusing it of attempting to "supplant parliament." In a seven-point communiqué issued on October 9, the Kataeb and the Lebanese ecclesiastical orders denounced the NDC for "trespassing on the prerogatives of the constitution and existing democratic institutions" instead of sticking to its "sole mission" which was "to restore sovereignty." This full-sacle rightist drive against the NDC ensured its collapse. On November 24, in what proved to be its final session, Karami declared: "I believe the state has ceased to exist."[8]

Karami absolved the Kataeb of blame, placing it squarely on "those in the presidential palace"—that is, the president and Chamoun.[9]

Toward Reconciliation of the Maronite and Muslim Right

This somewhat surprising conclusion to the NDC accorded with a shift in the prime minister's position concerning Muslim and NDC demands. His new stand pointed to an internal rift between the LNM and traditional Muslim politicians. Following the failure of the Arab League meeting on October 15, a strong anticommunist campaign fostered by Saudi Arabia's friends got under way in Lebanon. Saeb Salam, returning from a visit to Riyadh on November 22, denounced "communism" and the "international left" in terms clearly indicating the LNM. Sermons against "atheistic communists" and slogans scribbled on walls in Muslim quarters developed this theme. A principal target of this campaign was the effort of some LNM parties to provide schooling for children in quarters cut off from access to schools or in which schools had closed.

This movement toward rapprochement between the Maronite and Muslim right coincided with the first American approaches to Damascus and the appearance of a number of international "mediators" in Lebanon. One, from the Vatican, was concerned about the effect of the war on the 15 million Christians living in Arab countries. Cardinal Bertoli arrived to try to talk moderation to Catholics.[10] At a time when Maronite political and religious leaders were openly calling for partition, Bertoli put the Vatican squarely on the side of Christian–Muslim coexistence. He argued that Lebanon's true interest lay not in confrontation with the Palestinians but in helping them to achieve their human and national rights. The cardinal's grace and diplomatic skill in delivering this message succeeded for a time in lowering the tone of rightist talk of partition, thereby helping bring together the Christian and Muslim right.

Three days after Bertoli's departure, French President Valery Giscard d'Estaing sent a special envoy, Couve de Murville, for a ten-day visit. While criticizing Syrian, Libyan, and Palestinian involvement in the conflict, he reaffirmed France's rejection of partition and emphasized that his mission was one of conciliation. He succeeded in persuading Kataeb leaders to assume a low profile, and patched up relations between the president and the prime minister. On November 29, in his first broadcast since the beginning of the civil war, President Franjieh—followed by Karami—appeared on television to announce their agreement on a four-point peace plan.

This plan won a mixed reception. Its terms—ending the fighting, expanding the cabinet, talking with the Palestinians about their status, and unspecified social, economic, and political reforms—were too general and lacking in content to inspire confidence. Their consecration of sectarianism without making any commitment to reform made them unacceptable to the national and democratic forces. Nonetheless, Speaker Kamel al-Asaad established a parliamentary committee of all factions to study the plan, until difficulties of another kind hindered its realization.

Black Saturday

On December 2, Israel raided refugee camps and numerous villages in the north and south in one of its most punishing raids ever. The raid was intended not only to assist embattled rightist militias but also to answer the UN Security Council, which had approved Syria's proposal to link extension of the UN mandate in the Golan to Security Council discussion of the Palestinian question—with the PLO participating in the debate.

On the day of this attack, a truck carrying hundreds of copies of the Koran was overturned on the Beirut–Damascus road, near the Kataeb-controlled village of Kahhale: a big bonfire was lit to destroy the Islamic holy books. Moderate Christian leaders and even Chamoun condemned this act, but the Kataeb did not. Two days later, Damascus invited Pierre Gemayel to visit.

Syrian President Assad later told a Muslim delegation that he had invited the Kataeb for "the good of Lebanon," as the Kataeb had assured him of its readiness "to work for peace and unity."[11] The meeting facilitated Assad's goal of restoring traditional Maronite–Sunni collaboration and undermining the popular movement for democratic change.

Back in Beirut, however, Gemayel's militias were busy trying to abort a Syrian-sponsored solution, indulging in an orgy of random killing of Muslims and Palestinians—men, women, and children—on Saturday, December 6. Estimates of the number killed that day ran up to between 200 and 300. The operation was well-organized; kidnappings and killings occurred in many parts of the city at the same time. People were hauled out of passing cars at roadblocks or out of their offices and homes and, if their identity cards showed them to be other than Christian, promptly dispatched. Kataeb gunmen even invaded the Electricity Authority building in East Beirut, intent on killing its widely respected Muslim chairman, Fouad Bizri. He was saved only by the courageous delaying tactics of his largely Christian staff and the breathless arrival of Kataeb politbureau members come to rescue him from their own gunmen.[12]

The Second Battle of Beirut

Black Saturday touched off the second battle of Beirut (December 6–January 22) and the war for partition. That evening the LNM withdrew from the Higher Coordinating Committee until the perpetrators of the massacre could be brought to trial. Next day the Kataeb—with the complicity of the Internal Security Forces (ISF)—reoccupied the Holiday Inn, along with the Phoenicia Hotel and other buildings. In reply the LNM launched a "punitive offensive" in the hotel district, capturing the St. Georges Hotel and surrounding the Kataeb in the Holiday Inn and the Zeitouni night club block on the seafront. LNM forces also overran Kataeb positions in the downtown commercial district and won control of the main road linking this district to the coast. New and heavier weapons were used in these battles, and fighting was intense. Leading the attack in the downtown zone, the Mourabitoun penetrated almost to the Kataeb's main headquarters in Saifi near the port. Saiqa and al-Fatah—not the Kataeb—stopped the Mourabitoun from entering the Christian area, presumably following the Syrian president's directives.[13]

Almost all Lebanon now became involved in the war, a war for partition in which the Maronite right set out to "cleanse" mixed areas of Muslims and "foreigners." While Muslims in some rural areas responded by driving out Christians, in Palestinian–LNM controlled West Beirut Christians continued to coexist with the Muslim majority, for the most part without incident, demonstrating that the alleged Christian need for "protection" was a false issue.

On December 11, a 1,200-strong force of Kataeb and Chamounist militias (aided by the ISF) attacked a Muslim and Syrian Social Nationalist Party (SSNP) quarter on the northern outskirts of Beirut. The attackers paraded their prisoners, mainly Shi'a migrants from Baalbek, through Christian East Beirut. In Baalbek the next day, angry Shi'as attacked the Serail and freed all prisoners. On December 16, 500 Kataeb and Chamounist militiamen overran Sibnay, a Shi'a and Progressive Socialist Party (PSP) village south of Beirut, again parading prisoners through Christian quarters while the village was emptied of its inhabitants. This provoked a LNM offensive against Kafrshima near Beirut and the opening of a new front against Kahhale on the Beirut–Damascus road. In the south, Israeli troops moved across the border to set up a roadblock near Kafr Kila, stopping all Lebanese cars and checking on their occupants. In the north, heavy clashes resumed between Zghorta and Tripoli. Imam Sadr appealed to all Catholic prelates to use their influence to halt the eviction of the Shi'a population from their villages; failing a reply, he called his followers to arms. A Christian exodus from the Akkar Plain and Bekaa Valley then began.

In Beirut, Karami, with the help of Arafat and the Syrian-guided groups in the LNM, managed to achieve a cease-fire. The continuing rightist "purification" of "Christian Lebanon" by eviction of non-Christians made a mockery of the truce, but the relative calm in Beirut from mid-December to January 4 permitted the resumption of political efforts to end the crisis and revealed significant shifts in political alignments.

Karami's acquiescence in the deployment of the army in the hotel district widened the distance between him and the LNM. Sent into battle under orders of Chamoun, the army intervened more than once to help the rightist militias. To LNM protests, Karami replied that the troops were at Chamoun's disposal and were intended to protect banks and hotels. When, later, large army reinforcements sent into the Bekaa attacked Shi'a and LNM forces encircling Zahle, Jumblat commented: "In allowing use of the army Karami has made Camille Chamoun the real leader of Lebanon." Jumblat met President Assad in Damascus on December 15, but rejected his demand to "end the bloodshed" by declaring: "This is impossible without political, social, and economic reform."

$$\left[13\right]$$

Syrian Policy
and the National Movement

Succor for the Right

The visit of the Kataeb leaders to Damascus in December inaugurated a new phase in Syrian policy. And on December 9, 1975, the Syrian-guided groups—the Lebanese Baath, Kamal Shatila's United Forces of Working People (UFWP), and Imam Sadr's *Mahrumin*—effectively pulled out of the Lebanese National Movement (LNM), issuing a statement which disassociated their parties from the LNM's "punitive offensive," affirmed support for Prime Minister Rashid Karami's decision to use the army, and—almost as an afterthought—condemned Black Saturday. While attracting scant attention at the time, this statement proved to be central to the new phase of Syrian policy.

Black Saturday and the LNM's response convinced Syrian President Hafez Assad of the imperative of large-scale Syrian military intervention in Lebanon. He wanted first to prevent a Palestinian–LNM victory, since this could precipitate an Israeli invasion, undermine Syrian tutelage over the Palestinian resistance movement, and undercut his strategy for getting back the Golan by a negotiated settlement. Such a victory, by its radicalism, could also threaten his regime in Syria. At the same time, he wanted to prevent any rightist attempt at partition, hoping to persuade the Maronite right to look to Syria rather than to the West or Israel for "protection." The latter he apparently proposed to do by giving the right much of what it wanted in Lebanon.

The shift in Syrian policy promptly hardened the stand taken by the Kataeb and its allies. At the end of December, Karami presented his peace plan to the Maronite community. In essence the plan was a compromise, and its proposed reforms were moderate: fifty–fifty Christian–Muslim representation in parliament; reaffirmation of the

Maronite monopoly of the presidency, coupled with a more equitable balance between the powers of the executive and parliament; the creation of an economic-social council; and the creation of a parliamentary committee to deal with Lebanese–Palestinian relations.

At a meeting on December 31, Maronite political and religious leaders rejected the plan in toto, insisting the National Pact remain inviolate and Palestinian intervention in Lebanon be ended. Only President Suleiman Franjieh refused to sign this declaration, indicating he would accept the plan, but only if it contained (1) a written guarantee that the president would always be a Maronite, (2) a European or Arab guarantee of Palestinian observance of Lebanon–PLO accords, and (3) a referendum on the proposed fifty–fifty distribution of Christian and Muslim seats in parliament.

This intransigent Maronite position dismayed moderate Christians. Many Christians, Maronites among them, opposed rightist extremism but did not dare speak out. As the London *Economist* pointed out (January 24, 1976): "the Christian militants are not, according to all the evidence, supported by the majority of their own faith, who for years have lived peaceably alongside Moslem neighbours and would dearly like to do so again." Efforts undertaken by Raymond Edde and others to form an organization that would speak for the moderate Christian majority were quickly submerged by the resumption of fighting brought about by the Maronite declaration.

On January 4, 1976, the Kataeb militia blocked a food convoy en route to Tel al-Zaatar camp, starting a siege that was to end seven months later with the camp's fall. Simultaneously the right mounted an attack on the small Dbaye refugee camp ten miles north of Beirut, the home of about 200 Greek Catholic Palestinian families who had remained outside the conflict. These moves may have been intended to provoke al-Fatah into participating directly in the fighting, just as the PLO was about to take its seat in the UN Security Council for debate on the Palestinian question. If so, the strategem succeeded. Al-Fatah openly and for the first time in strength entered the war in response to these attacks on the camps.

"Cleansing" of Rightist Areas

Even as Syrian President Assad extended his "protection" to the Maronite extremists, their forces were effecting de facto partition, consolidating and expanding their domain in Beirut and evicting Muslims and Palestinians. Syrian Foreign Minister Abdul Halim Khaddam felt compelled to warn that Lebanon could either stay united or it would return to Syria—all four districts of it. The emphasis on the four districts was intended to make plain that Damascus did not subscribe to the Maronite claim that Mount Lebanon had never been part of Syria. Camille Chamoun reacted angrily. "Before thinking of annexing Lebanon," he retorted, "Syria had better try to liberate the Golan."[1]

Claiming to speak for the resistance movement, the pro-Syrian Saiqa leader Zuhair Muhsin stressed the "differences" allegedly dividing the Palestinians from the Lebanese National Movement. For the Palestinians, he said, "it is not necessary to deal a crushing blow to the right," since this would only produce "Israeli interference."[2] Four days later, Kataeb forces supported by Lebanese army artillery overran the refugee camp at Dbaye, slaughtering many of its Catholic inhabitants.

The LNM promptly retaliated by striking at the Kataeb in the Holiday Inn, the Hilton Hotel, and the downtown area of Beirut, while Jumblat's militia poured down from the mountain to join Palestinian–LNM fighters in besieging the well-to-do Maronite town of Damour on the coastal highway twelve miles south of Beirut. At the northern edges of Beirut, LNM militias, having won control of the two bridges over the Beirut river, severed the only remaining link between Beirut's Christian suburbs and Junieh, the "capital" of the Maronite right. But the rightist offensive against the camps and the destitute slum quarters of Maslakh and Qarantina, inhabited by Shi'as from the Bekaa and the south and a few Kurds, Syrians, and Palestinians, did not halt.[3]

On January 16, Prime Minister Karami and other Muslim leaders were meeting at the mufti's residence in Aramoun when the Lebanese air force intervened in Damour, in defiance of Karami's orders. Clearly visible from Aramoun, the Lebanese planes strafed LNM forces, killing thirty-five people. An angry Karami telephoned Syrian President Assad about the "grave rebellion of the air force." But it was not this call, contrary to Assad's later claims, that prompted the Syrian President to send units of the Palestine Liberation Army (PLA) into Lebanon on January 19; rather it was the successes of the LNM militia, both in Beirut and elsewhere in the country.[4]

Qarantina, home of some 27,000 people, fell to the right in January. Three thousand rightist combatants machine-gunned their way through the slum area's narrow alleys to trap and exterminate its late defenders. Male prisoners were executed, while the bodies of old men, women, and children strewn through the area testified to the slaughter of the innocent. One picture flashed around the world showed three militiamen dancing around the body of a young girl, strumming on their guns as if they were guitars.

In response, infuriated LNM–Palestinian forces attacked Damour on January 21. Before the assault they left open the road to Saadiyat, where Chamoun had a palatial home, to permit roughly half of the population to escape. But innocent people were killed, and the attackers, joined by peasants from the surrounding areas, indulged in an orgy of looting.[5]

Coincident with the fall of Damour, Syrian mediators arrived in Beirut on January 22 to impose a cease-fire that ended the second battle of Beirut, saving the right from almost certain defeat. The fighting had left scarcely a building in the downtown area and the hotel district unscathed. The cease-fire institutionalized a Syrian military presence in the Higher Syrian–Lebanese–Palestinian Coordinating Committee, set up to take charge of security, and in the many commissions created to supervise the truce. Some fifty Syrian officers were attached to the 5,000 PLA troops now in Lebanon, and about 230 Syrian intelligence officers also established themselves in the country.

The Syrian presence did not halt the systematic looting of downtown Beirut, where looters emptied shops of their contents without interference. Expert safecrackers brought from London blasted open vaults in the British Bank of the Middle East, reportedly making away with $5 million. It was an open secret that the Syrian-controlled Saiqa was the chief organizer of these hauls; Saiqa leader Zuhair Muhsin earned the nickname "Zuhair the Persian" owing to his predilection for Persian carpets.

Following a good word from Washington about his "constructive role in Lebanon," President Assad struck hard at the Lebanese institution most feared by other Arab regimes, its relatively free press. On the night of January 31, about a hundred Saiqa troops attacked without warning and without provocation the offices of *Al-Muharrer* (pro-Palestinian) and *Beirut* (published by the Iraqi Baath) with rockets and guns. They doused the offices with oil and set them on fire, killing seven people and wounding many others. Among the victims were the distinguished Egyptian author and journalist Ibrahim Amr, who was badly burned and died of his wounds, and *Muharrer's* deputy editor, whose charred body was found in the ruins.

As the truce was supposed to go into effect, a Syrian delegation arrived to meet all communities as well as the LNM and the Palestinian resistance movement. The talks proceeded against an ominous background. The army increasingly intervened in the fighting on behalf of the right, against Karami's orders, producing a growing unrest among soldiers and noncommissioned officers alike.

The Kataeb's "Political Triumph"

The right took advantage of the Syrian-imposed truce to organize itself as the Front of Freedom and Man in Lebanon, which after several name changes became known as the Lebanese Front.[6] The front proclaimed its support for Syria's "mediation" and on February 7 President Suleiman Franjieh went to Damascus, where he and Assad put into final form what had started as Karami's peace plan and which now became a seventeen-point Constitutional Charter.

Endorsed by Karami and his cabinet, the charter consisted in part of vague generalities in favor of social justice, though it included several secondary demands from the LNM program. It also granted the Sunni demand for a fifty–fifty Christian–Muslim distribution of parliamentary seats, and it promised an attempt to create a more equitable balance between the powers of the president and prime minister and to reform the naturalization law. Its chief thrust, however, was to consecrate sectarianism: it guaranteed a Maronite president in perpetuity, a Sunni prime minister, and a Shi'a speaker of parliament, as well as the sectarian distribution of parliamentary seats and all important administrative positions. Most significantly, perhaps, it carefully omitted any provision to de-sectarianize the army, and it insisted on censorship of the press. It also affirmed the unity and Arab character of Lebanon, and assigned to Damascus the task of guarantor of the Palestinian resistance movement agreements with the Lebanese state. In an unpublished protocol, Syria promised to execute a series of measures regulating Palestinian activities in the context of the Cairo Accord. Despite the fact that the resistance movement was thus squarely under Syrian tutelage, it took no public stand on the charter.

The charter won a lukewarm reception at best. Lebanon's foremost constitutional authority, Edmond Rabbat, called it an attempt "to complete the unwritten National Pact" and held it to be in violation of the constitution.[7] Despite heavy pressures, Jumblat refused to endorse those points that contradicted the LNM program.

The Maronite right accepted the charter, although it required some concessions to the Muslim right. In reality it had little choice since the recent fighting had been damaging to its cause. The United States, France, and the Vatican having failed to espouse its crusade, the right could only pursue rapprochement with Syria. Assad obliged the right in important respects. At its demand, he excluded from the charter all important LNM demands, and agreed to exclude from the new government any representative of the LNM or the moderate Christians.[8] The Kataeb had good reason to boast: "We succeeded thanks to our diplomacy in transforming our military defeat into a political triumph."[9]

The LNM–Palestinian Riposte: Break-up of the Lebanese Army

As a result of the Kataeb's political triumph the LNM–Palestinian alliance felt compelled to try to transform its own political defeat into a military victory. An effort in this direction was already underway as part of the regular army began to change sides, with more and more of its ranks joining the Lebanese Arab Army (LAA), which was formed by Lieutenant Ahmed Khatib after the army intervention in Damour.[10] The son of a notable Sunni family and cousin of a Progressive Socialist Party (PSP) deputy, Khatib's immediate goal was to compel the government to grant amnesty to the growing number of "deserters" and to accept the principle of "national balance" in the army. The LAA program issued on February 3 called for a nonsectarian army, a new democratic Lebanon based on secularism and Arabism, electoral law reform, and the abolition of all private militias. Al-Fatah provided its financing, and before long, with garrisons in the south, north, and east proclaiming allegiance to the LAA, Khatib's forces could operate with impunity in the Tripoli region, most of the Bekaa, and south Lebanon.

Syrian representatives hastened to Beirut, declaring that Khatib's movement was a threat to the peace plan and the security of both

Syria and Lebanon. In vain they tried to persuade Jumblat and the LNM to halt Khatib and, equally in vain, to persuade Franjieh to abandon his refusal to form a national unity government.[11] On March 11 they returned home, ordering the fifty Syrian officers assigned to the truce commissions to follow.

That evening, Brigadier General Aziz al-Ahdab, the Muslim commander of the Beirut garrison, broke into the television news to demand the resignation of the president and the cabinet within twenty-four hours. Proclaiming himself provisional military governor, he declared a state of emergency, and called on parliament to elect a new president within seven days.

The scion of a notable family and a friend of many Maronite and Sunni leaders, Ahdab took pains to proclaim his support for "brotherly Syria." But Damascus, not without reason, perceived the coup to be directed against the Syrian role in Lebanon. Without the cooperation of al-Fatah, Ahdab could not have used West Beirut's television and radio. Al-Fatah's intellegence chief, Abu Hassan Salama, escorted him to the television station.

Al-Fatah's role in the LAA initiative as well as in the Ahdab coup was part of a resistance effort to counter Assad's attempt to bring the movement under his control, an effort for which it had Saudi and Egyptian backing.

Ahdab called his "initiative" not a military but a media coup, "to activate the people." Although he called it a "salvage movement to save the army," his efforts further splintered the army. Commander-in-chief Hanna Said tacitly—but silently—approved the initiative in the hope that Ahdab, a Muslim, could stem the movement of Muslims out of the army and into the LAA.

Two days after the "coup," Colonel Antoine Barakat, one of the Franjieh clan, seized the Military Academy at Fayadiyah, on the road to Damascus, a strategic position to bolster the defenses of the presidential palace at Baabda. Taking with him a generous portion of the army's arsenal, Barakat and his troops fought in the same trenches with the rightist militias. The army was now split five ways: (1) those who remained loyal to the High Command; (2) those who fought with the rightists; (3) the LAA; (4) the small group around Ahdab; and (5) the many who simply went home to sit out the war.

Perceiving that Ahdab could not seize power even if he wanted to, Jumblat tried to bring Ahdab and Khatib together; as a result three LAA representatives were named to Ahdab's command council. On the right, confusion at first prevailed, with Bashir Gemayel and Kataeb military leader William Hawi supporting Ahdab, while other Kataeb leaders and the Chamounists opposed him. The Kataeb sent a representative to Damascus to consult with Assad.

In general Maronite deputies, reflecting the sentiments of their constituents, welcomed Ahdab's initiative. The people of the militia-controlled Maronite heartland had experienced something of a change of heart since the Syrian-imposed truce of January 22. For it was then that rightist militias began to systematically collect "taxes," a euphemism for blackmail and protection money, from the inhabitants of areas under their control. To many of the victims of these exactions, Ahdab's solution—the resignation of Franjieh—seemed the best way out. The fact that the president's domain was in the north rather than the Maronite heartland made him an ideal scapegoat in this area.[12]

Yet Ahdab's attempt to salvage the army was doomed to failure. The army was too discredited, and the war of the barracks had left too little to save. The one important result of the coup was the March 13 parliamentary vote demanding Franjieh's resignation. When he refused, the LAA moved against the presidential palace to compel him to step down. But Saiqa and Syrian army troops halted his drive, and President Assad summoned Lebanese leaders to Damascus in an attempt to halt the fighting.[13]

Karami, Saeb Salam, and Kamel al-Asaad journeyed to Damascus on March 20 to try to persuade Assad to compel Franjieh to resign. Their mission failed. Syria's two tough colonels—Madani and Muhammed al-Kholy—in charge respectively of Syria's military and intelligence operations in Lebanon, turned on their heels and on March 13 the Lebanese branch of the Syrian Baath violently attacked Jumblat as "a traitor and a mercenary."

LNM–Palestinian Victories

On March 13–14, the LNM, the LAA, and the resistance movement jointly launched well-planned, coordinated, and successful military offensives in Beirut and the mountains. The army's disintegration made the LNM–Palestinian alliance the principal military force in the country; the LNM held the initiative for the first time since the civil war had started.

The joint operations involved battles and advances in the north around Zghorta and the Akkar; in the south around Qlai'a; in the Bekaa, the encirclement of Zahle; and in Beirut an offensive in the hotel district directed at Ashrafiyya, one arm of a two-pronged offensive, the other arm launched in the mountains east of Beirut.

During the last week of March, in the fiercest fighting of the war so far, the Palestinian–LNM alliance took in rapid succession the Holiday Inn, the parliament and Starco buildings, the Normandy Hotel and the still unfinished Hilton, both crucial to the Kataeb's defense of the Beirut port area and the approaches to Ashrafiyya. This offensive then drove on into the labyrinth of alleys and narrow streets of the old commercial center behind the port. On March 25 the LAA bombarded the presidential palace, scoring eighty direct hits in four hours and compelling Franjieh to flee to Souk Mikhayil, fifteen miles north of Beirut.

The other arm of the offensive against Ashrafiyya started from Aley in the foothills above Beirut down toward Kahhale, straddling the Beirut–Damascus road, now defended by the Kataeb and Colonel Antoine Barakat's army units. Capture of Kahhale would put the entire Beirut–Damascus road in the hands of the Palestinians and the LNM. A mountain offensive, launched simultaneously from Aley, had succeeded in capturing a string of towns by April 2, putting the LNM and Palestinian joint forces at the approaches to—and on the mountain crests overlooking—the Maronite heartland.

The war assumed new dimensions in these March battles. Regular army units, now involved on both sides, used heavy, sophisticated weapons from the arsenal of the Lebanese army.[14] By the end of March the LNM–Palestinian alliance had restricted Maronite control to 18 percent of the land area of Lebanon and 27 percent of its population. The LNM's objective—to reduce the area controlled by the Maronite right so as to make partition impossible and thereby remove the right-wing veto of its reform program—had been achieved.

This was unacceptable to Syrian President Assad. Sending small units of his army deep into Lebanon, toward the end of March he massed large contingents on both sides of the frontier.

From here periodic forays were made ever deeper into Lebanon, while within Lebanon Syria's colonels tried to secure a cease-fire. Jumblat refused, rejecting repeated demands from Assad to come to Damascus. Assad then summoned Yasir Arafat to what was described

as "the toughest meeting ever" between the two men. Assad threatened to halt army supplies to the Palestinian resistance movement,
close commando facilities in Syria, and cease supporting the Palestinian cause internationally if al-Fatah did not at once halt its assistance to Jumblat and the LNM: Arafat must choose between
Jumblat and Syria. Arafat yielded to his pressure only in part. He
refused to give up his alliance with the LNM, but grudgingly con-
sented to withdraw Palestinian front-line support from the mountain
offensive.[15]

Under pressure from al-Fatah, Jumblat went to Damascus on
March 27. Assad later said Jumblat flatly rejected a cease-fire.[16] But
Jumblat's version was somewhat different: "I asked him only for a
three- or four-day delay, at most a week or two, to decide the armistice
. . . . We were sure that our military victory could put an end to the
war of the isolationists."[17] He then recounted Assad's reply:

> "Listen, he told me, "this is for me an historic occasion to turn the
> Maronites toward Syria, to win their confidence, to make them realize
> that their protector is no longer France or the West. It is necessary to
> help them so that they no longer importune aid from the foreigner. I
> cannot permit that you conquer the Christian camp in Lebanon: that
> would create among them a feeling of resentment."[18]

Jumblat argued that "the Christian camp" was not the issue: "the
Greek Orthodox, the Armenians, three-fourths of the [Greek] Catholics, and a third of the Maronites themselves are hostile to the ultras of
Maronite isolationism. . . . It is necessary to save them from the
fascist yoke: all the isolationists do not represent more than 25 percent
of the Christians."[19]

Assad Versus Jumblat and the LNM

Assad later maintained that he took the decision for direct military
intervention in Lebanon just after this meeting with Jumblat.[20] Yet at
the time of this encounter Jordan's King Husain was just arriving in
Washington—having met Assad en route—to plead for U. S. support
for Syrian military intervention.[21] The Lebanese war, he told a
congressional luncheon, was no longer a war between Christian and
Muslim but one between right and left, and only the intervention of
the Syrian Army could prevent Lebanon from being "overrun by

leftists." While still disclaiming having made an affirmative response to Assad's demands, the State Department praised Syria's "mediation" and affirmed support for "moderate elements" in Lebanon, as opposed to Jumblat's "radical elements." And on March 30 Dean Brown, President Ford's newly appointed special envoy to Lebanon, left for Beirut, coincident with the U.S. decision to approve direct Syrian military intervention. The United States had won Israel's agreement not to interfere so long as Syrian troops were limited in number and stayed north of the Beirut–Damascus road.

Pressed by the PLO, the Soviet embassy, and even Dean Brown, Jumblat agreed to a ten-day cease-fire on April 2, on condition that the fighters remain in place and that parliament amend the constitution to permit the election of a new president.

Still, the Assad campaign to discredit Jumblat intensified. Posters and handbills distributed in Muslim quarters caricatured the LNM leader as "the phony king of the left," "the traitor and American agent" conspiring with Washington to partition Lebanon. Damascus activated its Muslim friends, including Rashid Karami, to join in its campaign. Assad also acted to cripple LNM forces by cutting their supply lines through Syria, while Saiqa occupied strategic positions in Beirut and other ports to intercept incoming LNM munitions, fuel, food, and other supplies. Syrian patrol boats instituted a blockade of the Lebanese coast. By mid-April the *New York Times,* citing intelligence sources, reported that most of Syria's thirty-ship navy was engaged in this endeavor.[22]

Syria's unannounced military intervention began on April 9. A Special Forces unit seized the Lebanese customs post at Masnaa, while troops crossed into the Akkar and commando units moved on Tripoli. The intervention started on the eve of the important parliamentary session—opposed by Syria—to amend the constitution to permit election of a new president.[23]

While armed militias of both sides encircled the villa, parliament approved the amendment unanimously within fifteen minutes, with nine deputies absent. Two days later the LNM agreed to extend the truce until the end of April to permit the election to be held. Meanwhile, Syrian units took up positions at the crossroads leading to the besieged city of Zahle, while others advanced fifteen miles down the road to Beirut, and Syrian patrols fanned out to show the flag in Marjeyoun and other towns of the south.

Demonstrations against the Syrian intervention brought thousands into the streets of Sidon and Tyre, while hundreds protested in the towns and villages along the Beirut–Damascus road. Demonstrators carried banners and chanted slogans:

Move to the Golan, Oh Rulers of Syria

No to the American Conspiracy

No to the Brotherly Repression

The Syrian Army Must Not Be a Tool in the Hands of the Isolationists Against the Resistance and the LNM.

As full-scale fighting resumed in Beirut and the mountains, Syria's alliance with the right became more open. Kataeb militia besieging the Greek Orthodox town of Dhour al-Choueir, a long-time Syrian Social Nationalist Party (SSNP) stronghold, entered it unopposed. They followed Saiqa, which on the pretext of breaking the siege took in food and flour and then invited rightist forces to enter. In Beirut the so-called Hospitals War—with hospitals on both sides as targets—started with the heaviest bombardments yet.

The Presidential Election

On April 15 a PLO delegation went to Damascus for a fence-mending session that resulted in a seven-point agreement. This called for joint action by all parties against any party breaking the truce; reconstitution of the mixed truce commissions; and rejection of partition as well as American solutions and all attempts to Arabize the conflict. The crucial point was the PLO's apparent endorsement of the Syrian intervention—in direct contradiction to the first demand the delegation had taken to Damascus: the withdrawal of Syrian troops.[24]

While the LNM viewed withdrawal as the only way to ensure a free election, it agreed to take a "constructive attitude."[25] The Kataeb approved the accord, but both Camille Chamoun and Bashir Gemayel denounced it. In a defiant gesture toward Damascus, Gemayel announced the formation of a shadow government in rightist areas.[26] After an LNM threat to establish a revolutionary government, President Franjieh was finally persuaded to sign the constitutional amendment making possible an early presidential election.

Raymond Edde, an outspoken opponent of Gemayel and Chamoun,

won the LNM endorsement, while Elias Sarkis, the head of the president's office during Shehab's term, received immediate backing from the Kataeb and Karami. Jumblat announced that he would not participate unless Syrian and Saiqa troops were withdrawn. Edde, who saw Syrian intervention as the central issue, was promptly vetoed by Damascus, which backed Sarkis.

The election on May 8 assumed an unintentionally farcical character. When, three days earlier, Akkar deputy Suleiman Ali publicly announced that he would "at the request of our brethren in Syria" vote for Sarkis, Edde telephoned to congratulate him on his "frankness and courage." Less gentle Syrian pressures—when bribes estimated to total nearly $10 million failed—were applied to other deputies. A group of Bekka deputies told Edde that they were voting for Sarkis because "our districts are virtually occupied by the Syrian army."[27] Saiqa troops forcibly brought deputies of doubtful loyalty to Syria to the voting session. Of three who hid in the Carlton Hotel, one, Pierre Helou, escaped his would-be captors and fled to the airport, where he boarded a plane to Africa, declaring: "I shall never return." Lebanese National Movement attempts to prevent the election failed, owing in part to al-Fatah's non-participation. Sarkis was elected on the second ballot by sixty-six votes and three abstentions. Altogether thirty-nine deputies, including Jumblat, Edde, and Saeb Salam, joined the LNM boycott.

On the eve of the election, the Kataeb began an offensive against the positions in Mount Lebanon captured by the LNM in March. Its sophisticated, well-planned, and well-coordinated character suggested the participation of army command officers. To permit the Kataeb to transfer forces from the Beirut front to these mountain battles, Damascus interposed Palestinian Liberation Army (PLA) troops in the buffer zone in downtown Beirut, in violation of the April 15 accord. The Palestinian Liberation Organization (PLO) promptly sent units of the PLA's Ain Jalout Brigade, recently arrived from Egypt, directly into the battle raging in Mount Lebanon.

On May 12 the PLO, the LNM, and the LAA formed a joint command, with Jumblat as political director, and officially took the name Joint Forces. Next day these forces began an offensive against Faraya, a resort town in Kisrwan, and quickly captured Ouyoun al-Siman on the road to Faraya.

In the north, Saiqa, the Syrian-commanded Hittin Brigade (the PLA's largest), and Syrian army commandos tried to take control of

Tripoli, attacking Iraqi Baath headquarters and other LNM strong points, and touching off battles which left hundreds killed and wounded. Within a few days they captured most strategic posts in the city. Other engagements between Saiqa and al-Fatah were fiercely fought in Sidon, Tyre, and Beirut, where Saiqa bombarded the Bourj al-Barajney refugee camp. Commenting on these developments, the Israeli prime minister, Yitzhak Rabin, told an Israeli Labor Party meeting on May 12 that Syria was "at war" with al-Fatah.

On May 15 the PLO for the first time publicly and unequivocally denounced the Syrian intervention. It called on Syria to leave and on the Syrian-controlled PLA to withdraw from Tripoli or to "stand in the same trench" with the LNM in the north. Alarmed by the Syria–PLO conflict, Muslim leaders empowered Imam Sadr to go to Damascus to try to heal the breach. That evening, reports from Tripoli indicated that PLA troops were withdrawing with Assad's approval. Arafat, therefore, went to Damascus to meet Assad and the Libyan prime minister, Abdul Salam Jalloud, who had also come to mediate. After meeting Assad, Arafat and Jalloud traveled together to Beirut, where Jalloud called for Arabization of the conflict, as the PLO and LMN were now demanding. Assad first agreed to a prime ministers' meeting with Egypt, Saudi Arabia, and Kuwait, then at the last minute refused.

A Lebanese Solution?

Following the LNM's dramatic military successes in Beirut and the mountains, a new political current emerged in Lebanon, stirring hopes of national dialogue. The Joint Forces occupied almost half of Mount Lebanon, reducing the Maronite right's domain to less than 20 percent of the country's land area and barely 25 percent of its people. As a result, the right apparently saw that even partition had become impossible. Bashir Gemayel sharply criticized the February 14 Constitutional Charter and spoke of his accord with numerous points in the LNM reform program. Al-Fatah then arranged a series of low-level, secret contracts between the LNM and the Kataeb. The deep-seated suspicion that Maronite right retained toward its ally, Syria, assisted this new current.

President-elect Sarkis also appeared to put his hopes in dialogue.

On May 19, after meeting Jumblat for the first time since his election, Sarkis expressed optimism about a solution. The next day Bashir Gemayel strongly criticized traditional politicians, asserting that "the new Lebanon will be built by the combatants of both sides." Mourabitoun leader Samir Sabbagh responded with a call for a "round table" of the fighters to "find a political solution and build a democratic Arab Lebanon." In an interview with the pro-Palestinian *Al-Muharrer* on May 25, Bashir Gemayel reaffirmed his agreement with various points in the LNM program, while his brother Amin proclaimed the Kataeb's attachment to the Palestinian cause and its determination to "end political confessionalism."

Two days later, however, a Kataeb spokesperson asserted that "Bashir Gemayel does not express the opinion of the Politbureau."[28] That same day Jumblat's sister, Linda Atrash, was brutally murdered at her home in a Kataeb-controlled Christian quarter near the Green Line. The crime was interpreted as an attempt to halt the LNM–Kataeb exchanges. Hastening to deny any part in the affair, Kataeb officials arrested three of their men held responsible, and Pierre Gemayel made a point of publicly endorsing the propositions put forward by his sons. But strongly opposed to the Gemayel line were the Chamounists and the small, extreme rightist Guardians of the Cedars, who were already involved with a new ally—Israel.

On May 31 the Syrian army openly entered Lebanon. And on June 2, Jumblat and Bashir Gemayel met in West Beirut, formally to permit Gemayel to express his condolences on the death of Linda Atrash, but also to discuss the terms of a wholly Lebanese solution to the war. But the Syrian intervention had changed the balance of forces. Two weeks later, Bashir asserted:

> We were in the middle of negotiations when the Syrian military intervention took us by surprise. To my mind we (the warring parties in Lebanon) were on the verge of reaching an agreement when Syrian troops intervened and reshuffled the cards. This is also the view expressed by Kamal Jumblat yesterday. The intervention toppled everything.[29]

Was the Kataeb genuinely involved in trying to come to terms with the Lebanese National Movement, or was it simply stalling until the anticipated Syrian intervention would restore its fortunes? The question remained unanswered. Certainly Assad could not accept a solution that would deny his regime its now dominant position in Lebanon and would allow the Palestinian resistance movement to escape his tutelage. He had already obtained Washington's permission for direct military intervention, and saw that the time had come.[30]

To "Win the War"

The pretext for Syrian intervention occurred on May 29, when Major Ahmed Maamari began a savage bombardment of Qobayat and Andaket, Maronite villages in the Akkar two miles from the Syrian border. Maamari, a Muslim fanatic earlier identified with Ahmed Khatib's Lebanese Arab Army (LAA), had sided with Damascus at the time of its break with the LNM and thereafter joined the Syrian-orchestrated anti-Jumblat chorus. That Maamari persisted in his bombardment in defiance of orders from both Arafat and Jumblat suggested that he was acting to provide a pretext for Syrian intervention.

A 6,000-strong Syrian force crossed the frontier on May 31 at two points. Two thousand troops drove into the Akkar to halt Maamari's attack, while the bulk of the force moved down the Damascus–Beirut highway. One detachment turned off to lift the siege of Zahle in the Bekaa Valley, while the main column proceeded toward Beirut. It was brought to a halt about twenty miles from the capital by the stiff resistance of LNM-Palestinian units dug in at the narrow Dahr al-Baidar pass, the road's highest point.

In the Bekaa, where the troops fanned out from Zahle to occupy the Rayak Air Base and other positions, the Syrians quickly put together their own puppet army, known as the Vanguards of the Lebanese Arab Army. Lebanese air force officers stationed at Rayak (nearly all air force officers were then Christians, predominantly Maronite) formed the nucleus, joined by a number of "volunteers" from Khatib's LAA. Former LAA Major Ibrahim Shahine, who became commander of the Vanguards, explained to a reporter: "The Syrians told me to join the Vanguards or go to prison in Syria. So I took the former offer."[31]

With one column stalled on the Damascus–Beirut road, the Syrian command directed another southward, toward Sidon, while four Syrian jets made dramatically threatening passes over the Palestinian refugee camps in and around Beirut. In addition, Damascus had at its disposal even larger forces already in Lebanon: 2,000 soldiers of the Palestinian Liberation Army's (PLA) Syrian-commanded Hittin Brigade; Syrian army commando units operating in the country since

April; Syrian army regulars stationed just inside the Lebanese border in the Akkar and the Bekaa Valley since April; the militarily insignificant troops of the pro-Syrian Baath and Kamal Shatila's United Forces of Working People (UFWP); and, most important, some 7,000 Saiqa troops, most of whom were then either Syrian army regulars in Palestinian uniforms or Lebanese and Syrian mercenaries. These pro-Syrian forces went into action in coordination with the Syrian army. On June 5, Maronite rightist leaders—Franjieh, Chamoun, Gemayel, and Charbel Qassis, the head of the Lebanese Order of Monks and a leading rightist political activist—issued a declaration paying homage to Syria and endorsing Syrian intervention in Lebanon.

Al-Fatah's intelligence services succeeded in preventing a planned June 6 Saiqa operation which aimed to seize all LNM and Rejection Front offices and the military and political apparatus of al-Fatah. And many in pro-Syrian ranks voluntarily surrendered their weapons to al-Fatah's fighters. Troops of the Syrian-commanded PLA Hittin Brigade revolted, arresting their commander. Saiqa defectors joined al-Fatah in large numbers. Saiqa was driven completely out of the refugee camps and forced back to the airport, its principal stronghold. Its armories in the camps yielded huge stocks of weapons, "enough for a thousand soldiers." The pro-Syrian parties were also defeated, their leaders fleeing to Syria or taken prisoner, their offices closed.

That same Sunday, shortly after the Saiqa assault began, 6,000 fresh Syrian troops crossed into Lebanon. They were prevented from entering Beirut not at Algerian and Libyan insistence, as President Assad later claimed, but by the Joint Forces, who, entrenched in ditches and behind trees and overturned cars, fought them to a standstill.

The Syrian armored force, driven out of Sidon after heavy losses, pulled back to the environs, where its troops vented their frustration in artillery bombardments of Palestinian refugee camps, the old quarters of the city, and some villages in the Jezzine district. Saiqa took similar revenge on the Beirut front, bombarding the Shatila and Bourj al-Barajney camps.

The reinforcements of early June doubled the size of Syria's expeditionary army, but the intervention was not going according to plan. Overconfident Syrian officers had not expected significant opposition from the Palestinian resistance movement (from which Syria had grown accustomed to wringing concessions), much less from the scorned Lebanese National Movement. The Syrian stranglehold on the airport and the Khalde crossroads, blocking exits to the south and east, maintained an effective blockade of West Beirut. But Syrian setbacks were nonetheless humiliating, and probably contributed to President Assad's decision to accept a degree of Arab involvement in his Lebanese enterprise.

[14]

Arabization of the War:
Defeat of the Popular Forces

In intervening militarily in Lebanon, Syrian President Assad correctly calculated that other Arab states lacked both the will and the means to challenge him. He was aware that despite their loud complaints, these governments shared his aim to tame the Palestinian resistance movement and were content to let Syria do the dirty work. The apparent paralysis of the Arab League and of the Arab governments most closely concerned with the Arab–Israeli conflict—in the face of appeals from the Palestinians and the Lebanese National Movement (LNM) for Arab action to halt the Syrian offensive—did not derive from conflicts among these governments. However widely their motives differed, they were in accord both on the need to domesticate the Palestinian resistance movement and on the imperative of avoiding the appearance of complicity in this operation in the eyes of their own peoples.

Egyptian President Sadat, for example, had switched his support from the right to the left early in 1976, and in the spring dispatched the Palestinian Liberation Army's (PLA) Egyptian-dominated Ain Jalout Brigade to Lebanon to offset the Syrian-commanded Hittin Brigade. But Sadat always carefully refrained from doing anything decisive to hinder Assad's mission in Lebanon. Saudi Arabia objected so strongly to Syria's violent anti-Egyptian propaganda that it cut off all financial aid to Syria, persuading other Arab oil states to do the same. But the Saudis still backed Assad's objectives in Lebanon, although they were now concerned to ensure that Syria did not achieve domination there to the exclusion of themselves and other Arab states. Iraq's massing of troops on the Syrian border in June, when the Syrian army openly intervened in Lebanon, was no more than a propaganda gesture intended for internal consumption. Iraq had earlier sent Palestinian "volunteers" into Lebanon, mainly in order to strengthen its own influence there. It did not greatly object to Syria's "disciplining" of al-Fatah, since this might permit the Iraqi-backed Rejection Front to win control of the Palestinian resistance movement.

Libya, which had ceased its aid to al-Fatah, sent Prime Minister Abdul Salam Jalloud to reconcile Damascus and the Palestine Libera-tion Organization (PLO). During June and July Jalloud shuttled be-tween Damascus and Beirut more than twelve times in an attempt to fulfill this mission—while generous Libyan financial aid to Syria continued to pay a part of the cost of Syria's military operations in Lebanon. Jalloud maintained constant pressures on the PLO to nego-tiate with Assad, but abstained from any concrete efforts to moderate Assad's policy. His pressures did achieve a slight easing of the Syrian blockade of West Beirut, but Assad did not fulfill the terms of a June agreement providing for lifting the blockade and a Syrian pull-back. The only genuine pull-back of Syrian troops came in mid-July, with the Syrian withdrawal from the outskirts of Sidon to Jezzine.[1]

The silence of Arab states was broken finally by the unexpectedly effective resistance mounted against Syria; the Arab inaction became suspect to their own peoples. On June 8 Arab League foreign minis-ters met in Cairo and decided to send Arab League Secretary-Gen-eral Mahmoud Riad to Damascus to seek Assad's acceptance of a token Arab peace-keeping force. Two days later—coincident with the reinforcement of his expeditionary force in Lebanon—Assad gave his consent. But the project almost at once became bogged down in rhetoric and political maneuverings.

The first Arab contingents arrived at Beirut Airport on June 21: 500 Libyan and 500 Syrian troops. Saudi and Sudanese troops ar-rived a week later. The force succeeded in opening the airport on June 24, although the Syrian units stationed there did not withdraw as they were supposed to do. As soon as the new troops arrived, a rightist bombardment scored direct hits on the terminal building and on a 707 plane, killing its pilot. This bombardment closed the airport until November 19, when the war had officially ended.[2]

General Muhammed Hassan Ghoneim, the Egyptian commander of the Arab force, with the help of the League's special envoy, Hassan Sabri al-Kholy, succeeded in establishing a neutral zone embracing the airport and the Beirut–Sidon road. Later another neutral zone was secured on the Muslim side of the Green Line dividing Beirut, near the National Museum crossing point. But rightist shell fire prevented extension of this zone into the Christian sector. Rightist opposition also blocked other crucial provisions of the plan, such as protection in other hot spots, the return of displaced persons to areas from which they had been evicted, and so on.[3] General Ghoneim placed responsibility for the crippling of his mission squarely on the Maronite forces, which "approved agreements on these matters only to open fire on the Arab Force when it tried to carry them out."[4]

Despite Ghoneim's and al-Kholy's efforts, the Arab force proved to be little more than an attempt at Arab face-saving. Protracted negotiations over its composition and mission gave the Syrian army time to reorganize before continuing its offensives. These were ocurring all over: in the north, where the Syrian army surrounded Tripoli; in the southeast, where it captured Rashaya, at the foot of Mount Hermon, and Marjeyoun, twelve miles from the Israeli border, and cut the Palestinian supply line to Syria; and in the southwest, where it established itself on the heights above Sidon, its artillery commanding the port and the Zahrani oil refinery, the only source of gasoline and fuel oil for the Joint Forces and for West Beirut.

In the Akkar Plain and in the Bekaa Valley, both adjacent to Syria, the Syrians established an occupation force which destroyed artesian wells and blocked supplies of fuel oil for pumps, thus making irrigation of fruit trees and market gardens impossible, refused entry to Beirut newspaper reporters, and cut communications to the rest of Lebanon. These troops distributed food and medical aid to rightist sympathizers, while subjecting others to frequent searches and arrests. An organized popular resistance appeared within ten days of Syria's June offensive, specializing in attacks on Syrian armored vehicles and transports and the liquidation of local "traitors." The Syrian response was ruthless: hundreds were arrested and two hanged following a successful ambush of a Syrian military convoy on the Zahle–Baalbek road in August.

None of these Syrian operations provoked any protest from the Arab League or its members. PLO leader Yasir Arafat, accusing Arab governments of supporting the Syrian campaign against the Palestinians, told the Arab League Council in Cairo early in July: "Palestinian blood is cheap to you. There are 3,850,000 Palestinians living in your countries. You won't get away with it."[5]

Privately, many Arab diplomats at the Cairo meeting agreed that the Arab failure in Lebanon was not an accident but a "plot." One

high-level Arab diplomat pointed out that had Assad wanted to separate the warring parties, he could have done so by interposing his
troops between them in one quick step. Instead his army moved
slowly and in stages, "squeezing the Palestinians and cutting them off
from their land and sea supply routes, a tactic that could be aimed
only at destroying or at least reducing the military and political power
of the Palestinians."[6]

The Syrian blockade deprived LNM–Palestinian areas—including
West Beirut, already without water and electricity—of arms, munitions, and food.[7] Syrian shelling set the Zahrani oil refinery ablaze,
destroying the only source of gasoline and fuel oil and so crippling
military operations, hospitals, ambulances, and bakeries. The counterpart of this blockade was the free and undisturbed movement by
sea from Israel of heavy weapons and other supplies to the rightist
port of Junieh, and the opening of rightist supply lines through and
from Syria itself. Arms and ammunition to the right from Israel were
even delivered through Syria for a time.[8]

A Triple Alliance

The so-called Arabization of the Lebanese war coincided with the
formation of an unacknowledged, American-inspired working alliance
of Syria, the Maronite right, and Israel. Maronite rightist contacts
with Israel predated the civil war, and in early 1976, when the right
faced decisive defeat, its leaders received substantial Israeli assistance. In May a regular supply line began to operate between Haifa
and Junieh, delivering heavy weapons, rockets, tanks, armored personnel carriers, and small arms to the Lebanese front. Israeli officers
moved into rightist communities to provide military training and to
plan strategy. Several thousand Lebanese front troops were trained in
Israel that summer, and top Israeli officials met rightist leaders more
than once. A U.S. State Department official confirmed Israel's delivery of arms. "Of course they're doing it. Everybody knows that."[9]

By May of 1976 Israel was also deeply involved in the Lebanese
border region, where early in the year it had opened a so-called "good
fence" at the frontier, thereafter encouraging Maronites in the border
villages to cross into Israel to use two clinics set up for their benefit,
later to trade, then to work in Israel as tobacco sorters and unskilled

workers. Israel regularly sent patrols two miles inside Lebanon and sometimes Israeli reconnaisance missions went up to the Litani River. Israeli officers trained young men of the villages as "home guards." And, on July 2, 1976, Israel transported Lebanese Front militias from Junieh via Haifa to Qlai'a in the border strip, where Israel was already building a "security belt" on Lebanese territory.[10] This was the first of what soon became the regular transfer of rightist militias (and a few hundred regular army troops of southern origin loyal to the Lebanese Front) from the north to Haifa and on to Lebanese villages. By summer's end Israeli forces were stationed in Qlai'a, Rmeich, Ain Ebel, Dobbal, and Alma al-Shaab and maintained regular contact with other Lebanese villages. Israeli soldiers set up roadblocks on Lebanese roads and installed telephone lines from Maronite villages to positions inside Israel.

The Syrian government could not have been unaware either of Israel's military aid to the Lebanese Front or of its expanding control in south Lebanon. Yet it remained silent, choosing neither to try to halt this interference nor to denounce it. The Israeli–Lebanese Front alliance put no visible strain on the Syrian–Lebanese Front alliance.

Bolstered by the de facto support of both Israel and Syria, the Lebanese Front could now move in strength against the last Muslim, Palestinian, and refractory Christian areas in East Beirut: the Palestinian camps, Jisr al-Basha and Tel al-Zaatar, the Shi'a suburb of Nabaa, the small Armenian Christian Quarter, Badawi, and so on. The rightist assault on the Palestinian camps became possible when the Syrian army broke the LNM's siege of Zahle, whose inhabitants had served as hostages for the camps; the right had not dared to attack the camps so long as Zahle could be overrun by the LNM.

Jisr al-Basha, a camp of about 2,000 Christians, fell under an all-out assault launched several hours after its Kataeb attackers had agreed to a cease-fire. Tel al-Zaatar, which sheltered some 30,000 Palestinians and Lebanese within its defense perimeter, had been under an off-and-on embargo on food and medical supplies since the start of the civil war and under tight blockade for 119 days. It held out for fifty-two days more, under some of the most concentrated artillery shelling any area had experienced.[11]

Rightist offensives against the camps, the slums, and other enclaves were assured success by Syrian army attacks and by pressures on the Joint Forces on many other fronts, particularly around Sidon, in the mountains to the east, in the Upper Metn, and near Sofar. President

Assad's failure to honor an agreement made with Jalloud and the PLO to pull back his forces from Sofar and Jezzine meant that almost half the Joint Forces' effectives were tied down on these two fronts alone.

Heavy shelling by the Syrian army halted a Joint Forces attempt to break the siege of Tel al-Zaatar by a thrust through Ain-Remaneh and Monteverde. Another attempt to save the camp by drawing rightist forces away to a new front at Chekka, forty-five miles north of Beirut, initially succeeded, but was soon defeated by a rightist counterattack which recaptured Chekka and drove northward toward Tripoli through Greek Orthodox Kura, a Syrian Social Nationalist Party (SSNP) and Communist Party of Lebanon (CPL) stronghold. In over-running Kura, Kataeb militias pillaged and damaged churches and monasteries, including the twelfth-century Balamand monastery, looting its priceless manuscripts and icons. The Kataeb laid waste villages, torturing and massacring many Christians.[12] Most inhabitants, almost all Greek Orthodox, fled to Muslim Tripoli for refuge. Syria's contribution to this rightist offensive was to maintain a heavy bombardment of Tripoli and the two Palestinian camps just to the north.

In a desperate initiative to save Tel al-Zaatar, on July 20 a PLO delegation went to Damascus, despite Assad's failure to honor earlier agreements. Nine days of negotiations produced what appeared to be close to a PLO surrender: the Palestinian acceptance of a cease-fire and of Syria's dominant role in Lebanon, new restrictions on resistance movement activities, and a round table conference of Lebanese parties to negotiate a political settlement based on the February 14 Charter. All this was in return for still another Syrian promise to pull back from Sofar and Jezzine. Hardly was the document signed when Assad added new conditions, then repeatedly postponed further meetings until Tel al-Zaatar had fallen.

Fall of Nabaa and Tel al-Zaatar

On August 6, after a fifteen-day siege without food and water, the town of Nabaa—close to Tel al-Zaatar and crucial to the camp's defenses—fell to Lebanese Front militias. A group of Shi'a leaders including Musa Sadr and Kamel al-Asaad surrendered the quarter without consulting the defending garrison, which battled on for another two days before being overcome.[13] Lebanese Front militiamen then "cleansed" Nabaa of its inhabitants and fought each other over the spoils in two days' looting. The poor Armenian Christian quarter, Badawi, was the next to be "cleansed," the crime of its inhabitants having been to try to help the people of Nabaa.[14]

Nabaa's fall precipitated the fall of Tel al-Zaatar. Rightist forces—including some regular Lebanese army units but not the Kataeb—began the attack on the camp on June 22 but fared so badly in the first three days that the Kataeb sent its troops into the battle to avert a fiasco. During the camp's more than seven weeks of resistance its inhabitants lived on meager rations of lentils, and a drop of water became "worth a pint of blood." Each day some twenty-five people were killed and about a hundred wounded as they ventured out of shelters in search of water. For four weeks the Lebanese Front refused the International Red Cross (IRC) entry into the camp. When, on July 23, Jean Hoefiger and two other IRC officials were allowed in, they found 600–700 wounded and in desperate need of evacuation, together with children and others dying of dehydration, dysentery, and lack of medicine. Even the slightly wounded had developed gangrene. The Front's conditions for evacuation of the wounded meant that "they would be gunned down before they reached the IRC convoy."[15] Evacuation was brought to a halt after two days, when snipers fired on the wounded lying on stretchers on the ground, picking them off one by one with well-aimed single shots.

The camp fell on August 12, while al-Fatah was negotiating with the Kataeb for its evacuation. Rightist forces deliberately stormed the camp before these arrangements could be carried out—if, indeed, the Kataeb ever intended to carry them out—and also tricked the camp population into coming out into the open to face their fire. As the camp inhabitants streamed out, the rightist militias "fell on them like wolves," arguing over how many Palestinians each group was entitled to execute and slaughtering them in cold blood.[16] Entire families were killed. There was hardly a male between the ages of ten and fifty among those who managed to reach West Beirut. Boys of eight and ten were summarily executed. Girls no older than that were raped before being dispatched. All sixty camp nurses, women and men, were lined up two by two, marched out, and machine-gunned.[17] Looters—often families of the killers—wore masks to protect themselves from the stench of rotting corpses.

Damascus said not a word about the fall of Tel al-Zaatar, but quickly closed its borders to Lebanese to limit the Syrian repercussions of this massacre. Syrian opposition to Assad's alliance with the right was erupting in bomb explosions, sabotage, and murders. During the camp's final days Assad sent Lebanese Front leaders assurances of his continuing support, and Syrian army artillery fire on the camp assured its fall.[18] Syrian troops were then also besieging the two Palestinian refugee camps north of Tripoli, where the rightist drive to take that city had by then reached within five kilometers of the southern approaches to its ports.

The fact that throughout the seven-and-a-half-week siege not a single Arab government had lifted a finger to save the people of Tel al-Zaatar underlines the real meaning of the Arabization of the Lebanese civil war. As al-Fatah's Abu Iyad pointed out: "You can't make me believe that a hundred million Arabs were incapable of breaking a blockade imposed by several hundred men, that they could not even lift their voices to put pressure, if not on the militias, at least on Syria who protected them."[19] Arab regimes were united, if nothing else, in bringing about the defeat of the Palestinian resistance movement and the Lebanese National Movement.

Maneuvering Toward a Settlement

The fall of Tel al-Zaatar represented the turning point of the war. Between then and a major Syrian offensive in late September, three very different projects were launched to try to influence an eventual settlement.

The first was Assad's renewed drive to divorce both the Palestianian resistance movement and the traditional Muslim leadership from the LNM. From the PLO he demanded acceptance of new conditions to the July 29 Accord, reducing the LNM to a negligible role in his projected political settlement. From the Muslim right, whose leaders he now invited to Damascus, he sought a reconciliation with the hardline Maronite right—no easy matter.

Running counter to this was the second initiative of Arab League envoy Hassan Sabri al-Kholy and the Arab force commander General Muhammed Hassan Ghoneim to achieve a cease-fire on terms that would constitute the groundwork for a political solution. The third initiative was the call issued by Saudi Arabia and Kuwait for convocation of an Arab Summit on the Lebanese crisis. At first sight this undertaking also seemed intended as an alternative to Damascus' policy.

President Assad did not want the LNM involved, either in the committee that under the terms of the July 29 accord was to end the fighting and supervise the truce, or in the negotiations for a settlement. "There could never be a reconciliation with Kamal Jumblat," he told his Lebanese visitors. He would treat Jumblat as "no more than a deputy from the Chouf." Jumblat—answering the question "Why did Syria let us down?"—touched on the core of the matter. "They found us too independent. We were never in the pay of the United States, the Soviet Union or whoever. . . . In the main they were alarmed by our real and moral independence and our growing influence in Arab opinion. And finally they knew that to try to subject the Palestinians they had first to make us wise."[20]

In August, Syrian Foreign Minister Abdul Halim Khaddam served an ultimatum on the PLO, ruling that the LNM could be a party to cease-fire negotiations only if the Syrian-sponsored National Front—whose leader, Assem Qanso, had been living in Damascus since June—were also included. He demanded the immediate Palestinian–LNM withdrawal from the mountains, an end to the "information war" against Syria, and the application of the Cairo Accord. The PLO rejected these terms. Abu Iyad explained:

> If the Palestinian Revolution must consider the Lebanese Front and the isolationists in general an opponent with whom it must dialogue, then whoever claims to be a mediator in the conflict, in this case Syria, must also keep the channels of communication open with the Lebanese National Movement. The Damascus Agreement was stillborn because Syria insisted on having the National Front represented in the cease-fire talks. . . . Since the talks were aimed at putting an end to the fighting, the big question, of course, was: Where is [Syria's] National Front fighting?[21]

The al-Kholy–Ghoneim plan was of a different order, proposing to treat all belligerents on an equal basis and in an even-handed manner. It also called on Syria to fulfill its commitment to withdraw from Sofar and Jezzine. Damascus and the right both rejected this plan.

For Arab rulers, a rapprochement between Syria and Egypt had become indispensable to end the war on their terms. Thus, when Riyadh, Kuwait, and Cairo decided to postpone their proposed summit conference, Assad had a free hand to settle the conflict on his terms. The decision to postpone the conference reflected the emergence of a consensus among Arab rulers that the war was holding up an overall settlement of the Arab–Israeli conflict and must be ended as quickly as possible.[22]

Thus reinforced, Assad subjected the Palestinians to stronger pressures. Syrian envoys Naji Jamil and Colonel Muhammed al-Kholy presented Abu Iyad with Assad's "final offer" on the LNM Movement issue on September 11. Since it merely repeated the standard Syrian denial of the LNM's legitimacy, the PLO rejected it.[23]

Sarkis' Inauguration

The week preceding Lebanese President Elias Sarkis' inauguration was marked by an outbreak of fighting all along the northern coastal area as different rightist factions of the Lebanese army battled for control of certain army barracks, with the Kataeb and Chamoun's National Liberal Party (NLP) supporting opposing factions. By the eve of the inauguration fighting had subsided; the Kataeb mounted an impressive military parade to make certain all recognized its preeminence.

At Syrian insistence, the inauguration took place in Chtaura, in the Syrian-occupied Bekaa close to the Syrian border. This was against the wishes of most Lebanese, but in fact the inauguration appeared more Syrian than Lebanese. Hundreds of Syrian tanks and soldiers occupied Chtaura and its environs, while Syrian MIGs flew overhead. Syrian intelligence officers lined up the sixty-seven deputies who attended (thirty of them driving from Damascus, where they now lived) for identity checks and searches. Raymond Edde, Rashid Karami, Kamal Jumblat, and their supporters boycotted the ceremony.

To mark the inauguration PLO leader Yasir Arafat proclaimed a unilateral cease-fire, and the next day he met two Lebanese officers designated by the new president—Brigadier Mussa Kanaan and Colonel Ahmed al-Hajj—in the presence of the Arab League's Hassan Sabri al-Kholy, to draw up a working paper. Arafat pledged to withdraw Palestinian forces from the mountains once an agreement had been reached. This was the first clear indication that the PLO was ready to make concessions to the new Lebanese president, concessions that it had refused a Syrian regime intent on bringing the

Palestinian resistance movement under its tutelage. Preparations therefore began for a Sarkis–Arafat meeting.

Resolved to prevent a Lebanese–Palestinian settlement without Syria, Assad looked for an excuse to abort these promising negotiations. He found it in a September 26 attack by four Palestinian commandos on the Semiramis Hotel in Damascus. The fact that the commandos belonged to a pro-Iraqi group did not prevent Damascus from pinning the attack on al-Fatah. The Syrian media waged a violent campaign against the "deviationist al-Fatah leadership," identified as "the main enemy" of the Syrian regime. Assad had found the pretext for his long-threatened mountain offensive, which was intended, as al-Nahar commented, "to head off possible agreement between Sarkis and Arafat."[24]

The Palestinian resistance movement knew that a confrontation with Syria would be politically damaging and that the Joint Forces could not stand up to the superior power of the Syrian army. It had refused to withdraw from the mountains only out of solidarity with Jumblat and the LNM.[25] Jumblat's conviction that Syria would not dare send its army beyond Sofar was based on assurances he had received from United States envoy Dean Brown that the United States opposed any outright Syrian military intervention in Lebanon.[26]

When the Syrian offensive began, the outgunned and outnumbered Joint Forces—no more than 1,500 men, against two brigades of about 6,000 and a few thousand Lebanese Front militiamen—after an initial stiff but token resistance, drifted down the mountainside to strong points in and around Aley to escape encirclement. Within two days the battle was over. Damascus called for a cease-fire, while the Lebanese Front continued an offensive toward Joint Forces headquarters in Aley, now being bombarded by both the Lebanese Front and the Syrians from their newly captured mountain positions. The Joint Forces threw back this attack, but fighting came to a standstill when Saudi–Egyptian efforts to end the war were stepped up.

Did Syria obtain President Sarkis' consent before starting this offensive, which torpedoed peace initiatives then under way? While noting that such consent would be "a significant turnabout in Sarkis' position," Jumblat added that if he had not given consent "the consequences are also grave, since as head of state he is unaware of what is taking place in the country he heads."[27] Sarkis remained silent. Damascus was, in fact, already preparing a new military drive in a fashion now become standard: Damascus Radio repeatedly broadcast appeals from southern villages for "help to drive out the Palestinians," followed on October 12 by a large-scale Syrian offensive westward from Jezzine toward Sidon and southward toward Nabatiye. The next day an armored Syrian force rolled down the Damascus–Beirut road from Sofar toward the Joint Forces stronghold just below Aley.

These new Syrian offensives came right after the resumption of Lebanese–Palestinian talks. Meeting on October 9 and 11, the participants had reached agreement on a joint working paper which was notable for its degree of coordination. The draft accord proposed the following: cease-fire, to be followed by withdrawl of both Lebanese belligerents from confrontation lines and tense areas and their replacement by Arab forces; the establishment of buffer zones controlled by Arab forces between the belligerents, among which the Syrian army was included; and the application of the Cairo Accord and political dialogue among Lebanese parties, with all sides pledging not to resort to violence.[28]

At the conclusion of the second Chtaura meeting Arab League envoy Hassan Sabri al-Kholy told reporters: "There was 100 percent agreement."[29] He added that the draft would be presented to Presidents Assad and Sarkis and PLO leader Yasir Arafat for approval and would be signed at the next meeting on October 13. However, a Syrian offensive down the Damascus–Beirut road started on the very day the Chtaura meeting was to reconvene, making the meeting a physical impossibility.

One Syrian offensive reached within four miles of Sidon, subjecting the city and port to heavy bombardment, while another seized the heights overlooking Haitoura on the way to Nabatiye. But in their offensive drive down the Damascus–Beirut road, Syrian forces met strong resistance outside Bhamdoun. The battle for Bhamdoun—with the possible exception of Tel al-Zaatar, the most intense and murderous of the entire war—cost the Syrian army hundreds of killed and wounded and compelled it to engage in house-to-house fighting. The Joint Forces' stand at Bhamdoun stalled the Syrian army's march on Beirut. During this battle Arafat telephoned several Arab leaders to ask for their intervention to halt the fighting. All were "too busy" to receive his calls.[30] On October 14, however, he succeeded in speaking with Saudi Prince Fahd who asked for a few hours delay "to settle the problem." Next day Fahd announced that a summit restricted to

Syria, Lebanon, the PLO, Kuwait, Saudi Arabia, and Egypt would meet in Riyadh on October 16, to be followed by a cease-fire.

The Arab Summits and a Cease-Fire

President Assad tried to stall convocation of the summit on various pretexts, first by vetoing Lebanese and Palestinian attendance, then by insisting on Jordan's King Husain's presence, then by declaring he would send his foreign minister in his place. But at 1:15 a.m. on October 16, Damascus Radio interrupted its program to announce that Assad would attend. This abrupt reversal followed an ultimatum from Prince Fahd, who threatened that if Assad did not attend the summit would meet without him, would ostracize Syria, and would cut off all financial and economic aid.[31] The fierce Palestinian–LNM resistance at Bhamdoun, offering as it did convincing evidence that an assault on the last Joint Forces' strongholds in West Beirut would be costly and bloody, may also have influenced Assad's decision. Attendance cost him nothing; the summit provided him with almost total victory without further bloodshed.

The Riyadh summit decisions, endorsed by a full Arab summit in Cairo on October 25, in effect allowed Syria to occupy all Lebanon. Syria would hold the whip hand over the Palestinians, under only nominal Arab supervision. In return Assad muted his criticism of the Sinai Accord and implicitly acknowledged Sadat as the front runner in the Arab drive for a settlement with Israel. Syrian–Egyptian relations were restored.

The peace plan provided for a cease-fire from October 21. It also stipulated the formation of a 30,000-strong Arab Deterrent Force (ADF)-under the personal command of President Sarkis, for which, it was later revealed, Syria would provide the bulk of the troops. Finally it provided for a four-power committee (Saudi Arabia, Kuwait, Egypt, and Syria) to supervise and guarantee execution of the Cairo Accord within forty-five days of the ADF's formation.[32] Heavy arms were to be collected from militias; the press and other media were to be censored. The Palestinian resistance movement was ordered to withdraw to positions held before April 13, 1975, and to readmit Saiqa to the PLO. The sole dissent at the full Cairo summit came from Iraq, which rejected the plan because it did not call for withdrawal of Syrian troops from Lebanon.

These decisions were intended to assure a measure of Arab, chiefly Saudi, control over Assad's Lebanese and Palestinian enterprises and to secure common Arab interests, not Syria's alone. The Arab leaders dealt only with the Palestinian aspect of the Lebanese crisis, and in so doing put their weight on the side of perpetuating the old order. Even the Palestinian question was restricted to such problems as Arab leaders found convenient to recognize. In a secret session Arafat was bluntly told that the resistance movement must abandon the goal of a democratic and secular state in all Palestine and be prepared to accept, if this could be achieved, a West Bank–Gaza state committed to peaceful coexistence with Israel. He was even pressed to make some gesture toward PLO recognition of Israel in anticipation of the (hoped-for) Geneva Conference.

More significant than what the summit did about the Palestine problem was what it did not do, and was afraid even to talk about. On three different occasions during the Riyadh summit Arafat tried to raise the issue of Israel's expanding military intervention in south Lebanon and the dangers it posed to the Palestinian resistance movement, Lebanon, and Syria. Israel's military activities in south Lebanon, then being reported to the world press, were plainly directed to making implementation of the Cairo Accord impossible. The rightist militias that Israel had organized, trained, armed, and now directed and supported in battle provided the cover behind which Israeli control was being extended over south Lebanon. Even as the summits met, Maronite rightist militias with Israeli support were occupying Marjeyoun and a number of villages near the frontier. Yet Arab leaders refused to discuss this issue, although Sarkis and Sadat had spoken about it at length in Cairo in September. Cairo's al-Ahram at that time quoted Sarkis as identifying Israel as one of the principal political and military participants in the civil war.[33]

The Assad regime did not break its silence, either on Israel's activities in the south or on Israel's alliance with Assad's own allies, the Lebanese right. Yet soon after the summit, Syria began to facilitate the transfer of PLO effectives to the south.

The war in the south was under way before the October summit conferences. As the civil war died down in the wake of the summits, then sputtered out in the rest of Lebanon, the war in the south escalated, with Israel, the Maronite right militias, and a faction of the old Lebanese army on one side and the Palestinians and the LNM on the other.

The End of the War

The summit conferences touched off some of the heaviest shelling of the war in Beirut and periodic outbursts of fire along traditional confrontation lines. Fighting subsided only when the Arab Deterrent Force (ADF) virtually completed its occupation of all but the south in the last week of November.

Syria's rightest allies greeted Syrian ADF troops coldly, while Muslim areas often showered them with rice and flowers. Lebanese Front attempts to keep the ADF out of its area were eventually overcome, but not before a protest demonstration in East Beirut—complete with barricades, roadblocks, and burning tires—vented its opposition. The rightist faction of the Lebanese army loyal to Commander-in-Chief Hanna Said threatened to fire on ADF troops.

The presence of ADF troops, stationed only on main roads and at certain strategic points, did not end the violence. Each day brought its quota of dynamited cars, bomb explosions, hit-and-run raids, kidnappings, and assassinations. Terrorism replaced large-scale combat. Now 8,300-strong in Beirut with several thousand more effectives elsewhere, Saiqa was one of the chief authors of the terror. Its operations, directed against the Rejection Front and Arafat's followers in the PLO, provoked recurring battles. "We won't tolerate the present PLO leadership, they must all go," Syrian and Saiqa authorities avowed.[34] A Syrian-instigated schism in the Popular Front for the Liberation of Palestine (PFLP) general command, erupting into clashes between pro-and anti-Syrian factions, gave Syria the pretext early in February to encircle and shell the Shatila and Bourj al-Barajney camps in West Beirut. In two days of fierce fighting, twenty-three Palestinians and five Syrians were killed.

Defeat of the Popular Forces

This engagement marked the beginning of an attempt to impose restrictions on the Palestinians. Devised by the four-power committee, these limited the arms in the camps to the automatic rifles of the Palestine police forces, themselves reduced to five police for every thousand camp inhabitants. Freedom of speech and activities of Palestinian leaders were drastically curtailed, Palestinian radio stations were banned, and all Palestinian publications subjected to drastic restrictions. The number of Palestinians in Lebanon was to be reduced to those registered with UNRWA in 1969, i.e. 200,000, requiring some 150,000 to leave the country. The Palestinian armed presence was to be limited to a still unspecified area in south Lebanon.

Under these and other pressures the Palestine General Council, meeting in Damascus in mid-December, endorsed a Palestine state without defining its borders. A five-hour discussion between President Assad and Arafat and other Palestinians led to a Palestinian decision to "cooperate" and "show flexibility" in negotiations for an Arab–Israeli settlement in return for a measure of relaxation in the restrictions imposed on them in Lebanon.[35] Yet Arafat was careful to avoid making formal compromises, refusing to compel the Palestinian resistance movement to take final decisions while giving the impression that it would be willing to compromise if invited to a summit conference at Geneva. PLO policy was essentially to gain time in the hope that Israel's intransigence would ease pressures on the PLO.

Domesticating the Palestinian resistance movement proceeded in step with concessions proffered on its behalf by Arab leaders bent on a settlement with Israel—at almost any cost to the Palestinians. Egyptian President Sadat affirmed his preference for Jordanian tutelage over a Palestinian mini-state; Syrian President Assad insisted on a Palestinian reconciliation with Jordan's King Husain; Presidents Sadat and Assad agreed, in advance of all negotiations, that the projected Palestine mini-state must be demilitarized; both presidents proposed to submerge the Palestinians in a pan-Arab delegation to Geneva; and, finally, when even this proved unacceptable to Israel, Assad, seconded by Zuhair Muhsin, declared that a Palestinian presence at Geneva was not after all necessary.[36] Syrian officials stated the situation clearly: "The Palestinians will just have to be practical and accept what can be achieved. This is being made clear to them, not only by us but by all other Arabs as well. The interests of the whole Arab nation are involved."[37]

Even as the Syrians were battering the Palestinians in Beirut and as 500 Syrian soldiers and tanks moved south to Nabatiye, nine miles from the Israeli border, Israeli troops accompanied by the Kataeb and other rightist militias were fighting the Joint Forces for control of a number of villages near the border. When the Israeli government issued a strong warning against the Syrian approach to its borders, Israeli Prime Minister Yitzhak Rabin almost immediately received assurances that the Syrian forces would withdraw.

By February 15, the Israeli–Lebanese right forces had taken possession of a string of Lebanese villages along the border. Israeli participation was established both by eyewitness reports and by classified data from electronic monitoring.[38] Western analysts concluded: "Israel has succeeded in drawing a security belt of Christian-controlled towns around its border." Rightist leaders in Beirut were at this time recruiting volunteers for the south, while others shopped in Israel and Europe for weapons. The Assad regime, while tightening restrictions on the Palestinians, allowed the Maronite right prerogatives that it used to help construct an Israeli buffer zone on Lebanese territory. The more concessions Arab leaders offered Israel at Palestinian and Lebanese expense, the harder became Israel's stand and the more concessions it demanded.

Israel's stance made a mockery of the Arab civil war that Arab rulers had waged in Lebanon. Arab rulers did succeed in weakening the Palestinian and Lebanese popular forces, but the Geneva conference they counted on to achieve a settlement with Israel rapidly receded beyond the horizon. Their major achievement proved to have been to undermine their own bargaining position vis-à-vis Israel. Food riots and social violence in Egypt in mid-January exposed the fragility of the social base on which these rulers operated. Menachem Begin's election in May 1977, putting an end to any hopes of a relaxation of Israeli intransigence, underscored the extent of the Arab rulers' miscalculations and their failure, even as their opponents—the Palestinian, Lebanese, and Arab popular forces—met defeat.

The national and popular forces were also victims of postwar terrorism. Raymond Edde, the most outspoken critic of Syria, escaped two assassination attempts, then left the country. A bomb blast near Kamal Jumblat's home in Beirut killed five people and wounded nineteen. LNM activists in the Bekaa, the Akkar, and Tripoli were imprisoned. Major Ahmed Khatib, the leader of the Lebanese Arab Army (LAA), was jailed in Damascus and other LAA officers treated as mutineers, while army officers who fought with the right resumed their posts, some in the Army Command. In the south the inhabitants of Khiyyam were massacred by Maronite militias in a seventy-two-hour orgy of torture and killing. And on March 16 Kamal Jumblat, his chauffeur, and bodyguard were ambushed close to a Syrian army checkpoint on their way home to Mukhtara and shot dead. Both inside and outside Lebanon, Syria was held responsible for this crime.

The loss of Jumblat at this moment could hardly be measured. "Without Jumblat," said his political enemy, Kataeb politbureau member Karim Pakradouni, "Lebanon will suffer a political and intellectual vacuum. He was one of those rare men who are bigger than their nation. . . . Hence his drama and his influence."[39] To a friend and ally, Samir Franjieh, "Jumblat was an uncontested democrat. So much so that he was considered the Lebanese incarnation of 'socialism with a humane face,' that is a democratic socialism which abhors all limitations to fundamental liberties."[40]

Internationally, tribute was paid to Jumblat as "an independent and dedicated socialist who was progressively radicalized by his confrontation with Lebanon's social reality . . . and by the Palestinian problem in its Lebanese context."[41] The *New York Times* declared, "It is a tragedy that he is dead," while *Le Monde* concluded: "With the death of Kamal Jumblat, the future is dead in Lebanon."

Jumblat's assassination guaranteed the continued opposition to any significant change in Lebanon. Despite the efforts of his Progressive Socialist Party (PSP), and his son, Walid, to prevent sectarian outbreaks, some of Jumblat's Druse followers sought revenge in violence. More than a hundred Christians were killed in the Chouf before the situation could be brought under control.

Silencing the Popular Forces

Following the cease-fire, when President Sarkis did not move quickly enough to impose censorship, Syrian troops occupied and closed down seven newspapers, all published in West Beirut, and one magazine. These included the widely read *Al-Nahar*, the conservative *L'Orient-Le-Jour*, and the progressive *Al-Safir* and *Al-Muharrer*. Only three papers remained, one directly controlled by Syria and two others by rightist organizations allied to Syria. During its occupation of the newspaper offices, the Arab Deterrent Force (ADF) removed files relating to Syria, the Palestinians, and President Sadat as well as such equipment as took the Syrian fancy, including new modern presses installed by *Al-Nahar* just before the war.

This operation, coupled with the arrest of journalists (two *Al-Safir* editors were imprisoned in Damascus), showed scant respect for President Sarkis, the nominal commander of the ADF, who was then trying to help publishers win Assad's consent for a system of self-censorship. The solidarity of publishers and reporters and the impressive support lent by liberal opinion to the cause of a free press took Damascus by surprise. The Press Syndicate, a publisher's association, provided *Al-Safir* and *Al-Muharrer* with an office in which their joint staffs put out the papers. The association's president, Riad Taha, went himself to Damascus to secure release of the *Al-Safir* editors. In one way or another presses were made available for all the closed papers. Only *Al-Nahar* suspended publication for a time.

Syrian troops withdrew from the newspaper offices on January 3, two days after the government adopted a sweeping censorship law aimed at the Palestinians and the LNM. Officials explained that Lebanon should cease "to be used by the Palestinians as a platform for their information and propaganda activities." The Palestinian news agency, WAFA, lost the right to file reports and commentaries. Correspondents were ordered not to quote WAFA and not to file statements or interviews with Palestinian leaders. The London *Times* correspondent reported from Nicosia that Lebanon was "taking on the appearance of a police state. The public voice of the Palestinians, for more than a quarter of a century freely heard in Beirut, has been effectively and totally silenced within the last three days."[42]

The censorship blacked out the LNM's existence. Kamal Jumblat's name could no longer be mentioned. People could no longer be designated as left or right, Muslim or Christian, making understandable reporting by the foreign press almost impossible. In the censor's view, the war had been strictly between Lebanese and Palestinians and the Palestinians must leave Lebanon. It was "as if the largely Muslim Lebanese left who fought alongside the Palestinians never existed."[43] Of the twenty censors, eighteen were Christians; some had even been affiliated with the Kataeb during the war.

The grotesque partiality of the censorship proved to be its undoing. Western diplomats, foreign correspondents, and business people all complained sharply. Bankers and business people told the government that they could not do business without the information needed to operate. The censorship suggested that there was something to hide; it implied a lack of stability that made them reluctant to invest. Within three weeks the censorship of outgoing dispatches was lifted. Internal censorship remained, but—owing to a proliferation of political party newspapers distributed freely, hence not requiring a government license and so not subject to censorship—soon became ineffective. Some of these party papers, like the LNM's *Al-Watan*, for a time won a wide audience. On the other side, the Kataeb's *Al-Amal* remained the leading privately published paper.

Tension on the Right

The postwar period saw growing friction between the Arab Deterrent Force and the Maronite rightists, who were themselves divided by a power struggle between the Kataeb and the Chamounists. Nevertheless, the Assad regime and elements within the Kataeb tried to maintain their alliance on a political level as the basis for keeping Lebanon united under a "benevolent" Syrian tutelage. But these elements did not now command majority support within the Kataeb leadership. During the war, when Syria became its ally and the way seemed open to domination of all Lebanon, the right had dropped talk of partition to call for "liberation of all Lebanon from the Palestinians and international communism." But with the war's end the right feared that its aims had not been achieved. Instead of "restoring Lebanese sovereignty over every inch of Lebanese land" it had a Lebanon with sovereignty over almost nothing, a Lebanon controlled by a foreign occupation army—and a Muslim and Arab one at that. Meanwhile, Christian sectarian fanaticism had reached a new intensity, feeding on the minority fear complex the Kataeb had deliberately nurtured among its followers. In this ambience the goal of "liberation of all Lebanon" was retained as an option, while the case for partition was made ever more openly.

President Assad quickly dashed Lebanese Front hopes, declaring that partition was out of the question. A Lebanese Front conclave therefore discussed the future of Lebanon in terms of "pluralism," again insisting on the distribution of Lebanon's Palestinian population among other Arab states and on citizenship for Lebanese emigrants. The conclave showed that the right, in spite of its continuing dominance in what remained of the state's structures, had also lost the war. It therefore became more dependent on Israel.

President Assad was hailed in the West as having "come out a winner." But if, as he told Kamal Jumblat, his aim was to turn the Maronites toward Syria, "to win their confidence and make them realize their protection no longer lies in France or the West," he miscalculated. The Maronites turned for "protection" not to Syria but to Israel. Assad's war against the Palestinians and the Lebanese National Movement permitted—indeed virtually invited—Israel's entry into and control over south Lebanon.

Israel and its backers proved to be the real—and the only—victors of the Lebanese war.

$$\left[\begin{array}{c} \text{PART} \\ \text{III} \end{array}\right]$$

FRAGILE PEACE

[15]

The Reckoning

The toll exacted by one of the most savage civil wars of the century cannot be precisely estimated. The number of war dead has been put at 25,000 to 40,000 (20,000 to 25,000 Lebanese and 5,000 to 15,000 Palestinians). Another 5,000 to 7,000 Lebanese and Palestinians were killed in the 1977–80 fighting. Some 60,000 were wounded. The majority of victims, around 70 percent, were under 20 years old.[1] Roughly 600,000 people, a fifth or more of the total population, were evicted from their homes and districts. Of the displaced, 500,000 were Muslims, both Lebanese and Palestinians, who lost everything: their camps, quarters, suburbs, shantytowns almost all razed to the ground. The remaining 100,000 were Christians, including 30,000 Greek Orthodox run out of the Kura district by the Maronite Kataeb, and some 30,000 Maronites evicted from Damour by the Joint Forces in retaliation for the rightist massacres of Maslakh and Quarantina. The remaining 40,000 had fled, either from the fighting or from the mixed districts to which they feared to return.

Crowded into partially destroyed houses, beach cabins, tents, suffering from malnutrition, gastritis, rheumatism, and diarrhea, the refugees endured great hardships. The Lebanese National Movement (LNM) demanded the return of all displaced persons, both to alleviate their conditions and to end the de facto partition of the country achieved by the rightist eviction policy. The Lebanese Front adamantly refused to allow any non-Christian to return to areas it controlled, its sole concern being to oust the 12,000 Lebanese and Palestinian refugees of Tel al-Zaatar now settled in Damour.

Between 625,000 and 700,000 Lebanese left the country during the war, some 200,000 to Syria and 100,000 to the Gulf.[2] Although during 1977 roughly half the wartime emigrants returned home, between 1975 and 1980 Lebanon suffered a net loss of 500,000 inhabitants.[3] The war's end did not bring reconstruction and jobs. Promised large-scale aid from Arab oil states did not materialize, and Lebanese businessmen did not bring back capital in significant amounts for investments at home. Insofar as they invested at all in Lebanon, they tended to do so in rapid-return ventures and speculation, awaiting "stabilization of the security and political situation." As a result, a postwar exodus of job-seeking young people accelerated.

Shortages of skilled labor were acute, especially in industry and building, each of which lost roughly a third of its workers. Even so, the jobless remained legion. The de facto division of the country so circumscribed the mobility of labor that one district could experience a severe labor shortage while another faced widespread unemployment. Much of the working class and a part of the lower middle class had long been without wages. While the minimum wage was raised as living costs spiraled, economic need continued to fill the ranks of the private militias, which paid regular wages.

In a largely urban civil war, in which the symbols of the country's rentier and catering economy were the chief targets, greater Beirut, the home of nearly half the population and the workplace of many more, suffered the greatest devastation. The port of Beirut, source of most of the dynamism of Lebanon's economy, was crippled. Much of Lebanon's tourism infrastructure, including forty-five of its most important hotels, was destroyed, as was roughly 50 percent of its industrial capacity. The war also took its toll on schools, hospitals, government offices, and on sewage, phone, electricity, water, and transport systems. The country's productive capacity was reduced to 40–50 percent of what it had been in 1974.[4]

The year 1977, moreover, proved to be no more than a breathing spell. In March of 1978 Israel invaded and occupied the south of Lebanon. Battles between Syria and the Lebanese Front periodically broke out in Beirut the same year. Together these were as destructive to the economy as the entire nineteen months of civil war. Syrian heavy artillery destroyed the greater part of East Beirut's electricity system, including underground cables and sub-stations which had escaped unscathed in the civil war. And for two months after the 1978 fighting greater Beirut suffered draconian electricity rationing.[5]

Syrian bombardments compelled the evacuation of some 300,000 people from East Beirut and its suburbs between July and November. The 1978 battles uprooted almost as many people as had the 1975–76 civil war. The Israeli invasion and occupation of the south drove some

250,000 people to the north. Arriving at the rate of about 20,000 a day, 100,000 or more crowded into West Beirut, sleeping on sidewalks and in vacant lots until the LNM and other organizations could place them in requisitioned apartments and the government could erect tents on vacant lots. As the refugees, mainly Shi'a Muslims, poured into West Beirut, armed Lebanese Front militia took to the streets to block their entry into East Beirut. Many refugees returned home during the next months as Israel slowly withdrew from all but the border strip. Yet altogether at least a million people—fully a third of Lebanon's entire population—had been displaced since 1975.[6]

Peripheral Gains—Natural Losses

Yet through all these misfortunes the Lebanese managed to survive, some quite comfortably. As *Le Monde Diplomatique* has pointed out, three principle resources fueled the postwar economy: remittances from emigrants, enormous financial subsidies from abroad to the many militias, political organizations and propaganda operations on both sides; and the transfer of wealth accumulated internally by looting, wartime profiteering, theft, and smuggling.[7]

Remittances from emigrants rose from $100 million a month in 1977 to about $150 million a month, or $600 per resident, in 1980.[8] With no counterpart in production, remittances spurred inflation and represented a substantial loss in human resources. In 1975, 98,000 Lebanese workers (13.1 percent of the total labor force), almost half of their industrial workers, had been employed in foreign countries.[9] By 1980 the number working abroad had grown to approximately 220,000.[10] The most serious consequence was not the emigration of doctors, engineers, and other professionals, but of trained manpower, "people with minor skills who really make the difference between an industrial and a non-industrial country."[11] Emigration was both a result of and contributed to a marked decline in the economically active population. This numbered 426,329 in 1979 compared to 597,778 in 1974, a fall of about 29 percent. At normal growth rates, the economically active population would have reached 791,359 in 1979, yet the actual figure was 46 percent lower.[12] The war made Lebanon's economy more of a rentier economy than it had been before: the foreign contribution to gross national product increased from 25 percent before the civil war to 47 percent in 1980.[13]

The second major resource—money regularly flowing into the country to subsidize militias, political organizations, propaganda, and so on—defies estimation. The Order of Maronite Monks, which during the war played a key role in mobilizing foreign financial support for the Lebanese Front through its links with the Vatican and Western churches, continued to do so after the war. Contributions from Maronite emigrants, often through the Lebanese World Cultural Union, did not cease with the war's end. Israel's subsidies to the cause of "Christian Lebanon" became substantial. Libya, Iraq, Saudi Arabia, and later Ayatollah Khomeini's Iran financed certain Shi'a or Sunni Islamic organizations, some LNM parties, and Palestinian resistance movement groups, while the Palestinians brought large sums into the country to underwrite their operations, as did Syria, the Arab Deterrent Force (ADF), and the United Nations Interim Forces in Lebanon (UNIFIL) and their personnel.

Transfer of wealth accumulated internally by looting, wartime profiteering, and theft—along with smuggling, which developed into big business when the war ended—constituted the third resource. This transfer was part of a larger process: the decentralization which resulted from the wartime movement of population from Beirut to the provinces and the country's splintering into politico-sectarian-geographic zones. Provincial cities such as Sidon, Zahle, Junieh, and Tripoli developed to provide a variety of goods and services in each zone. Movement within each zone increased, drawing these cities closer to their respective hinterlands and spurring new transport systems. Local building boomed with the construction of shops, hotels, offices, factories and the establishment of branch offices of trading companies and other enterprises in the provinces.

Such fragmentation of development made for higher prices and the ineffective use of resources. Moreover, the anarchic multiplication of similar production and service units within partially closed areas could not foster either national cohesion or national growth, both of which were vitally needed in postwar Lebanon. It did encourage contraband trade, however, and the expansion of such trade after the war robbed the government of resources it needed to function. If during the 1975–76 war contraband trade was carried on by both sides, such trade in the postwar period became big business for the victorious Lebanese Forces. According to customs officials, in the eight years from 1975 to the middle of 1983, the Lebanese Forces robbed the state treasury of more than five billion Lebanese pounds by simply retaining control of the government's pier five in Beirut port.[14] Since goods entering Lebanon through pier five paid no customs duties, only ships with cargoes carrying less than one percent customs tax used the government pier next door. By 1983–84 the government pier was handling one or two ships a day compared to the eight to twelve unloaded daily at the Lebanese Forces pier. In the early 1980s the Lebanese Forces, handling about 50 percent of all Beirut's shipping commerce, still flatly rejected all government attempts to close the illegal ports on the pretext that ports in the Syrian-controlled north—i.e., Tripoli—must be closed first.[15] Customs receipts, once the largest revenue item in the state budget, now provided only 14 percent or less of state income.[16]

Contraband trade gradually affected almost all aspects of the national economy. The industrial sector could not compete in price with illegally imported foreign goods, especially because its own costs rose continually in pace with rising energy costs, erratic power cuts, and frequent staff absenteeism owing to lack of transport and the always uncertain security situation. According to the president of the industrial association, Fouad Abi Saleh, the industrial sector in 1981 employed only 55,000 workers, barely half its prewar labor force, had an industrial capacity only 75 percent of that of 1975, and could not use even that.[17]

The Lebanese Forces also engaged, as did many other militias, in the highly lucrative export of hashish. In 1977, the area planted to hashish in the Bekaa reached 100,000 donums or about three-fourths of the Bekaa's cultivated land, as compared to about 25,000 donums before the war. The big profiteers in this lucrative enterprise were the politicians and influential people who owned much of the land along with the mafia that developed to handle transportation, distribution, and so on.[18]

Rampant corruption, bribery, and favoritism in government agencies contributed to government impotence, making substantial inroads in government revenues. No institutions existed to supervise government spending, and the national deficit skyrocketed, threatening the value of the Lebanese pound.

A New Class in Formation?

In decentralizing and fractionalizing power, the war produced a newly rich and locally powerful social stratum of war profiteers, contraband traders, big-time looters, and city and regional military and political *zuama* and their clienteles.[19] This evolution took place on both sides of the barricades. In the extensive peripheral Muslim and mixed areas of the LNM and the Palestinians, the near collapse of the traditional Sunni political class permitted local power centers to arise among the broad variety of currents in these areas. Here no attempt was made to centralize power, and no one group was in a position to impose its domination over the rest. Lebanese National Movement policy, moreover, was directed toward trying to strengthen the state, not to replace it, as decisions it adopted in June 1967 made clear. Abandoning its demand for the abolition of political sectarianism, it called only for "political balance" to be achieved through redistribution of power among the sectarian communities and for the dissolution of "private entities" (sectarian "statelets") to permit Lebanon's unity under a central government. Its efforts to create an "enlarged front" to achieve this goal, however, proved unsuccessful.

In the Lebanese Front's compact heartland, the civil war completed an earlier shift of power from the traditional, historically dominant Maronite families to a middle and small bourgeoisie increasingly oriented toward the Kataeb and other rightist parties. The financial and commercial bourgeoisie remained prominent in the leadership of the Kataeb, but the impulse for a Maronite ministate, already under construction, came for the most part from its radicalized middle and lower ranks.

A Maronite State in Construction?

In 1977 the Lebanese Front served notice of its plans: "We have fought the war and we have won," declared Bashir Gemayel, adding that the Lebanese Forces "will not hesitate to take up arms once more. In any case, we have created our own government which is carrying out studies and executing projects."

One of these projects, largely ignored in the West, was an ideological guidance program centered in the Maronite Ruh al-Kuds (Holy Spirit) University, a program in which Father Boulos Naaman, head of the university's history department and architect of the Lebanese Front's alliance with Israel, had a leading role. Soon after the war's end, Naaman articulated the Lebanese Front's goal of transforming Lebanon into a Christian homeland in these terms: "Muslims and Christians cannot live together in Lebanon or anywhere else."

Even before the war Kaslik University had become a center for propagating the conviction that Christian-Muslim coexistence is impossible and for instilling contempt and hatred for Muslims. University brochures always presented Muslims as "the enemy" and employed the terms racists always use in describing human groups held to be inferior: "the Muslims sexual life is instinctive lewdness," "the Muslim God is a god of violence," and the like.[20]

In Kaslik publications, Muslims appear as an ethnic group shaped for all time during the Caliphates, their characteristics unchanged throughout history. Kaslik dismisses any calls for national unity or any efforts to unify the country or temper its inequalities as attempts to destroy Lebanon's identity. And it has repeatedly brandished the "looming threat" of Lebanon's transformation into an Islamic republic and of the reduction of Christians to "a small minority." Kaslik therefore demands the partition of Lebanon to create a Maronite "national home" to be linked to Israel.[21] All of this fostered a climate of opinion in which compromise was ruled out.

Lebanese Front leaders spoke in the same vein. Bashir Gemayel, the commander of the Lebanese Front's military arm, the Lebanese Forces, and the spokesman most effectively reflecting the views of the Front's extremists, held the civil war to have been "a challenge to the very existence of Christian Lebanon . . . a war of desecration and eviction against Christians." Insisting that the militias be promoted as "a hedge against the perfidy of the future," he warned that Christians must either "firm up the war" or "revert to the coexistence formula" which means "plunging into a sectarian abyss."[22] In other words, the Maronite right must either reestablish its ascendancy or precipitate another civil war.

The result can be seen in popular reaction in areas under Front control to failed assassination attempts against Bashir Gemayel in April of 1979 and against his father Pierre in June. Portraits of Bashir—wreathed in Biblical inscriptions and foretelling the coming of the Messiah: "Hosanna! Blessed be he who comes in the name of the Lord"—hailed his "miraculous" escape. Pierre Gemayel's even more "miraculous" escape—when a 50-kiloton remote control bomb destroyed the car in which he was riding—brought out his pictures with Biblical verses concerning the resurrection, and his followers thronged to the spot to kiss the ground.

The holocaust was another cherished theme. Following Israel's lead, the Kataeb equated the situation of Lebanese Christians with that of the Warsaw Ghetto in World War II, and casting Syria in the role of the Nazis. A series of articles entitled "The Lebanese Holocaust" in *al-Amal* in February 1979 featured such subjects as "Syrian brutality," plots to settle the Palestinians in Lebanon, the threat of Lebanon's transformation into an islamic republic, and the consequent reduction of the Christians to "a small minority."[23]

The unceasing dehumanization of Muslims by Maronite clerics and political leaders recalls the Hitler–Goebbels dehumanization of Jews and its consequences, and goes part way in explaining the atrocities of the civil war and after. The Christian right inspired a fanatical hatred and fear among the Lebanese Front's constituency and, despite official discouragement, to an extent evoked similar atrocities from certain groups in the NLM.

As important as ideology was the financing of this Maronite project. A Common Financial Committee, set up in 1975–76 to collect taxes in Lebanese Front areas to finance the war effort imposed a comprehensive and highly lucrative postwar tax system throughout their area: a personal income tax on all residents; sales taxes on a wide range of consumer goods and services; taxes on business firms, corporations, banks, etc.[24]

By 1978 the Lebanese Front had constructed a virtually complete state infrastructure. Commissions for health, information, education, economy, justice, foreign relations (and offices abroad resembling embassies) reportedly operated much like government departments. The Front also boasted its own official radio station, its own Lebanon News Agency, its own police, legal institutions, and, of course, its own army, the Lebanese Forces.

This tightly organized "statelet" within a state, however small its population and area, owed its power to the substantial leverage its leaders continued to command within the Lebanese state machine, holding key posts in the army command, the civil service, and the educational system. Moreover, President Elias Sarkis was, in the words of Rashid Karami, "the executor of Lebanese Front plans." Sarkis barred the Arab Deterrent Force (ADF) from certain important Front-controlled areas and withdrew it from others so that the Front could enjoy "auto-security." He, more than anyone else, blocked army reform, thus keeping the army under the control of the Maronite right. Deputies involved in drafting a new army law in

1978–79 disclosed that Sarkis stubbornly refused to give up any presidential prerogatives in military matters because "it would diminish my prestige in the Maronite community." Finally, Sarkis confined his political consultations almost exclusively to the Front and its friends, leaving Muslim and LNM leaders to meet with Prime Minister Selim Hoss.

In sharp contrast, Hoss, a former professor and banker, by acting on the principle that all Lebanon was his constituency, soon won respect as "the best prime minister Lebanon has ever had." His first government was for the most part one of technocrats, an implicit admission that a unified policy was impossible and that the government's task was to get the country running again.[25]

The War Continues

After 1976 the war simply shifted to the south. To the Lebanese Front troops already in place were added army soldiers transported by Israel from Junieh. Commanding these combined forces were Majors Saad Haddad and Sami Chidiac, the former long known for his violently anti-Palestinian orientation. If Israel's then defense minister, Ezer Weizman, is to be believed, Haddad became part of the Israeli forces in the late summer of 1976.[26] Yet these officers still drew their pay and received their orders from the Lebanese Defense Ministry. Lebanese Front militias, some brought from the north by Israel and some recruited locally, soon came at least nominally under Haddad's command.

A number of Israeli-directed offensives had given these forces control of much of the frontier zone, leaving the Palestinian–LNM joint forces confined to a small area in the central sector around Bint Jbeil. The Israeli involvement persuaded Syrian President Assad to reopen the Palestinian supply line through Syria, provide the joint forces with heavy weapons, and send Saiqa to enter the battle on their side. The Palestinian–LNM joint forces recaptured Taybe and Khiyyam in the first half of April, then froze operations at the direction of Assad, who apparently hoped to inspire in Israel a comparable moderation. Israel predictably escalated the fighting; Israeli Foreign Minister Yigal Allon warned that any attacks on Lebanese border villages (under Israeli control) would touch off a Middle East war.

The Likud election victory that brought Menachem Begin to power in May of 1977 sapped Syrian hopes for a peaceful Arab–Israeli settlement. It also emboldened the Lebanese Front, which promptly declared the Cairo Accord "null and void." Before the end of May the Begin government deployed Israeli ground troops *inside* Lebanon directly against the Palestinians.[27]

Early in August of 1977 Israeli artillery attacks on Nabatiye, Bint Jbeil, and other towns initiated the heaviest fighting in five months. Begin acknowledged that Israeli ground troops were involved in these battles in support of "the Christians" threatened, he said, by "annihilation" at the hands of the Palestinians just as the Jews had been threatened by the Nazis during World War II.[28] Promising to save the Christians from this fate, he told an American delegation that without Israel's support the Christians of Lebanon would have been "wiped out long ago."[29] Israeli military operations in south Lebanon thereafter received wide publicity in Israel, and leaks from "high Israeli officials" permitted the American press to publish details of Israeli military aid to the Lebanese Front in both the north and the south. These revelations undermined the authority of the Lebanese government, serving notice that Israel intended to control south Lebanon and through south Lebanon the whole country.

The Chtaura Agreement: Israel Fights On

Under heavy pressure from both Beirut and Damascus to implement the "Lebanese interpretation" of the Cairo Accord, the Palestinians accepted the Chtaura Agreement of July 25, 1977, under which the accord would be implemented in three stages. The first two—completed with dispatch and without incident—called for the Arab Deterrent Force (ADF) to take up positions around the Palestinian camps and collect arms over and above the limit allowed by the Cairo Accord. Syrian authorities, the UN, and the Lebanese government all praised the Palestinian resistance movement's cooperation in fulfilling these terms.

The third and most difficult stage concerned the south, from which *all* combatants, with the exception of a token number of Palestinian commandos, were to be withdrawn. Once demilitiarized zones were established, Lebanese army troops would be stationed in the area;

both sides would withdraw coincident with an effective cease-fire and the arrival of Lebanese army regulars. These stipulations met Israel's long-standing demand for removal of the Palestinian military presence from its border. Hardly was the agreement signed when Begin made his promise to "save the Christians of Lebanon from genocide" and multiplied his military operations in the south. The Lebanese Front then promptly rejected the formula for "balanced withdrawal" by both sides.

In late August, Major Saad Haddad launched artillery and missile attacks on villages in the south, followed by a ground offensive. Although supported by Israeli artillery, his forces' position became so critical that on September 16 an Israeli infantry battalion accompanied by armor and artillery drove openly and officially five miles into Lebanon, occupying military posts and strategic positions (later turned over to Major Haddad) and besieging the village of Khiyyam. Although the Israeli bombardment of this village reached an intensity of more than a thousand artillery rounds a day, Israeli ground forces proved incapable of taking it. Two weeks after invading Lebanon, Israeli troops withdrew under American pressure. A cease-fire went into effect on October 10.

Israel continued to block execution of the Chtaura Agreement by refusing to provide assurances of safety for Lebanese army units scheduled to move in as the Palestinians and other forces moved out. The *Washington Post's* Jonathan Randall reported: "The Israelis are changing the rules and demanding a new ball game. They extracted the maximum concessions from the Lebanese and the PLO through the U.S. and now want to go beyond what Lebanon and the PLO can live with."[30]

Although responsibility for wrecking the Chtaura Agreement was clear, both Beirut and Damascus now demanded complete withdrawal of the Palestinian–LNM forces from the south. The government remained impotent, however, owing to its failure to use its emergency powers either to purge the army of such men as Major Haddad or to reform the army's organization and bring it under civilian control.

Failure to cashier officers serving with the Israeli puppet forces in the frontier zone made a mockery of government pretensions to extend its sovereignty over the south. Prime Minister Hoss proposed to cashier all Muslim and Christian officers who had played important roles in the civil war, along with all officers who collaborated with Israel. But President Sarkis and Defense Minister Fouad Boutros maintained that only Muslim officers who "defected" to the LNM should be discharged since the Christian officers were "still serving within the legality of the state during the civil war." The army command and officer corps therefore remained highly partisan, and the army in large part outside of government control.

Unusually heavy Israeli air and artillery attacks on Palestinian refugee camps near Tyre and Sidon killed at least 150, including many Lebanese. In the wholly Lebanese village of Azziya, the Israelis killed fifty or more Lebanese, provoking angry demonstrations in early November. The United States refused to condemn this attack. And Sadat did not mention it during his visit to Jerusalem a week later.

[16]

Sadat's Journey to Canossa and the Wars of 1978

Egyptian President Anwar Sadat's peace initiative radically altered the premises of the Lebanese and Palestinian situation. Until that time American policy had included at least verbal respect for the "legitimate rights of the Palestinian people" and promised to ensure their participation in the peace process, a promise reaffirmed by U.S. President Jimmy Carter in the joint United States–Soviet Union Declaration of October 1, 1977. Sadat's trip to Jerusalem canceled all this. On December 15, 1977, following Menachem Begin's visit to Washington and Sadat's to Jerusalem, Carter specifically excluded the Palestinian Liberation Organization (PLO) from any part in the "peace process."

Sadat's eagerness to come to terms with Israel, together with Carter's vacillation, encouraged Israel's aggressions against south Lebanon, especially its March 1978 invasion and subsequent takeover of the frontier zone. Similarly heartened were the Lebanese Forces, who continued to harass the Syrians, the Palestinian resistance movement, and the Lebanese opposition. A week after his Jerusalem visit, Sadat predicted that "blood will flow in Lebanon and Syria."[1]

The PLO and the Arab states opposed to Sadat's initiative (Syria, Algeria, Libya, South Yemen) pressured Damascus to put an end to the Lebanese Front's alliance with Israel so that a strong defense line could be established on Lebanon's southern border. But Syrian President Hafez Assad adhered to his policy of maintaining a stalemate in Lebanon that kept Syria in command.

Sadat's visit did reassemble the Lebanese National Movement (LNM)—in disarray since Kamal Jumblat's assassination. The Egyptian president had hardly left Jerusalem when movement leaders

239

formed a Committee of Reunification. For the first time since Syria's 1976 military intervention in Lebanon, Damascus contacted LNM leaders to secure their cooperation in organizing an anti-Sadat rally. LNM leaders defined its tasks as working to unite Lebanon under a central authority; assuring its Arab identity; closing the Israeli border; and protecting the Palestinian resistance movement from liquidation.

In 1978 blood flowed in more than one war in Lebanon. The "Syrian–Lebanese War" (in the phraseology of the Lebanese Front, which deliberately provoked it) began on February 6 at the Fayadiya army barracks in East Beirut, when a Lebanese officer fired an anti-aircraft gun at a roadblock erected by the predominantly Syrian Arab Deterrent Force (ADF) and killed at least six Syrian soldiers. The ADF had set up the roadblock upon hearing that the barracks commander planned to transfer to the Lebanese Forces a shipment of newly arrived U.S. military trucks intended for the Lebanese army.[2] Heavy fighting touched off by the killing spread during the next three days to other parts of the city. Much of the fighting could have been avoided had Commander-in-Chief Boutros Khoury complied with ADF demands for the handover of the officers responsible for the attack on the Syrian soldiers, but he did not.

The Fayadiya affair brought to the surface the festering question of the unreformed army. President Assad told a Lebanese parliamentary delegation on February 9:

> The Lebanese army . . . is a factional and splinter army . . . not a national army. This army must, therefore, be dissolved so that a new army may be built. Most of the recruits belong to the political parties of the Lebanese Front. Political balance must be re-established and the Lebanese Front must stop acting as if it was the victor vis-à-vis other Lebanese groups.[3]

He was merely stating the obvious.

Israel's March 1978 Invasion

Barely a month after the Fayadiya affair, Israel invaded the south. This combined air, sea, and ground assault came three days after a Palestinian resistance movement operation inside Israel that left thirty-seven Israelis dead and eighty wounded, mostly by Israeli police bullets.[4] The Palestinian operation itself was a reply to Israel's ever more aggressive involvement in south Lebanon and its highly publicized alliance with Major Saad Haddad's forces, as well as its expansion and speed-up of Jewish settlement in the West Bank, and the exclusion of more than 4 million Palestinians from any part in deciding their own future and that of their homeland.

Israel did not long pretend that its invasion was a retaliation for the Palestinian operation. Its objective was to establish a "security belt" along the border, as Ezer Weizmann told a press conference five hours after the invasion started.[5] Other Israeli sources revealed that a military incursion into Lebanon to set up such a belt had been under study for two years.[6]

Yet another objective proclaimed by Weizmann was "to wipe out the Palestinians once and for all."[7] Here Israel failed dismally. The Palestinians—outnumbered roughly fifteen to one and without tanks, heavy anti-aircraft guns, or planes—for six days stood up to an Israeli army equipped with the world's most sophisticated weapons, including U.S. cluster bombs. These it used with devastating effect, against, among other places, two Palestinian refugee camps south of Tyre.[8]

Nowhere did Israeli forces succeed in breaking Palestinian resistance. Five days after Israeli leader Menachem Begin announced that Israel had achieved its goals, the Israelis were still fighting all along the line. When compelled to withdraw, Palestinian fighters did so in disciplined fashion, and most succeeded in reaching the north with their heavy weapons intact. Fewer than 100 Palestinian fighters were killed in the invasion's first eight days, but some 500 Palestinian noncombatants lost their lives.[9] The battle put up by the Palestinians made Israelis increasingly see the invasion as "a failure and a mistake," and forced them to abandon their attempts to take Tyre.[10] The Israeli newspaper *Davar* called the invasion "Israel's Vietnam," which caused more suffering to the civilian population than to its intended target.[11]

Nevertheless, Israel's round-the-clock bombardments killed at least 2,000 Lebanese civilians, caused some 200,000 Lebanese and 65,000 Palestinians to flee to the north, and left a broad swath of death and destruction from the slopes of Mount Hermon in the east to the heights overlooking Tyre in the west. *Washington Post* correspondent H.D.S. Greenway reported: "There is hardly a town left undamaged. Some have been all but flattened by air strikes and shelling. . . . The damage belies Israeli claims of surgical strikes against Palestinian bases and camps."[12]

Muslim civilians were a favorite target—the victims of Maronite massacres. The most notorious massacre occurred at Khiyyam, where Major Saad Haddad's forces dragged forty-two men and women, too old and frail to flee, out of their houses and the village mosque (where some had huddled to escape the invaders), shot them, and threw their bodies into a garbage truck. An Israeli officer—speaking after the cease-fire of Israel's determination "not to leave a vaccum" in the 450 square miles it then occupied—admitted: "We cannot turn [control] over to local Christian forces, not after all the Muslims they have massacred."[13] Yet Israel did just that.

American officials reacted calmly to the invasion, judging that it "would ultimately make a solution easier."[14] Then U.S. Secretary of State Cyrus Vance dismissed Israel's unauthorized use of America weapons as "a complex question" and Begin's hints that his troops might remain in Lebanon as a matter for "U.S. counseling." Ze'ev Schiff, senior military commentator of the Israeli paper, *Ha'aretz*, reported on March 21, 1978: "There is no doubt the Americans knew about the operation beforehand. . . . If they had wanted to, they would, undoubtedly, have been able to delay and probably to prevent the operation altogether. . . . American silence was tantamount to endorsement."

Yet when Begin declared his mission accomplished with the occupation of a "security belt" along the border, Washington secured a UN Security Council resolution demanding Israeli pullback to the frontier. Washington was concerned that open U.S. compliance with Israel's takeover of the border strip might torpedo Sadat's "peace effort." When Begin then ordered Israeli troops to advance to the Litani River, the Security Council adopted another U.S.-sponsored resolution ordering its withdrawal and the setting-up of an UN Interim Force in Lebanon (UNIFIL).

UNIFIL faced a complicated task, primarily due to each party's different interpretations of its mandate. Although UNIFIL's relations with the Palestinian rejection front militias were at first troubled, the main body of the resistance by and large cooperated, and by mid-May Israel had withdrawn from all but the frontier zone. This it turned over to Major Saad Haddad's forces in June, ordering local mayors and mukhtars to cooperate with him because "he represents the Israeli army."[15] U.S. State Department spokesman Tom Reston, however, asserted that "Saad Haddad is an officer of the Lebanese army and has been in liaison with the Beirut authorities on how best to cooperate with the UN."[16] American observers interpreted this stand as "indirect approval of the Christian conservatives taking over the border zone." Reston's assertion clearly indicated that President Sarkis also approved. The UNIFIL commander, General Emmanuel Erskine, confirmed this in announcing that "on the instructions of the Lebanese government" he was dealing with Haddad and his forces as "legitimate representatives of the Lebanese government." Angrily denying any such instructions, Lebanese Prime Minister Selim Hoss called "this kind of talk . . . irresponsible, unfounded, and rejected." It soon became clear, however, that Foreign and Defense Minister Fouad Boutros had indeed issued such instructions, presumably with Sarkis' approval.[17]

This was to say the least astonishing. Sarkis had promised Assad on May 31 that he would cashier Majors Saad Haddad and Sami Chidiac and fifty other officers *before* sending a regular army unit to the south. Assad had then agreed to this dispatch and undertook to secure Palestinian cooperation. Elevating Haddad and his men to the rank of "legitimate government representatives" (called thereafter in UN and official Lebanese parlance the "de facto forces") was the more curious since their only distinction, as Israeli officers themselves had pointed out, was their torture and mass killings of Lebanese Muslims—men, women, and children.

On May 31 the newly created 650-strong Litani Brigade of the Lebanese army, put together under Hoss's direction, marched through the Israeli–Haddad enclave toward Tibnine in the UNIFIL zone, but was halted by shellfire from Haddad's forces, and under orders not to return fire. Thus by mid-August all but 130 of its effectives had been redeployed. A senior Lebanese officer declared that the UN, Israel, and the United States all broke their pledges about the brigade's deployment, and that only Syria and the Palestinians kept their word and assisted its advance.[18]

The most significant aspect of this affair remained the relations of the government with Majors Haddad and Chidiac. UN spokesmen over the next three and a half years indicated that UNIFIL was still bound by the Lebanese authorities to consider Haddad and his forces as legitimate, and that the government's failure to clarify their status obstructed fulfillment of its mission.

A UN diplomatic report, cited by *Al Liwa* on January 13, 1981, referred to the original Lebanese government request that the UN cooperate with the "de facto forces in the South." It spoke of efforts to persuade the Lebanese government to take a clear stand on these forces, and of UNIFIL's inability to cope with the situation in the border zone until it did so. Six months later, when Kuwait and Saudi Arabia were attempting to settle the Lebanese crisis, Kuwaiti Ambassador Abdel Hamid Bouajane declared flatly: "We expect that relations between the Lebanese Authority and Saad Haddad will be broken."[19] They were not.

The role of the two officers was part of the larger problem of the character of the Lebanese army. It is significant that neither the Army Command nor the Defense Ministry ever denied the frequent assertions of Major Haddad that he received his orders from the Lebanese Army Command. Albert Mansour, a Greek Catholic deputy and a member of parliament's Defense Committee, revealed that "there is a Special Operations Room in the Deuxième Bureau to give orders and information to these majors."[20]

The scandal of the two officers, apparently serving at the same time in both the Israeli and Lebanese armies, spurred parliament's determination to draft a new army law. A joint parliamentary commission under Colonel Fouad Lahoud's chairmanship set out to do so. At its second meeting, Defense and Foreign Minister Fouad Boutros, speaking "in the name of the highest authorities," opposed *all* restrictions on the commander-in-chief and on the creation of military and defense councils, among the most important of the proposed reforms. Since Boutros' statement did not have the desired effect, Sarkis ordered the commission to freeze its activities, provoking angry deputies to document instances of the army command's illegal promotions and other illegalities by which the Maronite right retained control of the army.

The Lebanese Front Versus the Syrians

The Israeli invasion also gave new impetus to the Lebanese Front's war against the Syrian presence. Less than a month after the invasion, provocations against the Arab Deterrent Force (ADF) by Camille Chamoun's Tiger militias, linked to his National Liberal Party (NLP), set off a fierce battle between the civil war's traditional flashpoints, the Muslim stronghold of Shiah and the Christian district of Ain-Remaneh. Heavy artillery and rocket launchers, some used for the first time in the city, killed or wounded nearly 300 people.

The Lebanese Front's highly vocal outrage over "the Syrian attack on Ain-Remaneh" prompted Hoss to resign on April 19, only to be reappointed eleven days later, with his non-political cabinet reinstated on May 15. The Front's conditions for forming a political government would have assured a nearly two-thirds Christian majority and totally barred representation of the national forces. The goal of achieving "national accord" was therefore set aside for the time being.

The growing Lebanese Front involvement with Israel also whetted internal animosities that had developed mainly as a result of Kataeb efforts to expand its hegemony in the north, at the expense of traditional *zuama* such as Franjieh. The Front's worsening relations with Syria and its ever more blatant collusion with Israel brought open war between it and Franjieh on May 1, when a car bomb explosion in Zghorta wounded forty people. Muslim Tripoli generously donated blood for the wounded, opening the way to reconciliation between Tripoli and Zghorta, Karami and Franjieh. In losing Franjieh, the Front lost the Maronite north, the loyalty of several army units, and the altar of Maronite nationalism, the Cedars of Lebanon.

On May 23, 1978, Franjieh's son Tony declared the break with the Front final, and a series of killings and counter-killings followed. These represented only a fraction of the fierce fighting among the Front's various militias, however, resulting in part from the ADF's pullback from certain rightist domains.

The Ehden Massacre

"During the first half of 1978," Franjieh told *Al-Nahar* on February 5, 1979, as "I heard personally from Camille Chamoun, the Kataeb assassinated or killed 400 people from the NLF. . . . Now the Christians are endangered by the Kataeb more than by anyone else." The president knew whereof he spoke. On June 13, 1978, just after Maronite militia leaders signed a pact renouncing further fighting, 600 elite Kataeb troops surrounded Franjieh's summer home in Ehden and massacred Tony Franjieh, his wife, and their three-year-old daughter. Their bodies were mutilated and riddled with bullets. In nearby Zgharta these troops killed more than 30 people.

This operation, masterminded by Bashir Gemayel and led by Samir Geagea, was intended to eliminate those Maronites seeking a solution for Lebanon within an Arab context and to bring the entire Maronite community under Kataeb command. Instead, it provoked what the Kataeb itself admitted was "an earthquake of popular reaction." Thousands crowded into Zgharta for the mass funeral of the victims, expressing revulsion over an act that shocked even war-hardened Lebanon. The Maronite League moved slightly away from the Lebanese Front while in the Greek Catholic town of Zahle political, religious, and business leaders proclaimed their neutrality. A month later, when Chamoun insisted "there will be no renewal of the ADF mandate," Joseph Iskaff, Zahle's wealthy Greek Catholic member of parliament, declared: "Nothing justifies divergences on the renewal of the ADF. Lebanese are not in disagreement on the need for the ADF. We in the Bekaa prefer to avoid the agonies of bloody conflict and propose to neutralize Zahle and the entire region."[21]

Lebanese Front war Against Syria

The Lebanese Front's war against the largely Syrian ADF erupted periodically in East Beirut and its suburbs in the period from July 1, 1978, when Kataeb and army elements from the Fayadiya and Sarba barracks joined the battle started by Chamoun, and early October, when the Western powers ended it. Chamoun early on appealed to "the civilized world" to halt "Syria's extermination of 600,000 Christians in Lebanon," but only Israel responded. Israeli propaganda obligingly equated "Syria's slaughter of Christians" to the Nazi slaughter of the Jews in World War II, while Israeli ships almost daily unloaded munitions and sophisticated weapons in Lebanese Front ports. The number of Israeli advisers stationed in militia camps near Junieh rose to 1,200; Israeli troop reinforcements ostentatiously rushed to the border; Israeli gunboats and helicopters appeared off the Lebanese coast; and on July 6 Israeli planes sweeping low over West Beirut broke the sound barrier, smashing windows and spreading panic. This exercise was intended not to frighten Syria but to raise Lebanese Front morale. Israeli officials were at this time holding almost daily talks—indirectly and through the United States—with Damascus.[22]

After consulting with U.S. Ambassador Richard Parker, President Sarkis told Damascus he would resign if the bombardments were not halted. Assad reportedly said, "Let him. We can always find another president." Assad insisted on an end to the Lebanese Front's alliance with Israel and on the cancellation of its partition plan. On July 6, almost coincident with Israel's sonic booms over Beirut, Sarkis resigned.

This did not have the intended effect. Sarkis' failure to provide leadership, and his obvious partisanship, had generated a certain despair among many Lebanese. When deputies quickly prepared to elect a new president, Sarkis withdrew his resignation, and in a message to the nation flatly refused to disarm the Front militias so long as the Palestinians remained armed. Indirectly, he absolved the Front of responsibility for the battles.

Yet in the early summer of 1978 the Front clearly found its prospects far from bright. The summer battles prompted a new wave of emigration which the Maronite community, already diminished since the start of the civil war, could not afford. Official figures showed the Lebanese population shrinking by about 180,000 persons, or 6 percent a year.[23] The most telling comment on Front policy came from one of Sarkis' closest advisers and a member of the Kataeb politbureau, Karim Pakradouni, who said: "They speak of genocide, of massacre. No, it simply the slow death of political Maronitism that is in process of committing suicide."[24]

Israel to the Rescue

Lebanese Front leaders did not heed his warnings. In the last week of August, a delegation led by Bashir Gemayel and Camille Chamoun secretly visited Jerusalem to demand direct Israeli intervention "to save the Christians of Lebanon." Begin promised, as his office revealed nearly three years later, that the Israeli air force would intervene if Syria used its air force "against the Christians." Another boost to Front fortunes came on September 17, 1978, with the conclusion of a separate Egyptian–Israeli peace at Camp David.

This accord combined with Front attacks on Syrian soldiers in Beirut provoked a new explosion of violence. From September 23 to October 7 Beirut experienced the most devastating battle in its history. For Damascus the imperative was to rupture the Israeli-Lebanese Front alliance. Fighting raged over an area stretching from

Antelias in the north to Hadath in the south and eastward to Broumanna in the mountains. ADF pounding of Ashrafiyya—producing hugh craters, destroying buildings and water and electricity systems—left the district's remaining inhabitants without water or food.

When calls for a cease-fire by both Assad and the UN Security Council met no response, Sarkis flew to Damascus for a long-postponed meeting with Assad, taking with him an all-Christian delegation. This unprecedented step angered the other communities: the president appeared to be cutting himself off from precisely that part of his constituency—the Muslims and the Lebanese National Movement (LNM)—that had tried consistently to uphold his authority.

Insisting on hearing the views of those ignored by Sarkis, Assad invited Muslim and LNM representatives to meet with him in Damascus, where Sarkis continued to shun them. These discussions produced agreement on the need for prompt army reform and a total end to the Front's collaboration with Israel.

Rebuffed in Damascus, Sarkis and his delegation visited Arab Gulf states financing the ADF. Out of this round of visits came the October 15–17 Beiteddine Conference, which brought Syria and Lebanon together with the foreign ministers of Saudi Arabia, Kuwait, Qatar, Sudan, and the United Arab Emirates. Saudi persuasion was credited with the Front's observance of a truce during the conference.

The Beiteddine Conference

The Beiteddine Conference reaffirmed and updated the decisions of the October 1976 Riyadh Summit. A follow-up committee (Saudi Arabia, Kuwait, and Syria) a week later established a timetable for collection of weapons, an end to armed manifestations, and the scrupulous application of censorship regulations. It urged parliament to complete the new army reform law and called on the government to give parliament "a conception of a comprehensive political settlement." The Army Command was told to take legal steps against army personnel dealing with the Israeli enemy.

The conference did not address itself to the problem of how these decisions were to be carried out. Aware of the government's impotence, the Front and Fouad Boutros greeted them with contempt. The government tried to make a start by moving against Israel's collab-

orators in the army, Majors Haddad and Chidiac, and by completing
the army reform law. However, the Army Command promptly sabotaged the first initiative by issuing court martial orders against Lieutenant Ahmed Khatib and four of his aides and against a small far
right faction led by Captain Samir Ashqar (responsible, according to
Franjieh, for the killing of Syrian soldiers at the Fayadiya barracks).
And in trying to enforce the court martial order against Ashqar the
Deuxième Bureau's Special Forces accidentally or intentionally killed
him.

More significant than the conference decisions—neither new or for
the most part enforceable—was the strong condemnation by both
France and the United States of the Maronite militias and of Israel's
promotion of Lebanese Front intransigence. French Foreign Minister
Louis de Guiringaud, in an address to the Anglo-French Press Club in
Paris on October 16, bluntly accused the Front of starting the fighting,
warning that it was not supported by the Christians as a whole and
that its course could only lead to partition. U.S. State Department
spokesman Tom Reston promptly announced American accord with
de Guiringaud's position. He pointed out that it was in Israel's interest
for Syria to be tied down in Lebanon while the Israeli–Egyptian peace
was negotiated. Both Washington and Paris told Israel not to encourage the Christian militias, who "were pursuing an unobtainable and
suicidal dream of an independent state inside Lebanon." Israel paid
no heed.

The Army Reform Law

The Beiteddine decisions could not be implemented without basic
army reform or action against Major Haddad and his forces in the
south. On March 14, 1979, fifty-eight out of fifty-nine deputies approved a proposed army law, over the opposition of Sarkis, Boutros,
and the Lebanese Front—all of whom rejected any military reform
touching the prerogatives of the Maronite president, the Maronite
commander-in-chief, and the Maronite head of the Deuxième Bureau.
The reforms demanded by parliament were hardly radical, designed
only to bring the army's structure into line with the structures prevailing in most West European armies. Strong Arab and international
pressures were exercised on behalf of these reforms, in particular by

Washington and Paris, which had undertaken to sell the reformed army equipment and weapons. French leaders told Sarkis during his official visit to Paris in November 1978 that the army must be restructured without delay so that it could assume its national responsibilities.[25]

In January 1979 France also helped push through the UN Security Council resolution 444, prolonging UNIFIL's mandate for five months and calling on the Beirut government to present a plan to extend its authority over all its territory. This pressure was aimed at compelling Sarkis to take action against Major Haddad's forces in the border enclave, action he refused to take without parallel action against the Palestinians. Additional pressures came from Arab states: the Sudan withdrew its 600 troops from the ADF in mid-February; Saudi Arabia took out its 1,200 men in mid-March; the United Arab Emirates (UAE), its 750-man contingent not long after.

Such pressures, however, did not prevent the president from introducing loopholes into the army law that allowed its purposes to be thwarted. The Military Council was still to be formed on a sectarian basis; the commander-in-chief was to retain virtually all authority; the role of the minister of defense was to remain negligible; and new provisions concerning the army's organization were to be canceled, with this prerogative restored to the executive authority. Sarkis, moreover, delayed issuing the relevant decrees for more than a year, and Khoury delayed even longer before presenting a decree on command structure. This attached to the commander-in-chief's office a number of agencies duplicating exactly those the new law established *outside* his control, and attached the army intelligence directorate to the Army Command, giving it authority in the political domain, something even the old law had not done. Hoss and Muslim members of the Council rejected this decree.

Adoption of the army reform law compelled the government to fill the security vacuum left by the Arab troop withdrawals from the ADF. Damascus agreed that the Lebanese army should replace the departing Saudis in certain positions in East Beirut. The Lebanese Front, for so long the champion of the army's deployment in place of the ADF, rejected the government plan to deploy Lebanese troops in East Beirut, taking exception to their numbers (too many), their weapons (too heavy), and their positioning (anywhere inside East Beirut). Sarkis and Khoury conceded virtually every Front demand: only 120 army troops and 75 Internal Security Forces (ISF) members, equipped with light weapons, were positioned exactly as demanded by the Front (which took the most strategic positions for itself). East Beirut and its suburbs remained firmly in the hands of the Lebanese Forces.

This affair gave free rein to the Chamounist and Kataeb chieftains of the eastern suburbs. Warlord battles in May and June killed some 100 civilians, wounded many more, and totally disrupted the lives of residents, who were compelled to flee or take refugee in cellars for days on end. The fighting provoked unprecedented outcries of anger and disgust from inhabitants. In mid-May several hundred women carrying placards inscribed "Neither Kataeb or NLP! We want Lebanese state authority" took to the streets with rare courage to demand—even in front of the parties' main offices—"a total end to gangster rule." Bashir Gemayel and Camille Chamoun hastily declared still another fusion of their parties, but fusion did not materialize and fighting continued. As the battle intensified in June, they were reduced to appealing for army intervention to stop it, perhaps the most significant concession made by the Maronite right since the beginning of the civil war. At least it permitted Hoss to lay down the terms of the army's intervention: the deployment of an effective force without limit as to number, weapons composition, or positioning. The army for the first time entered and assumed control of the eastern suburbs.

Army to the South

The Western powers had set mid-April of 1979 as the deadline for the dispatch of an army contingent to establish a symbol of authority in the south. And in early April the government sent an army unit to the south to meet this deadline. The government hoped that the army's presence in the UNIFIL zone would free UNIFIL to move into Haddad's Israeli-controlled enclave. Yet as Hoss pointed out, Israel had only to oppose this arrangement for the Western powers to withdraw their support for the Lebanese initiative. And on April 12, 1979, Prime Minister Begin handed the border strip to Major Haddad. Six days after receiving this bounty, Haddad proclaimed his independent "Free Lebanon," at the same time attacking the Lebanese army contingent moving to the south by way of the coastal road. Under orders not to return fire and without heavy weapons, the unit managed nonetheless to push ahead to Tibnine in the UNIFIL zone. There UNIFIL itself was subjected to one of the most violent attacks ever by Haddad's forces. "No one aided us in the UNIFIL zone," Hoss said later. "Major Haddad brought Israeli forces into the enclave which UNIFIL could not repress. The problem of the south demands an international decision which has not been taken."[26] It never was taken.

Haddad's state, an area eight to ten kilometers deep stretching ninety kilometers along the border, contained, he said, some 60,000 Shi'as and 40,000 Maronites. His armed forces, roughly 3,000 strong, included militiamen brought by Israel from the Maronite heartland. To Beirut's accusation that Haddad was partitioning Lebanon, Chamoun retorted: "This is an uprising to liberate Lebanon. . . . We need a force like that one that struggles in the South to liberate all Lebanon."[27]

The next day a presidential decree expelled Haddad from the army. The court martial order against him was reactivated and new charges—of mutiny, attacking the Lebanese army, and detaching part of Lebanon to annex it to another state—were added. The Army Command quickly reactivated the court martial orders against Khatib and the LAA officers, adding a charge of contacts with Israel. The examining magistrate assigned to both cases declined, explaining that he could not treat the two groups on the same basis as ordered. No more was heard of the court martial cases.

[17]

Destabilization and Its Consequences

On March 26, 1979, Israeli Prime Minister Menachem Begin and Egyptian President Anwar Sadat signed the Camp David agreement, providing for the return of the Sinai to Egypt in exchange for Egypt's tacit desertion of the Palestinian cause and acquiesence in Israel's retention of the remaining occupied territories (Syria's Golan and the Palestinian West Bank ruled by Jordan). The accord made no mention of the Israeli settlements planted throughout the occupied territories—seventy-seven in the West bank alone—where on the very day of the signing ceremony Begin authorized construction of twenty-two new settlements. Camp David included an autonomy plan for the Palestinians, but only for those of the West Bank and Gaza, that is, for less than a third of the Palestinian people, much of whose land Israel had already confiscated. This so-called autonomy carefully excluded the right to national self-determination and statehood. It was to be implemented sometime in the future through a step-by-step process, with Israel reserving to itself a decisive veto power over any agreement and the right to demand annexation of the West Bank and Gaza after a five-year transition period. Camp David, in the words of a distinguished Palestinian writer, Fayez Sayegh, condemned Palestinians "to permanent loss of Palestinian national identity, to permanent exile and statelessness, to permanent separation from one another and from Palestine, to a life without hope and meaning."[1]

The Camp David accord had profound repercussions in Lebanon, where Palestinian political and military forces were concentrated. In mid-January of 1979, Israel's biggest incursion into Lebanon since the March 1978 invasion struck refugee camps in the vicinity of Tyre and in villages north of the Litani River, provoking a five-day heavy battle with the Joint Forces.

253

Israel's War Against the South

The UN Interim Force in Lebanon (UNIFIL) zone now became the target of stepped-up Israeli bombardments and aggressions by Colonel Saad Haddad's troops, who stormed into villages to compel young men to join his army. The United States and the UN refused Beirut's demand for military action against these incursions, although UNIFIL officers admitted their troops were "totally inadequate for the task assigned and not even sufficient to halt Israel's incursions into the UNIFIL zone."[2]

These attacks proved to be the opening salvo of a five-month Israeli war of attrition against the south. Three weeks after the start of the Israeli onslaught, Begin proposed peace negotiations, the departure of "the Syrian forces of conquest," and the pursuit of "operations against the Palestinian commandos in Lebanon." Selim Hoss called this proposal "amazing," coming as it did after "barbaric Israeli aggression. . . . The aim of these aggressions is blackmail in its ugliest form."[3] Lebanese President Elias Sarkis, as usual, remained silent.

From April until the end of August, Israel turned southern Lebanon into a free-fire zone, subjecting it to almost daily pounding by heavy artillery and bombers. These attacks emptied and devastated villages, farmlands, and towns, including Tyre; like the March 1978 invasion, it ruined tobacco and other crops. UN observer records at the end of August showed that shelling by Israel and the Israeli-controlled Haddad forces had occurred on an average of four or five days a week since April, while Palestinian fire into Israel was insignificant. UNIFIL officials admitted that the Palestine Liberation Organization (PLO) was disposed to facilitate its mission, but that a Palestinian decision to withdraw from southern villages to spare them from Israeli retaliation brought not a softening but a hardening of the Israeli position.[4]

A Lebanese government report submitted to a conference of Arab foreign ministers of social affairs in January of 1980 summarized Israel's achievements in the south: 250,000 driven from their homes; 25,000 houses partly damaged; 10,000 houses totally destroyed; 3,046 families left without a breadwinner; 10,810 children orphaned; 36,000 pupils left without schools; five towns (Tyre, Nabatiye, Hasbaya, Bint Jbeil, Tibnine) badly damaged; and ten villages wholly destroyed. According to the International Red Cross, 80 percent of all villages were damaged.[5] A PLO official put the number killed in southern Lebanon during the single month of June at 200, with another 450—mostly women and children—wounded. Sidon and Beirut again overflowed with displaced families squatting in empty lots, hovels, or whatever they could find.

In an area where agriculture was the mainstay of life, 11,000 dunams of tobacco land, 51,000 of orchards, and 70,000 of orange groves were totally destroyed by 1980 (1 dunam = .618 acres). Millions of trees and saplings were uprooted. Ports in Sidon and Tyre, highways, telephone installations, and power stations were damaged or demolished. Public services valued at 1.4 billion Lebanese pounds were destroyed.[6]

Subversion of the Lebanese State

If Israel was the prime mover in the destabilization of the south, its chief Lebanese ally, Bashir Gemayel, masterminded the destabilization of the legal Lebanese state and Elias Sarkis' presidency. This was accomplished even though Gemayel in 1976 had joined with Damascus to make Sarkis president, and in spite of the fact that his party traditionally posed as the defender of the existing state and its institutions. By early 1979, however, Christian state-building was proceeding successfully in the area between the Beirut-Damascus highway in central Lebanon and Zghorta in the north, an area he had "cleansed" of Muslims (with the exception of a few Shi'as left in Byblos as a source of cheap labor). Gemayel's state could already boast its own army, police forces, and judicial, fiscal, and tax systems, along with a few "ministries." His policy throughout this period was one of blocking any and all attempts to reunify state institutions or to extend the authority of the Sarkis government.

At the same time Gemayel reinforced his own authority by imposing his control over the Christian militias and parties. Following his operation against the Franjieh clan in the north, Camille Chamoun's National Liberal Party (NLP) and its Tiger militia became his chief targets. "During the two years 1978–80," Lebanese Front President Chamoun later asserted, "each month registered bloody battles between the NLP and Kataeb," battles in which "the militias killed each other without reason, without any valid motive."[7] The reason, however, was plain enough: Gemayel's determination to seize and monopolize power and to subject all other Christian militias to his control.

The climactic battle between Gemayel's and Chamoun's militias came on July 7, 1980, when, in a surprise onslaught of great brutality in East Beirut, along the coast to the north, and in the mountains to the northeast, the Lebanese Forces broke the back of the NLP militia. During this operation Gemayel's men deliberately mowed down countless innocent bystanders, including women and children, killing several hundred people—all in Maronite areas.

Yet Chamoun refused to break with Gemayel's forces, which in turn needed the former president as a political cover. Chamoun explained his calculation: "If we succeed in this [unification of the two militias], the question of government will become secondary because the cabinet will have nothing more to do than expedite current affairs while the political future will be in the hands of the two parties and, as is well understood, of the Lebanese Front."[8]

During the July 7 operation Gemayel's militia slaughtered some twenty or twenty-five Syriac Christians. Three days later, Gemayel served notice on the far-right Guardians of the Cedars and al-Tanzim militias to join his Lebanese Forces or dissolve. He then warned the Armenian Tashnag, a long-time Kataeb ally, to stand with his Lebanese Forces or face the consequences. To the Armenian votes delivered by the Tashnag, Pierre Gemayel had owed his first election to parliament in 1960 and his subsequent terms as well. But the Tashnag and the Armenian community—Catholic and Orthodox, established in Lebanon for some sixty years and accounting for about 10 percent of its population—by opting for neutrality during and after the civil war, had become "non-Lebanese" to the Kataeb. Three times in little more than a year (from the autumn of 1978 until September of 1979) the Kataeb attacked Armenian quarters because the Tashnag refused to join the Kataeb war against the Arab Deterrent Force (ADF), and because many in the community managed to avoid paying taxes to the Lebanese Front.

Following his July 7 triumph, Gemayel forced the other Christian militias to dissolve themselves into his own Lebanese Forces. This created at least the semblance of an organized army with which Gemayel was ready to challenge the Lebanese army itself. Still resisting his control, however, were NLP centers in the eastern suburbs of Hadath and Ain-Remaneh, which surround the Baabda-Yarze area, seat of the presidential palace and the defense ministry. This area was one of the few parts of the rightist domain under the control of the Lebanese army. In September, therefore, Gemayel launched a drive to seize this strategic area, battling both the Lebanese army and the NLP. At Hadath the army stood firm, provoking Gemayel to threaten to deal with this problem "with the mechanics and mentality of July 7th . . . pending the war of liberation whose date is not yet fixed."[9]

In late October, when Gemayel's forces struck at Ain-Remaneh, Chamoun's main stronghold, army units entrusted with its security either joined in fighting against the NLP, withdrew without resisting, or were evicted by Gemayel's troops. This confirmation of Syrian–LNM charges of the partisan character of the army compelled Chafik Wazzan to order "a full investigation" of the army's defiance of government orders and to promise its return to Ain-Remaneh. The investigation did not materialize, however, and when in early January of 1981 the army did return, it did so on terms negotiated with and satisfactory to Gemayel. He demanded that the Hadath military district be joined to that of Ain-Remaneh, and that the new district thus formed be placed under the command of an officer loyal to himself. Fouad Lahoud dryly recommended that the state adopt Gemayel's methods in security matters since "these permitted Bashir to dominate the Lebanese Front regions and then to become effective commander of the Lebanese army."[10]

Perceiving early on that a small Christian state was not viable, Gemayel set out to become president of the Lebanese state, using his Maronite mini-state as a springboard. His march to the presidency began on July 7, 1980, when he converted the Christian militias (Franjieh's excepted) into an organized army under his command, established a governing body independent of the existing Lebanese state, and assumed direction of the Kataeb political bureau, a function performed until then by his brother Amin. Bashir's project for a Christian state, however, faced some basic dilemmas, since at least two-thirds of all Lebanese Christians lived outside the projected state, and some 150,000 Christians living within it daily crossed the green line to work in West Beirut.

Christian Opposition to Gemayel's Ambitions

Moreover, widespread Christian support for Gemayel's project could not be taken for granted. Christian opposition to the Maronite

political right—which has always claimed to speak for all Christians—
was a constant element in every Christian community, including the
Maronite. Lebanese Christians never have been socially or politically
homogeneous. The 1975–76 civil war sharpened the contradiction
between the Arabist and universalist vocation of the Greek Orthodox
and the anti-Muslim, anti-Arab doctrine of Lebanese Front Maronites
(who are themselves Arabs, although they claim descent from the
Phoenicians). Only the Orthodox bourgeoisie of Ashrafiye have joined
the Maronites. The Greek Catholic community split after the 1975–
76 civil war; a rightist current remained in East Beirut. But other
currents existed: businessmen who had profitable relations with Syria,
itself the home of a substantial Greek Catholic community; Greek
Catholics of Palestinian origin who live mainly in West Beirut; and
many of Syrian origin in Zahle and elsewhere. Traditionally, much of
the Greek Catholic community has supported the Palestinian cause.

The most outspoken Maronite opponent of the Kataeb and its
Lebanese Forces has been Raymond Edde, in self-exile in Paris since
1977. Remarking that most Lebanese "cannot possibly approve theft,
looting, protection rackets, and piracy," Edde insisted that the conflict
was not a sectarian war:

> The proof is that the Christians living in West Beirut, Sidon and Tripoli
> live in understanding with the Muslims and enjoy greater freedom of
> expression than the Christians who live under the fascist Kataeb system
> in Kisrawan, half of Byblos, half of Metn and, of course, Ashrafiye.[11]

One of the most dramatic rejections of the Kataeb thesis that Christians need special privileges (called "guarantees") as a protection
against Muslims came in April and May of 1981, when thousands of
Christians fleeing the fighting in Zahle, Lebanon's third largest city,
sought refuge in West Beirut and other mainly Muslim areas.

Damascus Brakes Gemayel's March to Power

Syrian President Hafez Assad's policy since the beginning of the
1975–76 civil war was to insure that his army maintained a balance of
power in favor of the Christian rightist militias. At the same time, he
was also adamant in preventing these militias from going what he
considered to be too far. The Gemayel-concocted Battle of Zahle was
one such case.

Emboldened by his 1980 triumphs, Bashir Gemayel early in 1981 set out to provoke an Israeli attack on the Arab Deterrent Force (ADF) in Lebanon, which then stood in the way of his ambitions especially because of Assad's efforts to achieve Lebanese "national reconciliation." Gemayel chose predominantly Greek Catholic Zahle—with a population of about 220,000 and the capital of the Bekaa—as the site for his provocation because of the city's strategic importance to the defense of Damascus. To give substance to his assertions to the Israelis that Syrian army commandos were preparing to occupy Zahle, he sent nearly a hundred Lebanese Forces militia into the city. In an apparent attempt to provoke Syrian retaliation, the militia killed Syrian soldiers, shelled Syrian army headquarters in Chtaura, near the border, and started to cut a road from Zahle to the Maronite capital of Junieh. Damascus responded by shelling and besieging Zahle and started construction for the installation of SAM-6 missiles nearby. But Assad simultaneously offered to lift the siege the moment Kataeb militiamen left the city, an offer Bashir concealed from the Israelis and rejected out of hand.[12] His dire warnings that Zahle's fall would lead to the Syrian capture of "the entire Maronite mountain range" as well as to the "fall of East Beirut" brought Israeli ships to Junieh.

Dissent within the Israeli military establishment became apparent during the battle's first week, when "a senior Israeli military officer"— later identified as the Israeli Defense Force (IDF) chief of intelligence, Major General Yehoshua Saguy—told foreign correspondents in Tel Aviv on April 14 that Israel had delivered large quantities of arms, munitions, and equipment to Gemayel's forces in Zahle. Saguy also denounced Kataeb charges of Syria's genocide of Christians as "pure propaganda," and took pains to point out that the Bekaa was "a part of Syria's defense line" to protect Damascus, making clear his opposition to Israel's involvement there. He further disclosed that Major Saad Haddad's bombardments of towns and villages in the south coincident with the Zahle battles were carried out "on instructions from his superiors in the north" (who always denied such relations with Haddad).[13]

In fact, as Haim Hecht explained in the April 1983 issue of the Hebrew monthly *Monitin,* the real battle over Zahle was fought within the Israeli military establishment, between Mossad (the external intelligence service), which tried to get the Israeli army involved in the fighting, and Military Intelligence, which enlisted Washington's help to cancel a planned April attack on the Syrians. Saguy, a long-time opponent of Israel's sponsorship of the Kataeb, conveyed his suspicions of the Zahle maneuvre to Begin, but to no avail. He and other intelligence officials suspected that a high-ranking Israeli official—probably Chief of Staff Rafael Eytan—had given the Kataeb assurances that Israel would come to its aid if need be.[14]

In any case, Eytan arrived in Junieh for a final review of the projected offensive with Gemayel. But the offensive met with strong reaction from ADF forces. Begin later revealed that on April 7, 1981, he had received a desperate appeal from his Lebanese clients, who declared that without outside intervention they could no longer hold Zahle or even East Beirut. In reply, Begin urged them to fight on, but promised only diplomatic and material support.[15] Reagan administration officials later explained that a planned Israeli intervention in behalf of the Lebanese Forces had been called off under pressure from U.S. Secretary of State Alexander Haig during his visit to Jerusalem in April.[16]

The Lebanese Forces carried the fighting—the fiercest since the end of the civil war—to the port of Beirut and to the Green Line, while in the south Haddad's artillery pounded Sidon. On all these battle fronts the Lebanese Forces suffered defeat. An abrupt change in the rightist tone toward Syria underscored the extent of the setback; Gemayel now declared his willingness to talk to the Syrians—"whom we respect and ask to respect us." The Zahle battle made clear that Syria would not permit any further extension of Lebanese Front control beyond the traditional Maronite enclave, and that Syria was determined to halt any expansion of Israeli influence in Lebanon. Syria's victory compelled Arab states which had for some months withheld payments owed the ADF to rally once again around Damascus.

The Zahle affair was crucial, as journalist Michael Jansen pointed out, "because the 1982 invasion followed directly from it." Israeli Defense Minister Ariel Sharon's 1982 plan—to drive the PLO from the south, destroy its base in Beirut, and put the Kataeb in power—was "an adaptation of the Zahle operation which was on Sharon's desk when he became defense minister in August 1981."[17]

The Missile Crisis

In the Zahle fighting Syria finally dislodged Kataeb forces from the Frenchman's Chamber, a formidable rock fortress on Mount Sanin's highest peak and the only point linking Kataeb forces in the Bekaa to their Kisrwan bases. The Syrian–LNM capture of Mount Sanin on April 26 disturbed both Washington and Tel Aviv; the former professed that it threatened "Russian domination of the eastern Mediterranean," whereas Israel saw it as a threat to its work-in-progress: achieving a protectorate over Lebanon. The only response Israel could find was an air strike against Syrian helicopters harassing Kataeb troops still on Mount Sanin. Following Eytan's warning that "any plane that enters [the Bekaa] will be shot down," on August 28 Israel downed two Syrian helicopters provisioning ADF troops in the Bekaa.[18]

Begin's aggression (in his own words) sent the morale of the Lebanese Front militias, which "had been on the verge of giving up to Syria, skyhigh."[19] The helicopter incident occurred at the very moment that Syrian Foreign Minister Abdul Halim Khaddam was driving to Baabda for his second round of talks with Lebanese political leaders on the terms of national accord. The Front promptly reverted to intransigence.

Assad quickly installed surface-to-air missiles in the Bekaa, a calculated risk that took into account his friendship treaty with the USSR, on the one hand, and American fears that an Israeli attack could touch off an explosion damaging to American interests in the Gulf oil states, on the other. Begin's threat to remove the missiles by force prompted Reagan to dispatch a special envoy, Philip Habib, to defuse the crisis. Although Habib failed to get the ADF–LNM forces down from Sanin and the missiles out of Lebanon, he did persuade Begin to refrain from attacking them, as well as to abandon his demands that Assad remove missiles from *inside* the Syrian border and concede Israel's long-claimed "right to freedom of the Lebanese skies."

The Israeli–Palestine War

Begin did not confine his aggressions to the Bekaa and the north. In June his planes destroyed Iraq's nuclear reactor near Baghdad. And on July 10 he launched large-scale air, naval, and artillery attacks against Palestinians and Lebanese in southern Lebanon. These attacks followed on similar aggressions May 28 through June 3, to which the Palestinian response had been restrained. Five days after the July 10 aggression the PLO abandoned its restraint and shelled the Israeli town of Nahariya. Israel's response was to send its planes, gunboats, and artillery to blanket-bomb densely populated areas in the south, deliberately slaughtering fleeing women, children, and men, battering the port of Tyre, and setting Zahrani oil refinery ablaze. The Joint Forces fought back with the largest rocket barrages to date against northern Israel, forcing its inhabitants into shelters for the entire two weeks of the war. And on July 17 Israeli bombers struck at one of West Beirut's most heavily populated areas, the Arab University and two nearby refugee camps. For Beirutis this became Operation Infanticide, so many were the small children and infants among the more than 300 killed and 800 wounded.

The Joint Forces did not have an effective anti-aircraft network, yet they were the victors in the July battles. As Lebanon's UN delegate, Ghassan Tueni, emphasized, they were victorious militarily "because they resisted and survived and because Israel could not achieve its declared aim of destroying them."[20] The cease-fire which went into effect on July 25 constituted de facto Israeli recognition of the PLO, despite Israel's denials and Habib's inventive obfuscation that the truce was concluded "between Israeli territory and Lebanese territory." The pattern of Israeli attacks, Tueni warned, pointed directly to a future invasion to realize the frequent threats of Israeli generals to occupy all of south Lebanon.

The July 1981 cease-fire was an American–Saudi achievement, based on the understanding that its observance by Israel and the PLO would be guaranteed by both sponsors respectively. The PLO accepted the cease-fire, condemning it to virtual military paralysis, only under great pressures. Another achievement for Washington was that the Saudis implicitly assumed responsibility for bringing the Palestinians into line in attempts to make the cease-fire permanent. The Saudis understood that the United States in return would prevent Israeli attacks on Lebanon and the Palestinians. But this understanding proved to be mistaken. Washington's immediate aim was merely to strengthen UNIFIL, expand its zone of operations to include areas held by the Joint Forces, and halt the flow of arms to the Palestinians. This occurred while the United States still refused to talk to the Palestinians, or to recognize any Palestinian rights. By resuming war deliveries to Israel, after a sixty-eight-day suspension following Israel's destruction of Iraq's nuclear reactor, the United States virtually invited Israel to continue its attempts to liquidate the Palestinians.

Political Arrival of the Shi'as

The arrival on the political scene of Lebanon's nearly one million Shi'a Muslims for the first time in the country's history contributed indirectly to the undoing of Gemayel's ambitions. The Christian-dominated Lebanese state established in 1920 had driven the Shi'a community—which in Ottoman times had lived for the most part wherever it liked in Lebanon—into the poor and peripheral areas of the south and the Bekaa Valley. It was not until the beginnings of industrialization in the 1950s and the demand for cheap labor that Shi'as from these deprived areas could move into Beirut's southern suburbs, Shiah and Ghobeiri, where they soon constituted 75 percent of the country's industrial workforce. Later, Shi'as expelled from East Beirut during the 1975-76 civil war also settled in these suburbs, which developed as the power base of a community in the process of urbanizing.

By 1973, a nascent left-wing political movement, led by the small Lebanese communist parties, was gaining strength among the Shi'as. That year Shi'a leader Imam Sadr created his Movement of the Disinherited, dedicated to raising the living standards of *all* the deprived, not only the Shi'as. While an important purpose was protection for the population in the south, the main purpose of Sadr's group was to halt and reverse this leftward trend. The movement presented itself as being in the direct line of Shi'a tradition, going back to the early centuries of Islam when Shi'ism was the standard of social revolt against the Sunni ruling class, a political as well as a theological movement. Sadr's decision two years later, in July 1975, to establish a military and social movement called Amal, suggested that the Movement of the Disinherited had not achieved significant success in winning Shi'as away from the left parties. Sadr's explanation was that in Lebanon a movement without a militia could accomplish nothing.

The Amal Movement

Founded, according to its leaders, as a private social organization one-fifth of whose membership was originally Christian, Amal carried on the social welfare of the Movement of the Disinherited. A decade later it still had Christian members, though far fewer, according to Dr. Ghassan Siblani, a Lebanese University professor and a member of Amal's four-member presidential committee led by Nabih Berri. Siblani defined Amal as a "self-help" organization, with much of its work done by volunteers.[21]

Amal, which means Hope, is also the acronym for brigades of the Lebanese Resistance *(Af waj al-Muqawama al-Lubnaniyaa)*. As a military organization, its main goals were to oppose Israel's aggressions, and, later, to drive the Palestinian-LNM Joint Forces out of the south and to force the Shi'as out of the left parties and the LNM. By the early 1980s, although its leaders claimed it could mobilize 30,000 fighters, its maximum fighting strength was closer to 10,000, still an impressive number on the Lebanese scale, and roughly equivalent to the PLO fighters then in Lebanon.

During the 1975-76 civil war and until 1978 Amal and the Shi'a community had received substantial financial and political support from various sources, including al-Fatah, although Amal was then militarily incapable of fighting. This early Palestinian support did not prevent Amal in the years 1978-82 from repeatedly attacking Joint Forces militias in the south, in particular, the Iraqi-backed Arab Liberation Front (ALF), the Communist Party of Lebanon (CPL), and the Organization of Communist Action (OCA). Its moves against the ALF derived from the escalating Iran–Iraq conflict, as Ayatollah Khomeini marched toward power in Iran. Amal's attempt to undermine the communist parties and their secular orientation was—given the strength of these parties among the Shi'a poor and disadvantaged—an imperative if Amal was to reach its goal of monopoly representation of its community. Amal also stood with the government and the Lebanese Front in demanding that the Joint Forces withdraw from the south, as did a growing number of southerners who suffered increasingly from Israeli retaliation.

In its early years Amal made little progress in its efforts to wean Shi'as away from the left parties and the Palestinian resistance movement. Owing to Israel's escalating aggressions against the south, Amal later became more successful. As Western diplomats in the area pointed out, these Israeli aggressions were intended to turn the local population, once among the strongest supporters of the Palestinians and their Lebanese allies, against the Joint Forces. In these years many southerners fled the south: some 300,000 as of the summer of 1979, according to then Lebanese labor and social affairs minister,

Nazim Qadri. This figure included 100,000 driven out of Major Saad
Haddad's enclave either "because they refused to collaborate with the
Israeli invaders and their puppets or because they had allegiances the
Israelis didn't like."[22] A Palestinian leader, however, speaking of "the
insupportable situation of the population of south Lebanon," admitted
(in something of an understatement): "The Joint Forces have not
succeeded in establishing with the masses of the south the good
relations that would have permitted mobilizing the masses around
these forces."[23]

In the two years following Imam Sadr's mysterious disappearance
in Libya, from August of 1978 until 1980, when Nabih Berri became
its secretary general, Amal's leadership consisted chiefly of wealthy
men of religion; its base of the disinherited, a heterogenous collection
of families, clans, and pressure groups, flourished. Some of these were
dependent on one or another of the traditional Shi'a *ulema;* others had
ties with the Kataeb, which in this period was reported to have trained
some 600 Amal militiamen in its camps. Still others, following the rise
of Ayatollah Khomeini's revolutionary Shi'a movement in Iran, were
drawn to his banner. Some of these later settled in and around
Baalbek, a Syrian-controlled area that became a center for Lebanese
and non-Lebanese of this persuasion. The most important and dura-
ble of Amal's connections in this period, however, proved to be that
established with the Deuxième Bureau, a connection rooted in its
anticommunism and its armed opposition to the Palestinians, the
Lebanese National Movement, and the left in general.

Nabih Berri brought to Amal a seemingly more modern leadership.
In 1955-56 he was elected president of the General Students Union of
Lebanon, the first Shi'a to hold such a post. A graduate of the Arab
University, a French-educated lawyer, and a highly successful dia-
mond merchant in Sierra Leone, his birthplace, Berri was one of a
then-nascent class of Shi'a business and professional men that originally developed in emigration—chiefly in Africa—owing to their
exclusion from such fields in Lebanon by the dominant Maronite and
Sunni bourgeoisie. Unfavorable conditions in Africa in 1970s
prompted many Shi'a emigrants to return home, where they invested
their capital for the most part in real estate in Beirut's southern
suburbs, and later and to a lesser extent in industrial projects. Some
became engaged in a broad attempt to overcome their community's
backwardness by financing efforts to make education available to all
Shi'a young people, providing funds for the construction of schools

and for university and other scholarships. As a result, Shi'as since the early 1980s have constituted the largest single group graduating from Lebanon's universities; more recently a growing, if still very small, number of Shi'a women have become university students.[24]

These developments expressed and reinforced the determination of the rising class of Shi'a professional and business men to assume leadership of their community—Lebanon's largest—and achieve for it a commensurate place in the sectarian political system. Amal's frequent battles with the LNM and the Palestinian resistance movement in the south, West Beirut, and its suburbs—all areas of predominant Shi'a population—responded to this imperative. Amal, moreover, had become stronger owing in part to the help of the Lebanese army command, which at the end of the 1975–76 civil war had inducted many Shi'as into the army, and now seconded some of them to join Amal in its battles against the Joint Forces. Amal itself, however, unexpectedly faced a stronger opponent in 1981, when Yasir Arafat for the first time sent PLO units into battle in support of the smaller Joint Forces militias then under frequent attack by Amal. This meant that in a period when Israel and Bashir Gemayel's Christian army together were openly preparing an invasion to make war against the PLO and the LNM in Lebanon, the Lebanese left and the Palestinians were engaged in defending themselves against Amal attacks.

Following Amal's fourth congress early in April 1982, Nabih Berri explained the platform it adopted. This emphasized the imperative of achieving a common Lebanese, Syrian, and Palestinian stand and Lebanese unity on the basis of equality, liberty, and justice. The Amal movement, he insisted, was for "every dispossesed person," not only for Shi'as. Official Lebanese practice, he pointed out, "has always been that of equalizing between those who are needy and those who enjoy economic well-being; the Lebanese Front fights for the privileges of those at the top, Amal fights for the dispossessed." Challenging the Lebanese Front imperative, he stated Amal's conditions: the Front must end its dealings with Israel and Saad Haddad; must allow those driven from their homes to return; must drop its claim to represent all Christians and accept the fact that Christians opposed to the Front have a voice; must end confessional politics in Lebanon; must agree that equality and justice govern all inter-Lebanese dealings; and must abandon all ideas of partition. Berri characterized Amal as "a nationalist force," "a protector of the Palestinian revolution," and declared the liberation of Palestine to be its first duty.[25]

Such positions suggested that Amal and the LNM shared a certain common ground. But Amal used armed force in January of 1982 to prevent the application of the LNM's proposed—and sorely needed—security measures in West Beirut; and again, in April, Amal defeated a carefully prepared LNM project to hold elections for local councils that were intended to aid West Beirutis overcome the many war-imposed difficulties they faced. These events demonstrated that for Amal the issue was one of power.

Amal's drive to achieve exclusive representation of the Shi'a community inevitably reinforced the sectarian political system. Yet, as the military arm of the higher Shi'a Council, Amal was committed to the resolutions it adopted in 1977. While rejecting total secularism, these resolutions proclaimed the Council's support for modernization based on eradicating political sectarianism and for a democratic parliamentary republic in Lebanon.[26] This stand was at least verbally, not far from that taken by Kamal Jumblat, who called "at the present stage" not for secularism but for the elimination of both the sectarian political system and the sectarian allotment of public posts.

The issue at stake between Amal and what was left of the LNM was control of the south, where the LNM had long fought politically and militarily beside the Palestinians, and control of West Beirut, where the LNM had been more or less in command since 1975. (Israeli occupation of both areas in the summer of 1982 made Amal and the LNM on-and-off allies in efforts to oust the invaders and end the dominance of Israel's Lebanese allies in political life.)

Amal's efforts to win Shi'as away from the communist parties and the LNM in time proved successful, even though Amal made no real attempt to challenge the social order. Moreover, its practice of resorting to political legalisms (such as its insistence on deployment of the army in the south "even if it were 100 percent Maronite") was clearly a weapon against the left, the LNM, and the Palestinians. Amal found it useful to maintain the fiction of the state, however feeble, since the state would be the framework for any future dialogue among the sectarian communities, which Amal could attend, but from which the LNM and the left would be excluded. Moreover, in the south "the fiction of the state served as a rampart against the Palestinians."[27]

The Faltering National Movement

Under Kamal Jumblat's leadership the LNM represented a genuine popular movement dedicated to the total elimination of political sectarianism in the electoral system and in all public offices. Its defeat in the 1975–76 civil war and Jumblat's assassination, both at Syria's hands, dealt it a crippling blow. In Lebanese terminology, the LNM constituted "the left," a term used in Lebanon to designate any person or group opposed to the sectarian political system. The LNM was not "leftist" in the European sense of the term, and did not pretend to be. Only the two communist parties were "leftist" in this sense. In the political climate of the Kataeb-dominated Sarkis regime, and without Kamal Jumblat, the wide disparities among LNM member parties tending to go their own ways proved crippling.

The LNM did not repudiate Jumblat's 1975 reform program, which defined the conditions for building a modern democratic state, but it now advocated only a more equitable balance within the sectarian state and "support for the legitimate authorities" in the hope of strengthening these authorities against the Lebanese Forces' partitionist thrust. This hope did not materialize. In practice, the LNM gave priority to the defense of the Palestinian movement and the preservation of Lebanon's Arab identity. This was in a period when, as a result of the civil war's outcome, sectarianism was on the march and the need for social, economic, and political reform ever more urgent.

The selection of Walid Jumblat—Kamal's son, who had already become head of the Druse community—to lead the LNM in 1980 was intended to underscore the LNM's commitment to his father's legacy, which commanded respect far beyond the LNM, especially among independents. But Walid became the target of presidential palace intrigues designed to provoke frictions within the Druse community and to undermine his leadership; these intrigues compelled him to reaffirm his communal commitment.

A new LNM political charter, adopted on April 3, 1981, for the first time unequivocally defined its goal as "a united, democratic and secular Lebanon based on equality and social integration as opposed to a fascist, sectarian Lebanon based on discrimination, partition and dependence."[28] Bashir Gemayel's unification of the Maronite militias under his leadership in November 1980, which stripped the Sarkis regime of its last shred of authority, prompted this evolution in LNM policy. The new charter asserted LNM independence of both Syria and the Palestinian resistance movement in working for a Lebanese solution to the Lebanese crisis. It sounded a new note by claiming that reliance "on the present legitimate authorities" to achieve a political settlement was "impossible," and placed on these authorities "the greater part of the responsibility for the continuing ordeal of

Lebanon." Yet, in demanding that the government confront Israel's "isolationist plans for Lebanon," it pledged to support these authorities because "they symbolize the country's unity." Secularism in Lebanon is a revolutionary goal, but the LNM's adoption of this goal came too late to affect the accelerating crisis.

Absent from the new program was any demand for economic and social reform. This was astonishing in a period (1977–82) when internal production in real terms fell below that of 1974. The minimum wage depreciated sharply in value, more than a quarter of the active population emigrated, and 20 percent of the workforce was unemployed by 1978, a percentage that continued to rise thereafter. During this period, also, consumer prices increased fourfold, bringing a drastic fall in living standards while the profits of banking and commercial capitalists soared. The banking system—under foreign control since the Intra Bank crash in 1966—directed local savings abroad or into commercial activities. Soaring imports of consumer goods deprived Lebanese industries of their markets, and deindustrialization in the 1977–82 period proceeded apace. Industry imported 80 percent of its inputs, and produced at a rate 40 percent below that of 1974; importers won control of roughly half the internal market for industrial products. The profiteers of the 1977–82 period, as for the 1975–76 civil war, were the banking and commercial capitalists in highly profitable alliance with the military warlords throughout the country. This alliance directed a large part of local savings to investment outside of Lebanon and the rest to commercial activities alone in Lebanon.

All this went unchallenged by the LNM or any other political group. The LNM's neglect of social and economic reform reflected its order of priorities: the defense of the Palestinian resistance movement and the Arab identity of Lebanon came first and second, with social and economic reform taking third place. This order of priorities reflected the fact that the LNM lacked a homogeneous base, independent of the PLO.

Israel's Terrorist War

The LNM's alliance with the Palestinian resistance movement made it, the inhabitants of national areas, and the Palestinians the targets of an Israeli-directed war of terrorism that killed or maimed hundreds of civilians. The terrorist war, chiefly in the form of power-ful car bombs and other explosions, went into high gear in the summer and fall of 1981 and continued into the early weeks of Israel's 1982 invasion. In the three weeks from mid-September to mid-October of 1981 more than 130 people—Lebanese and Palestinians—were killed, and more than 400 wounded, all in LNM areas in Beirut. In southern Lebanon in the same period the toll was eighty-three Pales-tinians killed and 225 injured. Local surrogates of Israel carried out these operations. West Beirut and its environs had been infiltrated on a large scale, as cabinet member Marwan Hamade pointed out, with the aim of thwarting a LNM security drive then under way and destabilizing the opposition.[29]

This infiltration was facilitated by the almost incredible confusion caused by the presence of some fifty-eight armed organizations in West Beirut alone.[30] West Beirut paid the price of its increasingly anarchic atmosphere. In the early weeks of Israel's 1982 invasion, one Kataeb and two Haddad militiamen then captured publicly confessed they had planted a bomb in West Beirut in June which killed more than fifty people.[31] Propaganda issuing from Lebanese Front and Kataeb radio stations appeared to be skillfully coordinated with such explosions, sowing divisions among different groups, political and non-political. Lebanese security forces later reported that more than 60 percent of the car bombs that exploded in West Beirut before Israel's invasion were rigged in Saad Haddad's enclave in the south, then driven to East Beirut and at the moment desired planted in West Beirut.[32]

The no-war/no-peace state prevailing since the civil war's end made ever more difficult the LNM's search for an effective strategy to confront the problems issuing from that unresolved war. For Syria's 1976 rescue of the sectarian state had arrested secular currents at a time when patron–client relations, interwoven with kinship and sec-tarian loyalties, were reinvigorated by the importance these webs of relations had assumed for survival. Until the Syrian intervention, the banner of political secularism had been on the rise under the LNM, and the LNM's own evolution toward horizontal, class-based political relations appeared to be slowly advancing. The LNM's demoralizing defeat at the hands of the Syrian army contributed to regenerating the traditional currents within the LNM, and to the failure of some of its constituent organizations to overcome essentially tribal structures which inhibited the development and practice of internal democracy.

Eruptions of armed clashes among its own organizations, as well as between these and other groups, indicated the continuing importance of such allegiances.

The LNM's refusal to usurp governmental prerogatives in the hope of strengthening the government against the Lebanese Front's partitionist thrust meant that large areas under its control, deprived of government services, received little if any help from the LNM. The LNM therefore did not secure the relations of confidence with the people of its areas that such a sorely needed effort to improve security and daily life could have produced. The LNM's military function was thus enhanced at the expense of the political, a situation underscored by LNM inability to put an end to the irresponsible, trigger-happy behavior of some of its diverse parties.

The LNM's structure was a "Big Five" of more-or-less authentic political parties (the Progressive Socialist Party, the Communist Party of Lebanon, the Organization for Communist Action, the Syrian Social Nationalist Party, and the Independent Nasserist Movement), plus a variety of small groups mainly financed by and owing some degree of allegiance to external powers. Such groups compromised the LNM in the eyes of the people whose needs and concerns did not rate highly in their priorities. This was a dramatic change from the earlier period, when the Palestinian resistance movement and the LNM stimulated a progressive conscience among the people, giving support to popular demands for social and economic reforms and so decisively helping to erode the power of traditional *zuama* and the army's Deuxième Bureau.

The people of West Beirut, the most important LNM area, experienced both the advantages and disadvantages of an open society. At one level, this society was democratic, permitting many freedoms and a wide diversity of opinion. In West Beirut alone, in addition to establishment newspapers and magazines, some thirty-nine "illegal" (uncensored) publications and several party radio stations offered news and comment. Lebanese Front publications devoted mainly to pillorying the LNM and the Palestinians could be bought at almost any news stand, although East Beirut banned LNM publications.

At another level near-chaos prevailed, since LNM attempts to establish order were not successful. Militarily the LNM was outweighed by both Syria and the Palestinian resistance movement; politically, as Syria's ally, the LNM had to contend with the ambiguities of Assad's policy in Lebanon. Assad's sights were focused on a coming Middle East settlement. This priority dictated his maintaining an army in Lebanon and his tutelage over the Palestinian resistance movement and the LNM, as well as his avoidance of any decisive action against the Lebanese Front that could provoke Israeli intervention. Rational as this policy might be from Damascus' point of view, it resulted in what many Lebanese perceived as a seemingly endless cycle of indecisive battles between the Arab Deterrent Force and the Lebanese Front. These aroused popular resentment and inevitably reflected on Syria's ally, the LNM.

In the 1977–82 period, the active opposition included mainly the Muslim communities—Druse, Shi'a, and Sunni—as well as the secular parties, the CPL, OCA, and Baath, and a number of Christian personalities (notably the Maronites Raymond Edde and Suleiman Franjieh and Albert Mansour, a Greek Catholic). But battles between the different opposition parties in the 1979–81 period, especially between Amal and the communists, as well as non-political clashes, contributed greatly to the disarticulation of the LNM. So did the fact that in practice not a few of the LNM parties succumbed in one degree or another to the sectarian disease, as each tried to establish control over its "own" area demarcated by sectarian criteria.

"Countdown for Liberation"

Recurrent battles in national areas prompted Bashir Gemayel to hail what he called "Amal's uprising against the Palestinians" as "another Ain-Remaneh" (the incident that touched off the 1975 civil war). Bashir launched his drive for the presidency on November 29, 1981. Early in December Israel annexed Syria's Golan and later imposed a tight blockade on Druse villages there. And, during the second week of January, Bashir Gemayel served as escort for Israeli Defense Minister Ariel Sharon and his entourage on a "secret visit" to East Beirut to plan the Lebanese Forces role in Sharon's projected invasion. On March 20, 1982, Gemayel boasted that "the Christian people of Lebanon" were preparing "to take a serious decision bearing on the country's future." He did not bother to conceal the fact that the decision concerned "collaboration of the Maronite people" with Israel in an invasion of Lebanon. *Al-Nahar* pointed out that a Kataeb military offensive against national forces would have little chance of success unless it was coordinated with an Israeli invasion of the south. American press and radio reports concerning a probable Israel invasion thereafter proliferated. And in New York, the United States vetoed a UN Security Council resolution condemning Israel's annexation of the Golan.

Early in April of 1982, Gemayel's Lebanese Forces held an "international conference" in Beit Meiri in the mountains behind Beirut. Some 130 delegates from abroad (North, Central, and South America, Australia, and several European countries), six Lebanese cabinet ministers, and many Lebanese political figures heard Gemayel announce that "the countdown for liberation" (from Syria and the PLO) "has begun." Not all delegates applauded Gemayel's thesis. Some provoked his anger by urging a Lebanese–Palestinian reconciliation. His constant talk for many months before as well as during the conference about "the Christian people of Lebanon" and about his militia as "the symbol of Christian nationalism," "the guarantee of Maronite power," and so on alienated so many that his brother, Amin, found it necessary to assure delegates that Bashir had no intention to partition Lebanon. The president of the American Lebanese League, Robert Barid, moreover assured them that United States policy "was no longer one of containing violence but was based on a strong Lebanese state." And, as if to underscore this assertion, leading American radio networks for two nights' running discussed multiplying reports of an imminent Israel invasion. A few days later, Bashir Gemayel hailed fierce fighting between Amal and the Joint Forces in both West Beirut and the south as "an uprising against the Palestinians," and offered to place his forces at Shi'a disposal. Amal ignored this offer.

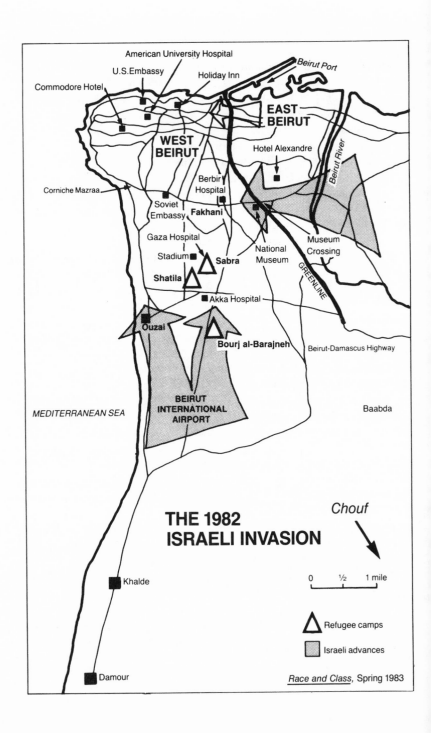

American University Hospital

U.S. Embassy

Holiday Inn

Beirut Port

Commodore Hotel

EAST BEIRUT

Hotel Alexandre

WEST BEIRUT

Beirut River

Corniche Mazraa

Berbir Hospital

Soviet Embassy

Fakhani

Gaza Hospital

Museum Crossing

Stadium

Sabra

National Museum

Shatila

GREENLINE

Akka Hospital

Ouzai

Bourj al-Barajneh

Beirut-Damascus Highway

BEIRUT INTERNATIONAL AIRPORT

Baabda

MEDITERRANEAN SEA

Chouf

THE 1982 ISRAELI INVASION

0   ½   1 mile

Khalde

△ Refugee camps

▪ Israeli advances

Damour

Race and Class, Spring 1983

[18]

The Summer of 1982: David and Goliath

The Invasion

On June 5, 1982, Israel launched its long-threatened invasion of Lebanon "with the total accord of the United States," according to Israeli Foreign Minister Yitzhak Shamir.[1] Israeli Defense Minister Ariel Sharon told Israeli TV on June 6 that American officials he saw in Washington in May "understood we had no choice but to strike." Yet the Palestine Liberation Organization (PLO) had strictly observed the cease-fire of July 24, 1981, and absolute calm had prevailed on the Lebanese–Israeli border ever since.

A peaceful border, however, was not the issue preoccupying Israeli decision-makers. Their objective was to exterminate Palestinian nationalism in the West Bank and Gaza by destroying the Palestinian infrastructure in Lebanon—a Palestinian state-in-embryo—and so once again disperse the Palestinian people. Israel's heavy-handed repression and the intensifying persecution of Palestinians in the West Bank and Gaza had failed to stem the rising tide of Palestinian nationalism. Thus from the outset the target of the invasion was West Beirut, where the Palestinian infrastructure was centered; Israel merely called it "the nerve center of international terrorism.' "[2] Western intelligence sources from the beginning identified West Beirut as the Israeli goal, and revealed that the whole operation was to have been successfully concluded within a week.[3]

Three months later, Israel's army was still stalled outside West Beirut. In the south it had by then partially destroyed and thoroughly looted the cities of Tyre, Sidon, and Nabatiye; had razed seven Palestinian refugee camps, destroying the homes of some 111,000 Palestinians and Lebanese; and had "wiped out the United Nations

275

Relief and Work Agency's work of 32 years, leaving all schools, clinics, and installations of the agency in ruins."[4] In all, the southern operations killed 20,000 or more and wounded double that number, while herding 15,000 into two concentration camps (one near Nabatiye, the other in Israel); some 600,000 people were left without shelter. Israel denied Palestinians prisoner-of-war status, asserting it would try them as criminals.[5] According to the eyewitness testimony of foreign doctors, themselves imprisoned for a time, Israel had beaten some Palestinian prisoners to death, left others to die for lack of food and water in the summer heat, and killed sixty to eighty under torture.[6]

Israel repeatedly used phosphorus rockets and cluster bombs against civilian concentrations in the south and in West Beirut, in violation of both the United States–Israel Mutual Defense Agreement of 1952 and the 1961 Arms Export Act.[7] The acid in phosphorus bombs burns through skin, tissues, muscles, and organs, causing bodies of victims to smolder, puffs of smoke often issuing from lungs. Water intensifies the burning. Survival is possible only if burning is confined to limbs that can be amputated.

The so-called concussion bomb Israel introduced in Lebanon causes buildings to collapse inwards, flattening large buildings in seconds. Such a bomb—used against an eight-story residential building in the Sanayeh gardens on August 7, on the pretext that PLO leader Yasir Arafat might be inside—killed some 250 people, mostly women and children. Of the fourteen such bombs given to Israel by the United States, seven were used in Lebanon (three in West Beirut and one in Sidon) but three of the seven did not explode.[8]

The chief target of these and other weapons was the civilian population: hospitals, hotels harboring the overflow of wounded, medical clinics, and institutions; any building flying the Red Cross or Red Crescent flag; Palestinian refugee camps, many of which were almost completely destroyed; residential districts; the southern suburbs where most of the working class lives; schools, orphanages, and government and PLO offices. In West Beirut, where 1 to 4 percent of the population could be considered combatants, at least 80 percent of casualties were civilians, both Lebanese and Palestinian. Use of such weapons accounts for the exceptionally high proportion of wounded who died: two deaths for every three wounded, compared to a normal ratio of one death for every four wounded.[9] In Tyre, Israeli bombardments destroyed or severely damaged four hospitals and eleven schools; in Sidon, nine hospitals and sixteen schools.[10] In the shelter of one school, some 150 civilians, many of them children, were killed. Robert Fisk reported in the London *Times:*

> The bodies lay on top of each other to a depth of perhaps six feet, their arms and legs wrapped around each other, well over 100 of them, congealed into a strangely unnatural mass.[11]

Later in West Beirut Israel demonstrated its ability to rip open shelters in cellars and underground car parks by firing its rockets at the base of buildings. In Sidon, Tyre, and Nabatiye, Israel closed down all Palestine Red Crescent Society (PRCS) hospitals, closed down all clinics and dispensaries in the refugee camps, and arrested all PRCS medical teams.

Four of West Beirut's five large hospitals—Barbir (almost totally destroyed), Maqasid, and the PRCS Gaza and Akka hospitals on the edge of the Sabra and Shatila refugee camps—were severely damaged. Gaza hospital, called by Israel "a military target," was so often and so savagely attacked that it had to be evacuated. Only the American hospital, the largest, was for the most part spared bombardment by American-made bombs. In the government-funded Islamic Psychiatric Hospital in South Beirut, 400 out of 800 patients remained because they had no place else to go; they lacked both food and care, owing to the frequent heavy bombardments which prevented the arrival of government funds and staff. In the Dar al-Ajaza Hospital for the mentally handicapped, the walls of three wards were partially destroyed, water and food was almost unobtainable, and some of the most severely handicapped children—kept in a basement and suffering severe malnutrition—were dying at the rate of two or three a day. Nine Israeli bombing raids on June 10 and 11 destroyed the year-old Development Organization for Human Abilities (DOHA) Center at Aramoun south of Beirut, which in normal times cared for 650 blind, deaf, physically handicapped, and mentally retarded children. American-donated cluster bombs were used in this attack.[12] Israeli bombardments from the sea also destroyed the DOHA's orphanage at Ouzai.

Israel adopted the strategy of waging war against the civilian population when it realized—as it quickly did—the high cost of attempting to take West Beirut by storm, which was apparently its original intention.[13] By making the civilian population its main target and by imposing a total blockade of the city, Israel expected to inflict so much suffering on and so terrorize West Beirut's civilians that they would turn against their Palestinian and Lebanese defenders.

Not more than 15,000 Palestinian and Lebanese National Movement (LNM) fighters defended the city against the combined forces of Israel and its Lebanese Maronite allies, which by June 13 had completely surrounded West Beirut. An Israeli takeover of the Green Line on July 3 drew the noose tighter.

The Blockade

The blockade began on June 13, when Israeli warships prevented the arrival of hundreds of tons of Red Cross medical supplies for West Beirut, which was already under almost daily bombardment, and doctors, nurses, and other medical personnel were denied entry to the city. Some 150 doctors and nurses were turned back during the siege, but others managed to reach the city by unofficial routes. West Beirut is totally dependent for its water and electricity on East Beirut, where the pumping station and distribution centers are located. Electricity and water, earlier turned off for relatively short periods, were completely cut off on July 4 and 5 and remained so until the end of the siege. (Occasionally water would be restored for an hour or two, periods too brief to make much difference.) Fuel, medicine, medical supplies of all kinds, staple and fresh foods, soft drinks, alcoholic beverages, all were barred entry into West Beirut.

Without fuel, garbage could not be collected. Without electricity, medicine, and water, hospitals could not adequately care for the sick and the wounded. Many surgical operations became impossible owing to inadequate lighting, the impossibility of sterilizing syringes and instruments, or for lack of instruments. The need to re-use syringes, dressings, and so on, the impossibility of washing gloves, dressings, sheets, clothes, or even of keeping hospital premises clean—all these contributed to the hazzards facing the wounded and to the high death rate.

The Israeli siege caused much suffering, but it did not succeed either in breaking the spirit of West Beirutis or in turning them against the Palestinian and LNM defenders of the city. People were free to leave if and when they wished, and many did so, often only to return in periods of relative calm. Rough estimates of the number who left vary between 100,000 and 200,000 out of a population of 500,000. Israel's psychological warfare—its mock air attacks, dire warnings and threats in radio broadcasts, and in leaflets dropped from planes urging Beirutis to flee or meet certain death—evoked fear among some but, as often as not, derision and scorn. On the whole West Beirut met Israel's all-too-real bombardments from air, sea, and land with fortitude mixed with fatalism.

The efficiency, dedication, and élan with which the PLO, the LNM, and other popular organizations working together to meet the emergencies created by the siege contributed much to the solidarity that developed among fighters, their active supporters, and the general population.

During the siege's first week the Red Cross, the Lebanese Committee for Popular Action (Amel), and LNM medical personnel set up more than twenty small "hospitals" or clinics with a bare minimum of equipment in basements near heavily bombarded districts. Owing to the devotion of their all-volunteer staffs, as well as the help provided by foreign nurses and medical personnel, also volunteers, this effort proved remarkably successful. Set up close to—sometimes in—areas suffering the most punishing attacks, the ability of these units to provide immediate care to the wounded saved many lives.

The PLO and the LNM also undertook to provide shelter, food, and water for those experiencing deprivation as a result of the blockade, and for the thousands made homeless by Israel's bombardments by air and sea as well as by mortar fire, rockets, and sniping from Israel's Lebanese allies close by. Dividing the city into six districts, the PLO and the LNM established a central refugee center in each district. These centers found shelter—or at least a place to camp out—in safer districts for many of the homeless. The PLO supplied the refugee centers with staple foods (flour, beans, canned meat, sardines, and the like from its stockpiles) to be distributed to the needy. Similar assistance was given, when possible, to the few hospitals still operating. At times, the PLO managed to get fresh fruits and vegetables into the city by paying bribes at Kataeb and Israeli checkpoints. When supplies permitted, a part of this food was sold on the market to relieve the plight of the ordinary citizen. Before the end of the siege, however, Israeli troops tightened controls and so ended the occasional import of fresh food into the city.

Except during periods of the heaviest bombardments, the PLO also managed to operate bakeries located in or near the refugee camps.

Working twenty-four hours a day, these bakeries fed many in such areas, civilians as well as fighters. Part of the benzine and fuel-oil supplies stockpiled by the PLO before the invasion was used for its own vehicles; the rest was given to hospitals to power generators or pumps. Together the PLO and the LNM tried to find and supply water to those most in need by digging some 150 new wells and reopening old ones; they also bought oil-operated generators (necessary in the absence of electricity), attaching these to cars in order to pump water into buildings that had wells.

Many volunteers participated in these and a host of other activities: cleaning hospital premises; helping to feed the wounded unable to feed themselves; providing physical therapy for the injured; holding classes and organizing other activities to keep children occupied and as far as possible out of danger; collecting and keeping records of all possible information on Israel's treatment of prisoners and civilians; and so on. As result, a remarkable feeling of solidarity developed between fighters, their active supporters, and the civilian population, and a high morale prevailed throughout the siege.

The Enemy Within

The Israeli Defense Force (IDF), ranked fourth in the world by Israeli General Ariel Sharon, enjoyed overwhelming superiority in men, arms, and equipment, as well as the advantage of collaboration by sectors of the Lebanese population as well as members of the government. Although the Lebanese cabinet at the start of the invasion called on the army to oppose the aggression by all means at its disposal, Gemayel and Commander-in-Chief Khoury failed to order the army to resist; it remained in its barracks throughout the invasion.[14] The president neither protested nor condemned Israel's blockade of West Beirut, or its use of outlawed weapons of mass destruction to devastate large parts of the capital and to kill or maim hundreds of Lebanese as well as Palestinians. He did not even protest Israel's occupation of Baabda, the seat of the presidential palace.

Part of the population of East Beirut welcomed the aggressors with flowers and kisses, and in the south that part of the Shi'a population in and around Major Saad Haddad's army collaborated, these gangs moving in under Israeli protection to kidnap and kill Palestinians and their Lebanese allies. Israel's rapid advance in the south owed much to the weight of its offensive but also something to the flight—on the first day—of the Joint Forces' Sidon-based southern commander, the PLO's Haj Ismail, and the consequent inability of the Joint Forces to coordinate efficiently their defense. To make matters worse, the PLO's South Bekaa commander, Abu Hajem, also fled on the first day. (Arafat's later appointments of the former to command the Tripoli area and of the latter once again in the Bekaa—both men widely known as corrupt and incompetent—was one of the grievances that contributed to the split in al-Fatah that erupted into the open in May 1983).

On June 15 the Israeli cabinet approved the Lebanese Forces' participation in the invasion. And, although Bashir Gemayel reportedly rejected a demand by Israeli Prime Minister Menachem Begin that his men assume the task of invading West Beirut, the Lebanese Forces and other rightist militias acted during and after the invasion as auxiliaries of the IDF, kidnapping, torturing, and often summarily executing their victims. Moreover, a plan long cherished by Gemayel, described as a "cleansing" or "purification" of the Sabra and Shatila refugee camps in south Beirut, was now put on the Israeli–Lebanese Forces' agenda. The inspiration for this operation was the Deir Yassin massacre of April 9–10, 1948, when Begin's Irgun killed 254 defenseless inhabitants of this Palestinian village and so provoked the panic flight of more than 600,000 Palestinians living in what became Israel. "On several occasions," *Time* reported, "Gemayel told Israeli officials he would like to raze the camps and turn them into tennis courts." Gemayel, who initially planned to use his troops in West Beirut, according to *Time,* had sent 500 of them to Israel in early 1982 for special training. These troops were selected for "cleansing" the Sabra and Shatila refugee camps, where Sharon insisted "2,000 terrorists" were hiding.[15]

Implementation of this plan required the prior ouster of Palestinian fighters from West Beirut. The steadfastness of both its civilian population and its defenders made this no easy task. Yet almost from the start of the invasion the PLO realized its departure would sooner or later become inevitable. The almost total inaction of other Arab governments—as well as the near absence of popular Arab demonstrations in their support in these countries—confirmed this perception. The PLO fought on in order to exact a high price from Israel, to ensure its own ability to fight again, and to secure guarantees for the safety of the Palestinian population in Lebanon.

By the last week of June 1982 the PLO agreed in principle to leave the city. This was part of a "peace plan" negotiated by U.S. President Reagan's national security adviser, William Clark, and a "special situation group" through Saudi King Fahd with Arafat in Beirut. The plan, however, was promptly abandoned at the insistence of then U.S. Secretary of State Alexander Haig, who instructed Philip Habib "to represent the maximalist Israeli position as official United States policy," an order against which Habib reportedly submitted an official protest.[16] Thereafter, Reagan put heavy pressures on the PLO to make further concessions while applying none at all on Israel. And in the last week of July and first twelve days of August, Israel subjected all parts of West Beirut to the most punishing bombardments of the war. The most devastating took place on August 12, when a negotiated settlement was already virtually achieved.

The War Ends

On August 13 the war ended with the agreement on a plan for evacuating Palestinian fighters. And in the last week of August, according to U.S. counts of actual departures, 8,300 Palestinian fighters and 3,600 Palestine Liberation Army (PLA) and Syrian troops left Lebanon. Once the PLO fighters had been evacuated, there were no military forces in the camps, as *Time* correspondent Robert Suro, who visited Sabra and Shatila a few days before the massacres, confirmed.[17]

The agreement negotiated by Habib with the PLO on the departure of its fighters contained American guarantees for the future safety of the half-million Palestinians living in Lebanon, as well as a firm statement of Washington's opposition to Israel's entry into West Beirut, including the camps. And on August 25 some 800 American Marines arrived in Beirut to constitute with French and Italian contingents a multinational force (MNF) to supervise the PLO withdrawal and to assure the protection of the Palestinians remaining in Lebanon. The MNF, which was scheduled to remain until September 26, departed on September 13—as if its mission had been accomplished when the PLO evacuation was completed. In so doing, it unilaterally repudiated the second part of its mission: the protection of Palestinian and other civilians.

Death of a President

Two days before the MNF's arrival, Bashir Gemayel had been elected president of Lebanon in an Israeli stage-managed election as farcical as that of Elias Sarkis directed by Syria in 1976. Relations between the president-elect and his Israeli sponsors, however, did not develop smoothly. Conflict arose over Gemayel's reluctance to conclude a peace treaty as demanded by Israel. Such a treaty would spell economic and political disaster for a Lebanon highly dependent both on its transit trade with the Arab world and on the sale of its own industrial and agricultural products to Arab countries, as well as on Arab tourism. Moreover, the Maronite business and upper class would be among those most adversely affected. Summoned to a secret meeting with Begin, Sharon, and Israeli Foreign Minister Yitzhak Shamir in northern Israel on September 1, Gemayel rejected their pressures to change his mind and was reportedly outraged because the Israeli leaders treated him disrespectfully. When Sharon, two days later, leaked an account of the "secret meeting" to the press, a furious Gemayel hastened to meet with Saeb Salam to declare that only parliament could decide the question of a treaty. Gemayel then started to call for the withdrawal of *all* foreign troops from Lebanon. And Sharon, in turn, threatened in the absence of a peace treaty to establish an Israeli security zone in south Lebanon, in which Saad Haddad would have the leading role.

In the late afternoon of September 14, Gemayel and some thirty of his associates were killed by a powerful bomb explosion in the Lebanese Forces' Ashrafiyya headquarters where Forces leaders met weekly. Absent from this meeting were Elias Hobeika, leader of the Lebanese Forces' extreme pro-Israeli faction and the man in charge of Gemayel's security, and Fadi Frem, who had on Gemayel's election to the presidency succeeded him as Lebanese Forces commander. The street word in both East and West Beirut pointed to Israel and the extreme pro-Israel faction of the Lebanese Forces as the assassins. Contrary to its usual behavior in such matters the Kataeb accused no one and, moreover, arrested hundreds of its own members.[18] And, when the Kataeb later revealed that it held in custody the man who had planted the bomb, it refused to allow him to be questioned by government authorities or to reveal the results of its own investigation.

The assassination, following on the heels of the MNF's departure, provided Begin and Sharon with the pretext to order the IDF to move immediately into West Beirut and surround the Sabra and Shatila camps. Israel's entry into West Beirut violated commitments given by Israel in the Habib agreement. Two earlier violations of the agreement—its movement into Bir Hassan to establish observation posts overlooking the Sabra and Shatila camps, and its failure both to withdraw its troops from the outskirts of West Beirut and to cease use of the airport—proved to be the preparatory stage for its third violation, the drive into West Beirut and the encirclement of the two Palestinian camps. LNM militias, who had accepted as binding the American guarantees and Israel's pledges that it would not enter West Beirut, had in the previous fortnight withdrawn from most of their positions and removed their barricades. The staunch resistance some LNM defenders managed to put up in a few districts could not halt the Israeli advance. By noon on September 16 Israeli troops had occupied West Beirut.

Sabra and Shatila

Only hours after the explosion that killed Bashir Gemayel, at a 3 a.m. meeting on Wednesday, September 16, Israeli Chief of Staff Rafael Eytan and IDF Commander General Amir Drori, in a meeting with Elias Hobeika, Fadi Frem, and other Lebanese Forces leaders, planned the "mopping-up" of the alleged terrorists in the camps. Hobeika, who personally supervised the Kataeb massacre of some 3,000 Palestinians and Lebanese in the Tel al-Zaatar refugee camp in East Beirut in 1976, was chosen to lead this mission.[19] Hobeika's unit in the Kataeb had never participated in battles. Its specialty was massacre, as Israeli leaders knew well.

Two hours after this meeting Israeli planes started making low-level flights over the camps, which later in the day were also subjected to artillery and tank shelling. The first wounded were brought to Gaza hospital around noon, and at this time camp inhabitants learned that Israeli troops were surrounding the camps and setting up check points. The rapidity with which the IDF and its closest Lebanese Forces allies exploited Gemayel's assassination lent credence to the rumor that the Israelis and Hobeika's extremist pro-Israel faction had killed him. Israeli leaders certainly knew exactly what the Hobeika–Fadi Frem forces had in mind. General Eytan told an Israeli cabinet meeting on the evening of September 15: "I see in their eyes what they [the Kataeb] are waiting for. It is enough that Amin Gemayel used the word revenge and the whole lot of them were already sharpening their knives."[20] At a meeting of top Israeli commanders with Hobeika and Frem the next day, both emphasized that a "Kasach" (slicing) operation would be carried out in the camps.[21]

Israeli forces prepared the staging area for the Kataeb murder squads which assembled under its auspices at the airport on the afternoon of September 16. Israeli paratroopers were ordered to facilitate their entry into the camps.[22] The Israeli Defense Force (IDF) supplied these squads with aerial photographs and maps of the camps and with other essential assistance during the operation, in- cluding issuing loudspeaker orders in Arabic to camp inhabitants, resupplying militias, and, on the second day, allowing reinforcements to enter the camps; this insured a new wave of killings on Friday afternoon. Moreover, as Shimon Lehrer, IDF reserve commander and jurist, has recently documented, the IDF command post 200 meters from the camp had received information that a massacre was under- way just after the beginning of the slaughter the day before.[23] The IDF command post did nothing to stop the slaughter when it first received the information on Thursday, and on the second day actively assisted it, permitting fresh reinforcements of killers to enter the camps.

IDF–Lebanese Forces radio contact was maintained throughout the massacre. During the night of September 16 Israeli troops fired flares at the rate of two a minute to light up the killing ground. These flares were clearly visible from many parts of Beirut, including the Amer- ican embassy which, however, betrayed no curiosity about this matter. The *New Statesman's* Claudia Wright reported that Reagan and other American officials also knew of the carnage in time to stop it but chose not to do so; Israel had identified the victims as "terrorists."[24]

The carnage was carried out in forays: one murder squad entered the camps and after a round of killing returned to relax—in some cases, to eat and drink with Israeli soldiers just outside—while another squad entered to continue the slaughter. This mode of operation in itself—small squads of militias equipped with knives, hatchets, axes, and rifles entering the camps in rotation to make house-to-house searches—reveals that the killers knew well that there were no terrorists in the camps, let alone 2,000 of them.

The victims of Israel's version of the "final solution" were killed not only by shooting but also—especially at the beginning so as not to alert other parts of the camps—by knives, axes, and hatchets; their throats were slit, their bellies ripped open. Even children were often tortured before they were killed. Some were dragged behind cars before being dispatched. One young man was tied to a wooden door and burned alive. At 11 o'clock Thursday night, Hobeika reported to the IDF Command in Beirut that "until now 300 civilians and terrorists have been killed." Twenty senior officers in Tel Aviv, as well as the Israeli command in Beirut, saw this report, but not one moved to stop the slaughter.[25]

The sector of the camps where the greater part of the killing occurred was clearly visible from the top of Israel's seven-story command post nearby, as anyone who bothered to go there could testify. Israel's Kahan Commission appointed to investigate the massacre did not visit the site (the IDF had by then withdrawn from Beirut), nor did it hear testimony from Palestinians or Lebanese. Also in plain sight of the command post was the ditch dug by the Lebanese Forces into which bulldozers (lent by the IDF to the Forces after all IDF identification markings had been removed) dumped hundreds of bodies. Bulldozers also razed houses and so buried the bodies of many victims in rubble. This was of great importance, permitting Israel, along with its agents and friends, to deliberately minimize the number slaughtered. Significantly, too, as Shimon Lehrer revealed, it was a representative of Mossad (Israel's external intelligence service) who recommended the loan of the bulldozers, and who also took part in all contacts concerning the operations of the Kataeb and the Lebanese Forces in the camps. Lehrer also pointed out that "the Kataeb command might well have received the impression"—from General Eytan's remarks during a meeting with Fadi Frem on the second day of the slaughter—"that they were free to continue their operation in the camps without interference until Saturday morning."[26]

Israeli soldiers stationed around the camps could not have been blind to the loads of bodies hauled away, or to the killings themselves.

But if protest there was, it was discouraged. An Israeli tank commander who reported to his commanding officer that he had seen the killing of five women and children in Shatila was told "not to worry."[27]

The massacre continued until around 9 a.m. the next morning (Saturday), when militias took survivors to the Israeli-controlled sports stadium where they were dealt with harshly, and where some were also killed. Killing also continued in Sabra, where reporters entering the camp around 10 a.m. saw among the heaps of corpses people whom they had passed early that morning. Perhaps most damning for Israel was the fact that its soldiers turned back, or blocked the way of, people trying to escape from the camps. The International Commission, citing specific cases, concluded:

> Israeli soldiers seemed to be operating under orders not to allow any inhabitants of the camps to escape, despite Israeli awareness that civilians were being killed in large numbers and that a massacre of some sort was under way.[28]

Even had there been 2,000 terrorists, as Israel and its Kataeb allies pretended, their presence would not have justified Israel's entry into West Beirut and the camps in violation of the Habib agreement. There were, in fact, no terrorists, no military personnel whatever in the camps, as both Israeli and Kataeb leaders knew. Had PLO fighters remained, the Lebanese Forces and the IDF would not have dared to carry out their "final solution." The International Commission stated that it "does not believe that Israeli Intelligence, which had manifestly accepted the numbers of departing PLO fighters as accurate, could have subsequently estimated in good faith that such a large number of fighters remained." The International Commission stated the most conclusive evidence of the intentional deceit of the Israeli and Kataeb allegations about the "2,000 terrorists":

> There was absolutely no resistance to the massacres. . . . The militiamen suffered virtually no casualties in their execution of the massacres . . . there were no signs of even the slightest resistance . . . an Oxfam field worker cites a sporting pellet gun lying beside the corpse of a young boy as epitomizing the total defenselessness of the camp population.[29]

In a Saudi Arabian television interview September 21, Yasir Arafat declared that more than 3,200 Palestinians were killed but that the exact number could not be determined because "most of the bodies were buried in the rubble of houses razed by bulldozers." As near as could be determined, he added, 1,800 people had been killed in the two camps themselves, another 1,099 died in Gaza hospital, and 400 more in Akka hospital. The gist of Arafat's interview was published in Beirut's *Middle East Reporter* the next day. The availability of this information did not prevent persistent efforts in both Lebanon and the West to minimize the number of victims. For months both the Lebanese and Western press spoke of "*only* 300 killed," though the figure was later raised to between 800 and 1,200. The 300 figure corresponds to that given by Hobeika to the IDF command in Beirut when the slaughter had just begun. It was also close to the number of bodies identified and buried by the International Red Cross: 302. Certain Lebanese government sources, who felt it necessary in the prevailing climate to remain anonymous, tried to correct the "*only* 300" refrain, giving these figures to the press: of 762 bodies found inside the two camps, 212 were buried in common ditches and not identified, and 302 were identified and buried by the International Red Cross. Another 1,300 bodies were taken away by relatives and buried privately, making a total of 2,062 massacred.[30] A respected and well-known Israeli journalist, Amon Kapeliouk, after a careful investigation, found the number killed to be between 3,000 and 3,500, 700–800 of whom were Lebanese.[31]

The Kahan Commission

In an analysis of the report made on the massacre by Israel's official Kahan Commission, Kapeliouk underscored the admission that "all forces operating inside the camps were under the authority of the IDF and acting according to its directives." Among the documents included in the report, he cited one issued by the Ministry of Defense on September 16, 1982, which stated that the Kataeb would be sent into the camps and that "only one element, and that element is the Israeli army, will command the forces on the terrain." Another document quoted the chief of military information as explaining: "This means that all forces on the ground including the Kataeb are under the authority of the IDF and acting under its directives."[32]

The Kahan report admitted that Kataeb leaders did not hide the fact that violence would be necessary to provoke the flight of the Palestinians from Lebanon, and noted that Bashir Gemayel had spoken of "resorting to extreme means" to "liquidate" the Palestinian problem. The report also conceded that Israel knew of earlier massacres committed by the Kataeb under Hobeika's direction, pointing out that these earlier massacres had reinforced the belief of Israel's most experienced intelligence officers that the Kataeb would seize "the slightest occasion to massacre the Palestinians." Knowing all this, the IDF and Mossad planned with Hobeika and his men the "purification" operation in the camps and cooperated in its execution.

The government of Amin Gemayel, elected to replace his assassinated brother, has never admitted in any way that the massacre was a crime. Following Israel's appointment of the Kahan Commission, the Lebanese government appointed a committee to investigate the massacre. Nothing was heard of the work of this committee—if any—until June of 1983, when the Kataeb news agency *al-Markaziah* reported that it had cleared the Kataeb of any involvement and that there would be no prosecutions. If such a report existed, it was never made public. Meanwhile Fadi Frem had become a welcome guest at high-society functions in East Beirut. Elias Hobeika more discretely transferred his operations to the south, returning to East Beirut only toward the end of 1983. But the calvary of the Palestinians in Lebanon did not end with the massacres.

Aftermath: The Effect in Israel

The Israeli invasion did not succeed in annihilating the PLO. As *Newsweek*'s Tony Clifton pointed out in *Monday Morning:*

> The Palestinians . . . fought off one of the most powerful armies in the world. I have no doubt having seen the intensity of the bombing and shelling of West Beirut, that the Israelis wanted to get into West Beirut to kill or drag PLO fighters into captivity. . . . I do not think that Israel spent billions of dollars, sacrificed hundreds of its young men and blackened its name in the civilized world just so that Yasir Arafat and George Habash and their men could fly off as heroes to the capitals of the Arab World. The guerrillas . . . did what all the combined Arab armies have never been able to do: they denied Israel its victory.[33]

The atrocities that blackened Israel's name were neither accidental nor spontaneous. Shortly before the invasion, Kapeliouk called attention to "an alarming phenomenon" in his country: the writings and teachings of certain rabbis—former military chaplains—who insist that the Bible orders the expulsion of the Arabs and in wartime the killing and extermination of non-Jews, including babies and their mothers.[34] "No religious authority, no rabbi has spoken against this kind of racist talk," he added, "any more than they have spoken against the abuses suffered by the Palestinians in the occupied territories." For General Avigdor Ben-Gal, then commander of Israel's northern district, Palestinians within Israel are "a cancer in the body of the country"; to Ariel Sharon, who threatened them with expulsion, they are "foreigners." General Eytan likens Palestinians in the West Bank to "drunken cockroaches in a bottle." In this vein, Begin told the Knesset on June 8, 1982, that Palestinian fighters were "beasts walking on two paws."

"If they are equal to animals on two paws, that's actually saying we should exterminate them." So Gideon Spiro, an employee of Israel's Ministry of Education and a former reservist who refused to serve in Lebanon and the West Bank, told the International Commission. "I think," he said, "that Israeli society went through—and is still going through—a process of dehumanization and fascisization of its values." He explained:

> As long as Israelis don't have to pay the price . . . don't have to stand in queues and decide either sugar or settlements, either petrol for the car or control of Lebanon—as long as you don't have to choose you can support everything. . . . Israel gets more than 50 percent of the foreign aid of the United States . . . in absolute figures more than India with its 600 million people. . . . [As long as this continues] Begin can do whatever he wants. That's all. It's very simple.[35]

Crimes such as those committed by Israel in Lebanon, the West Bank, and Gaza do not issue from the cold brutality of a Sharon or a Begin, but are inherent in, indispensable to, and have indelibly marked the history of the Zionist settler movement and its state. This is because the land rightfully belongs to the Palestinians, descendants—as Sir James Frazer has pointed out—of the pagan tribes which dwelt there before the Israeli invasion, and who have clung to the soil ever since, being submerged but never destroyed by each successive wave of conquest that has swept over the land."[36] As Arabs, their homeland has been Palestine for more than thirteen centuries, "a period of time conveying such evident and absolute ownership that anywhere else in the civilized world a kindred title would only be questioned by lunatics and disregarded by knaves."[37] The enduring validity of the Palestinian title to Palestine means that

Zionist "legitimacy" requires the extinction of the Palestinian people. The plan to do this involves a combination of physical extermination and dissolution as a people for those outside Israel, and for those inside Israel, reduction to a status that permits their profitable exploitation by Zionism's master race.

Israel's refusal to recognize the Palestinians and their national rights in Palestine is an attempt to conceal the terrorism and violence necessary to establish and maintain the Zionist settler state on a land belonging to another people. This violence, "never recognized, never registered, expelled from the collective memory, covered by biblical myth and 'legitimated' by the tragedy of genocide, haunts the collective unconscious of Jewish Zionism and prohibits taking notice of the Palestinians."[38] Hence Golda Meir's dictum: "The Palestinian people do not exist."

The Palestinians

The Palestinian people, some 5 million strong, meanwhile affirm their inalienable rights in Palestine ever more strongly. As an aide to Yasir Arafat pointed out:

> After the massacres of Sabra and Shatila, it is clear that in the Middle East there is either one people too many or one state too few. Either it is necessary to exterminate the Palestinians or to create. . . . an independent Palestinian state.[39]

Prior to Israel's 1982 invasion of Lebanon, that state structure was developing successfully. Without a land of their own, dispersed throughout the world for more than thirty years, the Palestinians have yet managed—under PLO leadership—to weld themselves into a national community and to assert their national identity. The PLO has spoken for and mobilized virtually all Palestinians, who through the PLO have expressed, worked for, and fought for their aspirations. And when the PLO has been under attack—as it has been so often, and was so fiercely in the summer of 1982—Palestinians have come from all parts of the world to serve in its ranks.

Over the years, bringing together all the institutions of the Palestinian people, the PLO has acquired many of the functions and something of the structure of a state: an executive power; a parliament representing Palestinians in the different countries of exile; and departments equivalent to ministries (education, public health, intelligence, social services, economy, finance, information, internal security, defense). Reflecting the fact that the Palestinians have become the most highly educated people of the region, the PLO has provided scholarships for many Palestinian students and maintained cultural institutions of high standing. Internationally, this national liberation movement has achieved extraordinary prestige: recognition by 117 states, roughly double the number that recognize Israel; observer status at the UN and its organs; the overwhelming support of the UN General Assembly, where the United States and Israel often stand alone on questions concerning the Palestinians; membership in the Arab League, the Islamic conference, the nonaligned movement, and observer status in the conference of African states.

In the course of a long and highly complex struggle, marked by searing defeats as well as notable achievements, the Palestinian liberation movement has to a significant degree freed itself from traditional primordial ties of religion, kinship, and tribalism, which still characterize of much of the region today, reaching a national, secular, and (to a much lesser extent) social class identification. This is a higher form of social consciousness than prevails in either Israel or Lebanon. This social consciousness found expression in Arafat's formulation and advocacy of the idea, as noted author and scholar Edward Said put it, that "Palestinian Arabs and Israeli Jews would—indeed must—seek a future together on an equal footing in a shared territory." To this day, as Said pointed out, "no Israeli leader has responded to the moral challenge and humane audacity of this vision."[40]

This higher form of social consciousness also explains, in part, the resentment Lebanese sectarian defenders hold for the Palestinians, whose interaction with Lebanese society contributed to exposing the bankruptcy of Lebanon's outworn social order and thus accelerating its breakdown. Sectarianism and Zionism are much alike, ideologies "based on primordial sentiments and committed to rigid orders that foster dominance of one religious community over the others."[41] Both have provided bases for imperialism historically, and both continue to do so.

$$\begin{bmatrix} \text{PART} \\ \textbf{IV} \end{bmatrix}$$

ASSAULT FROM THE RIGHT

[19]

The Right Triumphant:
Toward a New Lebanon?

On September 1, 1982, a week after his brother's assassination, Amin Gemayel was elected president of Lebanon, winning the votes of seventy-seven of the eighty members of parliament present. Muslim parliamentarians who refused to vote for Bashir conditioned their support for Amin on his pursuit of a policy of national reconciliation, for an end to the Israeli occupation, and achievement of Lebanon's territorial unity. The new president retained as prime minister Chafik Wazzan, by then enjoying rightist support but no longer the support of most of the Sunni community. And when the president's attempts to form a cabinet of politicians failed, he selected nine ministers without political or governmental experience, among them some of his business friends.

The state structures that Bashir Gemayel had appropriated for the Kataeb in the years of civil war served as the basis for Kataeb command of key state institutions, especially as it now controlled the presidency and soon would control the army and the judiciary as well. The powerful post of director of general security went to Zahi Boustani, Bashir Gemayel's chief lieutenant in the Lebanese Forces and a member of its Command Council. In order to make Ibrahim Tannous—for the past nine years the head of Kataeb military training—the army commander-in-chief, the president passed over forty-one officers of higher grades and qualifications and greater length of service. All forty-one resigned.[1] Tannous' lack of experience, if nothing else, made him totally unfit for this position. His sole qualification was his commitment to the Kataeb and the Lebanese Forces.

Rule by Decree

President Gemayel insisted that parliament grant him exceptional powers, including the power to legislate by decree. Most parliamentarians agreed with Selim Hoss that this demand far exceeded "what is necessary and required for the present stage" since such powers would cancel parliament's role. But, under the pressures of parliament speaker Kamel al-Asaad, they granted these powers in sixteen of the thirty areas demanded. The first decree issued by the president introduced press censorship for the first time in Lebanon's modern history, and many publications moved elsewhere.

Over the following year, of 161 legislative decrees issued by the president, fifty were in areas not included in the parliamentary mandate. Saeb Salam, among the most pliable of Sunni politicians and one of the most supportive of the new president, charged that he had used the emergency powers "to set up dictatorial rule."[2]

Decree Law 10 restored the commander-in-chief's absolute authority over the military establishment, which had been somewhat reduced by the March 1979 defense law. Tannous promptly used these powers to make a series of what Fouad Lahoud called "unjust promotions," provoking more resignations. An all-ranks purge of officers considered politically undesirable by the Kataeb opened the way to staffing the army with officers favored by the Lebanese Forces. Entering the army in large numbers, Lebanese Forces militias won rapid promotion and often assignments to instruct conscripts. American advisers assumed the task of training the new army; Washington supplied it with a great quantity of arms and military equipment, much of it apparently designed for police operations.[3] The army was again used to "enforce security" in the parts of Lebanon it controlled, and Decree Law 10 gave the commander-in-chief wide powers of search and arrest.

Fouad Lahoud sharply criticized the government's use of the army "in repressive actions in West Beirut, the southern suburbs and the mountains," and insisted on the imperative of "building a balanced army and one not subjected to the interests of one faction only." The praise Washington lavished on Lebanon's so-called new army, then being trained by the American military, contrasted sharply with the conclusions of a March 15, 1983, U.S. congressional study which found the army "in very poor condition . . . existing mainly on paper . . . and requiring two years to equip and train five brigades."

Misuse of the exceptional powers granted by the Lebanese parliament was not confined to the issue of the army, however. Decree 41, lifting the immunity of judges, opened the way for the Kataeb to achieve dominance in the judicial system, subverting the independence of the judiciary and provoking the resignation of the president of the Higher Council of Magistrates, Yussef Gebrane. Decree 42, lifting the immunity of civil servants, permitted purges in government departments and resulted in the appointment of Lebanese Forces and Kataeb stalwarts to crucial posts at home and abroad.[4] Directors-general in a number of departments were often selected from these same organizations, facilitating the circumvention of any ministers who might develop a tendency to independence. Even on the long-established basis weighted in favor of the Maronite community, power-sharing among the different communities no longer satisfied the Kataeb. It therefore decided that the National Pact had served its purpose and must be set aside, since it stood in the way of Kataeb–Lebanese Forces hegemony. The Kataeb instead raised the slogan "liberation before reconciliation" as a means of buying time during which it could establish an enduring political structure. An early casualty was the August 1970 decree issued by Kamal Jumblat, which had lifted a twenty-three-year-old ban on all groups upholding ideologies extending beyond the Lebanese entity and had introduced a significant measure of political democracy. Decree Law 153 of October 1983 canceled the August 1970 decree.

The rapidity with which the Kataeb achieved domination over the state machinery owed much to the existence of its own fully functioning "state." This, coupled with its control of the presidency, army, and other key sectors, gave it decisive power in virtually all state institutions. There were several reasons. For one thing, parliament's reluctant abdication of its prerogatives at the beginning of Amin Gemayel's presidency had shifted power to the president's team of advisers, the most influential of whom was his adviser on security matters, Wadi Haddad of the Ford Foundation. Prime Minister Wazzan's acquiescence in the ongoing Kataebization of the state facilitated this process. The Reagan administration also promoted the identification of Kataeb and state institutions. In April of 1983 high-level American officials in Washington told a visiting delegation of the French National Assembly's foreign affairs commission, led by Maurice Fauré, of the administration's satisfaction over the "rapid progress" made by the Lebanese army, and in particular over the fact that "the army's cooperation with the Christian militias has become very good." These American officials added: "The ensemble of the organized forces (army, militia, and gendarmerie) will be capable of maintaining order in two-thirds of the country."[5]

In assigning the Lebanese army the role of bolstering the Lebanese Forces militias, the Reagan administration stripped it of any pretension to a national identity, reducing it to no more than an auxiliary of the Kataeb militias. This approach also meant that the American Marines soon appeared to many Lebanese much like just another local militia.

The writ of Amin Gemayel's government ran only in West Beirut, comprising only 1 percent of Lebanon's land area but including a large proportion of its population. The Lebanese Forces commanded by Fadi Frem ruled in roughly 10 percent of the land—including East Beirut and the area to the north—an area from which the Kataeb and the Lebanese Forces (90 percent of whose members were also members of the Kataeb) totally excluded government authority and the Lebanese army. The army was not even allowed to take over the Barbara checkpoint on the coastal road between the "Christian state" of the Lebanese Forces and the Madfoun bridge in the north, gateway to the roughly 48 percent of Lebanon then under Syrian control. (In 1985 the Samir Ja'Ja' faction of the Forces still controlled this checkpoint, one of its most lucrative sources of revenue.)

The "Missing"

Both the army and the Lebanese Forces enjoyed carte blanche to enter West Beirut and terrorize its population. For many months the army conducted search-and-arrest operations in West Beirut, cordoning off one section of the city after another, storming into houses and apartments, taking into custody almost any Palestinian they encountered as well as many Lebanese. According to the Paris-based International Center for Information on Prisoners, Deportees, and Disappeared Palestinians and Lebanese, the Lebanese Forces kidnapped at least 800 Palestinians and Lebanese between September of 1982 and January of 1983, while the army seized 1,500 or more. Of those taken into custody, it reported, 85–90 percent were civilians, not fighters. An investigation by the International Federation of the Rights of Man (IFRM) soon after determined that the Lebanese

Forces alone were responsible for the disappearance of 1,500 Lebanese and 500 Palestinians since June of 1982. Most had been kidnapped from their homes or at roadblocks in the mountains, the Bekaa, or on the Beirut–Sidon road. The IFRM found that the Lebanese Forces systematically used torture in their detention centers, especially in their notorious military command office in Qarantina, near the Green Line.

Although it had signed the 1949 Geneva Convention creating the International Commission of the Red Cross, the Lebanese government, unlike the PLO, Syria, and Israel, refused to allow the ICRC— or anyone—access to its prisoners. The government's stand gave substance to the many reports of torture, mistreatment, and killings that filtered out of the Lebanese army as well as the Lebanese Forces and Kataeb detention centers. The "disappeared" after nearly a decade of civil war numbered several thousands. (Attempts after the events of February 1984 to secure release of the missing held by one side or the other failed. Only Walid Jumblat had the honesty to admit: "We killed them.")

The Remaining Palestinians: Precarious Existence

Women, children, the aged, the sick, the wounded, widows and orphans, the destitute and homeless—these constituted the Palestinian community left in West Beirut refugee camps after the departure of Palestine Liberation Organization (PLO) fighters. All were isolated and vulnerable, haunted by the Sabra–Shatila massacres and the years-long Kataeb propaganda campaign holding them responsible for all the ills of Lebanese society. Their harassment by the government and the Lebanese Forces came on the heels of that experienced at the hands of the Israeli troops, which had arrested among others anyone who had ever been employed by, or received help from, a Palestinian institution, including hospitals and clinics. Palestinians now faced a government that far from considering the Sabra–Shatila massacres a crime, openly proclaimed its determination to achieve the massacre's still unfulfilled goal: the ouster from Lebanon of the entire Palestinian community. This was the Gemayel government's over-riding concern. As one of Amin Gemayel's retinue put it: "Lebanon's chief problem is the presence of Palestinian civilians."[6] The government's announced decision that Palestinians who had arrived in Lebanon in 1948 would be allowed to remain was in many cases vitiated by the "proof" required. Chafik Wazzan reportedly told four Italian senators that the government planned to expel all Palestinians in Lebanon, putting the number at 500,000.[7]

In West Beirut, virtually its sole domain, the government persecuted Palestinians inside and outside the camps and gave free rein, even assistance, to the Lebanese Forces to do the same. Israeli bombardments had left the camps in ruins: houses without roofs or walls; water, sewage, and electricity systems disrupted or totally destroyed; broken drainage pipes turning streets and alleys into rivers of sewage. The government denied Palestinians the right to repair or rebuild their homes and sent bulldozers into the camps to bring down houses still standing, even some already rebuilt. Until well into 1983 the camps lacked both electricity and water, and the pressures to force the Palestinians to leave did not cease. The Lebanese army joined with the Maronite militias in terrorist attacks aimed at stampeding Palestinians to flee, and arrested or kidnapped Palestinians and their friends inside and outside the camps, holding them without charge in secret detention centers, denying them contact with the outside world and denying their families any knowledge of their whereabouts or even of their continued existence. Between October of 1982 and February of 1983 the Kataeb kidnapped more than 200 Palestinian women in the Beirut area, according to a committee of prisoners' families. Relatives and friends of prisoners, mainly women, held sit-ins and protest marches demanding the release, or at least news, of the missing, but met no response either from the authorities or the Lebanese Forces. Not one of the missing was located or released in the first six months of the effort, and fears grew that most of the missing had been killed.

The government and army joined in the aggressions intended to destroy the entire Palestinian infrastructure in West Beirut, striking especially at the network of services the PLO provided for disadvantaged Palestinians and often for disadvantaged Lebanese as well. The PLO's social affairs office in West Beirut—the target of both official and unofficial harassment—managed to maintain its services, but had to limit these to persons already on its lists. Many now fatherless families could therefore not be helped. The Palestinian Red Crescent Society hospitals and clinics, especially the Akka and Gaza hospitals on the edge of the Sabra and Shatila camps, suffered unceasing harassment, clearly intended to force their closure. The army "confiscated" medical supplies paid for and brought into Lebanon by the

PRCS. Electricity to PRCS hospitals was cut off for long periods. The government refused to renew work and residence permits for foreign doctors and medical personnel working in PRCS hospitals and clinics. Of twenty-two foreign doctors working in the Akka and Gaza hospitals in January of 1983, only two remained in August of that year. Three Belgian doctors, expelled in the summer of 1983, testified that attacks on Palestinians were made every day and that arrests in the camps by the army, police, and Lebanese Forces (often posing as official police) had become daily routine. They concluded that the government intended to drive all Palestinians out of Lebanon and wanted no witnesses to this operation.

Official media pictured the Palestine Research Center as the hub of a terrorist network. An explosion in the Center in February 1983 killed the wife of director Sabri Jiryis, who with three other high-level Palestinian officials was later arrested and subsequently deported. All institutions that employed, aided, or represented Palestinians came under attack.

Palestinians living in West Beirut outside the camps, including some holding Lebanese passports, also suffered. Palestinian shops and buildings were often blown up. Police bulldozers razed the homes of Palestinians in the area of the Kuwait embassy. Palestinian families were faced with demands for exorbitant rent increases and evicted if they did not pay. Tightened labor laws denied Palestinians employment in a number of fields. Inability to find work combined with the constant threat of arrest or worse led many young men to try to leave Lebanon.

The some 300,000 Palestinians living in the occupied south fared even worse. There Israeli troops encouraged a proliferation of Palestinian-hating militias, the proclaimed objectives of which were to drive back refugees from the Ain-al-Hilweh camp and to terrorize those living in the camps into mass flight. Throughout Sidon, the Kataeb posted notices calling on every Lebanese to fulfill "his duty to kill at least one Palestinian" and toured the city warning Palestinians through loudspeakers "to leave or face extermination." The threat was not an idle one. Three Palestinians were soaked in oil and burned alive; others were hacked to death with hatchets. Still others were mutilated and then shot. Some thirty Palestinians were killed at the beginning of 1983. By that time, roughly half the Palestinians living in the Sidon area outside the camps had been expelled. And more were evicted from its eastern suburbs in the first months of 1983.

Fear drove many back into the Ain-al-Hilweh camp, but Palestinian camp dwellers were not spared. Bullet-ridden bodies, found near the camps, spread terror. No one had ever been told not to work outside the camp. Yet those who did faced death on their way to and from home, and work outside had to be abandoned. The fact that Israel allowed these murderous militias to operate openly and freely and did not bother to conceal its official relations with them—combined with the memory of Israel's role in the Sabra–Shatila massacres—kept Palestinians in the camps in a state of fear. The "national guard" the Israeli Defense Force (IDF) formed inside the camp offered no comfort since these guards were introduced to spy on and police the inhabitants. They engaged primarily in harrassing or extorting money from their charges, who suffered the more because these guardians were often themselves Palestinians.

An unexpected result of this murderous campaign was that workers formerly employed outside the camp, which had been 90 percent destroyed, joined with others inside to rebuild it. This project had to be carried out quickly before a new government law banning permanent accommodation inside the camps came into effect. Certain American Jewish organizations donated bags of cement which the IDF distributed to the people, and UNRWA eventually provided necessary funds. An Israeli popular committee, headed by former IDF colonel Dov Yeremia, who had been dismissed for refusing to fight the Palestinians, provided a prefabricated school. A year after the start of the rebuilding project, it was almost completed, and Ain al-Hilweh was more comfortable and in better condition than it had ever been.[8]

At the beginning of 1984, however, no part of Lebanon was safe for Palestinians. UNRWA Commissioner General Olaf Rydbeck once again on January 21 expressed UNRWA's alarm over the resurgence of violent incidents directed against Palestinians in Lebanon, and called on all parties to do everything possible to protect the lives of civilians.

The Occupied South

In addition to its military and political goals in the south, Israel wanted to convert the region into a consumer market for Israeli products and integrate it into the Israeli economy. To do so it had to eliminate southern Lebanon's economic role as a consumer market for

Lebanese goods and as a production center for other Lebanese regions.

The expansion of Saad Haddad's enclave westward gave southern Lebanon an open border with Israel, from which all traces of the Lebanese state, including the Lebanese customs post, vanished. Here Israel established services to promote the sale of Israeli produce and goods in Lebanon and to persuade Lebanese to divert their imports from the ports of Beirut and Sidon to Haifa. Located on the first ten meters of Lebanese land north of the border, a branch of Israel's Hapoalim Bank offered Lebanese the opportunity to open a bank account in Israel without leaving Lebanese soil. Here an office of Israel's Ministry of Industry supplied Lebanese business people with lists of Israeli enterprises eager to trade with Lebanon and with a phone allowing them to place their orders for Israeli goods without crossing the border. By imposing exorbitant taxes, delays, and restrictions on Lebanese products, Israel "persuaded" Lebanese entrepreneurs to handle Israeli products. Goods traffic was all one way, however; Israeli markets were not open to Lebanese products.[9]

Israel dumped into Lebanon agricultural produce, in particular citrus and other fruits, benefiting from an export subsidy of up to 40 percent of its value at prices below Lebanese production costs. These were southern Lebanon's main crops and the chief support of its many farmers. For southern Lebanon, where agriculture normally employed 40 percent of the population, this spelled ruin. Moreover, by imposing a special duty on goods landed in Sidon for Lebanese importers, and by sharply increasing the prices of chemical fertilizers and other materials needed by farmers and industrialists, Israel raised costs for Lebanese farmers, merchants, and consumers; meanwhile Israeli products of all kinds, especially those similar to those produced locally, inundated southern Lebanese markets and "clandestinely" infiltrated into non-occupied Lebanon. Saudi Arabia and other Arab Gulf states—normally the biggest buyers of southern Lebanese exports—therefore imposed a widening boycott on Lebanese products.

Israel was soon selling each month in southern Lebanon $.5 million worth of agricultural products, while much of the south's citrus, orange, apple, and olive crops were left rotting on the ground. Local farmers did not even harvest their crops; either they were arbitrarily forbidden to transport agricultural products, or else transport costs exceded potential income owing to low market prices and the halt in Lebanese exports. Israeli troops also deliberately destroyed

Lebanon's agricultural resources. On one day alone in January of 1984, the IDF bulldozed 100,000 square meters of orchards as part of its "clearing" operations on the Tyre–Sidon road. Its announced intention was to uproot all orchards lining the main roads in the south.[10] It also destroyed meadow lands. By 1984 "a significant portion of agricultural land" had already been put out of production, according to a 1985 International Monetary Fund (IMF) study. Continuation of this policy would leave half or more of its farm labor forces without work.

The next phase in Israel's destruction of the south's economy was to close all its doors to the rest of Lebanon, isolating the south physically by establishing a de facto "frontier" along the Awwali River, where would-be travelers—especially merchants with perishable goods— were often held up for a week or more. At the Awwali Bridge, the sole crossing point, even people holding permits to cross suffered long delays. Their travails began in Sidon, when they sought passes permitting their return if they left the area. Here, as Sidon parliamentarian Nazih Bizri reported, if travelers were not deterred by long hours of waiting, police dogs were sometimes set upon them to drive them away. At the Awwali Bridge Israelis sometimes beat travelers with sticks, pelted them with stones, forced them to kneel for long periods on stony ground, or fired over the heads of those in the act of crossing the bridge.[11]

The situation became worse in early 1984 when Israel closed the Awwali crossing. A long, roundabout, pot-holed road through the mountains to Bater village in the southern Chouf became the south's sole link with the rest of Lebanon. At this crossing, as at the Awwali Bridge, Israeli military authorities speeded Israeli goods on their way while delaying Lebanese trucks and imposing exorbitant "taxes" on Lebanese produce.

Bizri called this treatment part of a deliberate campaign to drive Lebanese out of the south "so that Israel can establish settlements, as it has done on the West Bank, and so convert south Lebanon into Israel's North Bank."[12] In the meantime, closure of access routes erected a real frontier between the south and the rest of the country, multiplied the cost of transport six or more times, and put many Lebanese out of business. The IDF practice (adopted in 1983) of suddenly shooting in all directions in the streets of Sidon paralyzed economic activity there, and other towns were fearful the practice would spread, according to Halim Fayyad, governor of the south.[13]

By the beginning of 1984, southern Lebanon's industry had declined by 80 percent, owing to the difficulties of obtaining raw materials and the hardships of marketing and transporting output.[14] Restricted movement to and from the south deprived the area of its natural markets in the Chouf and Western Bekaa. (Similar restrictions were applied in the Israeli-occupied Bekaa with similar devastating effects.) Israeli road checkpoints were essential to this economic war: they not only multiplied the cost of transport six or more times but also gave Israeli trucks and produce a decisive advantage in reaching wholesale markets ahead of Lebanese trucks. Exports from the south had virtually ceased by early 1984 while, according to Nazih Bizri, millions of Lebanese pounds' worth of Israeli fruits, vegetables, industrial goods, and machinery were being sent through the south to all parts of Lebanon.[15]

Israel's rapidly developing exports into Lebanon, the products of large-scale production and modern packaging methods, posed a lethal threat to the small-scale, traditional Lebanese producer. This was especially true as Israel's military occupation allowed it to wage all-out economic war against a country which its invasion "had already splintered into tiny markets," in the words of Dr. Elias Saba, former Lebanese defense and finance minister.[16]

The Waters of Lebanon

For Israel, control of the south also meant acquiring the rivers that supply Lebanon's water. In the early 1960s Israel had seized the tributaries of the Jordan, to which Lebanon, Syria, and Jordan have recognized rights. In its 1978 incursion into southern Lebanon, Israel completed its control of the headwaters of the Jordan River. The 1982 invasion took control of the Litani River and all the technical data concerning the river, as well as the hydrographic charts pertaining to the Litani's Karoun dam.[17]

In the negotiations with Lebanon over Israeli withdrawal after its 1982 invasion, Israel did not demand the Litani waters. But, as Dr. Kamal Hamdan, a specialist in the field, noted, once Israel actually seized all the Jordan tributaries and all the water sources available in the foothills of Mount Hermon, "there remains only the Litani."[18] Raymond Edde also warned that Israel, simply by remaining in the south, controlled the waters of Lebanon's rivers, including the Litani.

The Litani River is the most essential to Lebanon, and to all the electric and hydro-electric stations in the Bekaa and south of the Awwali River; the Litani feeds the Bekaa, southern Lebanon, Beirut, and most of Mount Lebanon.[19]

Israel's Gateway to Arab Markets?

Israel hoped to use the rest of Lebanon as the gateway through which its products could penetrate Arab markets. This threat to Lebanon's economy developed after nearly a decade of civil strife, during which it had sustained, as Selim Hoss pointed out, "irreversible structural changes."[20] These included:

(1) The loss of its position as the Middle East's service center for trade, commerce, banking, and exchange, a loss the more serious because development of the service economy had compensated for Lebanon's lack of natural resources. The conditions for regaining Lebanon's role as the region's service center no longer existed, its former clients having developed their own circuits of exchange.

(2) The disappearance of cheap, seasonal foreign labor—mainly Palestinian and Syrian—on which agriculture as well as many industries were dependent. The civil war dispersed the Palestinian workers and ended the annual influx of some 300,000 seasonal Syrian workers.

(3) A precipitous fall in the inflow of "political money"—millions and millions of pounds that poured into the economic cycle every day. These included PLO expenditures as well as financial subsidies to the many militias and other groups by outside powers.

Moreover, the Israeli invasion cost the industrial sector alone 2.2 billion Lebanese pounds and a 70 percent drop in productivity. Lebanon's economic losses in eight years of civil strife were put at 125 billion Lebanese pounds (roughly $25 billion) by a Lebanese Trades Union Council study.[21]

The rupture of economic and social links between the regions of the country fragmented the national market and threatened Lebanon's cohesion and viability as a state. Both external and internal trade were paralyzed by the loss of accessibility between the various regions of the country and the loss of access to outlets to the outside world (ports, the airport). By preventing agricultural produce from the mountains, the Bekaa, and the south from reaching Beirut, and simultaneously dumping Israeli produce and goods on the Lebanese market, Israel ensured the wastage of Lebanese products and the bankruptcy of farmers and factories in these regions.

The government's inability to exercise authority throughout the country undermined public finances. Domestic debt—negligible before the 1975 war and mainly owed to the banking system—by 1984 "probably exceeded gross domestic production." according to an IMF–Lebanese government study dated January 4, 1985.

The economic slowdown in the Gulf in the early 1980s (as a result of the slack in the world oil market) added to Lebanon's woes, reducing remittances from Lebanese working abroad from a monthly average of $150 million to $65 million. Leading Lebanese economist Marwan Iskander pointed out that these workers, earning two to four times what Lebanese workers earn at home, represented a third of the total Lebanese workforce; their money transfers to Lebanon had a great impact on the level of income there.[22] The decline in these remittances contributed to almost a $1 billion deficit in Lebanon's 1983 balance of payments, the first such deficit since the early 1950s. Also highly damaging was the loss of Arab markets, which before the Israeli invasion attracted roughly 80 percent of Lebanon's industrial production. Of some 4,115 industrial establishments in Lebanon, a majority were geared to export to the Arab world, chiefly the Gulf states; but now fearing infiltrations of Israeli goods these states initially "cleared " only 177 firms.[23] In the first three months of 1984 industrial exports averaged only 60 million Lebanese pounds compared to 250 million Lebanese pounds in the pre-invasion period.

Israel's attempt to penetrate Arab markets via Lebanon was initially assisted by invasion-created scarcities, which permitted the sale in Lebanon of some $60 million worth of building materials and foodstuffs in the last half of 1982. At the war's end, Israeli commerce and industry minister Gideon Platt invited Lebanese businessmen to visit his country; they were received royally, offered airport facilities and the use of Israeli ports, especially Haifa, for their imports. Soon an estimated 42 percent of Lebanon's raw materials and manufactured goods were reaching the country through Haifa.[24] When in March of 1983 the government announced that the Lebanese army would take control of Beirut's port—including the Fifth Basin, from which the Lebanese Forces had long garnered a monthly income of up to $5 million—businessmen became more responsive to Israel's offer, believing the government would raise customs dues. [25] (In the event, however, the Lebanese Forces refused to return the Fifth Basin to the government.)

As Marwan Iskander pointed out, the Lebanese economy lacked all the elements essential for economic activity.[26] Government expenditures were almost all non-productive—mainly arms purchases from the United States—and such expenditures rose swiftly. Arms deals with the United States during the September 1983 Chouf war cost Lebanon more than a billion Lebanese pounds, and the arms were used mainly against Lebanese villages and towns in the region of Aley. Government arms purchases in 1983 brought Lebanon's import bill to 18 billion Lebanese pounds, while exports declined to 3.5 billion.

A sudden and steep rise in the exchange rate of the U.S. dollar in Beirut markets in early 1983 was attributed to the government's withdrawal of more than five billion Lebanese pounds from the Finance Ministry's account in the Central Bank and its transfer into dollars. This transaction pushed the dollar exchange rate vis-à-vis the pound to unprecedented heights; the pound lost 40 percent of its value, adversely affecting the entire economy. Such was the dramatic appearance of what came to be known as "the dollar mafia." Two years later, Greek Orthodox Deputy Speaker of Parliament Munir Abu Fadl attributed the then "stifling economic situation" to prohibitive prices and the appreciation of the dollar brought about by "the dollar mafia." This mafia, he said, "was Lebanese not external, and was "collaborating with Israelis and Zionists in Europe . . . to weaken the Lebanese economy and currency." Lebanese bank directors and other "pillars of Lebanon" were involved. He added that the general prosecutor had been ordered not to get near "these blessed persons." "Whereas a poor citizen who is caught stealing one loaf of bread is jailed for three months, a person who is wrecking the whole economy of the country cannot be touched."[27] He also held the state responsible for not closing the illegal ports, pointing out that a call to even one international insurance company to warn that Lebanon would sink all ships heading for an illegal port would have stopped all insurance companies from insuring such ships.

The public debt reached about 23 billion Lebanese pounds in 1983 compared to 11 billion Lebanese pounds at the beginning of 1982. Dr. Elias Saba predicted it would rise much more by the end of 1984. "What makes matters worse," he added, "is the cost of servicing this debt which exceeds the state's annual income."[28]

Huge expenditures on arms meant that almost nothing was done to restore the country's productive plant. Yet, at least a third of Lebanon's manufacturing capacity had been destroyed since 1975. A decade with little, if any, investment and so without technological advance had left industry (which accounted for one-fifth of the economy) in a poor position to recover, much less to advance. Much of the country's infrastructure had also been damaged or destroyed. Many roads had become unusable. Producing areas were cut off from markets. Links with foreign markets no longer existed; export and transit activity was slashed by half; the lack of raw materials and energy paralyzed industrial zones. The resulting sharp rise in Lebanese production costs meant that Lebanese products could not compete with the low-cost Israeli products pouring into the country.

By 1984 Lebanese industry operated at only 20 to 30 percent of capacity; 60 percent of the workforce was unemployed. Professional and skilled workers had emigrated. Industrial decline provoked a parallel decline in commercial activity. "Conditions are so miserable," *Al-Safir* reported, "that the trade unions have not asked and the government has not offered cost of living increments." Meanwhile, prices on twenty-five out of forty-one essential food items in the consumer food basket had risen sharply.

If the unemployed were legion, so too were the displaced and the homeless. The Ministry of Labor and Social Affairs in October of 1983 found the number of displaced families to be around 30,000, or roughly 150,000 individuals. These joined the 150,000 displaced in the years of civil strife before the Israeli invasion. Another 600,000 people, including housewives and children, had left the country. Altogether some 900,000 out of a total population of around 3.5 to 4 million—nearly a quarter of the population—had either lost their homes or emigrated in the 1975–84 period. (Population figures in Lebanon in the absence of a census, however, owe much to guesswork.) Social aid was almost non-existent; the workers' social security fund was non-operational; rents were at astronomical levels; real national income in 1983 was less than half that of 1974.

Lebanon's Lowest Ebb: The May 17 Agreement

On May 17, 1983, Lebanon signed a United States-negotiated agreement with Israel stipulating the terms of the Israeli troop withdrawal.

This agreement was crucial in Israel's drive to subordinate Lebanon's economy to its own and to use Lebanon as its door into the Arab world. Owing to American support for Lebanon on this issue, however, the agreement did not achieve its demands for "total normalization": a peace treaty, open borders, and a trade agreement. Yet the accord required negotiations on the free movement of goods, products, and persons during the first half-year after Israel's withdrawal. The free movement of Israeli goods across Lebanon's borders would destroy Lebanon's economy and with it the many merchants, mostly Maronites and other Christians, involved in such trade. Foreign Minister Elie Salem put it succinctly: "What would Lebanon gain by opening one door [to Israel] and closing twenty-two doors [to Arab states]?" Lebanon's exports to Arab countries had dropped by about half, and Syria threatened to close its borders to Lebanese products if Lebanon ratified the May 17 accord.

Israel's conditions for its withdrawal—supported by the United States and accepted by Lebanon—included the total departure of the Palestinians and the simultaneous withdrawal of Syrian forces, as well as the Syrian and Palestinian return of Israeli prisoners and war dead. The agreement ended the state of war, committed both countries to the cessation of hostile or terrorist activity against the other, and required the abrogation of laws and regulations in conflict with the agreement. Article 9—demanding that measures be taken within a year to abrogate treaties, laws, and regulations deemed in conflict with the agreement—would take Lebanon out of the Arab League. Articles 6 and 7 prohibited the entry into, deployment in, or passage through either state of the military forces or military equipment of any state hostile to the other. This prohibition applied to any state not having diplomatic relations with both parties—that is, to all Arab states except Egypt—and so required Lebanon's withdrawal from the Arab Defense Pact. In short, the agreement if implemented would remove Lebanon from the Arab world and place it in Israel's orbit. The agreement itself did not demand as a condition for Israel's departure the simultaneous departure of Syrian forces. But in a separate United States–Israel exchange of "letters of understanding" the United States agreed that Israeli troops should remain in Lebanon as long as did Syrian and PLO forces.

Implementation of the accord would transfrom southern Lebanon into an Israeli "security zone" extending northward forty-five kilometers to the Awwali River. Within this zone a second zone would stretch fifteen kilometers north from the border. Provisions governing these zones clearly revealed Israel's intention to organize a buffer zone in south Lebanon where both its military and political control would be assured, a decisive step toward fulfilling its long-held claim to south Lebanon. Stipulations concerning the military forces to be permitted on Lebanon's side of the border would legitimize Israel's puppet troops in the south, then commanded by Major Saad Haddad, integrating them into the Lebanese army and placing Haddad in command of a "Lebanese territorial brigade" to be stationed in the south. No restrictions whatever were placed on Israeli military forces on its side of the border.

The accord was totally unrealistic, however, since it was negotiated without Syria. U. S. Secretary of State George Shultz visited Damascus on May 8 to present Syrian President Hafez Assad with a *fait accompli:* Syria must withdraw its forces without security guarantees, and Israeli ally Saad Haddad would rule the south. Six days later, U.S. Defense Secretary Caspar Weinberger threatened "Russia and whatever proxies it may have in Syria" if it tried to block the accord. Assad replied by refusing to receive U.S. special envoy Philip Habib when he came to Damascus on May 18. The Reagan administration's belief that Saudi Arabia would bring Assad into line proved mistaken. Assad remained adamant: the accord flagrantly violated the Arab League Charter and the Arab summit resolutions; it repudiated Lebanon's Arab commitments; it treated all Arab countries except Egypt as enemies; it granted Israel domination in Lebanese air space and territorial waters; it imposed economic, political, and information restrictions throughout Lebanon; and it established de facto diplomatic relations between the two countries by setting up "special bureaus."

An Israeli–United States memorandum of understanding contained additional concessions to Israel further diminishing Lebanese sovereignty. These included giving Israel the right to take measures of its own to deal with "terrorism" in south Lebanon if the Lebanese army failed to do so. This would give Israel a green light for new incursions into Lebanon and for renewed attacks on Palestinian refugee camps there if Lebanon did not totally eliminate the Palestinian presence in Lebanon by itself.

Damascus insisted that Lebanon could avoid the loss of its sovereignty only by demanding the implementation of UN Security Council resolutions 508 and 509 in June of 1982, which called for

Israel's total and unconditional withdrawal. Raymond Edde carried this argument further. Terming the accord a "serious error," he pointed out that the government could and should have stuck to the 1949 Armistice Convention, which defines Israel as an occupant without title. The Lebanese–Israeli agreement would make Israel a legal occupant. As Edde emphasized, the Lebanese–Israeli agreement "hides a peace treaty. It is only necessary to read the annexes to be convinced." He also stressed that ratification of the accord would close the door to any possible reconciliation among Lebanon's warring factions, and would prevent an understanding with Syria that would allow it to withdraw its troops. Matters stood at an all-too-familiar impasse.

[20]

Popular Revulsion:
The Reemergence of the Opposition

When U.S. Secretary of State George Shultz traveled to Damascus in early July to win President Assad's acceptance of the May 17 agreement, the Syrian president replied that his troops would remain in Lebanon until every Israeli soldier had left and Beirut had abrogated the agreement.

Even before Lebanon signed the accord on May 17, Assad mobilized its Lebanese opponents to fight it. A meeting on May 14 at former Lebanese President Suleiman Franjieh's home in Zghorta brought together many key figures: former Lebanese Prime Minister Rashid Karami; Druse leader and Progressive Socialist Party (PSP) president Walid Jumblat; his close adviser Marwan Hamade; Communist Party of Lebanon (CPL) leader George Hawi; the National Syrian Socialist Party's (NSSP) Mahmoud Abdul Khalek; Assem Qanso, the leader of the Syrian Baath Party in Lebanon; and Franjieh's men. This gathering gave birth to the National Salvation Front (NSF), led by Franjieh, Karami, and Jumblat. The NSF had two principal objectives: to block ratification of the May 17 accord and to undermine the hegemony the Kataeb had achieved by its takeover of the state machine.

The many who dismissed the NSF as an incongruous mix of leaders representing minor currents soon proved mistaken. The NSF appeared at a time of rising dismay and anger against the government in the non-Maronite communities. Jumblat pointed to the main reasons for the erosion of the government's credibility: its acceptance of the May 17 accord; its failure to carry to a conclusion the official inquiry into the Sabra–Shatila massacres; its refusal to make public the commission's final report, so allowing the Kataeb to claim that the report cleared both itself and the Lebanese Forces of any responsibility for the massacre; its assistance in Lebanese Forces' attacks on the Druses in the mountains; its granting of many advantages to the Kataeb, the Lebanese Forces, and the Maronite hierarchy at the expense of all other communities; and, above all, its attempt to establish a one-party state.

The president's refusal even to discuss reforms, coupled with ongoing arrests and disappearances, assured the NSF a large constituency. To President Amin Gemayel, then in the United States, the NSF was "a new conspiracy from without . . . an opposition from a foreign helicopter"—because Jumblat often used a Syrian helicopter—that would soon disappear because "there are a Lebanese people and Lebanese officials determined to destroy the conspiracy."[1] In any event, the Jumblati Druses constituted the real force in the NSF; the informal alliance that proved significant was that between the Druse-led NSF and the Shi'a Amal movement led by Nabih Berri, which did not join the NSF. These two movements shared basic objectives and were led by the rising generation as opposed to the traditional *zuama* of 1943 National Pact vintage. Representing the largest community in Lebanon (33 to 40 percent of the total population), Berri tried to go beyond sectarian rhetoric, declaring: "Forty years after the National Pact, we should all reflect together about a participation formula based on the slogan: One Lebanon for all its sons without discrimination."[2]

Like the NSF, Berri demanded the replacement of the 1943 National Pact by a new pact "based on the effective participation of the Muslims in power." Berri and other Amal leaders insisted that Amal's goals were not sectarian.[3] Akef Haider, head of its political bureau, explained that "our aim is to achieve not sectarian goals but comprehensive social reforms." Berri, moreover, insisted that dialogue must include the state, "the first responsible and the one that will have to implement the decisions reached." In a "national paper" defining the future Lebanese framework, Amal demanded "abolition of political sectarianism." If this proves impossible, the paper went on, "we insist that all sects be equal. The criterion for jobs must be merit. If this proves impossible, the criterion for distributing posts must be fair and apply to all sects without discrimination."[4]

Amal posed a real challenge to Kataeb hegemony, due not only to the Shi'a community's numerical preponderance, but to Berri's stand as a Lebanese nationalist. Berri consistently tried to persuade those in the Shi'a community of their identity as *Lebanese* Shi'as, not just members of a religious sect. Poverty and discrimination, as well as long years of bearing the brunt of Israel's land, sea, and air assaults on the south, had forged the community into a militant political force. The Khomeini revolution in Iran heightened Shi'a militancy, and a faction led by Hussein Musawi, a protégé of Imam Sadr, wanted to establish itself as "Islamic Amal" under Khomeini's leadership. But Berri insisted on its Lebanese identity and that Amal not place itself under Khomeini's leadership. Musawi subsequently set up his small breakaway faction in the northern Bekaa.

The Shi'a political challenge may explain President Gemayel's persistent efforts to drive the Shi'as out of Beirut, as well as his army's periodic bombardments of Beirut's Shi'a quarters, in particular the indigent southern suburbs. One of his regime's first acts was to dispatch bulldozers to destroy the makeshift homes that Shi'a refugees had erected on the sand dunes of Ouzai and Bourj al-Barajney near the airport. The army fired on unarmed men, women, and children—who marched with placards asking that homes in their places of origin be assured before their present homes were destroyed—killing five and wounding many more. Many of these families had been driven out of East Beirut slums and the Tel al-Zaatar camp during the 1975–76 civil war. Others in the southern suburbs were victims of Israel's periodic attacks on the south. To the Gemayel regime, all were squatters, and their homes no more than shacks to be destroyed without warning.

Eight months later—on July 15, 1983—the army, joined by Lebanese Forces units, descended on West Beirut's now predominantly Shi'a (formerly Jewish) quarter, Wadi Abu Jamil, to evict some forty Shi'a refugee families from a school building. Since the school was not in use and homeless refugees were legion, Amal used it to provide shelter for the homeless. The army's eviction of these families touched off an eight-hour battle, in which the army and Lebanese Forces together attacked the people of the Wadi; this confrontation left fourteen civilian and eleven army casualties and some 500 people incarcerated in the Deuxième Bureau's post near the National Museum, notorious as the site of torture.

Nearly a fourth of Lebanon's total population, the Shi'as, lived mainly in the southern suburbs, which even before the civil war were known as Beirut's "Belt of Misery." An area of roughly 28 square kilometers in desperate need of housing, it was "a study area," where the construction of new housing was prohibited and where the Banque de L'habitat was instructed to refuse credits for the purchase of apartments. This, according to Berri, while 90 percent of the bank's credits went to East Beirut.[5]

True to Form: The Army in West Beirut and the Suburbs

Although the Lebanese army met a cordial welcome from the population when it entered the southern suburbs in the wake of the Israeli invasion, relations soured with the arrival on its heels of the Lebanese Forces, which harassed the population while the army carefully looked the other way. In August of 1983, as the Druse–Lebanese Forces war intensified in the mountains and army units gradually withdrew, the Lebanese Forces killed four Amal youths engaged in pasting Imam Sadr's pictures on a wall; the forces put up Bashir's picture in their stead.

Army units rushed to the suburbs to prevent Amal from responding to this attack. The army imposed an indefinite curfew on *all* Shi'a neighborhoods and announced its intention "to flush out" (as if they were garbage) all Shi'a militias, provoking nearly a week of clashes, the heaviest since the Israeli invasion. Amal fighters slipped behind the army and moved into West Beirut where, for the first time since the Israeli invasion, militias of the Lebanese National Movement (LNM) (Mourabitoun, PSP, and Communist) took to the streets to join the battle. Assisted by Syrian and Druse artillery from the mountains, Amal militias took over the green line, attacked two army barracks, and occupied the state television station; from the station for some hours they broadcast pictures and speeches of Imam Sadr, while the army occupied Amal's West Beirut headquarters.

Feverish bargaining between the government and Amal, in which Prime Minister Selim Hoss played a leading role, secured an agreement providing for the army's returning "amiably" to the suburbs on condition that the same measures be applied in East as in West Beirut. A declaration by the president would accept the restoration of "friendliness" and army officers would then contact Amal leaders to coordinate measures on the ground. Soon after, Hoss informed Berri that the prime minister, not the president, would proclaim the restoration of "friendliness," and Berri learned that the army was preparing a "massive bombardment" of the southern suburbs. Yet he still asked all leaders of the national forces to follow him in ordering their militias off the streets and roads.

The next day, a force of 10,000 soldiers began a three-pronged attack into West Beirut while the army command proclaimed an indefinite curfew; the army announced that all armed men would be shot on sight. This attack started at 4 a.m., exactly four hours before the time set for Berri's scheduled meeting with army officers to consider the army's plan for its *peaceful* deployment in West Beirut and the southern suburbs. The army succeeded in taking control of West Beirut but halted its advance at the gates of the southern suburbs, which it did not dare enter. Instead, it fired thousands of missiles and shells into the region, killing and wounding many people and devastating most of the area. Selim Hoss later commented:

> Why did the government order the army to withdraw from positions in West Beirut only to attack this region massively two days later? The army obeyed orders from above. . . . It is, therefore, the political authority which bears responsibility for the dimensions of the catastrophe that befell the capital.[6]

From this time onward Amal took total control of security and order in these suburbs.

The army's week-long, punishing attack angered West Beirut's population, whatever their sect. Already in July the dimensions of opposition—enveloping virtually all sections of the population, including many Christians—made itself felt. This was especially noticeable at both Sunni and Shi'a celebrations on the occasion of the Id al-Fitr ending the holy month of Ramadan. Spiritual leaders of both communities denounced the many arrests and kidnappings, declaring that no single sect, party, or group could remake Lebanon in its own image and ignore the other communities. Saeb Salam, originally a strong supporter of the president, now denounced the "insupportable behavior" of the government, especially that of the Deuxième Bureau, the public prosecutor's office, the security departments, and the official media. He demanded "radical measures to correct abuses committed by these government departments." The government, he said, must close all military headquarters not belonging to the army or the Internal Security Forces (ISF), close and suppress all military roads "reserved to certain quarters" (Kataeb and Lebanese Forces), release all persons arrested without legal authorization or held by illegal organizations, and take steps to aid the victims of such arrests or kidnappings.[7]

Other West Beirut leaders echoed these demands, noting that the state was present (administratively, judicially and militarily) in West Beirut but totally absent in other areas, where the Lebanese Forces remained in command. Kataeb leaders and the Lebanese Forces felt free to invite, welcome to their headquarters, and stage a parade in honor of Israel Defense Minister Moshe Arens. Illegal taxes were still collected and illegal ports still flourished to the profit of the Lebanese Forces and at the expense of the ordinary citizen. The critics stated clearly that they did not hold the Maronite community responsible for these abuses, explicitly blaming the Lebanese Forces.

The Mountain War

The Amal–army clashes in Beirut from August 28 to September 4 marked the beginning of a reversal in the victor-and-vanquished relationship that had prevailed between the Kataeb-controlled government and West Beirut since the Israeli invasion. These clashes coincided with the start of a new phase in the intermittent fighting in the Chouf mountains between the Druses and the Lebanese Forces that Israel had introduced into the area in the summer of 1982.

At the end of August Israeli troops prepared to move out of the Chouf to redeploy on the Awwali River line, forty kilometers to the south and about forty-five kilometers north of the Israeli border. Such a withdrawal threatened to precipitate fighting between the Druses and the uninvited newcomers to the area, the Lebanese Forces. Until this Forces' intrusion, Druses and Maronites under the leadership of Kamal Jumblat and Camille Chamoun respectively had lived peacefully together, even when the rest of Lebanon was torn by civil war. The one notable exception was the Druse killing of Christians following the assassination of Kamal Jumblat in March of 1977 when, in spite of Walid Jumblat's efforts to halt the massacre, many Christians fled from the Chouf. When Israeli troops occupied this area in the summer of 1982 and these Christians decided to return home, the Lebanese Forces ruled they could do so only under its protection. Israeli forces therefore allowed the Kataeb and the Lebanese Forces, never before present in the area, to accompany the returning refugees.

Once in the Chouf, the Forces established garrisons, imposed blockades around a number of villages, erected roadblocks and barricades, and generally behaved arrogantly toward the Druses, doing everything possible to humiliate them. Throughout they were supported by the Israeli army. Druses were arrested at roadblocks only because they were Druses and were beaten and tortured. To a Druse professor, kidnapped and beaten on a Sunday, the order to go to Syria was underscored by the threat: "We made Black Saturday. Now we will make Black Sunday."[8]

From the beginning of these troubles, Jumblat asked the president to withdraw the Lebanese Forces from the Chouf and negotiate this and other problems with the opposition. The president, relying totally on American support, saw no need to achieve accommodation with non-Maronite Lebanese and did not even bother to reply.

The Druses soon gained the upper hand in the mountain battles that ensued, driving the Forces out of Aley and the surrounding territory in February of 1983. Israel did not interfere to rescue the Forces, owing to the pressures of Israeli Druses and to the Gemayel government's failure to conclude the peace treaty it demanded. Battles between the Forces and the Lebanese army, on one side, and the Druses on the other, spilled over into Beirut; the army from a military base on the edge of the airport repeatedly shelled Druse positions in the mountains, provoking Syrian and Druse return fire on the base. Return fire hit the airport for the first time on July 22. Jumblat's promise that attacks on the airport would cease the moment the military base was removed met no response. Artillery and rocket duels between the Druses and the army continued, frequently closing the airport.

The Druse community—hitherto divided between the clan of Majid Arslan, the rightist parliamentarian from Aley, and the Progressive Socialist Party (PSP)—now united around Jumblat, the Arslan Druses joining their traditional PSP rivals to stand against the Lebanese Forces. Lebanese Druses also benefited from the political support of the 60,000 Druses in Israel and from financial assistance from the Druses in Syria. Pressures exerted by Israeli Druses persuaded Israeli troops to let weapons and munitions from Syria reach Druse fighters in the mountains, permitting them to challenge effectively the Lebanese Forces. The Israeli forces allowed Jumblat's fighters to take over stores of Druse weapons, confiscated when the Forces first entered the Chouf. (At one Israeli Druse rally in solidarity with Lebanese Druses, 1,333 Israeli Druse officers and soldiers signed a petition addressed to the Israel Defense Force chief of staff, demanding the release of Israeli Druse soldiers imprisoned for fighting in the Chouf beside the Lebanese Druses and insisting that "you let us cross the border to fight beside the Druses in Lebanon."[9] And, when the Lebanese army was sent into battle, it lost most of its Druse officers and soldiers, some refusing to fight, others joining up with Jumblat's forces.

In early September of 1983, Israel's preparations to withdraw from the Chouf led Jumblat once again to ask the president not to send the army into the Chouf until the Forces had departed and an agreement was reached on the army's role. Once more the president, who had earlier appealed to Israel (through Washington) to use its military forces against the Druses, did not respond, although Israel had already rejected his request. As David Lennon reported from Tel Aviv: "the Israeli government . . . consistently rejected the Beirut government's appeals to come to its aid against the Druses and its allies. . . . The last straw in disrupting Israel's unsigned alliance [with the Kataeb and the president] was the behavior of Kataeb militias in the Chouf. They were unable to hold positions handed to them and continued to demand Israeli troops do the job for them."[10] And on September 4, without advance notice to the Lebanese government, Israeli troops moved out of the Chouf area it had occupied for fifteen months to the Awwali River line, an operation completed in six hours.

As the Israeli withdrawal began, the Druses and the Lebanese Forces—both encouraged by Israel—started to seize vacated positions. Clashes followed. The Lebanese army entered the Chouf through Meshref, the main Lebanese Forces headquarters in this region, and thereafter assisted the Forces in assaults on a number of Druse villages and towns, including Abey, Biwirta, Kafrmatta, and Arsoun, winning strategic positions on the hills. The people of Biwirta and Arsoun were able to flee and so escaped massacre; those in the other villages did not. Five-and-a-half months later, on February 14, 1984, Druse militias regained Kafrmatta; they found many still unburied bodies, the flesh eaten away by foxes and birds. The Lebanese army, stationed in this area from September of 1983 to February 14, had not bothered to bury the bodies. Moreover, in September of 1983 this army had insisted to the International Red Cross, which had been asked by the Druses to bury the victims, that there were no bodies.

In September of 1983 news of the massacres in Kafrmatta, Abey, and Binnai spread quickly throughout the mountain, especially among Druse militias who were then in the third day of a violent battle marked by house-to-house and hand-to-hand combat for the strategically important town of Bhamdoun, which straddles the Damascus–Beirut highway and overlooks Beirut. And, when Bhamdoun fell to the Druses the next day, Druse fighters took revenge, massacring thirty Christians, according to an initial report by the Lebanese Forces. The Forces also charged that the Druses had killed forty Christians a week earlier in the village of Bmariam.

Massacres committed by both sides provoked a large-scale displacement of population. Some 25,000 Christians, many from Bhamdoun, took refuge in Deir Al Qamar. And 2,000 Lebanese Forces fighters, led by Samir Geagea—by trying to hide among these refugees and refusing to give themselves up—delayed for several weeks the refugees' safe passage to the Maronite mountain to the north, which Walid Jumblat had promised them from the beginning.

The Lebanese Forces intrusion into the Chouf at least temporarily put an end to the long-standing mixed Christian–Druse community in the Druse-dominated Chouf and the Maronite-dominated Metn. Maronites whose families had lived peacefully for generations side-by-side with the Druses lost everything and now found themselves homeless. Their anger and bitterness was directed not only against the Druses but also against the Lebanese Forces and the Kataeb which— because they had established garrisons throughout the Druse-inhabited Chouf and Aley districts—were widely held responsible for the catastrophe. A demonstration by some 3,000 now homeless Maronites against Maronite Cardinal Antonious Khreish at Bkerke because he had met with Walid Jumblat, "the butcher of the century," reflected what many perceived as a growing anger among the Maronites against their leaders. *Al-Nahar* columnist, Sarkis Naoum, found much of this widespread anger directed against the Lebanese Forces: "There is a tendency among almost all Lebanese factions to hold the Lebanese Forces responsible not only for what happened in the Chouf but for all the problems Lebanon suffered from in the past year also."[11]

Dominating Beirut, the Chouf is "the key strategic area in the country." Thus the victory won by the Druses (with Syrian support) in the three-weeks-long mountain war was a turning point. The outcome of the mountain war—in Jumblat's words "not a sectarian war against Christians but a national war for the defense of the Arab character and unity of Lebanon against Kataeb hegemony"—reflected a decisive change in the balance of power in Lebanon. It also underscored the total obsolescence of the power-sharing arrangements that had prevailed for the past forty-one years. This change in the balance of power provoked two responses: (1) a swift expansion of the American involvement in the Lebanese civil war in an effort to reverse this change; and (2) a genuine popular insurrection in area after area of Lebanon.

The Occupied South

No common attitude toward the Israeli occupation crystallized in the south in the early days. Some welcomed Israeli troops. Others suspended judgment. Opposition remained discrete. Yet the first call for operations against the Israeli forces came on September 16, 1982, and operations began four days later. In this period operations were the work of small groups that later came together in the National Resistance Front (NRF), formed in the words of leader Abu Hashem, "to fill the vacuum" left by the PLO's departure and the consequent disappearance of the PLO–LNM Joint Forces. Abu Hashem explained:

> We are the offshoots of a force that was present and of groupings that came into being with the Israeli occupation. The difference between today and the past is that we are not using artillery and rocket launchers but the most simple means that are available. . . . What is more important is that people have become fully receptive to offering a haven to whoever combats Israel and of hiding him. This is what enables fighters to make their hits.[12]

The entire south soon became a resistance front: part armed, the rest engaged in civil resistance. Shi'a religious leaders and Amal militants assumed a leading role in mobilizing the population to participate in a civil disobedience movement that rapidly expanded to embrace virtually all social strata. The Israeli troops' arrest of a Shi'a religious dignitary, Sheikh Raghib Harb, in early March of 1983, provoked among an already exasperated and tense population a remarkable solidarity movement throughout the south and Beirut, which won the sheikh's release in April. (Eleven months later, Israeli forces or their agents succeeded in murdering this immensely popular and influential sheikh, of whom it was popularly said: "When that man spoke, the ground shook.")

Enormous impetus was given the civilian resistance by an incident in Nabatiye, October 16, 1983. The most important Shi'a religious ceremony—Ashura, marking the martyrdom of Husain, Muhammed's grandson, at the battle of Kerbala—was deliberately disrupted by Israeli troops, who fired on religious marchers (wounding ten and killing at least one) and smashed in tanks through a crowd of some 50,000. Shi'a religious leaders called for "total civil resistance" to the Israelis and won an overwhelming response. Shi'a religious leader Sheikh Chamseddine repeated an earlier *fatwa* (religious edict), making collaboration with the Israeli enemy a sacrilege. Individual rejection of the Israeli enemy developed through common action into a common political concern over the community's future in Lebanon. Brutal Lebanese army attacks on Beirut's Shi'a quarters contributed to the growing political awareness of the community.

Resistance in the south, however, was by no means exclusively Shi'a. The resistance rallied Lebanese, whatever their sectarian identity. In the words of an Amal spokesman, widely quoted at the time, "None of us has the right to claim we are leading the resistance. This is a genuine national movement." Israel's failure to create local armed sectarian groups under its command in the south, as it had done successfully in the West Bank, testified to this.

Civil resistance in the south developed to include an effective boycott of Israeli goods, general strikes, and sit-ins and protest meetings in mosques and schools. People protested the arrest of national and religious leaders, some new and unsupportable Israeli exaction, or Israeli troops' wanton shooting and killing of young people whom it suspected, or pretended to suspect, of "terrorism." Villagers also developed what became known as the Allah Akbar (God is Great) Early Warning System: lookouts were posted to watch all access roads to the villages and warn (probably by walkie-talkie radios) of the Israelis' approach; loudspeakers in the village mosque immediately sounded the call to prayer and villagers swiftly flocked to the mosque to stand together against the invaders. Israeli troops' seizure of loudspeakers proved ineffective: villagers maintained well-hidden supplies. They also added the foul smell of burning tires, a traditional symbol of protest, to their "welcome" to Israeli soldiers.

The Israeli Defense Force (IDF) from the beginning had tried to create local armed groups under its command. One such effort was the attempt to organize village leagues, grouping village *mukhtars* in units of eight-to-ten members in each of ten areas (each comprising twelve villages) covering the entire Israeli-occupied south. Israeli officers and representatives of the ten areas constituted the general command of the village leagues. Another was the attempt to form national guard units in every village and town quarter, to be financed by illegal taxes on buildings, stores, cars, and so on. Extensive IDF contacts with notables and other influential persons in each locality supplemented these efforts. Yet the IDF won support only in Maronite centers such as Jezzine. The reply given by one *mukhtar* to Israeli pressures voiced the more common reaction: "Enlarge the Ansar concentration camp because we already reject your demands."[13]

An investigation by the newspaper, *Al-Safir,* the results of which were published April 6, 1984, provided evidence of the failure of this Israeli policy. In the largely Shi'a district of Nabatiye, efforts to establish militias and national guards failed in twenty-five out of forty villages, and in the fifteen villages where such units were formed less than five people joined up in three and less than ten in the remaining twelve. In the district of Zaharani, Israel proved incapable of establishing militias or guards in thirty out of forty-nine villages, and most units had less than ten members. Similar results were obtained in Tyre, where the units formed soon broke up and disappeared.

Local officials in towns and villages often refused under one pretext or another to give the Israelis the civil status information necessary to form the armed puppet groups. Such guards and militias as Israel was able to organize usually consisted of convicted criminals or similar types. According to Sidon parliamentarian Nazih Bizri, one Israeli-recruited national guard unit, for example, contained sixty to seventy convicted criminals. Such types were well-suited for their major duties—extorting money from businessmen and shops, harassing and terrifying the population by random shooting and bomb throwing—so giving the IDF a pretext for more arrests and harsher "security measures." Southerners were even subjected to additional taxes to pay the guards and militias Israel employed to harass, kidnap, the kill them.

The IDF's brutality, however, could not resolve the basic dilemma it faced in the south: its Lebanese ties were confined to the Maronites, who in the south numbered only about 50,000 compared to the half-million or more Shi'as. Some in the IDF command, therefore—prompted in part by the ignominious performance of its Maronite allies in the Chouf—gave much thought to the possibility of finding allies in the Shi'a community and forming a Shi'a army. The IDF chose a Shi'a officer, Abdel Amin Mansour (Abu Sateh) to head the Shi'a army it hoped to create. But Abu Sateh, reflecting the rapidly rising anti-Israel temper in the south, fled in November of 1983 to West Beirut, where he joined Amal. He denounced all who collaborated with Israel, and officially dissolved the Shi'a army (this he said, numbered only 120 men, all but thirty of whom had deserted). Israel's trigger-happy propensity for arresting Shi'a sheikhs at the slightest sign of trouble, and its inability to understand that these sheikhs were venerated leaders of their communities, contributed to the defeat of this project.

In Iqlim al-Kharoub in the southern Chouf, a Sunni area, Israel announced its intention to form a Sunni army in October of 1983, but the army did not materialize. In predominantly Sunni Sidon resistance—both civil and military—became so effective that Israeli troops were obliged to set aside for the time being the plan to withdraw further to the south. They feared that the Sunni militias led by Mustafa Saad—son of Marouf Saad, whose assassination precipitated the 1975 civil war—would join with Palestinian militants in Ain al-Hilweh camp to seize control of the city. The Christian community in Sidon was also involved in the expanding resistance.

The South Lebanon Army (SLA)

When Major Saad Haddad died in January of 1984, Israel picked another Maronite officer as his successor. This was a recently retired major general, Antoine Lahd, a long-time friend and business associate of army commander-in-chief Ibrahim Tannous. In the period just before his retirement and again in the early months of 1984, Lahd often visited the presidential palace.

On January 16 he met with Tannous, army intelligence chief Simon Qassis, and two of Haddad's officers; on January 19 he met with Tannous, Qassis, Elias Hobeika, the organizer and leader of the Sabra–Shatila massacres and now chief of Lebanese Forces intelligence, and Nazar Najarian, the Lebanese Forces commander in the south. *Al-Kifah al-Arabi,* which first reported these meetings, pointed out that provision for a regional brigade under Lebanese command to help protect Israel's northern border was included in the annexes to the May 17 agreement. And, although Defense Minister Boutros Khoury discounted charges of an existing relationship between his ministry and Lahd, popular suspicions persisted that the selection of Lahd was not made entirely behind the back of the Lebanese state and its top-level officials in the military institution.

In taking command of Haddad's army, rechristened the South Lebanon Army (SLA), Lahd bluntly declared his intention to crush escalating armed resistance to Israel's occupation of the south. The SLA thereafter stormed into mainly Shi'a villages, sowing havoc and destruction. This of course gave impetus to an increasingly determined resistance. Lahd's army, like Haddad's, was overwhelmingly Christian (about 80 percent) in an area where the population is about 80 percent Shi'a. The *Jerusalem Post's* military correspondent, Hirsh Goodman, commented: "All Israel's efforts were geared toward building up Christian hegemony in an area where there are no Christians." Israel's efforts to crush the resistance were not only fruitless but in an important sense self-defeating, as this comment by an "informed observer" suggests:

> It is the fear of Israeli soldiers of dying in Lebanon that some Israeli analysts see as the most damaging aspect of the invasion and occupation of the south. The myth of the omnipotent Israeli soldier is being shattered. The Israelis are being seen by the Lebanese not as supermen but as ordinary people with ordinary fears.[14]

In May of 1984 Israel admitted that during the previous twelve months 70 Israeli soldiers were killed and 376 others had been wounded, and that 508 acts of resistance had been serious enough to be classified as attacks. It also conceded that few resistance fighters had been captured, largely owing to the solidarity of the population and the effectiveness of the Allah Akbar Early Warning System. In late May of 1984 Israeli forces experienced more than forty ambushes, snipings, and bombings that killed four Israeli soldiers and wounded nineteen. The arrival in the Sidon region toward the end of 1983 of some 2,000 or more "graduates" of the Ansar concentration camp gave additional impetus to the resistance, and was reflected in the increasing sophistication of the bombs, radio-controlled explosives, and boobytrap devices it used. This was the beginning of a resistance that was ultimately to drive Israel out of the south.

[21]

The United States: A Belligerent in a Civil War

American Marines first became directly involved in the fighting at the end of August 1983, when fourteen Marines were wounded in a brief clash near the airport.

Early in September, roughly coincident with the fall of Bhamdoun and the Israeli troop withdrawal to the Awwali River line, the United States sent 2,000 more Marines to the Lebanese coast to reinforce the 1,200 stationed in Beirut as part of the multinational forces. More Marines were moved ashore. An American amphibious force assembled off the coast. The aircraft carrier, the *USS Eisenhower* (ninety planes), entered Lebanese waters, where its F-14 Tomcat fighters were soon engaged in flying reconnaissance missions over the mountains; the *USS Tarawa* with six jets arrived off Beirut from the Indian Ocean; and the *USS New Jersey* left the Panama Canal for the Mediterranean. The *New Jersey* was equipped with five-inch and sixteen-inch guns, the latter capable of hurling a shell of almost a ton and a half more than twenty-five miles; American officials boasted that these "powerful and accurate guns" could hit targets well inland. (As it happened, the shells dug up house-sized holes in the hills east of Beirut and caused Lebanese villagers uncounted losses in both lives and property, but they did not hit their intended targets.)

The American radio network CBS called "the massive airlift" of American munitions to the Lebanese army "the largest resupply operation since the 1973 Arab–Israel war." Declaring that "we have vital interests in Lebanon" (which he did not define) U.S. President Ronald Reagan on September 9 authorized the Marines to command sea and air strikes "to defend the MNF (multinational force)" while Vice-President George Bush ordered Syria "to get out of Lebanon." An official American promise that Marines and naval power would go

327

into action in the event of any threat to the Lebanese army that also threatened American forces delighted the Lebanese government. On September 17 Marines shelled Syrian-held positions in the Chouf, and two days later hit onshore targets in support of the Lebanese army, both with "the approval of the highest levels of the U.S. government."[1] These attacks, however, alarmed both houses of the U.S. Congress, still haunted by Vietnam, and both houses demanded restrictions on the use of American power.

The Pentagon explained that its concentration of military force in the Eastern Mediterranean was intended "to send a message to Syria." This signaled an American intention to tilt the balance of military power in Lebanon in favor of Lebanese President Amin Gemayel and so undermine both Syria and the Lebanese opposition. Syrian President Hafez Assad ignored the message, although American bombardments of Syrian positions in the mountain thereafter continued.

The short-term objective of U.S. policy was an attempt to prevent the fall of Souk al-Gharb, the Lebanese army's last stronghold in the Aley–Chouf mountains. Souk al-Gharb, fifteen kilometers southeast of Beirut, commands the road from the mountains to the presidential palace, the defense ministry, the American ambassador's residence, and East Beirut. Hence its strategic importance. This mountain town of some 2,000 mainly Greek Orthodox Christians, a once-fashionable resort, had become headquarters and second largest stronghold of the Lebanese Forces in the Aley district when they first entered this area on the heels of the Israeli forces in 1982. When the strategic mountain town of Bhamdoun fell in September 1983, it put the Druse in control of the mountain range all the way from the Upper Metn to the Chouf. Gemayel at that time tried still another appeal to Israel for help. Israel rejected these appeals from what it considered "the ungrateful Christians."[2] But the Christians had found "a new superpower to do their dirty work for them, in the shape of the misguided Americans. . . ."[3]

Army positions on a ridge running from Souk al-Gharb to a road junction south of Kafr Chamoun were held to be the key to the defense of Beirut. The American government appeared eager to use its impressive firepower against the Druses. Marine officers stationed themselves in Souk al-Gharb beside the Lebanese army to pinpoint targets and direct American and Lebanese return fire against Druse and Syrian positions. The Marines conducted all battlefield intelligence necessary to the direction of offshore and onshore fire, and took command of the war in an operation neither defensive nor minor. The battle was directed by a chain of command running from Rear Admiral Jerry Tuttle, the commander of the Sixth Fleet's main battle force, in the *USS Eisenhower's* operations room, down through the offshore commander of Task Force 61 (of which the Marines were a part), to the onshore Marine commander, Col. Timothy Geraghty. The latter explained that the "American military escalation is deemed defensive in the light of the success of the LAF [Lebanese Armed Forces] operation in the Souk al-Gharb area which is considered important to the security of the United States here."[4]

"We will not permit the fall of Souk al-Gharb," the White House proclaimed on September 20, at a time when the Marines were firing more than 600 shells a day on the town's attackers. American intervention saved Souk al-Gharb, but the shift of the American role in the multinational force from one of protecting Lebanese civilians to that of participating in the Lebanese government's war against its own people alarmed its partners in the multinational force. On September 21–22, the ambassadors of Britain, France, and Italy secretly visited the White House to implore the Reagan administration not to involve their countries in the expanding war in Lebanon.[5] And in Paris French Prime Minister Pierre Mauroy bluntly warned that the conflict in Lebanon was "one of civil strife which Lebanon tries to turn into an international crisis involving the United States and Soviet-backed governments." President Reagan, however, boasted that American naval power, especially the presence of the *USS New Jersey,* was the real reason for Druse and Syrian acceptance of a cease-fire on September 25.

The cease-fire negotiated by Saudi Arabia and the United States left the Druses in control of the Chouf. It also assured Syria, owing to its support for the Druses in the mountain war, a part in any discussion of a settlement. The ceasefire also demanded a "national dialogue" among the contending parties to settle the issue at stake. This was scheduled for October 31. On October 24, early on a Sunday morning, a suicide commando drove a truck laden with explosives into Marine headquarters near the airport; the explosion killed 241 Marines. Only minutes later, a similar operation demolished the French battalion's main center at Jnah near Beirut's southern outskirts, killing fifty French paratroopers. And, on November 4, another suicide attack destroyed the Israeli military governor's headquarters in Tyre, killing sixty people: twenty-eight Israeli troops and thirty-two Palestinian and Lebanese detainees held for questioning on "terrorist activity." David Kimche, the director general of the Israeli foreign ministry, traveled all the way to Geneva (where Lebanon's national dialogue conference was in session) to tell the world press that Syria was responsible for the explosion. President Reagan earlier had also placed "part of the blame" for the death of the Marines on Syria. Within six hours of the explosion, Israeli fighter bombers attacked Syrian-backed Palestinian forces near Bhamdoun "in reprisal."

The Sixth Fleet's bombardments of opposition forces fighting to take Souk al-Gharb could have been the immediate provocation touching off the attack on the American "peacekeepers," just as French fighter-bomber raids on opposition groups in the Bekaa could have been the immediate provocation for the attack on the French paratroopers. But the mainspring for these operations was in both cases found elsewhere. Opposition to France's pro-Iraq policy in the Gulf war explained the latter, while in the former case the explanation cut deeper: total rejection of an American policy distinguished by its contempt for the Arabs. American officials involved in forming and executing policy in the area were ignorant of both the countries and their peoples, personally hostile to Arabs, and well-known as "Arab baiters."[6] Most were one-time protégés or associates of Henry Kissinger. Following on the destruction of the American embassy in Beirut in April—when sixty-three people, including seventeen Americans, were killed in a similar suicide bombing operation—the killing of the Marines should have awakened the administration to the need to reexamine its policy. But both the Americans and the French preferred to hold either Syria or Shi'a extremists, or both, responsible.

An unidentified American official in the Gulf charged that Amal was responsible for the attacks, in conjunction with the Khomeini regime. Nabih Berri denied the charge. In fact, both Amal and the Higher Shi'a Council had from early 1983 moved away from the Khomeini regime. This was one of the reasons Hussein Musawi, a former lieutenant of Imam Sadr, had broken away from Amal to form an "Islamic Amal" closely linked to Iran, loyal to Khomeini, and based in Baalbek in the Syrian-controlled northern Bekaa.

Musawi denied that either he or Islamic Amal was involved, but he paid tribute to those who did it, whom he identified as "the orphans and widows of the victims and martyrs of Sabra and Shatila, of Beirut's southern suburbs and of north and south Lebanon." In short he placed the responsibility on American policy-makers. It was they, he pointed out, who approved and assisted the Israeli invasion, and supplied Israel with cluster bombs and other illegal weapons of mass destruction for use against the Lebanese, especially the Shi'as and the poor. It was the Americans who backed and supported Israel's Lebanese allies and their dominance over the Beirut government. It was they who armed and trained a Lebanese army which did not fire a shot against the Israeli aggressors, but rather did not hesitate to turn the full power of their weapons against the Lebanese people, especially Muslims and the disadvantaged.

Geneva Conference, October 31–November 4, 1983

The "urgent meeting to begin national dialogue immediately" demanded by the terms of the September 25 cease-fire compelled President Gemayel to drop his insistence that withdrawal of all foreign forces precede dialogue. This condition was intended to postpone dialogue indefinitely. The participants designated in the agreement included in addition to Syrian Foreign Minister Abdul Halim Khaddam, five Christians, all Maronites, and five Muslims.[7] Only one of these ten, Nabih Berri, came from outside the traditional ruling class. Only three were under fifty years old, the rest ranging in age from sixty-eight to eighty-four. Only two—Berri and Walid Jumblat—were present by virtue of the power they wielded on the ground. To many the conference appeared to be directed to saving not Lebanon but rather its aged and discredited clan-based leadership. The exclusion from the conference of any spokesman for the Greek Orthodox or Greek Catholic communities was designed to lend credibility to the Maronite pretension to speak for all Christians, and to the Maronite thesis that the conflict was between Christians and Muslims. Acceptance of this pretension prejudiced from the start any efforts to achieve a democratic solution.

While the conference was far from representative of either the political currents or sectarian composition of the country, its assigned task implicitly recognized the imperative of a new distribution of power. Most of the antagonists, who had been involved together in Lebanese politics for close to half a century, were soon amiably discussing and even reaching agreement on a number of issues. The issue that soon dominated the conference and gave it significance, however, was the insistence of Syria and the Lebanese opposition on the abrogation of the May 17 Lebanese–Israeli agreement. All those present finally concurred that President Gemayel must visit Washington and other capitals to win consent for the agreement's replacement by mutual guarantees of border security, in return for which Israel would withdraw from Lebanon. The new formula excluded all the political, economic, and military concessions wrung from Lebanon by American and Israeli pressures.

American–Israeli Strategic Alliance

The Lebanese "reconciliation meeting" in Geneva had hardly ended when President Reagan sent to Jerusalem Under Secretary of State Lawrence Eagleburger, considered the "most rabid" of the administration's "many Arab baiters," to conclude a new strategic alliance.[8] This alliance was intended to replace the strategic cooperation agreement Washington had suspended in December of 1981, when Israel annexed the Golan. Twenty-four hours before President Gemayel's December 1, 1983 arrival in Washington, to seek abrogation of the May 17 accord, Israeli Prime Minister Yitzhak Shamir and President Reagan signed the new strategic agreement in the White House. Gemayel's mission was stillborn. The Lebanese president heard only "tough talk" from his American counterpart, who ordered the Gemayel government to concentrate on the domestic situation and leave Syria and its supporters to the United States and Israel. His instructions were to establish close relations with Israel, and to rely on Israeli help in extending his government's authority over the Syrian-occupied parts of Lebanon. He was also told to discuss any revisions in the May 17 accord with Israel (Israel had already rejected any changes whatever in the accord).

The new American–Israeli strategic alliance angered and alarmed the Arab world, where it was perceived as an insult as well as a threat. The agreement provided for more American financial aid to Israel and even closer political and military ties. These included the formation of a joint commission to face "the Soviet menace to their common interests in the Middle East"; the stockpiling of American military supplies in Israel, making Israel a forward supply base for American and Israeli action in the area; the American purchase of Israeli-produced armaments and other American measures to improve Israel's financial position; and joint American–Israeli maneuvres in the Mediterranean. This American largesse appeared to the Arabs to be a reward for Israel's intransigence in refusing to halt settlement construction in the West Bank, or even for its rejection of Reagan's proposals for a West Bank solution.

By proclaiming the objective of the new agreement to be the ouster of Soviet influence from the Middle East, the United States and Israel advertised their intention to topple the Soviet-backed Syrian and South Yemeni regimes and to maintain an Israeli presence in Lebanon to help the United States fight Syria. Facing an American armada of three aircraft carriers boasting 300 war planes, President Assad called up 100,000 of his reserves, and on November 10 Syrian anti-aircraft batteries fired on American reconnaissance planes over Lebanon. Realizing that President Assad had already effectively vetoed the May 17 agreement—by refusing to withdraw his troops from Lebanon until all Israeli troops had departed—the United States and Israel set out to make him change his mind. On December 4, four days after the signature of the American–Israeli strategic agreement, a heavy American air attack on Syrian positions in the mountains east of Beirut was perceived throughout the Arab world as the closest the United States had ever come to war with an Arab country. The attack took place only twenty-four hours after Israeli fighter bombers had hit Syrian targets in central Lebanon. Arabs saw in these coordinated American–Israeli strikes the first product of the new strategic alliance. (These attacks on Syrian forces in Lebanon, coming on the heels of President Gemayel's talks with Ronald Reagan, prompted speculation as to Gemayel's role, if any, in this hardening of American policy.)

Two months before these Israeli and American strikes against Syrian forces in Lebanon, the Syrian government in a letter to the U.S. State Department had proposed that "the two sides work out a procedure for American surveillance flights over Lebanon that would provide Syrian batteries with advance notice and so avoid firing by either side." When the State Department finally replied, in December, it rejected the proposal, and the White House, brushing aside the objections of the Joint Chiefs of Staff, authorized the December 4 strike against Syrian positions in the mountains.[9] The outcome proved disastrous, two planes were downed by Syrian ground fire, and two others crashed in Syria. One pilot died of his wounds; the other—a black American named Robert Goodman—was captured.

Goodman was subsequently released by President Assad, who was recovering from a heart attack at that time, in response to the initiatives of black American presidential candidate Jesse Jackson. This compounded the Reagan administration's humiliation over this defeat.

Two days after the unsuccessful American air strike, a four-and-a-half-hour bombardment of Marine positions at Beirut airport by pro-Syrian Lebanese militiamen killed eight Marines. In retaliation—and determined to change the balance of power on the ground by weakening Syria and the Lebanese opposition—the Americans for the first time activated the *New Jersey's* sixteen-inch guns in order to hit at Syrian anti-aircraft positions deep inside Syrian-controlled territory in Lebanon's northeast hills. The guns, however, their targeting precision adversely affected by sea swells and atmospheric conditions, proved less than accurate.

The American and Israeli escalation of violence, including a second bombardment from the *New Jersey* shortly after the successful Geneva conference, underscored the U.S. refusal to reconsider the May 17 agreement and blocked the resumption of dialogue among the Lebanese factions. With the growing American participation in the war hard-line Maronite leaders—who had earlier perceived a need to make at least some concessions and come to terms with Syria—became once again intransigent. These American pressures, intended in part to persuade Assad to move away from the USSR, impressed neither Assad nor the Lebanese opposition. Assad continued to demand the withdrawal of Israeli forces as well as all four contingents of the multinational forces and insisted on the formation of a new Lebanese government favorable to Syria. Meanwhile, he mobilized his own people to stand up to Washington.

[22]

Syria, the PLO,
and the Battle for Tripoli

Despite their different long-term aims in Lebanon, the United States, Israel, and Syria share one short-term goal: the elimination of the Palestinian movement, particularly the PLO, as an independent political and military entity. Thus it is not surprising that the American-Israeli offensive against both the Lebanese opposition and Syria's role in Lebanon failed to deflect Syrian President Assad's own drive against the PLO. And in the midst of promoting the defense of Souk al-Gharb in September 1983, the then acting chairman of the U.S. Joint Chiefs of Staff, Admiral James Watkins, promised that once the Souk al-Gharb battle was won the United States would help the Lebanese army to wipe out the Palestinians in Tripoli.[1]

The September evacuation of more than 8,000 PLO fighters from West Beirut left as many, if not more, in the Syrian-controlled Bekaa and the Beddawi and Nahr al-Bared refugee camps on the outskirts of Tripoli in North Lebanon. In September 1983, following his expulsion from Syria in June, and from the Bekaa three months later, PLO leader Yasir Arafat established his headquarters outside of Tripoli. The expulsion move by the Syrian army was joined by PLO mutineers who saw in Assad's verbal militancy a chance to continue the armed struggle they accused Arafat of abandoning. Many Palestinians, at least in the beginning, shared the dissidents' criticism of Arafat's "go-it-alone" leadership and apparent progressive de-emphasis on the importance of armed struggle. Yet Arafat's position must be viewed in the light of the history of the past decade.

Almost from the start—and especially in the wake of the 1973 Yom Kippur war—Arafat perceived political compromise to be a regrettable necessity, even if for tactical reasons he preferred that Nayef Hawatmeh, leader of the Democratic Front for the Liberation of

335

Palestine (DFLP), be the first to advocate it. Arafat's resort to arms, starting in January 1965, was intended to persuade Arab governments, and world opinion, that Palestinian rights and the Palestinian claim to justice could not be ignored. His January 1968 declaration welcoming all Jews of Israel to live as equals in a democratic Palestinian state had posed a threat only to Zionist exclusivism. As Edward Said noted in the *New York Times,* Arafat and al-Fatah loyalists set out to shape the Palestinians as a "national community," making the PLO a "genuinely representative body." By 1974, Said argued, Arafat "had put the Palestinian people and their cause before the world. . . . he was the first popular Palestinian leader to formulate the notion that Palestinian Arabs and Israeli Jews could—indeed must— seek a future together on an equal footing in a shared territory."[2]

Israel's answer to this approach was incessant repetition of its claim that all Palestinian nationalists aimed to destroy the Jewish state and its people. Even the fact that in 1977 the Palestine National Council (PLO parliament) approved in principle a West Bank-Gaza Strip solution and in 1979 authorized negotiations on this basis did not halt Israel's propaganda. Yet almost alone in the Arab world, the PLO achieved a democratic and pluralist practice and distinguished itself as a secular political entity in a region where the few such entities that did exist were rapidly disappearing beneath a rising tide of fundamentalism.

Israel's rejection of every Palestinian initiative in time undermined Arafat's position, giving impulse to dissidents in the PLO and facilitating President Assad's drive to eliminate the PLO leader. Al-Fatah dissidents appeared to be blind to the mainspring of the Assad–Arafat conflict: the Syrian president's determination to win control of the PLO (and Lebanon), which explains his opposition to all of Arafat's initiatives. But Assad did not confront Arafat directly: he employed the Palestinian renegade, Abu Nidal, to destroy those Palestinians engaged in the search for "a peaceful and just solution." Two leading Palestinians active in this search, Sa'id Hammami and Dr. Issam Sartawi, met this fate. Sartawi's remarks about Hammami, at a memorial service for his colleague shortly before his own assassination, stand for his own position as well:

> He was quite aware of the military realities in the area and the position and importance of the super powers. This knowledge persuaded him that the purely military option advocated by some was merely a rhetorical

position unsupported by reality. He had the courage to advocate that a political option was needed in addition to the military one.[3]

This was also Arafat's position, although he was somewhat more cautious and for internal reasons did not deal directly with this sensitive issue. And, in the wake of the 1982 invasion, Israel, the United States, and Syria, each in its own fashion but not without complicity, set out to destroy Arafat—the only Arab leader elected by a representative assembly, a mandate renewed by the Palestinian National Council in February 1983. Syria's patron, the USSR, on this issue supported the PLO and Arafat, who after the PLO's departure from Beirut had embarked on a diplomatic strategy aimed at exploring President Reagan's September 1, 1982, "peace initiative."

This initiative called for substantial though not total Israeli withdrawal from the occupied territories and proposed Palestinian self-government in a West Bank entity linked to Jordan. Reagan's plan was widely perceived as a political and psychological plus for the Palestinians. For, although rejecting an independent Palestinian state, it also rejected Israeli sovereignty over, or permanent control of, the West Bank and Gaza. Reagan, moreover, called on Israel to immediately halt construction of settlements in the occupied territories. In reply, Israel accelerated its seizure of Palestinian land. By the end of 1984, it had taken 52 percent of the land of the occupied territories, chiefly for use by the military and by some 45,000 Jewish settlers already established in over a hundred settlements. Israeli plans call for installing 100,000 more Jewish settlers by the year 2,000, according to a report by Israel's West Bank Data Base Project, directed by Meron Benvenisti, former deputy mayor of Jerusalem.[4] This report pointed out that Israel is thus creating a "dual system" whereby the 800,000 Palestinians in the West Bank will be isolated "in a patchwork of hostile regions, alienated and severed" from each other.

Arafat, mindful of the growing desperation of the Palestinians in the occupied territories, insisted that Reagan's initiative must be explored even though it ruled out a PLO role, so making talk of self-government meaningless. Israel dismissed Reagan's plan out of hand. So, too, did President Assad, who wanted the Palestinian card in his own hands, not King Husain's, because in order to secure return of the Golan he needed the ability to "deliver" the Palestinians in any Middle East settlement.[5] He therefore opposed all Arafat's efforts to achieve a negotiated solution. If Arafat could be dispatched and the

Palestinian national movement crippled, Assad could reach a settlement with Israel and the United States (overlords in the area and thus necessary to any agreement) without regard for Palestinian rights.

Assad's minority regime, as Middle East expert Godfrey Jansen has pointed out, "desperately needs" to gain respectability and prestige from the PLO so as to "counter its unpopular and unrepresentative character."[6] Assad is an Alawi, a branch of Shi'a heterodoxy which represents only about 12 percent of the Syrian population, and he has drawn the members of his ruling clique from an even narrower base: the Alawis of his own family, clan, and village. For this reason, Assad has ceaselessly tried to subject the PLO to his own control and to use it to serve his own minority's interest, while presenting himself as the main defender of the Palestinian cause.

On the eve of Israel's 1982 invasion, the World Zionist Organization published its master plan for the future of the Middle East.[7] This calls for splintering existing Arab national states into sectarian mini-states: Alawi, Shi'a, Druse, Maronite, and so on. Assad's policy in Lebanon, by undermining PLO unity, accorded with this approach: his support of the Maronite minority throughout the 1975–82 period, his refusal during the 1982 invasion to aid the PLO or even to accept phone calls from PLO leaders, and his confiscation of Soviet arms shipments to the PLO. During the Israeli invasion, Syrian troops stationed in Lebanon were left on their own by a Syrian government whose main concern was to avoid being involved in the war. Syrian troops stationed in West Beirut, fought—but under PLO command—until the end, as did Syrian units in other parts of the country.[8]

In September 1982 Arab leaders met in Fez, Morocco, and put forth their own Middle East plan. This called for Palestinian self-determination and independent statehood under the PLO. PLO leaders decided to keep their options open. Two months later, Arafat and King Husain began a dialogue aimed at bridging the gap between the Reagan plan and the Arab Summit resolutions.

Meanwhile, however, Reagan's plan was slowly dying. Reagan's failure to support his own initiative demonstrated that it was intended only to mitigate Arab anger over American complicity in Israel's invasion. In fact, he promptly sabotaged his own plan by awarding Israel a large increase in American aid and the conclusion of the United States–Israel "strategic alliance." This meant that the United States would be financing Israeli settlements in the occupied territories in direct contradiction to Reagan's peace plan. On August 3,

1983, the State Department effectively buried Reagan's plan in announcing that dismantling Israeli settlements in the occupied territories was "impractical."

King Husain attributed the failure of his talks with Arafat to Reagan's failure to inject credibility into his own peace plan: his exclusion of the PLO from the proposed negotiations; and his refusal to recognize the PLO unless it accepted UN resolutions 242 and 238 and acknowledged Israel's "right to exist." Such a right does not exist in either international law or diplomatic practice. In establishing diplomatic relations de facto or de jure, states recognize no more than the fact that the state has control over the territory within its borders. And, if a state demands recognition in international law, it must, as Godfrey Jansen has pointed out, be prepared to abide by that law: "It is on this very issue . . . that Israel's claim that its right to exist be recognized falls to the ground because it is, in singular fashion, the outlaw of the family of nations."[9]

King Husain also pointed to Washington's failure to denounce Israel's illegal settlement policies or its increasing repression in the occupied territories. The Arab world shared the King's anger over what he termed "the total inadequacy of American constructive support for our position." Reagan's plan proved to be a fraud.

A Crisis in Al-Fatah

Both the Reagan and Fez peace plans contributed to a crisis that developed within al-Fatah in this period. Differences first surfaced at a closed meeting of al-Fatah's Revolutionary Council in Aden, January 27, 1983, when Arafat and his policies were severely criticized by one of al-Fatah's most respected military leaders. This was Abu Musa, a Sandhurst graduate and former Jordanian army officer who joined the resistance during the September 1970 battle of Amman, fought in the 1975–76 war in Lebanon, and directed West Beirut's defense in the summer of 1982. In opposing Arafat he insisted that the Arafat–Husain talks, Arafat's behind-the-scenes dialogue with Egypt, and PLO contacts with Zionist organizations and personalities be ended immediately.

A brave and honest man, Abu Musa spoke for a group of former Jordanian army—and now al-Fatah—officers who had made secret contacts with Syrian and Libyan leaders shortly after their departure from Beirut. The mutiny in al-Fatah's ranks in the Bekaa that erupted May 11, 1983, involved these colonels and Palestinian fighters dependent on Syria. Arafat's reappointment of the two discredited PLO officers, Abu Hajem and Haj Ismail, to command posts in Lebanon touched off the mutiny, and his subsequent cancellation of these appointments failed to halt it. Rebel leaders, based in Syria, held Arafat responsible for the Sabra–Shatila massacre because he had trusted American guarantees. They insisted his pursuit of an agreement with Washington could have equally disastrous results.

The validity of some of the rebels' complaints could not be denied.[10] Yet perhaps unwittingly, the rebels collaborated in Assad's drive to destroy the PLO's political independence and weaken its military strength. In the spring and summer of 1983 they drove al-Fatah loyalists out of the Bekaa to the Baddawi and Nahr al-Bared refugee camps near Tripoli, where Arafat had established his headquarters, and where the Syrian army was by far the strongest and controlling force.

Tripoli Conflicts

In the northern coastal city of Tripoli, isolated under Syrian Arab Deterrent Force control since the 1975–76 civil war, local conflicts rooted in the social upheavals of the early 1970s, and the defeat of the Lebanese National Movement (LNM) in the 1975–76 civil war, had by 1983 provoked the exodus of up to a third or more of the city's 600,000 people. Social strife opened the door to the rise of Muslim fundamentalism, which by the early 1980s had achieved dominance in a city now split into fiefdoms ruled by militias of one faction or another, a city—like Beirut—of street battles and car bomb explosions.

The majority of the city's population is Sunni. Yet, since many poor Alawi workers had migrated to the city from Syria earlier in the century, as well as more recently, Tripoli also has a substantial Shi'a Alawi minority, poorer and more exploited than the Sunni majority. The Syrian army presence in north Lebanon since the 1975–76 civil war, however, permitted Shi'a Alawis to improve their status and even to acquire a voice in local politics. The stationing in Tripoli in 1982 of

Rifaat Assad's Special Forces, the Pink Panthers (so-called because of the color of their uniforms), resulted in numerous clashes between the Panthers, assisted by the Saiqa-backed Arab Knights militia, and the multiplying Sunni fundamentalist groups.

Said Shaaban, a Sunni sheikh and leader of the Islamic Unification Movement (IUM), by repulsing an influx of Shi'a Alawi Muslims from Syria into what before 1920 had been a Syrian area just north of Tripoli, had recently achieved leadership of the Muslim fundamentalist movement in north Lebanon. Like most other militias, Shaaban's was financed in large part by the appropriation of customs dues collected at the port, in his case estimated at around 2 billion Lebanese pounds a year.

Tripoli was also a long-time stronghold of the sixty-year-old Communist Party of Lebanon (CPL). Over the years the CPL organized port workers in the harbor area, Al-Mina, who won higher pay and better working conditions. Al-Mina became a communist center, and Tripoli itself acquired a progressive aura. One of its deputies, Hashem Husseini, leader of the Partisans of Peace, also active in Tripoli, was awarded the Lenin Peace Prize.

In establishing his primacy in the city, Shaaban ruthlessly attacked the CPL. In mid-October 1983, his men, sporting black masks, killed at least sixty Lebanese communists in a four-day massacre at party headquarters in the dock area. Militiamen stormed into the homes of communist and non-communist workers in this area, killing all males, even the young and the old, in full view of their families, and rounding up others who were killed later, their bodies dumped into the sea. Shaaban's men then besieged CPL headquarters in the main Tripoli square, giving the some 200 people there the choice of departure from Tripoli or death. In these massacres, Shaaban violated his own favorite slogan: "Neither for Palestinians nor Syrians. For Lebanese only." Nearly all the workers killed were Lebanese-born and Tripoli natives. Shaaban at the time denied responsibility for the massacres, but two years later in Beirut he boasted that in three hours his movement had uprooted a party established in the city for sixty years.

Sunni political leaders in Tripoli (such as Rashid Karami and Abdel Meguid Rafi'i) and for the most part the Sunni upper classes did not support the bourgeoning fundamentalist militias and their frequent clashes with the Shi'a minority. In fact, they became increasingly concerned. The Sunni disadvantaged, however, responded enthusiastically to fundamentalist demands for social and political reforms, justice and equality for all Lebanon's citizens, and other similar slogans.

The rise of fundamentalist movements, here and elsewhere in the Arab world, owed something to the impact of the Iranian revolution, but in Lebanon their rise owed much more to the near decade of bitter Maronite–Muslim strife, the ever more fascist character of the Christian right militias and, last but not least, the devastating impact of the Israeli invasion and installation of a Christian government in Beirut. These trends provoked apprehensions that a return of government authority to the city would bring mass arrests like those made in West Beirut in the wake of the Israeli invasion, or even massacres like those at Sabra and Shatila.

In Tripoli, President Assad's Alawi regime was in open conflict with both al-Fatah and the Sunni fundamentalists, in particular Shaaban's IUM. His two enemies at times helped each other, a fact leading the CPL to hold Arafat responsible for the slaughter of the communists (without, however, supplying proof of this allegation). Both al-Fatah and the IUM denied the charge, which, intentionally or not, provided grist for the anti-Arafat mill then working overtime in Damascus.

The Battle of Tripoli

Soon after Arafat and PLO loyalists arrived in Tripoli in September 1983, Assad dispatched to the Tripoli front two armored brigades, as well as parachutists and commandos, altogether about 12,000 fighters to join Syrian forces already in the area. Several hundred Libyan troops bolstered the anti-Arafat front while some 2,000 PLO mutineers provided a thin cover for the Syrian and Libyan regulars. These were positioned on the hills surrounding the city and the camps on three sides, with Israeli warships off the coast completing the encirclement. Facing this formidable array of fire power, tanks, missile launchers, heavy artillery, and planes were Arafat's 3,000 guerrillas armed with light artillery, mortars, and rockets.

The Syrian-directed attack struck first at the Nahr al-Bared camp north of Tripoli on November 3, inflicting heavy casualties in a three-day battle. Separated from Arafat's main force at Baddawi by a ten-mile stretch controlled by the Syrian army, PLO fighters fell back to join in the defense of Baddawi camp which a few days later was itself surrounded. A cease-fire imposed by Arab states on November 10 was broken five days later by Syrian tanks and guns as the final assault on Baddawi began. Pitched battles, in which many of the defenders died, were fought at the entrance of the camp, which fell after a two-day onslaught.

Syrian bombardments did not spare Tripoli's suburbs, where many civilians were killed or wounded, or the oil storage tanks, which burned out of control for many days. Hospitals could not cope with the overflow of the wounded and the dying. And after arrangements for the evacuation of Arafat and his men were completed, Syria repeatedly bombarded Palestinian positions in and near Tripoli. Its relentless bombardments had one positive result. This was to hasten conclusion of long drawn-out negotiations, inspired by the Vatican, for an Israel–PLO prisoner exchange in which nearly 5,000 Palestinian and Lebanese prisoners in the Ansar concentration camp in south Lebanon were released in exchange for six Israeli military prisoners held by the PLO in Tripoli.

President Assad may have won the battle of Tripoli but al-Fatah mutineers did not. For Arafat's presence in Tripoli transformed the battle from one between opposing PLO factions to one between the PLO on one side, and Syria, Libya, and the PLO renegades on the other. Arafat's leadership, moreover, stimulated a wide mobilization of both Lebanese and Palestinian support for the PLO and against the Assad-controlled PLO dissidents.

The behavior of the dissidents during the battles for the camps lost them all credibility. In Nahr al-Bared camp, for example, they did not hesitate to fire into a crowd of camp residents demonstrating against them, killing twenty-five people and wounding seventy-five, according to the International Red Cross.[11] These murders brought virtually all the camp's inhabitants into the streets, where they held high Arafat's picture and tried to burn the cars of dissident leaders. Another demonstration during the burial of the victims next day rallied as many. Even in Syria, in the Yarmuk camp just south of Damascus, men, women, and children courageously took to the streets to protest Syrian attacks on Palestinians in Tripoli and to demonstrate against the al-Fatah rebels. Moreover, if many Palestinians may have originally sympathized with some of the rebels' criticisms of Arafat's leadership, this quickly changed when they perceived the rebels to be Assad's men and the issue to be that of the PLO's independence of Arab regimes.

In the Israeli-occupied West Bank and Gaza, reaction to the al-Fatah rebels was one of despair and confusion. A poll in the West Bank found 94 percent of those questioned opposed to the rebels. Elias Freij, mayor of Bethlehem, declared: "The PLO rebels have plunged us into a civil war before we even have our own state. It is a nightmare beyond our worst dreams." Arafat also received support from the elected mayors of the largest West Bank cities, the West Bank trade unions, and overwhelmingly from the Palestinians living in the camps.

Palestinian reaction to Arafat's defeat in Tripoli and subsequent reconciliation with Egyptian President Hosni Mubarak was comparable to that of the Egyptians to President Nasser after the humiliating Arab defeat in the 1967 war. Although aware of the PLO leader's shortcomings, Palestinians nevertheless reaffirmed their own commitment to the Palestinian cause and to the leader that symbolized that cause. For many, one of the first items on the post-Tripoli agenda was for the PLO and its leaders to come to terms with the rising political opposition within the organization. This opposition, spearheaded by the dissidents, the Popular Front for the Liberation of Palestine (PFLP), and the Democratic Front for the Liberation of Palestine (DFLP), rejected armed clashes against other Palestinians as a means of determining policy. Its aim was to make the Palestinian liberation movement more democratic, more effective, but ultimately more bound to Syria.

[23]

The Insurrection of February 1984 and Its Consequences

> The southern suburbs are pounded as if their inhabitants were not citizens of this country. The state by its actions in the last few days has committed suicide by seeking to eliminate its own citizens. The Muslim quarters are being suppressed while the Kataeb reigns supreme in other sectors of the capital.
>
> —Statement of Shi'a Community Supreme
> Council, December 17, 1983

As the Druse–Maronite war in the Chouf moved toward a conclusion at the end of 1983, the army and the Lebanese Forces savagely bombarded West Beirut's southern suburbs, a twenty-eight-square mile poverty belt known as "the suburbs of the deprived," leaving 300 dead. Crammed into this target were some 6–700,000 people, mainly Shi'as, many expelled from East Beirut's poorer suburbs during the 1975–76 civil war, and others driven from the south (300,000 in 1977 alone) by successive Israeli incursions and its 1982 invasion. Earlier army–Lebanese Forces attacks had provoked the flight of some 250,000 Muslims, leaving three suburbs almost totally uninhabited. Since the evacuation of the Palestinian Liberation Organization (PLO) in 1982 Amal had become the major political force in the area.

The bombardments became massive and methodical in January 1984, hitting West Beirut's Sunni quarters and the Sabra and Shatila camps, from which French troops had just been withdrawn. As a result the Lebanese Forces and the Lebanese army together were able to kidnap 150 or more Palestinians. At the same time former Prime Minister Saab Salam reported that more than a thousand residents of the southern suburbs were "arrested," many not to be heard of again.

In the first week of February 1984, a fierce joint army–Lebanese Forces assault on the southern suburbs shattered entire districts, killing 600 or more people, mainly women and children, and destroying hundreds of homes and water mains. This assault left some 400,000 people without electricity, running water, or food supplies, and condemned them to take shelter for days, even weeks, in basements so flooded with water from broken mains and so crowded that occupants were often unable to sit or lie down. Repeated UNICEF demands for a halt to the bombardments to permit repair of the mains met no response. Harsh winter conditions compounded the misery.

State medical services had never reached the suburbs. The only accessible hospital, a small one built in 1982 on the edge of the area, managed to treat many wounded although it was repeatedly shelled. Those treated were mainly refugees from the south or others experiencing once again the loss of their belongings, and the wounding or killing of families and friends.

The United States Withdrawal

American military officers remained in the Lebanese army's main operations room during the weeks when the American-trained Lebanese army, using American tanks, canons, and other equipment were pounding large areas of the southern suburbs to rubble. American warships, including the *USS New Jersey,* repeatedly struck at Syrian and Druse positions in the mountains while American Marines fought artillery battles with opposition militias. Israel's gains from the recently concluded U.S.–Israel strategic agreement now became apparent in the first killing of Arabs by the American armed forces (naval gunners at sea and Marines at the airport).

Fierce battles between the Lebanese Army and the Druse in the mountains, and between the army and the Shi'as in West Beirut and the southern suburbs, escalated in early February when President Gemayel tried to compel the opposition to abandon its demands and make important political concessions. Initially, opposition demands included the president's resignation, elimination of political sectarianism throughout Lebanon, and the withdrawal of all American forces. President Reagan, in an interview published in the *Wall Street Journal,* February 3, 1984, insisted that the withdrawal of American troops would mean the end of Lebanon and the end of overall Middle East peace prospects. In taking this stand Reagan disregarded Saudi Crown Prince Abdullah's unprecedented February 1 attack—before a group of visiting American businessmen—on the American role in Lebanon, which had the effect of withdrawing Saudi cover for the American presence and the American policies in Lebanon.

In a radio broadcast on February 6, Italian President Sandro Pertini explained the continuing United States mission in Lebanon:

> American Marines have become hostages to Israeli policy. If the United States had the political will to force the Israelis to withdraw in accordance with UN resolutions 508 and 509, there would be no need for the Marines. . . . Let us speak plainly, the Americans are remaining in Lebanon only to defend Israel, not peace.[1]

Despite this widespread perception President Reagan accused House Speaker Thomas P. O'Neill, who had initially supported the Marine presence in Lebanon but now demanded its immediate withdrawal, of being "ready to surrender," repeating that he would not. Three days later, seconded by Vice-President George Bush, the President reasserted his "firm and unwavering support" for President Gemayel. The next day, ready or not, Reagan "surrendered." Without a warning to Gemayel, he ordered the immediate withdrawal of the Marines to American warships off the coast.

Palestinians in the refugee camps greeted the American departure joyfully. When the Italian force withdrew on February 20 they cried. A young Palestinian told me: "The Italians protected us, tried to keep the Lebanese army from arresting us and when they failed, they took names to ensure the physical safety of the people arrested. They gave us a hospital and even made house calls. Truly they were our friends. Their presence was a real blessing for us."

The Battle for West Beirut and the Disintegration of the Army

The precipitous U.S. withdrawal was brought about by Amal leader Nabih Berri's call to all Shi'as in the armed forces to disobey combat orders, causing the swift disintegration of President Gemayel's 30,000 strong American-trained and American-equipped army: entire units defected to their respective sectarian communities while others fraternized with opposition militiamen.

Reacting to the American action, Raymond Edde blamed Gemayel for the Lebanese army's disintegration, noting that he preferred to use the army against a fraction of the population rather than use it to defend the country as a whole. In fact, Gemayel's mistake was the greater because he pitted the army not against a fraction, but against a majority of the population. He held Lebanon to be, as he had asserted in a TV broadcast on December 24, 1983, "the forward outpost of European security."

On the morrow of the uprising, the army's eleven brigades, although remaining administratively dependent on the Defense Ministry, were distributed among the major sects according to the sectarian identity of their officers and men. Confirmed at the Lausanne Conference of March 12–20, 1984, this system, while preserving a balance of forces on the ground, meant that the army had become no more than a collection of sectarian brigades often hostile to each other, incapable of establishing or keeping order, and frequently participating in battles between the sectarian parties and between the different regions of the country. A national army could issue only from a national state, which no longer existed, if indeed it ever had.

Colonel Fouad Lahoud, chairman of parliament's Defense Committee, asserted in late August 1985 that billions of Lebanese pounds were being spent for weapons intended for use "for repressive purposes"; that fighting brigades were "not properly organized and are dominated by a tribal . . . chaotic, confessional, even sectarian character. Discipline is lacking. Combat spirit, morale and mutual confidence are missing." Thousands in the army "had received no assignment and were doing no work." Waste of funds, "highly exaggerated prices" paid for arms, "irregularities" in making arms deals— these were "one of the chief reasons for soaring budget deficits."

The army's terrible bombardments of the southern suburbs, parts of West Beirut, and the Druse hills to the east in the twenty-four hours following the Berri call and its losing battle with Amal for control of the strategic corridor linking the suburbs to the Syrian-controlled countryside, provoked the fall of Chafik Wazzan's government on February 5. Both Walid Jumblat and Nabih Berri demanded Gemayel's resignation.

On February 6, Amal and Progressive Socialist Party (PSP) militiamen seized control of all West Beirut, thereby restoring the Green Line separating it from East Beirut. On February 14, Amal and Druse militiamen linked up at Khalde, eleven kilometers south of the city, thus gaining control of all access roads between the capital and the south and an unimpeded supply line linking the Druse mountains to the southern suburbs and West Beirut. The disintegration of the army's mainly Druse Fourth Brigade when it was sent to the mountains to repress the Jumblat forces assured this opposition victory. In the mountains, only Souk al-Gharb still remained in the hands of the Lebanese army.

By February 25 the opposition controlled all of West Beirut, the mountain regions southeast of the capital, and the coastal highway from Beirut south to Damour, an important outlet to the sea. President Gemayel had changed sides by this time, finding it more expedient to cast in his lot with Syria than with Israel. Gemayel's lack of qualifications for his post permitted President Assad, by a judicious combination of flattery and advice, to completely dominate him, encouraging the Syrian to ignore repeated demands for Gemayel's ouster.

The security plan for West Beirut, drawn up by Nabih Berri, assigned law and order duties to the predominantly Shi'a Sixth Brigade commanded by the Shi'a General Lutfi Jaber. One of Berri's first initiatives was the bombardment of the three Palestinian camps in South Beirut, Sabra, Shatila and Bourj al-Barajneh on February 24. This was only a few weeks after a Lebanese army "Christmas assault" that included massive fire into the camps and looting of homes, and forced many civilians to seek refuge in Jumblat-controlled areas and the Shatila Mosque. Following the February 24 aggression, Berri ordered Amal militiamen to encircle the camps, an action, as the weekly *Al-Shiraa* commented, that was "like putting gunpowder next to fire." A succession of Syrian-sponsored Amal offensives against the PLO followed—the same PLO that in the 1970s had provided Amal with the funds and organizational and military know-how that enabled it to become established. The "ideology of the deprived," hitherto predominant in Amal's propaganda, virtually disappeared after February 6, 1984, replaced by demands for the elimination of sectarianism—although Amal's own practice now became more sectarian than ever.

The American and Israeli failure to impose their own solutions on

Lebanon placed Syria in charge of any attempt to establish a new political order or to resuscitate the old. Syrian President Assad became the principal guardian of the Lebanese sectarian status quo. He thus deliberately perpetuated a system which had already brought more than a decade of seemingly endless civil war of ever greater brutality and devastation, a war that increasingly appeared to put the state's continued existence into question.

Assad was convinced that Lebanese national unity threatened not only his influence in Lebanon, but his own minority regime at home. This fear dictated his attempt to "reform" Lebanon's sectarian system, which amounted to little more than promoting Shi'a hegemony in Muslim areas at the expense of the Sunni community (hitherto the Maronites' junior partner in the sectarian political system), and preserving Maronite hegemony in the Christian areas. In Assad's scenario, the Maronite Kataeb and/or Lebanese Forces and the Shi'a Amal would rule Lebanon and, most importantly, function as the political police of their respective Christian and Muslim areas.

The Decline of the Sunnis

Traditionally and historically, West Beirut, home of the great Sunni families, was the Sunni capital. By the early 1980s, however, a Sunni decline was evident. The continuing influx of mainly Shi'a Muslim refugees from the south for over a decade had gradually "ruralized" the city's southern suburbs. The February 1984 Amal and Druse "insurrection" accelerated this process of ruralization, transforming even West Beirut itself into an increasingly Shi'a city. This evolution changed the very character of political discourse and political action as the line between sectarian and political identity was eradicated.

The Sunni community was the main loser in Assad's Lebanese strategy. Its largely urban enclaves were limited and scattered: West Beirut, Sidon, Tripoli, and a number of towns in the Bekaa. It did not command a unified militia, having relied on its excellent relations with Egyptian President Nasser and later with PLO leader Yasir Arafat and the PLO itself for protection and support. (Virtually all Egyptian and Palestinian Muslims are Sunnis.) During the 1975–76 civil war the PLO helped Ibrahim Koleilat organize and train a Sunni Lebanese militia, the Mourabitoun, the military arm of his Independent Nasserite Movement (INM). Driven out of Lebanon by the Israeli army in 1982, Koleilat and his men regrouped later, only to be attacked and defeated by Jumblat's Amal-supported Druse forces in a fierce west Beirut street battle on March 24, 1984.

The Sunni Mourabitoun's determination to bring the Palestinians back to Beirut was anathema to the Druse and Amal. On April 16, 1985, these forces struck again. These attacks on the Mourabitoun coupled with Amal's harassment of the camp Palestinians, who are also mainly Sunnis, angered and alarmed Sunni leaders. The strenuous efforts of the Sunni mufti, Hassan Khaled, and leading Sunni politicians on behalf of the Mourabitoun reflected the rapidly rising tensions among the Muslim communities.

Fundamentalism and the "New Islam"

Reforms long demanded by the opposition did not materialize in the wake of the February 1984 uprising. Initially Amal and PSP leaders appeared to be eager to perpetuate the tradition of Muslim–Christian coexistence that had prevailed for many generations in West Beirut, especially in the quarter known as Ras Beirut, where the American University of Beirut (AUB) is located. In the beginning these leaders even attended church services in what was perceived as an effort to reassure Christians frightened by the rapid rise of militant fundamentalist movements.

This tradition was dramatically undercut in January 1984 by the assassination of respected and popular AUB president, Malcolm Kerr. Born in Beirut, Kerr was a lifetime friend of Lebanese and other Arabs. His assassination—whether by Muslim fundamentalists or Christian extremists—underscored the seriousness of the campaign to close down the university. The February 1984 uprising inspired a fundamentalist move to kidnap and hold a number of university professors and officials. Fundamentalists also began to attack bars, theaters, liquor stores, and the like, in an effort to impose their "way of life." These militants included not only the Shi'a Hizbullah (Party of God) but also Sunni factions of the Muslim Brotherhood, who attempted to establish their own armed militias. The Christian militiamen of the Lebanese Forces, who themselves had long wanted to drive the AUB out of West Beirut, contributed to the fundamentalist efforts by occasionally subjecting its campus to rocket and artillery fire.

The AUB, however, stood its ground. West Beirut Muslims and Christians together formed the United Front of West Beirut in an attempt to maintain the area's long-standing tradition of peaceful coexistence and halt the exodus of frightened Christians, especially in the aftermath of the February 6 uprising.

These efforts were undermined by an influx of thousands of Shi'a and Druse militants. Amal and Druse leaders proved to be unwilling or unable to prevent them from ransacking homes and stores, appropriating whatever caught their fancy, and fighting their enemies and at times their allies—often in residential areas, without regard for the lives, belongings, or property of the inhabitants. Religious fanaticism gained further momentum and became more murderous. The United Front of West Beirut, lacking both an armed militia and political coherence, failed to secure sectarian coexistence. West Beirut sank into chaos.

Muslim Fundamentalism in Perspective

Muslim fundamentalism is not a new phenomenon in the Middle East. Indeed, as a reactionary bulwark against progressive secularism and democracy it has always been omnipresent. In the Nasserite years the fundamentalist Muslim Brotherhood had to go underground. During the ascendancy of the PLO, fundamentalism was widely considered to be synonymous with reaction and conservatism, primarily due to the traditional connections between fundamentalists and Western intelligence services. In the more conservative Arab states, the Muslim Brotherhood has often been the sole legal party.

The wave of fundamentalism throughout the Muslim world inspired by the Iranian revolution had an enormous impact in Lebanon, where it was fanned by both Christian sectarian fanaticism and the brutal Israeli repression that culminated in the 1982 invasion and its aftermath.

But regional factors other than the Iranian revolution also had an impact. Syria's campaign against its own fundamentalists throughout the late 1970s, culminating in early 1982 with the destruction of much of the ancient and beautiful city of Hama, brought a large influx of

Muslim Brotherhood into the northern Lebanese city of Tripoli. Many were former members of the Syrian army who had deserted rather than participate in Assad's assault against Hama and its people. Assad's determination to round up these deserters may have contributed to the savagery of his attack on Hama. (This was the more likely because PLO leader Arafat had financed, armed, and trained members of the Muslim Brotherhood who with a number of Muslim splinter groupings had established the Tawhid Movement.)

The fundamentalist drive against secularist organizations in Lebanon began in the months just before Israel's 1982 invasion. Many members of the Tawhid, an exclusively Sunni organization, left Tripoli following the expulsion of the pro-Arafat Palestinians and joined fundamentalists of the Jama'a Islamiyya in the predominantly Sunni areas of Sidon, where they have remained. Shi'a fundamentalism, on the other hand, rose to prominence when Iran became directly involved in Lebanon. Following Israel's 1982 invasion, Iran's Ayatollah Khomeini dispatched several hundred zealots or "revolutionary guards" to the Bekaa, where they propagated his fundamentalist interpretation of Shi'a Islam.

Early recruits came from the traditionally Shi'a and sectarian Amal militia. An "Islamic Amal" soon appeared in the Baalbek area headed by Hussein al-Musawi. At about the same time an Iranian-style Hizbullah was established in Beirut's southern suburbs. Its aim was to attract all Shi'a elements originating in the Bekaa who had become disenchanted with Amal's leadership.

The Syrian regime opposed not only fundamentalism at home but also a disproportionately powerful Shi'a fundamentalism in Lebanon. Fundamentalism was useful as a bulwark against the return of pro-Arafat Palestinian fighters, but not as a rival source of power. Assad therefore gave effective assistance to the Shi'a Amal but not to the extremist Hizbullah. Syria's intelligence service also apparently infiltrated groups oriented toward the Muslim Brotherhood. President Assad's ceremonious reception of his former arch enemy, Sheikh Shaaban, demonstrated the essential pragmatism of Syrian policy—and provoked speculation that Shaaban might become a Syrian instrument.

While fundamentalists have varying conceptions of how the "city of God" should be established on earth, all are theocratic. Sunni fundamentalists insist on a state based on the early Islamic Caliphate system; that is, a "prince of the faithful." Khomeinist Shi'as incorporate a brand of populism and "republicanism" more akin to the classical characteristics of oriental despotism. Sunni fundamentalists believe the Koran and ancient tradition provide guidelines, whereas the Shi'a doctrine is more hierarchical in perspective. The high priests of fundamentalism are usually simultaneously heads of prominent clans and families, and loyalty relations between them, their soldiers, and followers are based on regional, neighborhood, and kinship ties. The Shi'a Sayyids or masters (such as Hussein Fadlallah), thought to be descended from the Prophet's family, usually come from prominent families, while their followers tend to be drawn from urban petty traders or lumpenproletarians of rural peasant stock.

Fundamentalist organizations of all sorts seldom tolerate other political forces, especially secular ones, and aggressively infringe upon private freedoms when they have the power to do so. Opposition to everything non-Islamic manifests itself ideologically in an ingrained hostility toward communism, secularism, modernism, and anything Western in general; hostility to Israel emanates from Islamic anti-Jewish notions rather than anti-Zionism. Driven by blind fanaticism, various fundamentalist groups have engaged in indiscriminate terrorist campaigns against Lebanese Christians, Jews, Palestinians, Israelis, and more recently, foreign residents in Lebanon, a number of whom have been kidnapped and, in some cases, murdered.

Fundamentalist obscurantism also degrades the status of women, largely confining their mission to producing children. This is particularly true in rural and working-class sectors, where women have not been able to take advantage of the educational opportunities available to women in the business classes. Women's inferior status was long evident in the attitude of fundamentalist groups that women were not worth kidnapping. Eventually, however, one fundamentalist group announced that it was training a group of women for the specific task of kidnapping foreign women.

Fundamentalism's rapid rise owed not a little to the failure of the secularist Lebanese National Movement parties to challenge it. This may be at least partially explained by their weakness at the time. Before the Israeli invasion most of these groups, including the two Communist parties, maintained their headquarters in West Beirut's impoverished and overcrowded southern suburbs. Here they were physically close to the poor and exploited, aware of, and concerned with, their needs and problems, and the Communist parties at least pursued secular and national goals. On the eve of Israel's invasion, however, a series of attacks by heavily armed Amal militiamen destroyed the headquarters and offices of these groups, especially those of the Communists, killing many of their members or driving them out of the area.

Under such pressures the Organization of Communist Action (OCA), led by Shi'as and with a large Shi'a membership, in time indirectly adopted the theses of Muslim sectarianism. The Lebanese Communist Party's long history and well-established bureaucracy enabled it to keep its forces intact and withdraw to the Bekaa. Smaller left parties and groups, such as the Socialist Arab Action Party (formerly the Popular Front for the Liberation of Palestine) also maintained their political integrity. Most of the parties and groups of the now largely quiescent Lebanese National Movement, however, found it expedient thereafter to ignore or reject secularism. In time, this led them to set aside their program of reforms and adapt to the needs of the Muslim bourgeoisie, including sectarianism.

The response among all shades of fundamentalism to this conciliatory posture from the left was to attempt to destroy the parties of the national movement, even to liquidate them physically. The massacre of Communists, including the murder of party officials by the pro-Iranian Hizbullah, eliminated any illusions about the doctrine and practice of fundamentalist Islam.

Certainly the suffering, hardships, and fears inflicted on the civilian population by a seemingly endless war in which they were the main victims and received little if any help from anyone, also contributed to the popularity of fundamentalism. In such circumstances organized religion has traditionally provided consolation.

The Lausanne Conference: An End to Christian Hegemony?

If the Sunni community was now eclipsed by the Shi'a in Muslim areas, Maronite Christian hegemony over the Lebanese state also appeared to have been decisively weakened. This decline was precipitated by the Kataeb–Lebanese Forces' alliance with Israel before, during, and after the Israeli invasion and, perhaps most important, their decisive defeat by the Druse in the "mountain war" and the "loss" of West Beirut to the militias.

Yet, as the Lausanne "reconciliation conference," March 12–20,

1984, demonstrated, by refusing to acknowledge defeat the Christian right succeeded in blocking the opposition drive "to abolish the sectarian political system." (Actually, much of the opposition sought no more than a larger share of the sectarian pie.) The right owes this victory to former President Franjieh, head of the Syrian-sponsored National Salvation Front (NSF), comprising all major opposition parties except Amal. His defection to vote for the preservation of *all* Maronite privileges destroyed the NSF. Given Franjieh's loyalty to President Assad, this about-face raised questions about the real Syrian position.

Although not publicized at the time, Assad's contingency plan was to bypass the aging *zuama* (traditional leaders), concerned only to maintain their privileges. In their place, he would establish the leaders of the main sectarian militias—Maronite, Shi'a, and Druse—who would then negotiate a settlement among themselves.[2] After the Lausanne Conference this plan became Syrian policy.

The Lausanne "reconciliation" conference reconciled no one. It did not convince the Christian right that equitable power sharing with Muslims was imperative if the Lebanese entity was to survive. A strong current in the Lebanese Forces still clung to the belief that their old alliance with Israel would preserve "Christian rights." However, powerful evidence existed that this belief was unfounded. Israel's rejection of Lebanese Forces appeals for help in the Chouf war, a war it had instigated by encouraging the Forces to deploy in the Chouf, the Kharroub region, and the hills above Sidon, had demonstrated that it no longer needed Christian support against the Palestinians.

Ignoring this warning sign, the Lebanese Forces had established a permanent liaison office in Jerusalem on the eve of the Lausanne Conference. Nevertheless, the current within the Forces favoring alliance with Israel was beginning to lose ground to those advocating a shift toward Syria. Almost simultaneously with the opening of the Jerusalem office, Lebanese Forces Commander Fadi Frem re-established his army's control over East Beirut and the Christian area to the north, restoring Bashir Gemayel's "state within a state." Frem boasted that he would, if necessary, use military force to defend his "Christian canton," provoking both Amal and the Druses to establish their own cantons.

None of the Lausanne decisions were fulfilled. Defamatory campaigns continued—in defiance of Khaddam's insistence that they cease—and so also did the Amal–Druse drive for Gemayel's ouster. But one Maronite leader, Camille Chamoun, emerged from Lausanne convinced that the long-standing Christian claim that foreign intervention was responsible for the Lebanese crisis was false: "Let's say it candidly," he declared, "The conflict in Lebanon is sectarian." (And Chamoun continued to do his best to keep the sectarian fires burning.)

Syria in Command

By the beginning of the tenth year of civil war, April 1984, sectarian schisms were deeper, sharper, and more numerous than ever before, dividing not only Christians from Muslims but both groups internally, with each sect commanding its own area. A large part of the country remained under foreign occupation: 40,000 Syrian troops were in the north and east, and 15,000 Israeli troops were in the area between the Awwali river and the Lebanon-Israel border.

Bringing this splintered country together was the task assumed by Rashid Karami, a moderate Syrian-backed Sunni, when he was named prime minister (for the ninth time) in April and took the first steps toward formation of a "national union" government. Balancing demands was a problem from the start. Nabih Berri rejected the politically unimportant portfolios of water, electricity, and justice; as the leader of the largest sectarian community and of the triumphant February insurrection, his demand for creation of a new ministry for the south and reconstruction to be headed by himself, could not be denied. The exclusion of Saeb Salam, also many times prime minister, from the new government provoked Sunni resentment. But the choice of Selim Hoss as the second Sunni representative in the cabinet, demanded by the Grand Mufti Sheikh Hassan Khaled, was welcomed both inside and outside the Sunni community.

The government of national union—or as Raymond Edde christened it, "the government of the Father, the Son, and the Holy Ghost" (Pierre Gemayel, Amin Gemayel, and Syria)—won a vote of confidence from members of parliament elected in 1972; for most of the period since that time they had been drawing salaries without working.

The new government quickly proved impotent, incapable of halting the battles in Tripoli or the artillery duels in the mountains and along the Green Line dividing the capital. In fact, conflicts arising out of this misnamed "national union" government touched off frequent eruptions of violence that continued into July. On one day alone, June 11, more than 300 people were killed or wounded in bombardments. With the participation of Khaddam, Gemayel, and Karami, militia leaders on both sides prepared a security plan to open the crossing points between East and West Beirut and to reactivate the airport and port, both closed since February 6. However, this failed to produce either security or freedom of movement between the two halves of the city. A succession of similar plans met a similar fate.

The mainspring of the continuing violence was, and remained, the Christian right's rejection of any authority other than its own. Boasting that "confrontation lines are here to stay," Lebanese Forces leader Fadi Frem promised that if any army units were withdrawn from the Green Line, "Christian militias would take their place." In other words, the control exercised by these private militias would be formalized. Muslim, nationalist, and progressive demands for legislation to end the Christian right's domination of the army elicited no response.

During this period Damascus became the hub of Lebanese political life. Leaders of all persuasions frequently traveled there to discuss their problems, conflicts, and proposals for a settlement, usually with Vice-President Khaddam. It was also in this period that Muslim militia leaders achieved political as well as military domination over their respective sectarian communities, as the Maronite militias had done long before in theirs. By mid-1985, a Christian radio station in East Beirut, the Voice of Lebanon, claimed that nearly 20,000 militiamen were stationed in West Beirut: 14,000 Amal; 1,500 Hizbullah (Party of God); 900 Mourabitoun; 600 from the Assad Brigade of the Baath Party Organization in Lebanon; 300 Communists; 550 members of the Syrian Social Nationalist Party (SSNP); 1,000 members of the Organization of Communist Action (OCA) in Lebanon; and 500 Syrian intelligence operators. The Lebanese army's Sixth Brigade, overwhelmingly Shi'a, was also stationed in West Beirut and took its orders for the most part from Amal rather than the Lebanese government.

Maronite Class Conflicts and the Rise of the Lebanese Forces

In August 1984 Pierre Gemayel died. His death put an end to the Kataeb Party's monopoly on Christian decision-making, permitting

Lebanese Forces, long opposed to the party and its leaders—in particular President Amin Gemayel—to assert themselves. Early in February 1985, the Lebanese Forces command, led by Samir Geagea, declared its independence of the Kataeb in the areas of security, politics, finance, and information. This split stripped the party of much of its influence at a time when it was supporting the president's efforts to achieve an understanding with Syria and, to a move limited extent, with Lebanese Muslims. To this end the Kataeb had even agreed to return to the legitimate authorities a number of government departments it had taken over and operated in Christian areas.

The Kataeb also tried to persuade the Lebanese Forces to remove their roadblock at Barbara on the Beirut–Tripoli highway—without success. Taxes collected at Barbara on every vehicle and its contents provided the Lebanese Forces with financial wealth, and the kidnapping there of real or fancied political opponents often brought both political and financial profits as well.

On March 12, 1985, the Lebanese Forces proclaimed their *intifada* (insurrection), installing an Executive Council that did not contain a single leader from the Kataeb Party: Samir Geagea and his men took five seats and assigned the remaining five to Chamoun's National Liberal Party (NLP). The Lebanese Forces thereby declared their independence of the Kataeb, which in turn dismissed Geagea and his followers as "coup makers," declaring that they would henceforth not be allowed to speak or function in its name.

These developments underscored one of the ironies of the ten-year-old civil war: the traditional Maronite leaders who started it proved to be among the losers. To wage "total war" against other sectarian leaderships and preserve its ruling position, the Maronite comprador class which dominated the Kataeb politbureau had been compelled to rally middle, lower middle, and lumpenproletarian social strata of the Maronite community. In this total war the Maronite ruling class resorted to classic fascist techniques, the Palestinians becoming its favorite scapegoat just as the Jews had become the scapegoat in fascist Europe. The Palestinians, who are overwhelmingly secular, were blamed for all the nation's ills and evils, a practice quickly adopted by other Lebanese sectarian leaders, in particular the propertied and well-to-do Shi'a ruling class.

Unexpectedly, the Maronite leadership found its sphere of influence steadily eroding. This decline was noted in the structure of the sect and the interaction between internal subjective factors and external influences. Economically the absence of major breakthroughs and the pressures of repeated conflagrations spurred a huge and continuing flight of Christian as well as Muslim capital. This was an ominous warning sign to the Maronite elite. Another was the fact that their militiamen, most of lower middle-class origin, who bore the brunt of the fighting, had become keenly aware of their rights and potential power. Their military and political weight had already prompted them to organize the Lebanese Forces and to assert their independence vis-à-vis the Kataeb leadership. As the Maronite petty bourgeoisie gained strength politically and militarily, something close to a class struggle developed with the upper-class Maronite leadership. Class identification in time became stronger than the established code of family loyalty. This fissure in a party edifice that had long been based on loyalty to the Gemayel family soon became evident, even though Bashir Gemayel had assumed leadership of the Lebanese Forces' military apparatus and posed as its spokesman. Bashir and his father managed to hold the faction-ridden party together for a time, but after Bashir's assassination internal conflicts again surfaced. His father's death two years later opened the way for what might be a final split.

The expected confrontation between the traditional Maronite leadership and its militiamen emerged with a somewhat less violent character than that of the in-fighting among the Muslim militias. One reason for this was the disastrous defeats suffered by the Lebanese Forces in the south in the early months of 1985 at the hands of Druse and Amal militiamen, assisted by Abu Musa's dissident wing of the PLO. Another was the willingness of the Maronite leadership to make one concession after another to the Lebanese Forces in an attempt to save what it could—although ultimately it did not succeed in preventing the break.

The March *intifada* provoked confusion on all sides, especially as to Israel's role, if any, in Geagea's initiative. Israel publicly offered him its support in his efforts to change the Kataeb's leadership and to negotiate on behalf of "Christians liberated from Kataeb tyranny." Many suspected the insurrection was an Israeli play to out-maneuver the Syrians and diminish their influence in Lebanon. Prime Minister Karami called Geagea and his men "agents of Israel," and Sidon deputy Nazih Bizri held them to be a part of Israel's forces in Lebanon, "activated and helped" by Israel.

Without Kataeb representation, the Lebanese Forces Executive

Council consisted mainly of collaborators with Israel. When Syrian President Assad replaced Geagea with Hobeika on May 9, 1985, and called on Jumblat to confer with him, Jumblat flatly refused to meet "with that notorious guy responsible for Sabra and Shatila." But Assad's pressures soon prevailed. Raymond Edde continued the campaign from the safety of Paris. He revealed that in 1976 Hobeika, then already in liaison with both the CIA and Mossad, had been sent to South Lebanon by Bashir Gemayel (at Israel's request), where he assassinated many Lebanese and Palestinian civilians, and that he had participated in the Tel al-Zaatar massacres the same year.

Hobeika owed his rapid rise in part to his avoidance of ideology, to which the Lebanese Forces are allergic, and to his insistence that he supported a Syrian peace and was not a politician. He could therefore define his goals as "national reconciliation, Christian unity, and the return to our Arab environment," and sever all ties with Israel. This abrupt change in policy was the result of the crushing defeat suffered by the Lebanese Forces in the Sidon hills in the spring of 1985; Israel's announced decision to abandon its involvement in Lebanese politics and limit its support of the Christians to what was needed to maintain an Israeli security strip in the south; and not least, Damascus' threat that "the symbols of collaboration with Israel must vanish."

Once the Lebanese Forces changed policies, President Assad set up an interchange between its leaders and Berri and Jumblat. The resulting reconciliation of Druse, Shi'a, and Maronite militia demands permitted Hobeika and Geagea to seize the initiative from President Gemayel and the Kataeb, thereby excluding the traditional Maronite leadership from all policy decisions.

The War of the Camps

Early in January 1985 Israel announced a three-stage plan to withdraw its forces from Lebanon over a period of six to nine months: beginning within five weeks, it would withdraw south from the Awwali River to a line running from near the Litani River on the coast inland to Nabatiya; it would then withdraw from the Bekaa, where it faced Syrian troops, to a line near Hasbaya; and, finally, pull back all its troops. The Israelis declared, however, that they would retain a buffer zone in the south, where their puppet South Lebanon Army (SLA) would remain in control. To pay for this operation they asked Washington for $12 billion in grants over three years at a time when President Reagan had already requested a $400 million increase in military aid to Israel above the 1985 request. In support of this proposal, Israel disclosed that the economic cost of its occupation was about $240 million per annum, or $700,000 a day.

Israel welcomed Amal's May–June 1985 assault against the Palestinian camps in Beirut's southern suburbs—Bourj al-Barajneh, Sabra, and, most brutally, Shatila. The sponsor, however, was President Assad, who regarded the PLO presence in Lebanon as a major threat to his goal of a *Pax Syriana*. Tension between Amal and the Palestinians had been rising since Amal's April 16 West Beirut battle against the Mourabitoun, a militant defender of the Palestinian cause. Although nominally a Sunni organization, many of its fighters in this and other battles were Shi'as. The intervention of Palestianians loyal to Arafat in support of the Mourabitoun angered Nabih Berri, who decided the time had come to liquidate the pro-Arafat Palestinians.

The forces mobilized to bring the Palestinians to heel included Berri and his Amal militiamen, generously rearmed by Damascus; the Lebanese army's predominantly Shi'a Sixth Brigade; and even the Maronite Eighth Brigade, which supplied the Sixth with ammunition, tanks, and personnel carriers, and on at least one occasion (the battle for Bourj al-Barajneh) reportedly participated in the fighting.[3]

However, a crucial force did not join the campaign. Walid Jumblat was an ally of Berri, but not for an attack on the camps. The Druses are the smallest of Lebanon's six major sects, and Palestinians constitute a substantial part of Jumblat's military forces. Moreover, the efforts of his father on behalf of the Palestinian cause are not forgotten, and sympathy for the Palestinians remains strong in the Druse community. It was, therefore, no surprise that in defiance of Syrian pressure Jumblat's PSP militiamen blocked the coastal highway between Beirut and the south to prevent Amal reinforcements from reaching the camps, and assisted in the delivery of much-needed supplies to the camps through their positions in the hills. Most crucial of all, Jumblat allowed Abu Musa's forces and Nayef Hawatmeh's Democratic Front for the Liberation of Palestine (DFLP) to launch artillery and rocket barrages against Amal positions and Shi'a areas from the Druse mountains to relieve pressure on the camps. The contributions of Abu Musa and Hawatmeh proved to be a decisive factor in the defeat of Amal and its Syrian sponsors.

By the time the fighting died down, inhabitants who had survived the 1982 Israeli–Kataeb atrocities in Sabra and Shatila described the Shi'a massacres as even worse, "because they continued for weeks." Amal fighters took no prisoners, gunned down unarmed Palestinians, killed the wounded, and massacred Palestinian and other patients in the Gaza Hospital, while barring the International Red Cross from entering the camps.

Roughly 70 percent of both Sabra and Shatila were destroyed. But the battle was also costly for Berri's militia. Palestinian fighters not only fought off the Amal attackers they forced them out of the nearby Arab University area and the sports stadium. At the end of June, official figures put the number killed in the war of the camps at 650, of whom 500 were unofficially reported to be Amal militiamen. Some 2,500 were wounded. The successful defense of the camps was the more remarkable given the youth and inexperience of the Palestinian fighters. In Shatila, the 200-odd defenders were almost all secondary school boys 15 to 18 years old, many of whom were using arms for the first time. Their weapons were simple and mostly of their own fabrication. For example, they took detonators from defective enemy shells that landed in the camps and exploded them on the main road in a successful effort to keep enemy tanks from entering the camp.

Women and girls also participated in the camp's defense. A very few took part in the actual fighting; many cared for the wounded; others took charge of acquiring, preparing and distributing food to fighters, the wounded and other camp inhabitants. Some assumed the highly dangerous task of securing water from the camp's single operating tap, which was often under fire. These activities reflected the central role women had assumed in the camps after the departure of many of the men—first to the Gulf for work and later to Israeli detention in jails and the Ansar concentration camp—as well as the greater mobility they enjoyed because they were not considered a military threat.[4]

The Syrians, who for public consumption had to disapprove of the war, blamed it on their favorite scapegoat, Yasir Arafat. Politically, however, Abdul Halim Khaddam discretely supported Amal, portraying it as a victim, claiming (incorrectly) that it bore the brunt of the fighting in the south, and supplying it with still more arms and ammunition.

The Soviet press, in contrast, strongly opposed the war against the Palestinians. Unconfirmed reports stated that Moscow had threatened to cut off aid to Syria if the assault continued. Libya was reported to have made a similar threat, and Syria's relations with Iran were also strained.

Criticism, both national and international, of the role of Amal and its leaders in the war of the camps was somewhat deflected by the June hijacking of a TWA airliner to Beirut. Shi'a gunmen held thirty-nine American passengers hostage, demanding that Israel release 735 Lebanese who had been picked up in the south and were held illegally in Israeli jails. The resulting media circus in the West enabled Berri and his Amal fighters to bask for several weeks in an international spotlight, and their most recent attacks on the Palestinians were all but forgotten.

In mid-May, Yasir Arafat had stated his position on a peace settlement in an address to an Arab League seminar in Tunis. He was, he said, prepared to accept UN resolution 242 in return for the recognition of the full right of the Palestinians to self-determination. Resolution 242, he pointed out, clearly envisaged a global and regional peace settlement with full de facto and de jure recognition between the parties concerned. Turning to Lebanon, he asserted that an agreement existed between Syria, Israel, and the Shi'a community to guarantee the peace of northern Israel by preventing the return of the Palestinians to the south. Two days later Amal militiamen attacked the Palestinian camps in West Beirut.

Syria and Amal did not succeed in disarming the Palestinians. The agreement ending the war included a provision that the PLO would hand over all "heavy weapons," but they had none. Khaddam's attempt to define rocket-propelled grenades (RPGs) as heavy weapons collapsed when Ahmed Jabril of the Palestine National Salvation Front challenged him to produce a military dictionary that upheld his assertion.

However, neither Syria nor Amal abandoned their attempts to destroy the camps and get rid of the Palestinians. They launched a second major assault on the camps in November 1985, which also failed, as did a third in April 1986. These aggressions spurred Palestinian fighters to return to Lebanon to protect their families and camps—"the closest thing they have to Palestine." Early in 1986 al-Fatah's Abu Iyad revealed that thousands of its fighters who had been forced out of Lebanon in 1982 and after had filtered back into South Lebanon and West Beirut.

Assad's Peace Strategy

By the end of 1983, Israel's failure to achieve its pivotal aim of installing a strong rightist Maronite Christian government in Beirut had exhausted its patience. The Israeli strategy therefore shifted to an attempt to splinter the sectarian entities compromising the Lebanese state still further. The Israeli Defense Force also concluded that the Shi'a Amal movement would prove a more effective policeman than the South Lebanon Army. Uri Lubrani, coordinator of Israeli operations in Lebanon noted that Shi'a militiamen agreed to take .on the job of keeping the Palestinians and fundamentalist terrorists out.

Assad's strategy, on the other hand, as early as the 1984 Lausanne Conference had been one of attempting to achieve a negotiated settlement based on the three dominant sectarian militias: the Druse PSP and the Shi'a Amal, both in Syria's orbit, and the Lebanese Forces, which was at the time asserting its independence from the Kataeb. Assad calculated that in this way the traditional Maronite political establishment, dominated by political dinosaurs determined to hang on to their privileges whatever the cost, could be by-passed. Through an elaborate closed door intelligence effort Assad created his own lobby within the Lebanese Forces in order to encourage the militia's evolution into a political and military entity independent of the Kataeb party and attuned to his interests.[5]

The split between the Lebanese Forces and the Kataeb, proclaimed by Samir Geagea on March 12, 1985, established the Forces as "totally independent" of the Kataeb and the Lebanese Front. Geagea, was Israel's first choice to lead the Lebanese Forces, but Israel's allies were too few to secure his victory. His leading role in the 1978 massacre of Suleiman Franjieh's son Tony, his family, and thirty or more Zghorta citizens—killings of which he openly boasted at the time—excluded him, as did the ignominious defeat of the Forces under his command in the 1983 Chouf battle. Thus on May 9, 1985, Elias Hobeika, once linked to Israel's intelligence service and a leading participant with Geagea in both the Zghorta murders and the 1982 slaughter of Palestinians in the camps, assumed leadership of the Lebanese Forces.

Hobeika's subsequent visit to former president Franjieh, an initiative assisted by the Vatican, achieved a reconciliation, closing the seven-year breach between Franjieh and the Kataeb and by extension the Maronite community. This reconciliation was essential for Hobeika's rise to leadership of the Lebanese Forces as well as to his goal of excluding the traditional Maronite chieftains from decision-making. Hobeika, formerly an arch enemy of Assad's regime, also had to advocate the "Arab option," incorporating a leading Syrian role and serious dialogue with all parties to reach a political solution. Damascus, moreover, brought the Lebanese Forces to heel by compelling them in July 1985 to close their office in Jerusalem and recall their units stationed in Jezzine.

In response, Syria relaxed its blockade of the Christian enclave and withdrew Rifaat Assad's Special Forces from its northern edge. Damascus also gradually reduced its support for Amin Gemayel and invited a Lebanese Forces delegation to visit Syria.

Muslim and National Endeavors

Such developments prompted national and Muslim groups to renew efforts to organize their own ranks. Thus, on July 28, 1985, Berri and Jumblat announced the formation of a National Union Front (NUF) aimed at ending Kataeb domination of the Lebanese state and abolishing the sectarian basis of the political system in favor of a democratic and secular structure. Two days later, Assad presented Berri's Amal militia with a gift of fifty T-54 tanks, making it one of the strongest military forces in the country. Lebanese concluded that Berri's militiamen had become Syria's muscle men in Lebanon. This alliance between the Syrian president and Berri, both Shi'a Muslims, was in part rooted in their shared determination to destroy Palestinian political influence and military power in Lebanon, a goal also pursued by Israel. The Palestinians are mainly Sunnis and for the most part secular.

The Berri–Jumblat proposal for a democratic and non-sectarian political system won wide support from parties earlier active in the Lebanese National Movement—Nasserists, Communists, Socialists, Baath, etc.—and even from some middle-ranking Christian leaders. Fifteen political parties and sixty-seven parliamentary and independent personalities and leaders attended the NUF's birth at a mass rally at Chtaura in the Bekaa on August 6, 1985, the largest grouping of left and Muslim parties since the start of the civil war. The NUF's political platform focused on the imperative of building a modern state committed to equal opportunity for all its citizens. This required as a start a new electoral law, recognition of Lebanon's Arab identity, adoption of special relations with Syria, and escalation of attacks on Israel's forces in South Lebanon. This program was described as having "a national content within a sectarian structure," but like all earlier "solutions" the NUF was stillborn. Few prominent political leaders, not even the organizers of the first meeting, attended the second. This episode succeeded only in underscoring the power of the sectarian grip on Lebanon's political life.

Nabih Berri's proposals to the second meeting (from which he left early) were also stillborn. His plan envisioned formation of a presidential council composed of leaders of the six major sectarian communities, each sect to govern in turn. The Shi'a population is dispersed in pockets scattered throughout Lebanon. Thus canton solution such as the Maronites had constructed in the early 1970s in their areas or as Jumblat was accused of adopting in the Chouf and Aley would not be viable for the Shi'as. For this community, constituting almost third of the the total population, the goal can only be Lebanon's unification.

Yet Beirut continued to fragment as fierce battles between allies on both sides of the Green Line became the order of the day. On the East side, the Lebanese Forces and the Kataeb frequently fought each other for control of the Christian enclave. On the other side, the streets of West Beirut became battlegrounds for fierce hostilities between the allied militias of Berri's Amal and Jumblat's Progressive Socialist Party (PSP). One source of the conflict was the anger of both President Assad and Nabih Berri over the return of PLO fighters to Lebanon, where Jumblat, leader of the smallest of the six major communities and an ally of the anti-Arafat PLO, welcomed them into the ranks of his fighting forces. The inability of Amal, with its substantial superiority in numbers, to defeat Jumblat's Druse and Palestinian fighters further angered Berri and the Syrian president.

In 1985 the fourth Amal–Druse battle erupted on November 19, Lebanon's Independence Day. Heavy tanks fought in residential areas throughout the city in one of West Beirut's worst battles ever, christened the Flag War. On this day Lebanese, mainly the Christians, display the Lebanese flag. Jumblat regarded the flag as a heritage of French rule. On the eve of the holiday, to dramatize the need for a flag not handed down from colonial days, he ordered his men to remove the flags. This was hardly a revolutionary initiative. Many countries at one time or another have changed their flags. Berri not only rejected Jumblat's invitation to participate in this demonstration, he ordered his men to restore the flags. The inevitable battles that followed spread and became more ferocious as local bosses joined in, each determined to maintain control of his street or quarter. In five days of pitched battles over sixty people were killed and many more were wounded.

The Tripartite Agreement and its Collapse

In December, leaders of the major and more or less pro-Syrian militias—Amal, PSP, and the Lebanese Forces—met in Damascus at the invitation of the Syrian foreign minister, and drafted a "peace project" which included an end to the state of war, gradual reform of the sectarian political system, and an affirmation that Lebanon was in the Syrian orbit. This so-called Tripartite Agreement was clearly a victory for Damascus, provoking a swift response from both the United States and Israel.

For the first time since the evacuation of American troops from Lebanon, U.S. Secretary of State George Shultz publicly supported Lebanese President Amin Gemayel. Reiterating in an interview Washington's unshaken backing for "Lebanese legitimacy," Shultz underscored American confidence in Lebanon's presidency as the country's sole effective peace-making agency.

The Israelis, who had recently announced that they were abandoning Lebanon to fend for itself, sent jets to break the sound barrier over Beirut and the Bekaa. This gesture of support for Gemayel was in fact Israel's response to the recent deployment of Syrian long-range SAM-5 missiles. In the south the Jezzine–Sidon front was reactivated with the customary barrages raining down on civilian villages.

At the same time, as the other participants in the agreement had predicted, the accord quickly provoked dissension among the Maronite leaders. A January 1986 attempt by the pro-Israel element in the Lebanese Forces, led by Geagea, to kill Hobeika touched off a brief but fierce fracticidal Maronite war that claimed a heavy toll in civilian lives and property: 800 to 1,000 people were killed or wounded, and damage to property in the Maronite enclave was estimated at a million or more Lebanese pounds. The opposing forces used devastating firepower, including tanks, heavy artillery, and rocket launchers.

The conflict culminated in victory for the pro-Gemayel faction of the Lebanese army and the Kataeb militias under the command of Samir Geagea. Syria's man in the Lebanese Forces, Elias Hobeika, and a number of his lieutenants had to be flown out of the Maronite enclave. Once again, the Gemayel clan had regained a lost foothold.

The ouster of Elias Hobeika put paid to Assad's peace plan based on the Tripartite Agreement, since Hobeika was the only Maronite leader who had endorsed it. Almost coincident with this collapse, Israel carried out a vast "search and destroy" operation in South Lebanon which provided a cover for the murder of Lebanese communist leaders and activists, mainly by Hizbullah and Amal members. These organizations also assassinated communists in Beirut at the same time.

National institutions were rapidly disappearing. Not even the pretense of a national army now existed. In the period 1984-86 the army split along sectarian lines as officers and soldiers of the various sects were redistributed to brigades stationed in areas controlled by the militias of their respective sects. Most officers and soldiers transferred their allegiances to these sectarian militias. The largely Shi'a Sixth Brigade, for example, bore the brunt of the fighting in most of Amal's attacks against the Palestinian refugee camps although it was never allowed to participate in Amal's decision-making. General Ibrahim Tannous, one-time adviser to Bashir Gemayel and a former commander of the army's Eighth Brigade, automatically backed the Lebanese Forces in their battles with the opposition or the Palestinians. The Seventh Brigade remained loyal to, and took its orders from, former president Franjieh. The Tenth Brigade, one of the strongest and best equipped, in which Maronites affiliated to the Kataeb or Lebanese Forces also served, was under the command of Col. Nassib Eid Tannous, a Maronite loyal to President Gemayel. Most air force officers were Maronites affiliated to the Kataeb or Lebanese Forces.[6]

The collapse of the Tripartite Agreement marking the defeat of Assad's peace strategy accelerated Lebanon's progressive disintegration and the resurgence of the murderous feudal loyalties to family, clan, and tribe that have marked this area's history since ancient times.

[24]

South Lebanon: The Role of Syria, Israel, and the Palestinians

The Syrian Baath's involvement in Lebanon goes back to the early 1960s, when the fledgling Palestinian resistance was threatened with annihilation at the hands of both the pro-American Lebanese regime and Israel's repeated aggression. Spurred by its pan-Arab ideology, then taking a leftward turn, the Baath became increasingly concerned with the fate of the Palestinians. When hard-line Alawite leftists led by Major Salah Jadid took power in Damascus, they consolidated this left wing tendency. Jadid and his associates, among them Ibrahim Machos, who blended Baath pan-Arabism with a Fanon-like Marxism, alienated the more traditional Baath establishment that had become dominant in Iraq.

Jadid's commitment to safeguarding the PLO guerrilla presence in Lebanon and strengthening the Lebanese national movement expressed itself openly when Syrian regulars dressed in Saiqa uniforms crossed the border to relieve hard pressed PLO fighters during the 1969 battles with the Lebanese army. On several occasions the Syrian air force intercepted Israeli planes strafing PLO positions in Lebanon.

Jadid's involvement on the side of the Palestinians in both Lebanon and Jordan gave a pretext to right wingers in the Syrian military bureaucracy, the Hafez Assad group, to move against Jadid. As defense minister and chief of the air force, Assad was able to use the army against the party apparatus to become the absolute ruler of Syria in a bloodless coup in 1971. For clan and sectarian reasons Jadid and Machos, both Alawis and members of influential Alawi clans, were not physically liquidated, but they have remained in prison without trial ever since. Since Assad's ascent, his policies have consistently run counter to Palestinian national aspirations.

South Lebanon

South Lebanon became a major flashpoint in Arab–Israeli and Palestinian-Israeli conflicts in the late 1960s. When the PLO was driven out of Jordan in the wake of Black September, it concentrated its armed forces there. Since, as it publicly declared, Syria had decided not to confront Israel on the Golan Heights until it had achieved strategic parity, it attempted to use its influence in south Lebanon to further its aims.

Israel's intrusions in Lebanon, starting in the south, culminated in the all-out blitzkrieg of 1982. When its efforts to eliminate resistance to continued occupation failed, it decided to continue the war by proxy: that is, by limiting the Israeli physical presence as far as possible, and by exploiting existing religious and sectarian divisions among the south Lebanon population.

A major result of the 1982 invasion was Israel's expansion of the "security belt" it had occupied during its 1978 Litani invasion, when it seized all of South Lebanon below the Litani River, including the river and its waters—which it set out to divert into Israel. Moreover, by moving its so-called security zone in Lebanon northwards it was able to incorporate both Shi'a and Druse elements into its original Maronite militias to form its long-planned South Lebanon Army (SLA). Israel was at this point relying more on the Shi'a Amal militia than on its Maronite allies, who had been badly battered in their 1984 battles. However, it did retain the militia's Maronite command, with its strong ties to Camille Chamoun. On the death of Saad Haddad in 1984, it was Chamoun who had engineered the appointment of a long-time Lebanese army general, Antoine Lahd, as his successor.

Pursuing its traditional "divide and rule" policy, Israel also encouraged, trained, and financed other sectarian militias. They armed the Druses. They permitted the Shi'as, many of them Amal fighters, to keep their weapons. They also encouraged the formation of a "Shi'a army militia." In addition, Israeli intelligence formed the "National Guards," a "death squad" composed of Shi'as, to track down and liquidate Palestinian and Lebanese guerrillas. This squad included PLO dropouts and Amal members with Dieuxième Bureau connections. However in face of mounting popular resistance, these two militias collapsed, leaving the SLA as the only overtly collaborationist group.

The SLA was also in trouble. A senior Israeli officer admitted in February 1985 that one-third of its soldiers had deserted in response to death threats. Dozens of SLA fighters, Lebanese informers, and collaborationists had been assassinated in recent weeks, he added, with the word "collaborationist" hung around their necks. In this same period, there had been a marked increase in roadside bombings and ambushes.

South Lebanon and the Resistance

Organized armed resistance to the occupation began at the time of the Israeli invasion, spearheaded by Lebanese National Movement groups and remnants of PLO forces. These fighters operated under the name National Resistance Front. For the most part they came from the Lebanese Communist Party, the Organization of Communist Action (OCA), the Syrian Social Nationalist Party (SSNP), the Socialist Arab Action Party, and Nasserist groups. It was only late in 1984 that Sunni and Shi'a fundamentalist groups became active; they immediately captured the limelight from the more secular groups, partly because the Amal militia had taken control of the government's radio and TV stations in its February 1984 drive to seize power in West Beirut. Israel contributed to the fundamentalist build-up with frequent references to "the Muslim terrorist threat" while it remained largely silent about the nationalist "threat" as a whole.

Although Israel did not achieve its main objective in Lebanon, the destruction of the PLO, it did retard the Palestinian resistance there. Since its departure from Beirut in 1982, the PLO has been engaged in a gradual and laborious reconstitution of its forces. The main obstacle to this process has come from the factional rift between Arafat and the Abu Musa group.

Another kind of resistance to the Israeli occupation came from the Shi'a population of the occupied south. This grassroots sectarian opposition indirectly reflected the deep economic and social injustices implicit in the sectarian political system, in which the Shi'a community, the largest, occupied the bottom of the social-political ladder. Shi'a popular opposition, mainly of a fundamentalist and highly conservative character, found expression in mass demonstrations and uprisings against the Israeli occupation and attacks on Israeli personnel and Lebanese quislings. These actions, widely publicized in the foreign press and both humiliating and costly for Israel, were unquestionably an important factor in Israel's eventual decision to withdraw its troops from Lebanon.

In its efforts to secure a buffer zone, however, Israel achieved more than it at first expected. The original thirty-mile stretch seized in its 1978 invasion was now extended a further twenty miles north to Jezzine, putting three major Lebanese cities within its artillery range: Tyre, Sidon, and the southern suburbs of Beirut. Katyushas, nonetheless, continued to rain down on the Galilee panhandle. Where there had been one enemy, Israel succeeded in making many new ones, not only among the Lebanese national forces but also among the fundamentalist groups that now competed with them. At the same time, by its territorial advance Israel underscored its long-standing claim that all South Lebanon below the Litani was part of Eretz Israel, to which the Litani's waters therefore belonged.

Israel also now began to play a more intricate religious sectarian game, not only relying on the Shi'a Amal militia rather than its battered former allies, the Maronite forces, but attempting to create either a pro-Israeli or "neutral" lobby within the Druse community in Lebanon through its own Druse population. The PSP leadership, however, chose the Syrian–Libyan camp and, moreover, appears to have succeeded in neutralizing the Israeli Druse lobby itself.

Despite setbacks, sectarian fragmentation allowed both Israel and Syria—once Assad had underscored his support for the south Lebanese resistance—to influence internal Lebanese politics directly. Owing to Assad's general non-confrontational policy reinforced by Israeli threats, Syria's involvement appeared to be on a smaller scale than Israel's. The protracted Israel–Lebanon war in the south continued, given impetus by U.S. encouragement of Israel's "iron fist" policy, as Israel's defense minister, Yitzhak Rabin, the proud author of this policy, called it. As noted earlier, in September 1984 the United States vetoed a resolution presented by Lebanon that urged Israeli troops to respect international conventions in the south. And again in March 1985, following the slaughter of twenty-seven people in a single village, it vetoed still another Israeli Defense Force (IDF) Security Council resolution calling for condemnation of Israel's harsh practices in south Lebanon.

Rabin's "iron fist" policy proved to be an important factor in Israel's defeat in the south and eventual (although not complete) withdrawal.

The "iron fist" embraced actions including large-scale "preventive raids" on dozens of Shi'a villages; dusk-to-dawn curfews; massive attacks on towns and villages, one killing forty men in the town of Zrariyah; invasion of the main hospital in Tyre on March 4, 1985, seizure of its director and some ten blood donors; killing thirteen people including two key resistance leaders in a Shi'a mosque in Marakah village, an important resistance center. By January 15, 1986, however, one-third of the Israeli-backed South Lebanon Army had deserted in the face of death threats, according to IDF officers. On February 5, Rabin was compelled to admit, "If we eliminated PLO terrorism only to replace it with Shi'a terrorism, we will have to wonder about this war." Between January 14 when the Israeli cabinet approved its pullout plan, and February 19, 15 Israeli soldiers were killed and 150 wounded.[1]

In early April, Rabin told the Knesset he would pursue "a scorched earth" policy of all-out retaliation "if the attacks continued." Undoubtedly, Israel's "iron fist" policy accelerated the rise of Shi'a fundamentalism. Demands for the Islamization of Lebanon and the dismissal of President Gemayel, "the Shah of Lebanon," proliferated. Desertions from the SLA continued.

By September, Israel's army had completed its initial withdrawal, but still occupied more than seventy-two villages and 850 square kilometers of South Lebanon.

Iran's Stake

Yet the appearance and rapid growth in the south of the Iranian-sponsored Shi'a fundamentalist Hizbullah (Party of God) militia, 2–3,000 strong, threatened to wreck Israel's strategy of converting this area into a "security zone" patrolled by the IDF and its predominantly Maronite South Lebanon Army. Hizbullah was founded, financed, trained, and armed by Iran's Revolutionary Guards, some of whom had settled in the Bekaa in 1983. It repeatedly assaulted the Maronite SLA, the French troops in UNIFIL (because France, the only major power in UNIFIL, supported Iraq in the Iran–Iraq war), and the Amal militia. These attacks challenged both the UN role in Lebanon and Amal's influence among the many Shi'a Muslims in the south.

Hizbullah clerics soon moved into a dozen or more of the most impoverished Shi'a villages in the south, where they provided medical and other help to the needy. The organization continued its offensive against Israeli forces, whereas Amal reached a tacit understanding not to attack them if Israel did not attack Amal-controlled villages in the south. Multiplying Hizbullah attacks on Amal and UNIFIL presaged an eventual showdown with Amal. Many people both in Lebanon and abroad held Hizbullah responsible for the kidnapping of American and French journalists, AUB professors, an AUB librarian, and medical men attached to the AUB hospital, as well as some of the car bomb explosions in both East and West Beirut.

Hizbullah's ultimate goal was to transform south Lebanon into an Islamic republic on the Iranian model. Faced with this threat, not what Israel had wished to achieve by the 1982 invasion, Israeli defense minister Rabin promised to assist the South Lebanon Army with helicopter gunships and artillery.

The Palestinians

In December 1985 and again in May–June 1986, Nabih Berri's Amal militia, backed by Syria, made two further attempts to seize control of the Palestinian refugee camps in Beirut's southern suburbs and so eliminate the PLO as an independent political and military force. The assault was spearheaded by the powerful T-54 tanks given Berri by President Assad, apparently as a reward for Amal's earlier aggression against the camps. These attacks on the camps, inhabited mainly by Sunni Palestinians, followed an Amal assault on the Sixth of February Movement, a Sunni militia formed to replace the Mourabitoun. Amal maintained that the new force was merely a front for the Palestinians. In this one-sided battle the Sunnis had suffered heavy casualties and the Sunni areas of West Beirut had been severely damaged. The terms halting Amal's assault on the camps in May–June 1986 differed little from those that had temporarily ended its earlier attacks.

The PLO's assertion that Damascus was sponsoring Amal's repeated aggressions against the camps was widely believed since Assad vehemently opposed the PLO effort to rebuild its military strength. The presence of the Syrian-bequeathed tanks around Sabra, Shatila, and

Bourj al–Barajneh could not but remind the Palestinians of the fall of Tel al-Zaatar camp in 1976, in which Syria's role had been decisive.[2] Palestinians were convinced that the cease-fire would "last only as long as Amal needs to reorganize." Unlike all previous cease-fire negotiations, this time the PLO was denied representation. Its exclusion was clearly intended to reduce its status to that of one of the plethora of militias which had to be disarmed to halt West Beirut's disintegration into total anarchy. The Palestinian need for self defense was ignored. Although the cease-fire agreement stipulated total Amal withdrawal from the area surrounding the camps, these are neighborhoods inhabited mainly by Shi'as loyal to Amal, and policed by the army's predominantly Shi'a Sixth Brigade, also loyal to Berri. Amal's siege of the Palestinian camps in South Beirut has been continuous, while as the so-called progressive forces' reliance on Damascus has increased their support for the Palestinians has diminished.

This round in the continuing Amal war against the Palestinians left 110 killed and some 700 wounded. The agreement ending the fighting was signed by Amal and the PNSF (Palestine National Salvation Front) opposed to Arafat. SLA Commander Antoine Lahd declared in an interview his willingness to disband his militia if Amal undertook to keep the area quiet. His offer came just after Yitzhak Rabin asserted to the Associated Press that he would dismantle the SLA if a deal could be struck with Amal.

. . . And the Sunnis

Amal's renewed assault on the Sunni Palestinians in the camps in 1986 was part of a broader Shi'a offensive against the Sunni community that had constituted West Beirut's leadership before the 1975–76 civil war. During that war Beirut's Sunni leaders had for the most part maintained a low profile while the Lebanese National Movement and the PLO together defended West Beirut and its inhabitants. In the subsequent years the Sunni community never regained its former influence, but it strongly opposed (although not with guns) the takeover of West Beirut by Amal-led Shi'as in February 1984. Sunni resentment increased with the rising exactions and insulting behavior of what they perceived as Shi'a hordes of the poor, undisciplined, and uncouth. The Sunni community now felt threatened not only by Amal's dominance in West Beirut but also by its aggressions against the Palestinians, who are also mainly Sunnis and often secular. The Sunni grand mufti, Sheikh Hassan Khaled, on the occasion of the Id al-Fitr feast marking the end of Ramadan, charged that Amal and "gunmen" were waging war against the Sunni community in West Beirut to compensate for their defeat in their war against the Palestinians in the camps. Large-scale looting in West Beirut's Sunni districts and bomb attacks against the cars and homes of prominent Sunnis promptly followed. Many prominent on the left and right had left Lebanon in the preceding months, and more now followed.

$\left[25\right]$

Conclusion:
The Militias' War Against the Civilian Population

It was the Lebanese National Movement's drive for authentic political reforms that provoked the 1975–76 civil war. Syria's 1976 intervention, which denied victory to the LNM and led to the assassination of its leader, Kamal Jumblat, dealt the LNM a near mortal blow. Its most profound effect was the dilution of leftist and democratic currents, which weakened secular trends both within the LNM and outside it. By the early 1980s civil strife—as distinct from the guerrilla warfare waged by the PLO and the national parties against the Israeli occupation of much of the south—had degenerated not only into a war between different militias, but, more significantly, into a militia war against the civilian population, both Christian and Muslim.

In this undeclared anti-civilian war the identity of the fighters had changed by the mid-1980s. On the Muslim side, the university students and middle-class youth who had fought in the civil war had given way to a largely illiterate lumpenproletariat of Kurds and mountain Druses in Walid Jumblat's Progressive Socialist Party (PSP) and a predominance of Shi'as from the south and Beirut's southern suburbs in Amal. This evolution led to rising tensions and, soon, to bitter clashes between Shi'as and Sunnis, sparked by Amal's persistent attacks on the Sunnis, the Palestinians, and even on its own erstwhile "ally," the PSP. On the Christian side, especially after the death of Pierre Gemayel, the gangster-like Lebanese Forces assumed effective command.

Throughout the nearly twelve years of civil strife, the Green Line dividing East and West Beirut remained unchanged. The militia fighters of both sides seldom aimed their fire at each other. Their targets were residential and business areas behind the other side's militiamen: apartment buildings, hospitals, schools during school

378

hours—any gathering of noncombatants, even on occasion religious institutions. Most such targets were in an area, the Place de Canon, once renown as the city's favorite meeting place, welcoming people of all classes and creeds. The militas, moreover, appeared to be unconcerned about civilians behind their own lines. Fierce battles between the allied Amal and Druse militias erupted periodically in West Beirut, inevitably killing or wounding civilians, including Druses and Shi'as. Maronite factions in East Beirut similarly fought each other without regard for the fate of Maronite civilians.

The car bomb was a weapon of choice in the militia's anti-civilian war. Between January and August of 1986, for example, eleven car bomb explosions, seven of them in Christian areas, killed 225 people and wounded more than 800, maiming many of them for life, and caused material damage running into millions of Lebanese pounds. Victims trapped in cars burned to death, their charred remains unrecognizable. Explosions of bombs in or near markets and supermarkets were timed to go off at peak shopping hours, guaranteeing that most of the victims would be women and small children. Dynamite planted under parked cars or in garbage cans was also a favored weapon, the victims innocent passers-by.

Fighters survived, but their character had changed. The populace the militias claimed to represent now saw them not as protectors, as they had in the 1975–76 civil war, but as *Ghuraba,* outsiders, motivated primarily by sectarian loyalties and the prospect of loot.

The failure of the government's attempts to regain control of the most important ports deprived the Lebanese state of funds and the civilian population of much-needed goods and services. It also permitted the sectarian militias and their leaders to consolidate their power. As members of the government, Walid Jumblat and Nabih Berri demanded the return of the most important ports to government control. As militia leaders they ignored this demand. Camille Chamoun was simultaneously a member of the government, the leader of a militia, and the owner of a flourishing illegal port.

The presence of the largely hooligan sectarian militias in West Beirut, from which the police had long since vanished, was a major factor in the decision of many citizens to leave the country. The breakdown of public services also weighed heavily. Electricity and water shortages were frequent for a multitude of reasons—on one occasion the government explained it had cut off the water because peasants who lived near the reservoir were bathing and washing their laundry in it. In the frequent absence of garbage collection, huge mounds of refuse rotted in the streets. Corruption spread to a frightening degree. Residents had to live with the constant fear that their apartments or homes could be taken over by whatever militia controlled their neighborhood. Finally, the frequent battles between allied militias, sometimes lasting for days and endangering the lives and property of everyone who had the misfortune to live nearby, prompted the definitive departure both of foreigners and of Lebanese lucky enough to have somewhere to go and the means to get there.

While the Shi'as, the Druses, and the Sunnis were each attempting to win control of West Beirut, the Maronite Elias Hobeika and his fighters based in Syrian-controlled Zahle tried, for the first time and unsuccessfully, to invade East Beirut. Hobeika was not attempting to win control there; he wanted to impose himself as a factor within the Lebanese and Christian formula and ensure his inclusion in any Muslim-Christian dialogue. His proposed solution to Lebanon's conflict was an equal distribution of power between Christians and Muslims.

Hobeika's willingness, with Syrian prompting, to invade the "enemy territory" of East Beirut exposed the depths of the divisions among the rest of the Maronites, who were united only in their rejection of Muslim pressures for power sharing and their opposition to any Syrian role in Lebanon. At this time Israel was still equipping the 6000-strong Lebanese Forces led by Geagea, who portrayed themselves as "the protectors of Lebanese society." By the end of March 1986 Israeli weapons were flowing into Christian areas north of Beirut and the newspaper *Al-Safir* reported that Maronite leaders were once again discussing the resumption of relations with Israel. And Camille Chamoun's son Danny was out shopping for weapons again—in Jordan and Iraq as well as in Israel.

Economic Disaster

By the mid-1980s Lebanon's economy had come to a virtual standstill. Aside from intensifying the violence, the Israeli invasion had destroyed much of Lebanon's infrastructure, erected barriers throughout the South and other parts of the country, and forced the migration of much of the population. In the ensuing years the Israelis continued to instigate sectarian violence that promoted additional forced migration. The economic result was something close to collapse.

By mid-1985 almost half the adult labor force was unemployed. A large rise in government expenditures coupled with the deficit in Lebanon's balance of payments accelerated inflation, which put even more people out of work and made survival difficult even for many who still had jobs. Official figures showed that the cost of living for a person at subsistence level rose more than 100 percent in the first quarter of 1985. In 1986 conditions continued to deteriorate; economists began to warn of an "economic and social earthquake." Foreign banks had by this time left the country or drastically reduced their activities. Partly as a consequence, the deposits, loans, and transactions of the forty-nine banks under Lebanese management continued to grow. The Lebanization of the banking system, one of the goals of the Lebanese National Movement a decade earlier, was occurring, though not in the way the LNM had envisioned.

Victor Kassir, minister of economy and industry, warned in late March that "the economic situation will worsen. No one will risk money in the absence of a foreseeable political solution." No political solution was in sight, and in May and June alone, according to trade union officials and economists, the decline of the Lebanese pound pushed the monthly cost of the commodities needed to feed a family of five up from 6000 to 10,000 Lebanese pounds. At the time the minimum wage was 1,475 Lebanese pounds a month. Those fortunate enough to be employed and earn this much had to work nearly two days for the money to buy two and a half kilos of powdered milk. The price of bread, the basic staple, rose from 2.50 to 3 Lebanese pounds.

Two months later, a further decline of the Lebanese pound had boosted the cost of essential goods another 50 percent. Unemployment mounted as foreign enterprises closed down. Robberies and takeovers of occupied houses and apartments multiplied. Internecine battles raged between the nominally allied militas, who seemed to share only a total indifference to the sufferings of civilians. Many schools were forced to close down for shorter or longer periods, and in some cases permanently. Even when schools were operating, many children were unable to attend because of the dangers of getting to class and home again. People in the middle class left as fast as they could.

The militias did not restrict their attacks to the Lebanese civilian population. In West Beirut especially, attacks on Western institutions and individuals increased dramatically, most of them the work of religious fundamentalists. Airliners were hijacked to Beirut with distressing regularity. Western institutions such as airlines, banks, and most particularly the American University of Beirut (AUB) were threatened. Lebanese and Palestinians had been kidnapped and murdered since the very beginning of the civil war, but up to the mid-1980s, foreigners living in Lebanon had led an almost charmed existence. The rise of religious fundamentalism, inspired in part by the Iranian revolution, changed all this. Fundamentalist hatred of the West in general, and of the United States in particular, found expression (and significant international media coverage) in the seizure of Western hostages. Ironically, those kidnapped were for the most part long-term residents of Beirut, often associated with the AUB, who were sympathetic to the plight of the Lebanese and opposed to U.S. Middle East policies.

Although after many months or even years of captivity some of these victims have been returned following high-level negotiations and, one must assume, payoffs, others were not so lucky. The day after the April 1986 U.S. air raids on Libya the bodies of two British professors and an American librarian at AUB were discovered by a mountain roadside. They had been "executed" after varying periods in captivity in retaliation for the U.S. bombing.

These killings led to a further exodus of foreigners and Lebanese, and the downward spiral continued. Indeed, the very existence of the American University of Beirut, perhaps the most tangible symbol of the kind of cosmopolitanism which had once characterized the city, was in jeopardy since it was no longer possible to guarantee the safety of faculty and students—most of whom had departed anyway.

The violence, savagery, and intolerance which have characterized Lebanon in the mid-1980s tend to obscure both the origins of the conflict and several important issues which are its byproducts.

What began as a legitimate struggle for social justice enjoying the support of large and influential sectors of the population had degenerated over the course of more than a decade of fighting into little more than a bloody offensive by the militias against the very people they claimed to champion—the Lebanese and Palestinian populations in general. Admittedly this degeneration was the result in no small part of the intervention and power plays of Lebanon's regional neighbors

Israel and Syria, but the essential actors, the men with the guns and mortars, have remained almost exclusively Lebanese.

In the course of their fighting these men have wiped out much of the physical, economic, and financial infrastructure of the country in whose name they are at war, not to mention a good part of its human capital, the foundation stone of any society. Death and to a much greater degree emigration have constituted a "brain drain" of truly massive proportions. Even in the unlikely event that circumstances permitted, it would be almost impossible to repair this damage.

Beneath the seemingly random violence of recent years, however, other patterns have emerged. The militia's war against the people, and more especially the war of the fundamentalists against all things Western, has a North–South dimension which is ominous in the extreme. Even more ominous, however, is the potential for the "Lebanization" of other countries of the third world.

What has happened in Lebanon is so far unique in recent history. Indeed, not since the general acceptance of the concept of nation-state has a country disintegrated in quite this way, with the very population held hostage by the rival authority of marauding gangs, not for weeks or months but for years, with little end in sight.

Rather than being a tragic aberration in terms of social development, Lebanon may be a portent of things to come; its slide into barbarism may be the fate of other developing countries trapped by the current state of superpower rivalry, the debt crisis, and the lack of substantial progress in North–South negotiations for global redistribution in general. This is a chilling prospect indeed.

Notes

Introduction

1. "How many PLO Victims?" *Ha'aretz*, July 12, 1982. Cited in Sheila Ryan, "Israel's Invasion of Lebanon: Background to the Crisis," *Journal of Palestine Studies* 44/45 (Summer/Fall 1982).

2. *New York Times*, April 18, 1981.

3. Shamir statement cited by Jean Gueyran, "La hantise de la partition," *Le Monde*, July 25–26, 1982. Defense Minister Sharon told Israeli television on June 16 that American officials he saw in Washington in May "understood we had no choice but to strike." This was confirmed by the concentration of U.S. warships in the eastern Mediterranean that began five days before the invasion, apparently to forestall any possible Soviet intervention.

4. Cited by David Lamb, *International Herald Tribune*, July 18–19, 1982.

5. Edward Said, "Palestinians in the Aftermath of Beirut," *Journal of Palestine Studies* 46 (Winter 1983).

6. Begin in the Knesset, June 8, 1982, cited by Amnon Kapeliouk, "La liquidation de l'obstacle palestinien," *Le Monde Diplomatique*, July 1982.

7. See Livia Rokach, *Israel's Sacred Terrorism, A Study Based on Moshe Sharett's Personal Diary* (Belmont, MA.: 1980). Sharett was foreign minister from 1948 to 1955 and prime minister from 1953 to 1955; his diary, filling eight volumes, was published in Hebrew in Tel Aviv in 1979. All quotations from it are taken from Rokach's study. This quotation is from Ben Gurion's letter to Sharett, February 27, 1954; *Diary*, pp. 2397–98.

8. Sharett letter to Ben Gurion, March 18, 1954, cited in Rokach, *Israel's Sacred Terrorism*, pp. 24–30.

9. Salo W. Baron, *A Social and Religious History of the Jews*, vol. 2 (New York: 1937), p. 226.

10. Adel Ismael, *Histoire du Liban de XVII siècle a nos jours*, vol. 4 (Beirut: 1958), pp. 137–38, 310.

11. Philip Guedalla, *Napoleon et Palestine* (London: 1925).

12. Ismael, *Histoire du Liban,* pp. 160–61.

13. The signatories were Britain, France, Russia, Austria, and Prussia.

14. The sects are grouped as follows: Catholic Christian: Maronite, Greek, Armenian, Syrian, Chaldean, and Latin; Eastern Christian: Greek Orthodox, Syrian Orthodox, Gregorian Armenian, Nestorian, and Evangelical; Muslim: Sunni, Shi'a, and Druse (the Alawis and the Ism'ilis, both of the Shi'a branch of Islam, are not mentioned in the legislation and in matters of personal status must resort to Sunni or Shi'a Qadis); and Jewish or Israelite, primarily Sephardic Jews.

15. Although geographically the sectarian composition of Lebanon was somewhat mixed, sectarian concentrations remain as follows: Maronites in East Beirut, Kisrwan, Metn, Zghorta, Batrun, Ba'abdat, and (in the south) Jezzine; Sunnis mainly in West Beirut and its suburbs, Tripoli, and Saida; Shi'as in the South, the Bekaa, the Akkar, and the Beirut suburbs; and Greek Orthodox in the coastal district of Kura, Tripoli, Beirut, and Rashaya.

16. Joseph Moghaizel, "The Cross, the Crescent, and the Lebanon of Tomorrow," *Monday Morning,* May 6–12, 1974.

1: From Empire to Colony: Mount Lebanon and Grand Liban

1. Kamal Salibi, *Syria Under Islam 634–1097* (Beirut: 1977), p. 30.

2. Ilya Harik, *Politics and Change in a Traditional Society: Lebanon 1711–1845* (Princeton: 1968), p. 125.

3. Robert Haddad, *Syrian Christians in Muslim Society* (Princeton: 1970), p. 58.

4. By Bishop Nicola Murad in *Notice historique sur la nation Maronite* (Paris: 1844), p. 48. Cited and discussed in Harik, *Politics and Change,* pp. 139–43.

5. William Polk, *The Opening of South Lebanon 1788–1848: A Study in the Impact of the West on the Middle East* (Cambridge, MA.: 1963), p. 137.

6. Ilya Harik, "The Iqtaa System in Lebanon," *Middle East Journal,* no. 4 (Autumn 1965): 405–21.

7. The new provision called for the appointment of the *qa'im maqam* from one of the leading feudal families (Arslan for the Druses and Abillama for the Maronites) in consultation with the notables and the clergy. A council of twelve chosen by the heads of the religious communities (two each from the six major communities) assumed judiciary, tax assessment, and tax collection functions.

8. Georges Corm, *Contribution à l'étude des sociétés multi-confessionelles* (Paris: 1971), p. 338.

9. Kamal Salibi, *The Modern History of Lebanon* (London: 1965), pp. 111–12.

10. Toufic Touma, *Paysans et institutions féodales chez les Druzes et les Maronites du Liban du XVIIème siècle à 1914* (Beirut: 1971), p. 338.

11. See Boutros Labaki's important study, "La soie dans l'économies du Mont Liban et de son environment Arabe (1840–1914)," *Peuples Mediterranéens*, no 7 (April/June 1979).

12. Ibid.

13. Paul Saba, "The Creation of the Lebanese Economy—Economic Growth in the Nineteenth and Twentieth Centuries," in Roger Owen, ed., *Essays on the Crisis in Lebanon* (London: 1976).

14. Harry N. Howard, *The King–Crane Commission* (Beirut: 1963), pp. 130–31.

15. "Memorandum Presented in the Name of the Majority of the Inhabitants of Territories Illegally Annexed to the Autonomous Sanjak of Mount Lebanon" to the High Commissioner of France in Syria, Beirut, n.d.

16. Stephen Longrigg, *Syria and Lebanon Under French Mandate* (London: 1958), p. 252.

17. Samir Khalaf, "Primordial Ties and Politics in Lebanon," *Middle East Studies* 4, no. 3 (April 1968).

18. Edmond Rabbat, "Document de 14 Fevrier," *L'Orient-Le Jour,* February 24, 1976.

19. Roger Owen, "The Political Economy of Grand Liban 1920–70." In Owen, ed., *Essays on the Crisis,* pp. 23–32.

20. Major-General Sir Edward Spears, *Fulfillment of a Mission, Syria and Lebanon 1941–44* (London: 1977), p. 209.

21. Haut Commissariat de la Syrie et du Liban, *Rapport Au S.D.N.* (Paris: 1934), p. 30.

22. Jacques Couland, *Le Mouvement syndical au Liban 1919–1946* (Paris: 1970), p. 214.

2: The Early Years: Independence and the National Pact

1. Maurice Duverger, "Sects in Search of a Nation," *Guardian Weekly,* April 28, 1973.

2. Edmond Rabbat, *Formation historique du Liban politique* (Beirut: 1973), pp. 524–26.

3. See law #112 of June 12, 1959, which gives the president the right of appointment to all jobs for which the manner of nomination is not specified.

4. Michael Hudson, *The Precarious Republic: Modernization in Lebanon* (New York: 1968), pp. 262–64.

5. Samir Khalaf, "Changing Forms of Political Patronage in Lebanon," in Geller and Waterbury, eds., *Patrons and Clients in Mediterranean Societies* (London: 1977).

6. *L'Orient-Le Jour,* April 28, 1952.

7. See Sami Farsoun, "Family Structure and Society in Modern Lebanon," in L. E. Sweet, ed., *Peoples and Cultures of the Middle East* (New York: 1970). See also Bassem Sirhan, "The Qabadayat in Lebanon" (M.A. thesis, University of Alberta, Canada, Spring 1969).

8. Hudson, *The Precarious Republic,* p. 12.

9. Michel Ghorayeb, "Le Député au Liban recrutement et comportement" (Mémoire Doctorate, Beirut, 1966).

10. See Paul J. Klat, "The Ailment and the Cure," *Monday Morning* 6, no. 246 (February 28–March 6, 1977).

11. Kamal Salibi, "Lebanon Under Fuad Chehab 1958–1964," *Middle East Studies* 2, no. 3 (April 1966).

12. The National Pact's six-to-five Christian-Muslim ratio should also have obtained in the army, but no gesture was made in this direction until the 1958 civil strife, and then only to put Muslims in positions that were not effective command positions. The fact that in the early 1970s the ratio of Christian to Muslim officers in combat command was 85 percent to 15 percent is indication of continued discrimination against Muslims. Retirement of older and higher ranking Christian officers was deliberately delayed by the creation of new ranks in 1962 and again in 1972, in order to block Muslim accession to higher ranks. See Fouad Lahoud, *Ma'saat Al Jaysh Al Lubnani (Tragedy of the Lebanese Army)* (Beirut: 1976).

13. This practice continued at least until the 1975–76 civil war.

14. Fouad Lahoud, interview, Beirut, March 7, 1979. Col. Lahoud was closely associated with General Shehab in the early days of the Lebanese army.

15. Contradictions in the law's provisions have repeatedly given rise to conflicts between the president and the prime minister and defense minister. Another major flaw was the system of promotion: only graduates of military academies may become officers or noncommissioned officers with the result that the ordinary soldier is given no incentive and 90 percent of those who join the army remain ordinary soldiers. Interview with Lahoud, March 7, 1979.

16. For these and other details concerning the military zones, see George L. Keushguerian, "Civil-Military Relations in a Democratic Competitive System: A Case Study of Lebanon 1943–1970" (M.A. thesis, Beirut, 1975).

3: The Beginning of Nationalism(s) and the Emergence of Political Parties

1. See Robert Haddad, *Syrian Christians in Muslim Society* (Princeton: 1970), p. 86 and *passim.*.

2. Labib Zuwiyya, *The Syrian Social Nationalist Party, An Ideological Analysis* (Cambridge, MA: 1966), p. 168.

3. For Kataeb doctrine see its publication *Connaissance des Kataeb* (Beirut: 1948). See also Bahige B. Tabbarah, "Les Forces politiques actuelles au Liban (thesis, Faculty of Law, Grenoble University, 1954).

4. Michael J. Cohen, *Palestine, Retreat from the Mandate, the Making of British Policy 1936–45* (London: 1978), p. 33.

5. Ibid., citing Weizmann archives.

6. *Le Soir,* Beirut, September 29, 1947, cited in Labib Zuwiyya Yamak, "Party Politics in the Lebanese Political System," in L. Binder, ed., *Politics in Lebanon* (New York: 1966), p. 151.

7. A well-known Lebanese poet, Tewfik Awad, a Maronite, expressed this sense of belonging. In a veiled warning to today's Maronite leadership not to follow a Zionist policy of isolation from the Arab world, he said that if other minorities in the Orient "have their own fate, my fate as a Lebanese Christian under this sky is very different. I have my land, I have my history and I have my mission." For the Lebanese Christian he assumed "the biggest portion of responsibility" for the failure to build an integrated state, "because I have failed to convince the Lebanese Muslim that Lebanon is for his benefit as well as mine." *Nahar,* October 16, 1975.

8. *Connaissance des Kataeb,* p. 5. The Maronite community through many centuries considered itself—and was considered by the Holy See—to be a "nation" in the medieval sense of the term. Other sectarian communities also claimed nationhood in this sense, but in no other, perhaps, was the sense of identity so pronounced. The Maronite sense of identity, rooted in the Lebanese mountains, was greatly strengthened during the period 1291–1516, when the Mameluks controlled the entire Lebanese coast and the Maronites lived in isolation in north Lebanon, where they experienced a virtually autonomous political life. The role of the Maronite patriarch also contributed to the Maronite sense of nationhood: "The jurisdiction and power of the Maronite patriarchs have their origin and meaning in the power and jurisdiction given to the Superior of St. Maron's Monastery. This monastic origin explains the influence to the present day of the patriarch in civil and religious matters, making him in fact an actual leader of his people who often acts as the representative of the whole Maronite 'nation'." *New Catholic Encyclopedia* (Washington, D.C.: 1967), vol. 9, p. 245.

9. Charles F. Gallagher, *In the Wake of the Revolution,* American University Field Staff Reports, SW Asia Series, vol. VIII, no. 1.

10. *Qadiyyat al-Hizb al-Qawmi (Case of the National Party).* Document no. 1617, pp. 173–74, Ministry of Information, Beirut, August 31, 1949. This document was presented in the government's case against the SSNP for the attempted coup of July 1949.

11. Bishara al-Khouri, *Haqaiq Lubnaniyya (Lebanese Facts)* (Beirut: 1961), vol. II, p. 245.

12. Cited in Ilan Halevi, *Sous Israel la Palestine* (Paris: 1978), pp. 138–39.

13. See Walid Kazziha, *Revolutionary Transformation in the Arab World* (London: 1975), *passim.*

14. *Le Pacte du PSP* (Beirut: 1949).

15. Ibid., p. 41. See also Tabbarah, *Forces politiques,* ch. 3, sec. 5.

16. Michael Hudson, *The Precarious Republic; Political Modernization in Lebanon* (New York: 1968), p. 288.

4: The Shehab Experiment: The Failure of Reform

1. Drew Pearson, "Washington Merry Go-Round," *Washington Post,* May 24, 1958.

2. Desmond Stewart, *Turmoil in Beirut* (London: 1959), p. 111.

3. See, for example, the statement of the Opposition Delegation to the UN in August 1958, *L'Orient-Le Jour,* August 24, 1958.

4. Fahim Qubain, *Crisis in Lebanon* (Washington: 1961), pp. 176–77.

5. Throughout his term, President Shehab excluded Chamoun and his Ahrar or National Liberal Party (NLP), formed soon after he left the presidency, from any role in government.

6. Edde, the other Maronite in the four-man cabinet, quit within a year to go into opposition.

7. Frank Stokes, "The Supervigilantes: The Lebanese Kataeb Party as a Builder, Surrogate and Defender of the State," *Middle East Studies* 11, no. 3 (October 1975).

8. Many villages remained without; in the early 1970s Sidon had only two secondary schools, the rest of the south only four.

9. David and Audrey Smock, *The Politics of Pluralism, A Comparative Study, Ghana and Lebanon* (New York: 1975), p. 179.

10. Maurice Duverger, "L'Agonie," *Le Monde,* July 8, 1978.

11. Antoine Basile, "La vocation régionale de la place financière de Beyrouth," *Proche Orient Etudes Economiques,* January/December 1973. See also Pierre Nasrallah and Roland Pringuez, "Radioscopie du système bancaire libanais," *Proche Orient Etudes Economiques,* January/April 1975.

12. Riad F. Saade, "Réalité de l'agriculture libanaise," *Tiers Monde* 14, no. 54 (April/June 1973).

13. Ibid.

14. Ibid. A study made in the early 1970s found farmers in the Bekaa paying interest rates of 15 to 70 percent. R. Saab, "Some Problems of Lebanese Agriculture," *The Arab Economist* 6, no. 68 (September 1974).

15. Selim Nasr, "The Crisis of Lebanese Capitalism," *MERIP Report,* no. 73 (December 1978), and Elias Gannage, "Le crédit agricole au Liban," *Proche Orient Etudes Economiques,* July/December 1971.

16. Middle East Economic Consultants, *The Green Plan* (Beirut: 1972).

17. Ibid.

18. Nasr, "Crisis of Lebanese Capitalism."

19. The value of industrial exports thereafter rose at an even faster rate and by 1972 had increased five times over 1964, though inflation in the cost of imported raw materials accounted for part of this increase. See Ronald Farhana, "Export Industrial Expansion in Lebanon: An Evaluation" (M.A. thesis, Beirut, 1977).

20. Ibid.

21. Ministry of Planning, *Aspects de l'industrie libanaise 1962–64* (Beirut: 1965).

22. A. Y. Badre, "Economic Development in Lebanon," in C. A. Cooper and S. S. Alexander, eds., *Economic Development and Population Growth in the Middle East* (New York: 1972). See also L. Berouti, "Les problèmes de l'emploi au Liban," *Proche Orient Etudes Economiques,* January/December 1968.

23. Intra held more cash reserves as a proportion of total assets and carried a larger proportion of time and savings deposits; its assets ($230 million) far exceeded its liabilities ($170 million); its portfolio constituted a collection of valuable and sound assets.

24. Thomas Brady from Beirut, *New York Times,* October 22, 1966. See also *New York Times,* October 18, 1966, pp. 1 and 3; *The Economist,* October 17 and November 22, 1966; S. M. Salaam, "The Intra Crisis" (M.A. thesis, Beirut, 1970); Nizar Sakhini, "Intra Bank Crisis and the Development of the Lebanese Banking System" (M.A. thesis, Beirut, 1970); E. Ghattas, "Lebanon's Financial Crisis in 1966—A Systematic Approach," *Middle East Journal,* Winter 1971; and especially "Catastrophe of the Intra Bank" (Arabic), statement read to the meeting of the original shareholders, November 27, 1970.

25. Report prepared by Toufic Assad, minister of petroleum and industry, in January 1974, on the extent of foreign influence in the Lebanese banking system at the end of 1972 and submitted to the Council of Ministers for discussion. See *The Arab Economist* of March 1974 for an English translation of the first part of this report. The second part deals with suggestions for tackling the problem. The report also noted that negotiations were then under way for foreign purchase of four other Lebanese or Lebanese and Arab banks and that in 1973 alone the majority shares in four additional banks were bought by foreigners.

26. Dan Diner, "The Arab Bourgeoisie," *Khamsin,* no. 4 (1977).

5: The Forgotten South: Israel and the Palestinians

1. The Zionist Organization's Memorandum to the Supreme Council at the Peace Conference, February 3, 1919. J. C. Hurewitz, *Diplomacy in the*

Near and Middle East, A Documentary Record (New York: 1956), vol. 2, pp. 45–50.

2. The villages of Miskafan, Adas, Salha, Honine, Malkieh, Abef, Toula, and Manara.

3. Moshe Sharett's personal diary, cited in Livia Rokach, *Israel's Sacred Terrorism* (Belmont, MA: 1980), p. 7. Further excerpts from this diary are identified by date only.

4. Sharett, letter to Ben Gurion, March 18, 1954. Cited in Michael Bar-Zohar, *Ben Gurion, A Political Biography* (Tel Aviv: 1977), pp. 2398–2400 (in Hebrew).

5. Quoted in Rokach, *Israel's Sacred Terrorism*, p. 56.

6. Speaking at a cabinet meeting Ben Gurion declared that the United States was interested in toppling the Nasser regime, but did not want to use the methods it had adopted in Guatemala when it overthrew the government of Jacobo Arbenz, or in Iran when it overthrew Mossadeq; it preferred the work to be done by Israel. Israel therefore concentrated on preparations for the coming war with Egypt. The plan to partition Lebanon was not revived until after the 1967 war. Bar-Zohar reports that shortly before the 1956 Suez war Ben Gurion proposed to the French government Israel's annexation of south Lebanon, Syria's annexation of other parts of Lebanon, and the creation of a Maronite state in what remained.

7. Ghaleb al-Turk, "Mohafez of the South," in Halim Abu Izzedin, ed., *Lebanon and its Provinces* (Beirut: 1963).

8. Claude Dubar and Salim Nasr, *Les Classes Sociales au Liban* (Paris: 1976), p. 99.

9. The original twenty-five-year French concession expired in 1960, but after three years of irresolution it was renewed for another ten years in 1963 and again in 1973 for a similar period. The Régie's shareholders have been mainly foreign financial groups, banks, etc., much the same as those of the Régie of Tunisia. See Magda Rizkallah-Bouland, "La Régie des Tabacs et son syndicat," *Travaux et Jours* 44 (July/September 1972). Minister of Finance Fouad Naffah, however, told a press conference on February 10, 1973 that the "majority of Régie's shares are held by Lebanese."

10. See Vahe Karyergatian, "Monopoly in the Lebanese Tobacco Industry" (M.A. thesis, Beirut, 1965), for these figures.

11. From 0.14 Lebanese pounds in 1954 to 2.92 Lebanese pounds in 1963 and 7.54 Lebanese pounds in 1971; ibid., and Fouad Naffah, press conference.

12. Nicholas Kluiters, "La Vache et le Tabac," Beirut, 1968, mimeo.

13. Ghaleb al-Turk, "The South."

14. FAO–UNDP Project for Developing Hydro Agriculture in South Lebanon, *Preliminary Note on the Economy of South Lebanon* (Beirut: 1973).

15. The political boss of Baalbek–Hermel in the Bekaa was, until his death in 1976, al-Asaad's rich and landed brother-in-law, Sabri Hamade. The

Asaad and Hamade families together wielded enormous power, not only regionally but also on a national scale.

16. *Hawadess,* no. 968, May 30, 1975, p. 7, published "secret" statistics which, it said, Kamal Jumblat had received from "non civilian" sources: Shi'as, 980,000; Sunnis, 820,000; Maronites, 525,000. Many believe these figures to be somewhat exaggerated, but it is now recognized that the Shi'as have become the largest community in Lebanon. Such Lebanese population statistics as do exist are totally inadequate projections, based on a non-census count taken in 1943 for rationing purposes and modified by birth and death statistics. Births and deaths are poorly recorded outside the main cities. The figures do not take account of emigration.

17. See Marc Yared, "Le réveil du chiisme libanais," *L'Orient-Le Jour,* March 19, 20, 21, 23, and 26, 1974.

18. Yet as late as the early 1970s, Shi'a university students accounted for only about 8 percent of the total. Halim Barakat, *Lebanon in Strife* (Austin, TX and London: 1977), p. 36.

19. Christians constituted the majority of city-dwellers in Palestine and formed the nucleus of its middle class. See Edward Hagopian and A. B. Zahlen, "Palestine's Arab Population: the Demography of Palestine," *Journal of Palestine Studies* 3, no. 4, issue 12 (Summer 1974): 32–73. Palestinians brought about 60 million Lebanese pounds to Lebanon. Antoine Basile, "La vocation régionale de la place financière de Beyrouth," *Proche Orient Etudes Economiques,* January/December 1973.

20. Rony E. Gabbay, *A Political Study of the Arab–Jewish Conflict: The Refugee Problem (A Case Study)* (Paris: 1959), p. 216ff.

21. August 9 and 10, 1975, translated in *Journal of Palestine Studies* 5, no. 1/2, issue 17/18 (Autumn 1975/Winter 1976): 221.

22. Bassem Sirhan, "Palestinian Refugee Life in Lebanon," *Journal of Palestine Studies* 4, no. 2, issue 14 (Winter 1975): 91–107.

23. Rosemary Sayegh, *Palestinians: From Peasants to Revolutionaries* (London: 1979), p. 118.

24. Fawaz Turki, *The Disinherited: Journal of a Palestinian Exile* (New York: 1972), p. 58. See George L. Keushguerian, "Civil Military Relations in a Democratic Competitive System: A Case Study of Lebanon 1948–1970" (M.A. thesis, Beirut, 1975), p. 57.

26. Rosemary Sayegh, "The Palestinian Experience Viewed as Socialization" (M.A. thesis, Beirut, 1976), p. 338.

27. Keushguerian, "Civil Military Relations," p. 52.

28. Sayegh, "Palestinian Experience," p. 303.

29. Ibid., p. 382.

6: Winds of Change: The Emergence of a Sociopolitical Opposition

1. IRFED (Institut International de Recherche et de Formation en vue du Développement), *Besoins et possibilités de développement du Liban* (Beirut: 1961).
2. Ibid. Excerpts translated in *Monday Morning* 4, no. 178 (November 17–23, 1975).
3. NFLU constituent unions include printers, carpenters, construction workers, tailors, shoemakers, bakery workers, tramway workers and employees, cooks, hotel, restaurant, and coffee house workers, pharmacists' assistants, upholsterers, tannery workers of Beirut and of Mashghara, and taxi drivers.
4. Wadah Sharara, unpub. ms. (in Arabic) on the Shehabist period.
5. *Arab World*, September 27, 1965.
6. Michel Ghorayeb, "Le Député au Liban recrutement et comportement" (Mémoire Doctorate, Beirut, 1966).
7. *Arab World*, October 14, 1965.
8. See Paul Achar, "L'Université Libanaise," *Samedi*, October 21/27, 1972, and Edmund Naim (rector of the Lebanese University 1970–76), *Samedi*, April 29/May 6, 1972.
9. *Arab World*, February 20, 1967.
10. *L'Orient-Le Jour*, March 8, 1967, and *Havat*, March 8, 1967.
11. *L'Orient-Le Jour*, March 4, 8, and 14, 1967.
12. *Anwar*, March 29, 1967.
13. *Arab World*, May 11, 1967.

7: The Debacle: June 1967 and Its Aftermath

1. *Divrei Ha-Knesset* (Knesset Record), Jerusalem, 1967, pp. 2327 and 2330.
2. See William B. Quandt, *Decade of Decisions* (Berkeley: 1977), p. 50. See also Michael Bar Zohar, *Embassies in Crisis* (Englewood Cliffs, NJ: 1970), pp. 114–15.
3. *Ha'aretz*, March 19, 1972. See Amnon Kapeliouk, "Israel était-il réellement menacé d'extermination?" *Le Monde*, June 3, 1972.
4. General Peled's article in *Maariv*, March 24, 1972.
5. Ibid., April 4, 1972.
6. Godfrey Jansen, "The Shattered Myth," *Middle East International*, February 18, 1983, pp. 13–14.
7. See S. Abdullah Schleifer, "The Fall of Jerusalem, 1967," *Journal of Palestine Studies* 1, no. 1, issue 1 (Autumn 1971): 68–86.
8. *Al-Talia'a*, June 1969.

9. See Abu Iyad, *Palestinien sans Patrie* (Paris: 1978), p. 331.

10. Military censorship was replaced by self-censorship of the press on October 19, 1967.

11. *The Middle East Reporter* (Beirut), July 12, 1967.

12. *Arab World*, April 16, 1968.

13. *Le Monde*, May 8, 1968.

14. *Middle East Record*, 1968, p. 653.

15. *Arab World*, November 12, 1968.

16. See ibid., August 1 and 6, 1968.

17. Fouad Lahoud, *Mas'aat al-Jaysh al-Lubnani (Tragedy of the Lebanese Army)* (Beirut: 1976), appendix III, pp. 233–34. Lahoud, a former colonel in the Lebanese army, had been the chairman of parliament's Defense Committee since 1972.

18. *Arab World*, December 31, 1968, Report on Closed Parliamentary Debate on the Airport Raid.

19. Lahoud, *Tragedy*, pp. 233–34.

20. *Middle East Record*, 1969–70, p. 905.

21. Rosemary Sayegh, *Palestinians: From Peasants to Revolutionaries* (London: 1979), p. 160.

22. See Lahoud, *Tragedy*, p. 42.

23. See *Nahar*, June 6, 7, and 11, 1969 and *Middle East Record*, 1969/70, p. 908.

24. *Arab World*, August 15, 1969.

25. *L'Orient-Le Jour*, September 8, 1969.

26. After five heated meetings parliament approved the Accord by an eighty-eight to thirty vote of confidence (with three abstentions). The Kataeb voted affirmatively. Raymond Edde and his National Bloc voted against. Both Chamoun and Economy Minister Suleiman Franjieh were absent.

27. *Arab World*, March 3 and 6 and April 8, 1970.

8: 1970: The Tide Turns

1. Abu Iyad, *Palestinien sans Patrie* (Paris: 1978), p. 122.

2. Special Document, "Conversation with Kissinger," *Journal of Palestine Studies* 10 no. 3, issue 39 (Spring 1981): 187.

3. *The Middle East Reporter* (Beirut), November 1985.

4. The government of Saeb Salam, a resolute enemy of Shehab's Deuxième Bureau, won acclaim for finally disbanding the Joint Military Apparatus set up by Shehab to place all internal security organs under Deuxième Bureau control. Although its termination had been announced in April 1970 during Helou's term, the Joint Apparatus had continued to

operate illegally under army control. The Salam government's transfer of many Deuxième Bureau officers to embassies abroad as military attachés, and its arrest, trial, and conviction of a number of others, were widely hailed. Five high-ranking bureau officers who fled the country—four to Syria and one to Spain—were tried in absentia. They remained abroad until 1974, when Damascus's good offices opened the way for their return, retrial, and acquittal. The terms of this deal have never been revealed.

5. *Al-Jarida al-Rasmiyya* (Government Gazette), Beirut, 1971, p. 762.

6. Ibid., 1972, pp. 1413–14.

7. The law canceled the right that officers had hitherto enjoyed in military zones to verify and accept agreements reached in settlement of tribal disputes.

8. Nujaim was reportedly determined to keep the army out of politics and was not influenced by intercessions by politicians or others. See Fouad Lahoud, *Ma'saat al-Jaysh al-Lubnani (Tragedy of the Lebanese Army)* (Beirut: 1976), p. 45.

9. Revealed in parliament July 23, 1973 by Saeb Salam. Excerpts in Lahoud, *Tragedy,* pp. 79–81.

10. After his departure from the army during the civil war Ghanem turned up in an extreme rightist organization patronized by President Franjieh, the Front for National Struggle.

11. Rashid Karami in *Monday Morning,* no. 232, November 22–28, 1976.

9: The Gathering Storm: Political, Economic, and Social Crisis

1. The president, for example, held cabinet meetings without notifying the prime minister, presided over them in his absence, assumed functions properly those of the prime minister's office and tried to play lower ranking Sunni politicians against the "giants" of the Sunni community.

2. Saeb Salam, prime minister under Shehab from 1960 to 1961, owed much of his political power to his presidency of the Muslim welfare society, the Maqasid, with its unrivaled sources of patronage. But his retention of the society's presidency over the opposition of a reform committee provoked the resentment of Sunni notables. See Michael Johnson, "Factional Politics in Lebanon: The Case of the Islamic Society of Benevolent Intentions (al-Maqasid) in Beirut," *Middle East Studies* 14, no. 1 (January 1978).

3. See Robert Campbell, "Le problème du chômage du vendredi au Liban," *Travaux et Jours* 49 (October 1973).

4. Issued October 2, 1974. Text in *Travaux et Jours* 53 (October–December 1974), p. 158.

5. Jean Aucagne, "L'Imam Moussa Sadr et la communauté chiite," *Travaux et Jours* 53 (October/December 1974), pp. 31–52.

6. See Wadha Sharara, "Lebanese Spring," *Dirassat al-Arabiyya* 11, no. 12 (October 1975).

7. *Arab World,* August 17, 1970. Jumblat made his vote for Suleiman Franjieh conditional on Franjieh's commitment not to seek to abrogate this order. Franjieh won the election by one vote, which came to be known as "Jumblat's vote."

8. The Jumblat-led progressive grouping was formed in 1972 and was originally called the Front of National and Progressive Parties and Forces. It later became known as the Progressive Front, and with the outbreak of the civil war as the National Movement *(al-Harakat al-Watani),* literally the Patriotic Movement; it took this name officially in 1976. I will, however, refer to it as the Lebanese national movement or simply the national movement until it becomes the Lebanese National Movement (LNM).

9. Raymond Mallat, series of three articles on inflation, *L'Orient-Le Jour,* April 7, 9 and 10, 1974.

10. Ibid.

11. World Watch Institute, "Study for UN Conference on Desertification at Nairobi," August 29, 1977.

12. Figures on income distribution in this and the following paragraph from Mallat, *L'Orient-Le Jour,* June 17, 1973.

13. *Paul J. Klat, "The Ailment and the Cure," Monday Morning,* no. 246, February 28–March 6, 1977.

14. Salim Nasr, "The Crisis of Lebanese Capitalism," *MERIP Report,* no. 73 (December, 1978).

15. Ahmed Steitiyeh, in *Nahar Economic Supplement,* no. 8 (July 1968).

16. Ibid. Consumption accounts for 82 percent of local demand, investment for only 18 percent. Lebanon spends more per capita on transport and communication than the United States, and also more on cigarettes, home appliances, clothing, recreation, and amusement.

17. Klat, "Ailment and Cure."

18. Bureau des Documentations Arabes, *Le Rapport Higgins sur l'économie libanaise* (Damascus: 1960), ch. 3 (unpaginated).

19. *The Economist,* January 26, 1974.

20. See *Arab World,* January 9, 1973.

21. Cited in *Arab World,* April 4, 1974.

22. Salim Nasr, "Crisis of Lebanese Capitalism."

23. Rudolf Kareh, "Towards a Trade Union of Peasants in the Bekaa," *Samedi,* May 4–10, 1974.

24. See Paul Achari, "La Colère des Secondaires," *Samedi,* October 7–12, 1972.

25. Cited by Maurice Duverger, "Sects in Search of a Nation," *Guardian Weekly,* April 28, 1973.

10: National Crisis: Toward Civil War

1. Lebanese Association for Information on Palestine, Beirut, and *Arab World*, 1968–75.
2. Parliamentary Minutes of 1972, pp. 647–52. See also Fouad Lahoud, *Ma'saat al-Jaysh al-Lubnani (Tragedy of the Lebanese Army)* (Beirut: 1976), p. 65.
3. Lahoud, *Tragedy*, pp. 59–60.
4. Ibid., pp. 60–61.
5. Ibid., p. 230.
6. Selim Turquie, "Washington, La Syrie et les Maronites Libanais," *Le Monde Deplomatique*, November 1978.
7. *Arab Report and Record*, (Lebanon), April 11, 1973.
8. *Economist Foreign Intelligence Report*, May 9, 1973.
9. The *Economist*, May 19, 1973.
10. *Al-Muharrer*, September 30, 1973; *Arab World*, October 1, 1973.
11. *Al-Anwar*, September 2, 1973; September 11, 1973.
12. *Arab World*, September 12, 1973, pp. 3 & 4; press conference, September 17, 1973.
13. *Arab World*, September 18, 1973, pp. 1 & 5; *Nahar*, September 18, 1978.
14. *Al Hayat*, September 17, 1978.
15. The Kataeb and Ahrar blocked formation of a government for over a month in an effort to exlcude any "representative of the left." They accepted Takeiddine only after, at their demand, he swore he did not belong to the left and added, for his own satisfaction, "or to the right."
16. Text of U.S. Secretary of State Henry Kissinger's discussion with American Jewish leaders in June 1975 in *The Middle East* (London) 77, March 1981. (Klutznik later became President Carter's secretary of commerce.)
17. *Arab Economic Report, 1977* (Beirut: General Union of Chambers of Commerce, Industry and Agriculture for Arab Countries).
18. Beirut Office, Bureau of Labor Statistics. See also *L'Orient-Le Jour*, Supplement, March 27, 1980.
19. Among its other activities, the caucus published a series of social studies on such topics as the fight against monopolies, cultural imperialism, and the Arabism of Lebanon.
20. Gregoire Haddad, "Primum Vivere," *L'Orient-Le-Jour*, July 15, 1975; and "For A New Lebanon."
21. *Al-Nahar*, February 3, 1974, cited in Thom Sicking, S. J. and Dr. Shereen Khairallah, "The Shia Awakening in Lebanon," Center for the Study of the Modern Arab World (CEMAM) *Reports 1974*.

22. Little was heard of the ACO after five of its members (four Palestinians and one Syrian) were arrested and executed by the Syrian government in August 1975.

23. Seventy top posts in government administration, twenty-six in autonomous departments, and forty-four in the civil service.

24. See *Parliamentary Minutes,* 1974/2, pp. 2727–66.

25. Under Article 58 of the Constitution the president may promulgate by decree every urgent draft law that parliament fails to act upon within forty days of its being filed in the Parliamentary Record. The amendment became law by virtue of Decree 9640 of February 2, 1975.

26. *The Middle East Reporter* (Beirut), October 2, 1974.

27. See Marc Yared, "Une alternative au pourrissement?" *Samedi* 245, April 6–12, 1974; and Rudolf Kareh, "Comment gagner la paix sans perdre la guerre?" *Samedi* 257, July 5–12, 1974.

11: Flashpoint: The Outbreak of Hostilities

1. Rashid Solh to parliament, *Arab World,* April 4, 1975.

2. Parliament session of April 10, 1975. Fouad Lahoud, *Ma'saat al-Jaysh al-Lubnani (Tragedy of the Lebanese Army)* (Beirut: 1976), p. 171. At this point Lahoud, chairman of the Defense Commission, interjected: "If the Lebanese army has no right to move on Lebanese roads, then may the world rest in peace." Bizri replied: "The army may move—if it's just a question of moving."

3. The committee included the Communist Party of Lebanon (CPL); the Organization of Communist Action (OCA); the Progressive Socialist Party (PSP); the Socialist Arab Baath party; the Socialist Arab Baath Party Organization; the Arab Socialist Action Party; the Nasserite Organization (Marouf Saad's party); the Revolutionary Upsurge; the Union of Makasad Graduates; the Literature and Culture Group; the Federation of Trade Unions of the South; the Fishermen's Union; the Merchant's Union; the Chamber of Commerce; the Professional Union; and representatives of religious and political personalities.

4. Rashid Solh, interview in *Revue du Liban,* no. 1016 December 5, 1979, p. 16.

5. After the war, Abu Iyad reported evidence pointing to the Deuxième Bureau chief, Jules Bustani, and Camille Chamoun as the chief organizers of this massacre. Abu Iyad, *Palestinien sans Patrie* (Paris: 1978), pp. 249–51.

6. Full text in English is in the Center for the Study of the Modern Arab World (CEMAM) *Reports* 1975, p. 24.

7. They were Rashid Karami (Sunni); Adel Osseiran (Shi'a); Majid Arslan

(Druse); Camille Chamoun (Maronite); Philip Taqla (Greek Catholic); Ghassan Tueni (Greek Orthodox).

8. Cited in *Arab World,* April 11, 1975.

9. In Shiyah, a Shi'a group, Fityan Ali (Youth of Ali), led by Ahmed Safwan, became notorious. In West Beirut, a former Deuxième Bureau officer led a group of Sunni fanatics which committed many atrocities.

10. Cited in Edward Sheehan, "Step by Step in the Middle East," *Journal of Palestine Studies* 5, nos. 3 and 4 (Spring/Summer 1976): 3–53.

11. Iyad, *Palestinien sans Patrie,* p. 262–64.

12. For example, the United States' failure to support Chamoun in 1958. The inability of the Franjieh regime to stem the popular upsurge of the early 1970s or control the resistance movement apparently persuaded Washington of the desirability of a change at the top and implementation of some reforms sought by traditional Muslims.

13. Eric Rouleau, "La Syrie dans le bourbier," *Le Monde,* June 1, 1976.

14. Iyad, *Palestinien Sans Patrie,* p. 292.

15. CEMAM *Reports* 1975, p. 51.

16. Qawatli, "Islam, the State and Secularism," p. 175.

17. CEMAM *Reports,* 1975, p. 40.

18. Jumblat: *Pour le Liban* (Paris: 1978), p. 244.

19. Some of the groups and parties within the LNM, however, received financial and other aid from one or another Arab country. This was often conditional on their following the policies of their benefactors.

20. Organization of Communist Action (OCA), *Battle of National Destiny in the Middle East* (Beirut: 1977) (in Arabic). One of the LNM member organizations after the war defended this orientation as an imperative imposed by the international and regional balances of power in which "our democratic uprising would be more like a revolution swimming against the Arab tide."

12: Escalating War, Faltering Peace

1. The October 24 Movement was formed by Farouk Muqaddam, who became politically active in Tripoli in the 1960s in opposition to the sectarian system. Finding his support among the city's poorer classes and the Palestinians, he organized his own militia in 1969 and called it the October 24 Movement, after the date of the take-over of Tripoli. The Muqaddam family was the long-time rival of the Karamis for political leadership in the city.

2. See Fouad Lahoud, *Ma'saat al-Jaysh al-Lubnani (Tragedy of the Lebanese Army)* (Beirut: 1976), p. 181.

3. Ibid., p. 199.

4. See *Arab World,* Novbember 4 and 14, 1975 and *Arab World Weekly,* January 9, 1976. Many Lebanese Jews were descendants of Spanish Jews who came to settle in mountain areas in the fifteenth and sixteenth centuries. The Jewish synagogue in Wadi Abu Jamil was built in 1926. The Jewish schools were started in Ottoman times.

5. Interview in *Monday Morning,* October 20–26, 1975.

6. *Al-Mahadir al-Rasmiyya al-Kamila li-jalasat Hai'at al-Hiwar al-Watani wa Lijaniha al-Siyasiyya wa al-Ijtimaiyya wa al-Iqtisadiyya* (The Complete Official Minutes of the Meetings of the National Dialogue Committee and Its Political, Social and Economic Sub-Committees), in *Al-Tariq* 35, nos. 1–8 (January–August 1976): 101, 192, and 200. Gemayel insisted that "only the present formula can preserve national unity," threatened partition if the formula were in any way altered, and blandly refused to "discuss any topics until peace and order are enforced."

7. Ibid., pp. 285–303.

8. Ibid., pp. 187–89.

9. Ibid., p. 190.

10. Rashid Karami so informed Kamal Jumblat. See *Arab World,* November 12, 1975.

11. Kuds Press (Beirut) *Political Review,* February 20, 1976.

12. The Kataeb's butchery coincident with its leader's talks in Damascus with President Assad was explained as an attempt by extremists to block an understanding with Syria that could lead to something less than total victory. The Kataeb has always pursued a chameleon-like policy, moderate or extremist as strategy and tactics demanded, with members of the Gemayel family assuming specific roles: Bashir, the extremist, Amin, the moderate, and Pierre, "the honest but not unduly intelligent leader." Bashir was widely reported to have been the organizer of Black Saturday.

13. Lahoud, *Tragedy,* p. 187.

13: Syrian Policy and the National Movement

1. Khaddam's speech was widely reported and discussed in the Lebanese press of the following days. See *Arab Report and Record, 1975,* pp. 12–13.

2. *Al-Taliah,* reported in *Arab World,* January 10, 1976.

3. It was for Maslakh that the PFLP in June 1975 had asked for medicines, food, clothing, and building materials in return for release of U.S. Colonel Ernest Morgan, whom it had kidnapped.

4. Some 2,000 PLA troops were under Syrian command.

5. Jumblat, Saeb Salam, and others intervened to demand that Chamoun, believed to be in Saadiyat, be spared. A delegation therefore went to

Saadiyat to offer him a safe-conduct only to learn that he had fled days earlier in an army helicopter.

6. Present at the founding meeting were Pierre Gemayel, Camille Chamoun, Charles Malek (Orthodox), a philosopher, Fouad Chemali, a member of the board of the Maronite League and the reported financier of the militias known as The Organization, Said Aql, well-known poet and head of the Guardians of the Cedars militia until the summer of 1976, Shaker Abu Sulayman, president of the higher Maronite Council; and Sharbel Qasis, head of the Lebanese Order of the Maronite Monks. (The Maronite clergy took a decidedly activist role in the 1975–76 civil war, in contrast to its minor role in earlier civil wars.)

7. Edmond Rabbat, "Le 'Document Historique' du 14 Fevrier," *L'Orient-Le Jour,* February 24, 1976.

8. Eric Rouleau, "La Syrie dans le bourbier," pt. 2, *Le Monde,* June 2, 1976.

9. Ibid.

10. Kamal Jumblat, *Pour le Liban* (Paris: 1978), pp. 214–15.

11. Abu Iyad, *Palestinien sans Patrie* (Paris: 1978), p. 275–76.

12. See Samir Franjieh, "Post Ahdab Lebanon: New Balance of Power," *Monday Morning,* March 22–28, 1976.

13. Syrian Regulars in Saiqa uniforms participated in this operation according to the *New York Times,* March 24, 1976.

14. These included 155 and 130 mm. cannon and Sam, Grad, and Milan missiles.

15. Henry Tanner, *New York Times,* from Damascus, April 15, 1976 and July 7, 1976.

16. Assad, July 20, 1976 speech.

17. Jumblat, *Pour le Liban,* pp. 184–85.

18. Ibid., p. 185.

19. Ibid., p. 185.

20. Henry Tanner, *New York Times,* from Damascus, April 14 and 16, 1976.

21. *New York Times,* from Washington, April 1, 1976; "Syria's Gamble in Lebanon," *Newsweek,* April 26, 1976.

22. *New York Times,* from Washington, April 21, 1976, pp. 16–17.

23. Jumblat, *Pour le Liban,* pp. 252–53.

24. See statement of Kamal Jumblat, *Monday Morning,* Vol. 201, April 19–25, 1976.

25. Iyad, *Palestinien Sans Patrie,* p. 279.

26. Formation of eighteen administrative committees to function till the war ended.

27. Eric Rouleau, from Beirut, *Le Monde,* May 8, 1976.

28. This and previous statements cited were all published in the daily press.

They may be found in *Arab World,* April 23 and 27, 1976, and May 23, 26, 27 and 28, 1976.

29. Bashir Gemayel, interview in *Monday Morning,* June 14–20, 1976.

30. Eric Rouleau, "La Syrie."

31. *Newsweek,* June 16, 1976.

14: Arabization of the War: Defeat of the Popular Forces

1. According to the PLO, lifting the blockade of West Beirut was to have been one step in a ceasefire agreement that included withdrawal of Syrian troops within ten days, but the next day (June 13) Damascus announced that its troops would remain "until a political settlement" was reached.

2. See the *New York Times,* August 12, 1976, where Henry Tanner reported from Junieh that the right's determination to rob West Beirut of its international aura as the headquarters of embassies, international hotels, foreign residents and visitors promoted the bombardment.

3. The Arab League plan called for a cease-fire; a halt to all propaganda campaigns; the restoration of public services; the stationing the Arab Force in all hot spots; spelling out the three phases in applying the Cairo Accord over a three-month period; and the return of *all* displaced persons to the residential areas from which they had been evicted.

4. Interview in *Monday Morning,* September 2–12, 1976.

5. Henry Tanner, from Cairo, *New York Times,* July 4, 1976.

6. Ibid.

7. West Beirut survived the water cut-off owing to its many wells, much of the urban area having been orchard and farmland only a generation before.

8. Robert W. Stookey, "The United States," in P. Edward Haley and L. W. Snider, eds., *Lebanon in Crisis: Participants and Issues* (Syracuse, N.Y.: 1979), p. 235.

9. *Newsweek,* August 2, 1976.

10. *Arab World,* July 3, 1976.

11. *New York Times,* July 10, 1976.

12. After the war the Greek Orthodox church enlisted the help of the World Council of Churches and other organizations to secure the return of the icons and manuscripts. The Kataeb offered to sell back the icons for a large sum, but church authorities refused to pay anyone a single piastre. The icons had by early 1980 been delivered to the presidential palace.

13. Sadr's role in this affair was perhaps not surprising, since he had sided with Assad when Assad turned against his erstwhile allies, the PLO and the LNM. Even before this, Sadr and his Movement of the Disinherited—in striking contrast to their dramatic mobilization of the Shi'a community in

1974 and 1975—had become curiously inactive. On July 6, 1975, Sadr had announced formation of the Brigades of the Lebanese Resistance (*Afwajal al Muqawama al-Lubnaniyya* or Amal) to defend the south against Israeli aggression and, though this was not stated, to stem the rising influence of socialist and communist ideas among the Shi'as. For, at that time, the LNM and particularly the two Lebanese communist parties—the Organization of Communist Action (OCA) and the Communist Party of Lebanon (CPL)—attracted many Shi'as. On the eve of the civil war, roughly half the membership of these two parties and 40 percent of their sympathizers were Shi'as. In assuming a leading role in the defense of the south against Israel's escalating aggressions, these parties challenged Sadr's leadership whether they intended to or not. Amal made little impression during the 1975–76 war. It was only after Assad's turn against the Palestinians and the LNM and after the assassination of Kamal Jumblat and his "secular solution" to Lebanon's sectarian problems that Sadr again brought Amal to the forefront. For more on this development, see Yves Schemeil, "Sociologies du Systeme Politique Libanais," (Ph.D. thesis, Université de Sciences Sociale, Grenoble, 1976.)

14. Badawi was wiped out despite an offer by its LNM defenders to neutralize the area and entrust its policing to the rightist Armenian Tashnag party.

15. *New York Times,* August 1, 1976.

16. *Newsweek,* August 23, 1976.

17. This is, according to Dr. Yusif al-Iraqi, one of the camp doctors who was spared, apparently because he had once successfully treated a Kataeb official.

18. This message was reported in the press of August 10, 1976.

19. Abu Iyad, *Palestinian sans Patrie* (Paris: 1978), p. 291.

20. Kamal Jumblat, *Pour le Liban* (Paris: 1978), pp. 187–88.

21. Abu Iyad, interview in *Monday Morning,* September 27–October 30, 1976.

22. Kuwait's decision a week earlier to dissolve parliament, suspend the constitution, rule by decree and strictly control the press revealed a similar preoccupation. With a population that included some 200,000 Palestinians, an increasingly influential Arab nationalist movement and the only Arab press other than Lebanon's with a measure of freedom, Kuwaiti authorities acted, in part at least, to forestall opposition to the Arab consensus that was to be imposed.

23. A meeting at Chtaura, September 17, between president-elect Sarkis, Arafat, and Naji Jamil also proved futile, since Sarkis and Jamil in effect demanded PLO–LNM surrender, offering nothing in return.

24. *Arab World Weekly,* October 16, 1976.

25. Abu Iyad, *Palestinien sans Patrie,* p. 294–95.

26. Jumblat, *Pour le Liban,* pp. 215–17.

27. Jumblat, *Monday Morning,* October 11–17, 1976.

28. *Arab World,* October 11, 1976, pp. 7–8; October 12, pp 5–6; *The Middle East* 26 (December, 1976). Participants in the Chtaura talks were Colonel Michel Nassif and Colonel Ahmed al-Hajj for Lebanon; Colonel Muhammed al-Kholy and Muhammed Ghoneim, the commander of Syrian forces in the Bekka for Syria; and Hani al-Hassan for the PLO.

29. *Arab World,* October 12, 1976, p. 2.

30. Abu Iyad, *Palestinien sans Patrie,* p. 295.

31. *Arab World Weekly,* October 22, 1976.

32. The committee was composed of the Saudi Arabian ambassador in Beirut, Lieutenant General Ali al-Shaer; the Egyptian ambassador, Ahmed Lotfi al-Metwali; the Kuwaiti ambassador, Sheikh Abed Hamid Baijan; and Colonel Muhammed al-Kholy, representing Syria.

33. See Farid al-Khatib in *Monday Morning,* October 25–31, 1976 for this aspect of the summit.

34. Henry Tanner, from Beirut, *New York Times,* December 9, 1976.

35. Ibid., December 25, 1976.

36. Ibid., from Cairo, February 6, 1977.

37. Michael Parks, from Damascus, *Baltimore Sun,* February 6, 1977.

38. Stuart Auerbach, from Damascus, *Washington Post,* February 11, 1977.

39. Karim Pakradouni, interview in *Monday Morning,* March 28, April 3, 1977.

40. Samir Franjieh, "Lebanon After Junblat," *Monday Morning,* March 28–April 3, 1977.

41. Irene L. Gendzier, "The Assassination of Jumblat," *Nation,* April 2, 1977.

42. London *Times,* January 9, 1977.

43. *Washington Post,* from Nicosia, January 17, 1977.

15: The Reckoning

1. These figures from Fiches de Monde Arabe (FMA): Lebanese Economy, Population Data, 1698 1-L 16, September 24, 1980. A final official estimate by Prime Minister Hoss reported 25,000 Lebanese and 5,000 Palestinians killed.

2. Lower figure from the Lebanese World Cultural Union, *L'Orient-Le Jour* April 15, 1977; higher from Beirut Chamber of Commerce and Industry, *Les effets des evenements sur la population active au Liban* (Beirut: 1977).

3. Lebanese World Cultural Union, FMA 1698.

4. "L'industrie sur la defensive," *L'Orient-Le Jour* Supplement, March 27,

1980; *Middle East Reporter* November 22, 1978, pp. 9–10; *Middle East Money Market,* March 28, 1977.

5. Interview with Fouad Bizri, then president and director of the Electricity Authority, November 1978, Beirut.

6. Labor and Social Affairs Minister Assad Rizk, press conference in Paris, November 9, 1978. The forced exodus from the south in the eighteen months *after* the invasion added more than 200,000 to the number of displaced, as Halim Fayyad, governor of the south, told foreign ambassadors on an inspection tour of the south, September 4, 1979.

7. Selim Turquie, "De Quoi Vivent les Libanaise?" *Le Monde Diplomatique,* October 1979.

8. Central Bank estimate. Many remittances do not pass through the Central Bank. A substantial portion of this income is brought in by hand and neither the Central Bank or the commercial banks can count it.

9. Beirut Office, Bureau of Labour Statistics, *L'Orient-Le Jour* Supplement, March 27, 1980.

10. Dr. Abdullah Attiyah, "The Hostage Economy" (Arabic), *Al-Iqtissad wa Al-Amal (The Economy and the Worker),* May 1980.

11. Fouad Khouri, "Lebanon's Post-War Manpower Problems," *Monday Morning,* December 13–20, 1976.

12. Susannah Tarbush, "Expatriates Playing Varied Roles Abroad," *International Herald Tribune* Supplement, November 1980.

13. Attiyah, "The Hostage Economy."

14. "Activity Booming in Lebanon's Illegal Ports While Official Ports Almost Redundant," *Daily Star,* Beirut, September 3, 1984.

15. The ports in the north were operated by various local militias under the more-or-less benevolent eye of the ADF.

16. Henri Azar, "1981 Année Prospére pour le contrabande," *L'Orient-Le Jour,* January 22, 1982.

17. Fouad Abi Saleh, interview in *Monday Morning,* January 11–19, 1982.

18. See *Safir,* January 21, 1982.

19. Turquie, "De Quoi Vivent?"

20. See Hassan Dawud, "The Lebanese Muslim in the Brochures of Kaslik," *Al-Safir,* May 15, 1979; Dr. Daher Akkari, "Light on the Concept of the Maronite National Home," series of four articles in *Al-Safir* beginning July 8, 1978; Kaslik Committee of Lebanese Studies, statement of 8 May, in *Al-Safir* May 9, 1979; and the following Kaslik pamphlets: *I'raf Haqiqar Lubnan al-Siyasi* (Learn the Truth About Political Lebanon); *Al Islam Al Siyasi wa Wihdat Lubnan* (Political Islam and the Unity of Lebanon); *Shir'at al Jihad* (The Law of Jihad): *Lubnan Al Mustaqbal* (Lebanon, the Future); Amine Naji, *Reply to Muhsin Slim.* Also the Kaslik Monographs of 1975 and after: *Greater Lebanon, Agony of Half a Century* (Arabic and French) 1 (October, 1975); Abu Rami, *Lebanon Historical and Civilized Chain on the*

Neck of the Maronites, 18 (December, 1976); George Maroun, *Lebanon Unified with Fakhr al Din II,* 19 (January, 1977); Father Boutros Daou, *Tomorrow's Maronites in the Light of their History,* lecture of February 8, 1977.

21. See, among others, *Lebanon the Future,* above.

22. *Middle East Report* August 25, 1979.

23. *Al-Amal* February 16, 22 and 27, 1979.

24. *Al-Amal,* December 12 1979, interviewed a member of the Finance Committee, apparently in an attempt to still rising complaints about taxes and levies collected by the Front militias.

25. The government formed on December 9, 1976, remained in office until August 1979: Selim Hoss (Sunni) Prime Minister; Fouad Boutros (Orthodox), Deputy Prime Minister, Foreign Affairs, Defense; Dr. Salah Salman (Druse) Interior, Housing and Cooperatives; Dr. Ibrahim Sheyto (Shi'a) Health, Hydroelectric and Electric Resources; Amine Bizri (Sunni) Tourism, Public Works and Transport; Michel Doumit (Maronite) Planning; Assad Rizk (Greek Catholic) Labor and Social Affairs, National Education and Art; Farid Raphael (Maronite) Justice, Finance, Posts and Telegraph.

26. *Maariv,* November 17, 1977, cited in Amnon Kapeliouk, "La Securité d'Israel et la Glacis Libanais," *Le Monde Diplomatique,* April 1978.

27. Ibid.

28. *Maariv,* March 10, 1978.

29. Statement on Israeli television, April 12, 1977.

30. *Washington Post,* September 23, 1977. Israel's new demands included: Haddad must take over border security; the "good fence" must remain open; Lebanese would continue to work in Israel; the Palestinians must withdraw thirty kilometers from the border; and Israel should have the right to vet Lebanese army commanders assigned to the south.

16: Sadat's Journey to Canossa and the Wars of 1978

1. Sadat interview, *Financial Times,* November 27, 1977.

2. *Arab Report and Record,* 1978, pp. 90–91.

3. Ibid., and *L'Orient-Le Jour,* February 10, 1978.

4. The nine Palestinians arriving by sea commandeered a bus filled with many Israelis. A unit of Israel's special anti-terrorist police pursuing the bus directed fire into it inevitably killing many passengers. Much criticism of the police for not trying to rescue the passengers appeared in Israel.

5. Press conference broadcast by Israeli Radio on March 15, 1978; see also *Arab Report and Record,* 1978, p. 184.

6. Abraham R. Wagner, "Israel" in P. Edward Haley and Lewis W. Snider, eds., *Lebanon in Crisis* (Syracuse, N.Y.: 1979), p. 100.

7. *Sunday Times,* March 19, 1978.

8. Israel admitted the use of the cluster bombs both inside and outside the refugee camps when U.S. Congressman Paul McClosky presented a first-hand account of the attacks on the camps and the consequent misery and destruction. This was a violation of the condition the United States imposed on their use.

9. *New York Times,* April 1, 1978.

10. Israel attempted to hide this setback by putting it about that its forces had never intended to take Tyre. See "South Lebanon," *MERIP Reports,* no. 66 (April 1978).

11. Cited by Michael Parks from Jerusalem, *Baltimore Sun,* March 29, 1978.

12. *Washington Post,* March 25/26, 1978.

13. Michael Parks, *Baltimore Sun,* April 2, 1978. Other massacres occurred at Maroun al-Ras (forty men, women, and children killed) and at Bint Jbeil where all males were rounded up and shot, a massacre followed by raping and looting.

14. *Baltimore Sun,* March 16, 1978.

15. Wagner, "Israel."

16. *Arab Report and Record,* 1978.

17. Ibid.

18. Cited in *Ike* (Beirut), August 19, 1978.

19. *L'Orient-Le Jour,* June 12, 1981.

20. Albert Mansour's memorandum was addressed to the speaker of the house, the prime minister, the defense minister, and the deputies and was distributed to the press on August 22.

21. Muslim recruits assigned to the Front-controlled barracks of Sarba and Fayadiyah were so mistreated and harassed that they sometimes fled to save their lives.

22. *Middle East Reporter,* September 30, 1978.

23. Maxim Ghilan, "A Marriage of Convenience," *The Middle East,* September 1978.

24. *Reveil,* September 17, 1978.

25. Interviews in *Le Monde,* July 28 and August 8, 1978.

17: Destabilization and Its Consequences

1. Fayez A. Sayegh, "The Camp David Agreement and the Palestine Problem," *Journal of Palestine Studies* 8, no. 2 (Winter 1979).

2. Hoss's letter of resignation, May 16, 1979; *Arab Reports,* June 6, 1979, p. 25.

3. *Arab Reports,* May 23, 1979, p. 24.

4. Edward Cody, from Tyre, *Washington Post,* August 30, 1979.

5. *Middle East Reporter,* January 22, 1980.

6. "The Ordeal of South Lebanon," Ministry of Information, Government of Lebanon, Beirut, 1981.

7. See *Revue de Liban,* 1077, July 12–19, 1980.

8. *L'Orient-Le Jour,* July 31, 1980.

9. *Arab World,* September 15, 1980.

10. *L'Orient-Le Jour,* March 2, 1981.

11. Interview, *Le Monde,* August 12, 1980.

12. Ze'ev Schiff and Ehud Ya'arri, *Israel's Lebanon War* (New York: 1984), p. 33.

13. *Middle East Reporter,* April 15–30, 1981, *passim.*

14. Schiff and Ya'ari, *Israel's Lebanon War,* p. 33.

15. *International Herald Tribune,* June 4, 1981, p. 2.

16. *Middle East Reporter,* April 25, 1981, p. 10.

17. Michael Jansen, "Israel's Version," *Middle East International,* October 12, 1984.

18. See *Le Monde Diplomatique,* May 1981.

19. *Monday Morning,* May 11–17, 1981.

20. Ghassan Tueni, *Monday Morning,* September 7–13, 1981.

21. Dorothea Seelye Francke, "The Amal Movement—An Emerging Force," *AJME News* 9, no. 4 (March–April 1984). AJME stands for Americans for Justice in the Middle East.

22. Nazim Qadri, *Monday Morning,* August 12, 1979.

23. Bassam Abu Sherif, PFLP spokesperson, *L'Orient-Le Jour,* September 28, 1979.

24. Godfrey Jansen, "Berri, the Untypical Moderate," *Middle East International* February 24, 1984.

25. *Middle East Reporter,* April 5 and 9, 1982.

26. Ibid.

27. Samir Kassir, "L'etat libanais au miroir de la guerre civile," *Maghreb-Machrek* 10 (April–June 1984).

28. Documents of the Lebanese National Movement: Charter of the Politico-Organizational Front, April 3, 1981, Beirut.

29. Government reports, and in particular Albert Dagher, "La Grande Detresse de l'economie libanaise," *Le Monde Diplomatique,* January 1985.

30. Abu Iyad, interview, *Monday Morning,* October 5–11, 1981

31. See *Monday Morning,* July 12–18, 1982, pp. 46 and 48, for an account of the militia's press conference.

32. *Middle East Reporter,* January 1985.

18: The Summer of 1982: David and Goliath

1. Jean Gueyras, "La hantise de la partition," *Le Monde,* July 1982.
2. General Rafael Eytan, cited in *Review of Palestine Studies* 85, p. 107.
3. David Lamb, *International Herald Tribune,* July 18–19, 1982.
4. UNRWA Commissioner General Olaf Rydbeck, quoted in the *International Herald Tribune,* August 20, 1982.
5. Israel spokesman in Jerusalem in *Middle East Reporter Weekly,* November 2–3, 1982
6. Christophe Giannoa, Canadian director of the Red Crescent Hospital at Nabatiye, quoted by the Agence France Presse, July 1, 1982; Drs. Francis Capet (Belgian); Pascal Mathey (French); Madeleine Van Hoorst (Dutch); Jean Claude Pousin and Dominique Servais, *L'Orient-Le Jour,* August 23, 1982. For post-war torture and abus of prisoners see *Middle East Reporter Weekly,* November 2–3, 1982, and *Israel in Lebanon,* report of the International Commission investigating reported violations of international law by Israel during its invasion of Lebanon, Chairman Sean MacBride. Torture and abuse of Palestinian and Lebanese prisoners and the subhuman conditions to which they were subjected—especially in the notorious Ansar concentration camp near Nabatiye—still continued long after the war had ended, even though the Israeli commander of Ansar, Lieutenant Colonel Rosenfeld, admitted that of the 5,700 prisoners held there in spring 1983, 4,200 were civilians, most of them Lebanese. Clive Robson: "The Fate of 20,000 Prisoners," *Middle East International,* April 29, 1983.
7. In the case of the cluster bombs, it was also in violation of two special agreements. One in 1976 restricted cluster bombs to use in a defensive war; the other, a so-called secret agreement of April 10 and 17, 1978, set three conditions for use of such bombs: (1) only in the event of a land invasion of Israel by two or more Arab states which were two of those with which Israel was at war in 1967; (2) never to be used in an aggressive fashion; and (3) never in any event to be used against civilian concentrations.
8. See testimony of Franklin Lamb, *the MacBride Report,* pp. 226–36 for effects of these bombs and pp. 92–93 for conditions of use.
9. See International Commission on the Red Cross, John de Salis, cited in *Sunday Times* (London), August 8, 1982 for the figures on civilian casualties; and UNICEF's David Allen, *Guardian,* July 27, 1982 for the ratio of death among the wounded. Doctors reported similar, even higher, ratios.
10. Report of Lebanese Technical Commission on Tyre, *Al-Nahar,* July 13, 1982; UN High Commission for Refugees, Report on Sidon, July 12, 1982.
11. *The Times* (London), June 19, 1982.
12. *MacBride Report,* p. 95.
13. Ibid. pp. 143–45 for discussion of this question.
14. *L'Orient-Le Jour,* October 17, 1982.

15. *Time,* October 4, 1982. The International Commission commented: "Sharon's insistence on mopping up 2,000 terrorists . . . is virtually a mandate for the indiscriminate slaughter of 2,000 Palestinians . . . whether armed or not."

16. *Sunday Times* (London), September 27, 1982.

17. *Time,* October 4, 1982; *MacBride Report,* p. 164.

18. That Hobeika's pro-Israel faction was involved seemed likely to many. Israel's involvement remains a conjecture, though plausible: Israel's forces were poised for invading West Beirut and moved immediately.

19. Both Kataeb and National Liberal Party militia participated in the massacre at Tel al-Zaatar in 1976, where two to three thousand people were killed.

20. *The MacBride Report,* p. 179.

21. Ibid., p. 179.

22. *Jerusalem Post,* September 22, 1982.

23. See *also Amnon Kapeliouk, "La timidite d'une enquete ou l'art de s'arreter en mi-chemin," Le Monde Diplomatique,* November 1983.

24. Claudia Wright, "U.S. Silence during the Killing," *New Statesman, October 1, 1982, pp. 15–16.*

25. Hirsh Goodman, *Jerusalem Post,* September 1982.

26. Cited by Kapeliouk, *Le Monde Diplomatique,* November 1983.

27. The MacBride Report, p. 174.

28. Ibid., p. 178.

29. Ibid., p. 170.

30. *L'Orient-Le Jour* published these figures on October 12, 1982, p. 2.

31. Amnon Kapeliouk, *Enquete Sur Un Massacre* (Paris: 1982).

33. *Monday Morning,* August 30–September 5, 1982.

34. Kapeliouk, "Une strategie radicale," *Le Monde Diplomatique,* November 1982.

35. *The MacBride Report,* pp. 221–23.

36. Sir James Frazer, *Folklore in the Old Testament* (New York: 1923), p. 367.

37. J. M. N. Jeffries, *Palestine the Reality* (London: 1939).

38. Roger Nabaa, "Les Arabes et le refus de Israel," *L'Orient-Le Jour,* October 9, 1982.

39. Agene France Presse from Paris, September 24, 1982.

40. Edward Said, *International Herald Tribune,* November 17, 1983.

41. Hamlim Barakat, "Sectarianism and Zionism: Two Elementary Forms of Consciousness," in A. W. Kayali, ed. Zionism, Imperialism and Racism, (London: 1979), p. 250.

19: The Right Triumphant: Toward a New Lebanon

1. "Rebondissement de la guerre civile au Liban," *Le Monde Diplomatique,* October, 1983.
2. Saeb Salam, in press conferences on August 13, and September 4, 1983.
3. "Rebondissement."
4. Ibid.
5. Robert Solé, from Washington, *Le Monde,* April 12, 1983, p. 3.
6. "Rebondissement."
7. The Beirut press of March 2, 1983 reported that the prime minister so informed four visiting Italian senators.
8. Jean Gueyras, "Palestinians at the Mercy of Rival Militias," *Guardian Weekly,* October 23, 1983.
9. "Le danger de la pénétration économique Israeliénne au Liban se précise," *L'Orient-Le Jour,* December 1, 1982, Peter Francke, "Israel's Economic Invasion of Lebanon," *AJME News,* March 1983.
10. *Daily Star* (Beirut), February 1, 1984.
11. Nazih Bizri, interview by Mona al-Said, *Monday Morning,* November 28,–December 4, 1983.
12. Ibid.
13. South Lebanon Governor Halim Fayyad, interview by Mona al-Said, *Monday Morning,* January 16–22, 1984.
14. Fouad Abi Saleh, president of the Lebanese Industrial Association, in *Middle East Reporter* 16, January 1984.
15. Nazih Bizri, cited in "How to Kill an Economy," *Monday Morning,* January 23–29, 1984.
16. Dr. Elias Saba, in *The Middle East,* August, 1984.
17. John Cooley, "The Hydraulic Imperative," *Middle East International,* July 22, 1983.
18. Dr. Kamal Hamdan, "The Great Water Robbery," interview, *Monday Morning,* April 16–22, 1984.
19. Cited in *L'Orient-Le Jour,* July 31, 1983.
20. Selim Hoss, "The Way to Recovery," interview by Claude Khoury, *Monday Morning,* January 9–15, 1984.
21. "Economic Report," *al-Safir,* June 15, 1984. The losses in the 1913 Chouf war were put at 5 billion Lebanese pounds.
22. Marwan Iskander, interview, *Monday Morning,* September 26–October 2, 1983.
23. *Middle Eastern Reporter,* June, 1984.
24. Ignacio Klich, "Assault on Lebanon's Economy," *Middle East International,* May 13, 1983.
25. Ibid.

26. Cited in *Middle Eastern Reporter,* April 10, 1984.

27. Interview by Nadim Ghannan, *Monday Morning,* March 18–24, 1985.

28. Cited in *Middle Eastern Reporter,* April 21, 1984.

20. Popular Revulsion: The Reemergence of the Opposition

1. Amin Gemayel to a Lebanese–American audience in Detroit. See *Middle Eastern Reporter,* July 25, 1983.

2. *Middle Eastern Reporter,* August 21, 1983

3. Press conference, September 4, 1983.

4. "National Paper," issued Fall 1983.

5. Ibid.

6. *L'Orient-Le Jour,* September 4,1983.

7. Saeb Salam, interviewed on Lebanese television. See *Middle Eastern Reporter,* August 13, 1983.

8. Interview with Druse witness, Fall 1983.

9. Reported by *Ha'aretz,* cited in *Monday Morning,* September 12–18 1983.

10. David Lennon, "Israel and Lebanon," *Middle East International,* September 30, 1983.

11. Cited in *Monday Morning,* September 12–18, 1983.

12. Abu Hashem interview, Kuwait News Agency, September 7, 1983.

13. See *al-Safir,* April 6, 1984, for a documented account of Israel's inability to establish sectarian groups of any kind in southern villages.

14. Lennon, *Middle East International,* September 30, 1983

21: The United States: A Belligerent in a Civil War

1. William Lee, "Let Off the Hook," *Middle East International,* September 30, 1983.

2. David Lennon, "Israel and Lebanon, Awakening to Reality," *Middle East International,* September 30, 1983.

3. Ibid.

4. Claudia Wright, "Puppet Masters," *New Statesman* September 30, 1983.

5. Ibid.

6. Claudia Wright, "Balancing Act for Re-election," *Middle East International,* December 23, 1983.

7. The Maronites: President Amin Gemayel; Pierre Gemayel; Camille Chamoun; Suleiman Franjieh and Raymond Edde, who refused to

participate. The Muslims: Saeb Salam; former House Speaker Adel Osseiran; Amal leader Nabih Berri; Progressive Socialist Party leader Walid Jumblat.

8. Wright, "Balancing Act."

9. Ibid.

22: Syria, The PLO, and the Battle for Tripoli

1. Claudia Wright: "Blowing the Gaff," *New Statesman*. October 28, 1983.

2. *New York Times,* October 17, 1984.

3. "A Palestinian's Testament," address of Dr. Issam Sartawi, February 13, 1978, in *Middle East International*, April 15, 1983.

4. Meron Benvenisti, former deputy mayor of Jerusalem, cited in Reuter report, *Daily Star* (Beirut) April 2, 1985. All figures on Israel's confiscation of land in the West Bank are from Benvenisti's study.

5. The Israelis, backed by the United States and still convinced that they have an edge over Syria, rejected out of hand any settlement of the Golan issue.

6. Godfrey Jansen, "Arafat and Assad, the Inevitable Clash," *Middle East International*, July 8, 1983.

7. Oded Yinon, "A Strategy for Israel in the Nineteenth Eighties," *Kivunim (Directions),* journal of the World Zionist Organization's Department of Information. Translated and edited by Israel Shabak (Belmont, MA: 1982).

8. According to Jansen, Assad ordered Syrian troops stationed in West Beirut to withdraw from the battle but their Syrian commander rejected this order. (Jansen, "Arafat and Assad").

9. Ibid.

10. Samir Kassir, "L'OLP et les impératives de la legitimité," *Le Monde Diplomatique,* February 1984.

11. Madeleine Reveroux, *Revue d'estudes palestiniennes* 10.

23: The Insurrection of February 1984 and Its Consequences

1. Middle East Reporter, August 23, 1985.

2. *The Daily Star* (Beirut), October 17–24, 1985.

3. Nasser H. Aruri, "Syria's Master Plan for Lebanon?" *Middle East International,* June 28, 1985.

4. "Life in Lebanon in the Camps," *Middle East International,* December 6, 1985.

5. *Daily Star* (Beirut), May 21, 1984.

6. See *As Shiraa,* weekly issues of May 1986.

24: South Lebanon: The Role of Syria, Israel, and the Palestinians

1. *Washington Post,* February 19, 1986.

2. "The War of the Camps, A Truce Unlikely to Hold," *Middle East International,* July 11, 1986.

Index

33518

956.92 Petran, Tabitha
P

The struggle over
Lebanon

$12.00   j

DATE			
NOV 7 '89			